INTRODUCING SOCIOLOGY
A Guide to Sociological Concepts and Methods Covered

	CHAPTER TITLE	FOCUS	CONCEPTS	METHODOLOGICAL ISSUES
1	**A Day in the Life of Your Jeans:** **Using Our Stuff to Discover Sociology**	The SOCIOLOGICAL IMAGINATION inspires us to find new meanings in the stuff of consumer culture	**KEY: agency, sociological imagination, social structure, consumer culture** capitalism, conspicuous consumption, globalization, microsociological, macro-sociological, research method, social location, wage labor	*Founders of sociology*
	PART I: SURVIVING (AND THRIVING) IN CONSUMER CULTURE			
2	**You Are What You Eat:** **Culture, Norms, and Values**	Everyday food choices are illuminated through a SOCIOLOGICAL APPROACH TO CULTURE	**KEY: commodity fetishism, culture, cultural relativism, ethnocentrism, norms, values** deviance, Durkheim, empirical, ethnographic, femininity, feminism, Marxism, micro-sociological, macrosociological, normative, qualitative interviewing, subculture, theoretical perspectives, totem	*Qualitative interviews*
3	**Fast-Food Blues:** **Work in a Global Economy**	The WORLD OF WORK is explored through the lens of a fast-food burger	**KEY: alienation, class, ideology, McDonaldization, wage labor** bureaucracy, capitalism, commodity chains, commodity fetishism, cultural imperialism, ethnography, Global North, Global South, hegemony, iron cage, social location, social movements, transnational corporations, Weber	*Ethnography*
4	**Coffee:** **Class, Distinction, and "Good" Taste**	Your coffee order reveals the connections between CULTURE, CLASS, and STATUS	**KEY: class, conspicuous consumption, cultural capital, status** deviance, commodity chains, economic capital, ethical consumption, globalization, Global North, Global South, social capital, public space, quantitative research, sample, surveys, third place, upscale emulation	*Survey research*
	PART II: FITTING IN: BEING PART OF THE GROUP			
5	**Shopping Lessons:** **Consuming Social Order**	Shopping can teach us about SOCIAL GROUPS, SOCIAL SOLIDARITY, and SOCIAL ORDER: consumers go shopping to get stuff, but also to form group identity and deal with anomie	**KEY: anomie, individualism, social order, solidarity, social facts** agency, capitalism, collective conscience, consumer dupes/heroes, consumer sovereignty, cultural relativism, focus groups, functionalism, gentrification, longitudinal, mechanical solidarity, new consumerism, organic solidarity, public space, rational choice, social problem, social mobility, stigma, theoretical perspective, totems, upscale emulation	*Focus groups*
6	**Get in the Game:** **Race, Merit, and Group Boundaries**	The world of sports illuminates core concepts relating to RACE and SOCIAL GROUPS	**KEY: race, racism, racial discrimination and segregation; social constructionism** assimilation, bridging / bonding social capital, deviance, essentialism, imagined community, gender binary, in-group and out-group distinctions, laws, minority group, patriarchy, social boundaries, social capital, social location, social norms	*Field experiments*

	CHAPTER TITLE	FOCUS	CONCEPTS	METHODOLOGICAL ISSUES
7	**Barbies and Monster Trucks:** **Socialization and "Doing Gender"**	Toys shed light on gender SOCIALIZATION and DOING GENDER	**KEY: doing gender, gender roles/identity, patriarchy, sex/gender, sexism, socialization** agents of socialization, causation, correlation, cultural capital, (in)dependent variable, gender binary, ideology, intersex, pseudonyms, race, social stratification, stereotypes, cisgender, transgender	*Correlation versus causation*
8	**Dreaming of a White Wedding:** **Marriage, Family, and Hetero- normativity**	Weddings are an industry and a ritual that codifies our ideas of FAMILY and relationships	**KEY: marriage, family, heteronormativity, ritual** deviance, hegemony, heterosexual privilege, ideology, individualism, masculinity, new consumerism, nuclear families, patriarchy, second shift, social reproduction, socialization, stigma, upscale emulation	*Historical comparative research*
9	**I<3 My Phone:** **Technology and Social Networks**	Our relationships with technology reveal changing ways of making SOCIAL NETWORKS, SOCIAL CAPITAL, and COMMUNITY	**KEY: community, social capital, social networks, public sphere** alienation, anomie, Frankfurt School, hegemony, homophily, individualism, moral panic, social change, social problem, prosumers, technological determinism, virtual community	*Social network analysis*
	**PART III: STANDING OUT: INDIVIDUALS NEGOTIATING THE SOCIAL WORLD**			
10	**Branding Your Unique Identity™:** **Consumer Culture and the Social Self**	Brand culture is used to explore SOCIOLOGICAL THEORIES OF THE SELF	**KEY: brand, dramaturgical theory, identity, lifestyle, looking-glass self, stigma** brand community, collective identity, discrimination, generalized other, photo elicitation, prosumers, symbolic interactionism, status, stereotyping	*Photo elicitation*
11	**Looking Good:** **Ideology, Inter- sectionality, and the Beauty Industry**	Social ideas of beauty reveal the importance of an INTERSECTIONAL APPROACH IN SOCIOLOGY, and demonstrate how gender, race, and class work together	**KEY: body work, ideology, social constructionism, race, intersectionality, stereotypes** consumerism, content analysis, fashion cycle, gender, hegemony, lifestyle, racism, sexism, social location	*Content analysis*
12	**What's On Your Playlist?** **Subcultures, Racism, and Cultural Appropriation**	Musical tastes provide an insight into the formation of SUBCULTURES, as well as INSTITUTIONAL RACISM and CULTURAL APPROPRIATION	**KEY: cultural appropriation, institutional racism, subcultures, white privilege** art, color-blind ideology, commodities, discrimination, fashion, oligopoly, prejudice, status, social location, subcultural capital, taste, youth control complex	*Textual analysis*
13	**Our Love–Hate Relationship with the Car:** **Masculinity, Industry, and Environmental Sustainability**	Car culture is a way to understand SOCIOLOGICAL APPROACHES TO THE ECONOMY, and the connections between the economy, symbols, and the environment	**KEY: economic sociology, Fordism, post-Fordism, masculinity** archival research, aspirational good, bridging good, commodity, environmentalism, ethnicity, functionalism, globalization, hegemony, mass consumption, mass production, path dependence, post-materialist, sharing economy, social movements, stereotypes, subcultures	*Archival research*

INTRODUCING SOCIOLOGY USING THE STUFF OF EVERYDAY LIFE

The challenges of teaching a successful introductory sociology course today demand materials from a publisher very different from the norm. Texts that are organized the way the discipline structures itself intellectually no longer connect with the majority of student learners. This is not an issue of pandering to students or otherwise seeking the lowest common denominator. On the contrary, it is a question of again making the *practice of sociological thinking* meaningful, rigorous, and relevant to today's world of undergraduates.

This comparatively concise, highly visual, and *affordable* book offers a refreshingly new way forward to reach students, using one of the most powerful tools in a sociologist's teaching arsenal—the familiar stuff in students' everyday lives throughout the world: the jeans they wear to class, the coffee they drink each morning, or the phones their professors tell them to put away during lectures.

A focus on consumer culture, *seeing the strange in the familiar*, is not only interesting for students; it is also (the authors suggest) pedagogically superior to more traditional approaches. By engaging students through their stuff, this book moves beyond teaching *about* sociology to helping instructors teach *the practice of sociological thinking*. It moves beyond describing what sociology *is*, so that students can practice what sociological thinking *can do*. This pedagogy also posits a relationship between teacher and learner that is bi-directional. Many students feel a sense of authority in various areas of consumer culture, and they often enjoy sharing their knowledge with fellow students and with their instructor. Opening up the sociology classroom to discussion of these topics validates students' expertise on their own life-worlds. Teachers, in turn, gain insight from the goods, services, and cultural expectations that shape students' lives.

While innovative, the book has been carefully crafted to make it as useful and flexible as possible for instructors aiming to build core sociological foundations in a single semester. A map on pages ii–iii identifies core sociological concepts covered so that a traditional syllabus as well as individual lectures can easily be maintained. Theory, method, and active learning exercises in every chapter constantly encourage the sociological imagination as well as the "doing" of sociology.

Josée Johnston is Associate Professor of Sociology at the University of Toronto. She is co-author of *Foodies: Democracy and Distinction in the Gourmet Foodscape, second edition* and *Food and Femininity*.

Kate Cairns is Assistant Professor in the Department of Childhood Studies at Rutgers University. She is co-author of *Food and Femininity*.

Shyon Baumann is Associate Professor of Sociology at the University of Toronto. He is co-author of *Foodies: Democracy and Distinction in the Gourmet Foodscape, second edition*.

INTRODUCING SOCIOLOGY USING THE STUFF OF EVERYDAY LIFE

Josée Johnston
University of Toronto

Kate Cairns
Rutgers University, Camden

Shyon Baumann
University of Toronto

Routledge
Taylor & Francis Group

NEW YORK AND LONDON

First published 2017
by Routledge
711 Third Avenue, New York, NY 10017

and by Routledge
2 Park Square, Milton Park, Abingdon, Oxon, OX14 4RN

Routledge is an imprint of the Taylor & Francis Group, an informa business

© 2017 Taylor & Francis

Library of Congress Cataloging in Publication Data
A catalog record for this book has been requested

ISBN: 978-1-138-02337-6 (hbk)
ISBN: 978-1-138-02338-3 (pbk)
ISBN: 978-1-315-77650-7 (ebk)

Typeset in Minion Pro and Stone Sans
by Florence Production Ltd, Devon, UK

Test questions and a wealth of additional instructor support materials,
prepared by Ivanka Knezevic, Department of Sociology, University of Toronto,
are available on a password protected website www.routledge/cw/johnston
to faculty and administrative staff who have been approved to request review
copies by Routledge.

Printed and bound in the United States of America by Sheridan

CONTENTS IN BRIEF

CONTENTS

PREFACE: FOR INSTRUCTORS

THE CHALLENGES FACING SOCIOLOGY INSTRUCTORS: A STRATEGY OF "STUFF"

Anyone who has taught an introductory sociology class knows that this can be a formidable task. Such classes frequently bring together students who are at very different levels academically. Standard sociology textbooks sometimes introduce conceptual material in a dry (dare we say *boring*?) manner that is disconnected from students' lives. What's more, we face the challenge of teaching students to think *structurally* after years—or even a lifetime—of socialization within a culture of individualism that fosters simplistic responses to complex social problems. Our classrooms often reflect the narratives in mainstream media and elsewhere in society that prioritize individualizing, anecdotal reactions to multifaceted structural issues like racism, poverty, unemployment, and gender discrimination. Sometimes the Nike slogan—*Just do it!*—seems to resonate more in the classroom than Marx's famous aphorism, "Men [sic] make their own history, but they do not make it as they please." Sometimes, just introducing topics like Marx, history, or structure feels like a challenge.

These pedagogical challenges form the launching pad for this book. We suggest that one way to tackle these issues is to connect sociological thinking to the *stuff* of everyday life—stuff like cars, hamburgers, and basketball jerseys. Our fundamental goal—and challenge—is to showcase the utility of a sociological toolkit for understanding the world around us, starting with the cultural and material stories of our stuff. This approach opens up a range of opportunities for the introductory sociology classroom. To engage students from different academic levels, we provide examples from consumer culture that capture the attention of less prepared students, while prompting more advanced students to think deeply about sociological concepts and knowledge. Consumer culture is fundamentally rooted in a culture of individualism, and we use those examples to encourage students to reflect on the prioritization of the "self" in contemporary life. As we suggest in the introductory chapter, sociological thinking is fundamentally about *seeing the strange in the familiar*.

We believe that the best way to spark students' sociological imaginations is to invite them to see the strangeness of the familiar stuff in their everyday lives: the jeans they wear to class, the coffee they drink each morning, or the phones their professors tell them to put away during lectures.

Consumer culture is one of the most powerful tools in our teaching arsenal. We know from our work in the classroom that starting with the stuff of consumer culture is often seen as a more engaging entry point than seemingly dry academic concepts. In our experiences with students we have been struck by the powerful presence of consumer culture in their lives. They—we—live in a world where brands, products, and marketing pitches powerfully shape our sense of self, as well as our ideas about life possibilities, other people's identities, and the larger social world. Some of the most engaging stories shared in our classrooms are about the stuff students hope to buy one day, memories of stuff given and received, and the profound disappointment and frustration that can result from being denied access to desirable consumer experiences. These experiences are not simply personal shopping narratives, but entry points to the demanding work of sociological thinking. Using the stuff of consumer culture, this book encourages students to put sociological concepts and theories to work in order to make sense of the multiple contradictions of social life.

LEARNING THROUGH CONSUMER CULTURE: SEEING STUDENTS AS AUTHORITIES AND PROMOTING THE *PRACTICE* OF SOCIOLOGICAL THINKING

When you read about the centrality of consumer culture in contemporary life, it might be tempting to dismiss these observations as the lament of curmudgeonly, left-leaning professors ("Ah, kids these days! All they care about is online shopping, Kardadshian selfies, and Mixed Martial Arts matches—why won't they listen to me talk about Weber?"). To be clear, when we talk of consumer culture, we are talking about a relationship that is bi-directional. When we engage with students on topics of consumer culture, we understand their social worlds better, we gain valuable insights into the social relations and processes that surround all of us, and most importantly, we feel better equipped to deliver sociological concepts that help students make sense of their lives. This strategy also signals the rich intellectual possibilities opened up for the *sociology instructor* through a dialogue on consumer culture. This dialogue is frequently surprising, enlightening, and challenging. Many students feel a sense of authority in various areas of consumer culture, and they often enjoy sharing their knowledge with fellow students, and with us. One student has a vast understanding of sneaker culture, another is an expert on online make-up vloggers, while another can give an impromptu lecture on car modifications. Opening up the sociology classroom to discussion of these topics validates students' expertise on their own life-world. We, in turn, gain insight from the goods, services, and cultural expectations that shape their lives. (One of us—Josée—learned from her students how the word "basic" is associated with UGG boots, pumpkin spice Starbucks lattes, and white femininity. She also learned that masculine car owners talk about "modifying" their cars, and certainly do not "accessorize" them.) These insights provide us with valuable entry points to explore questions of agency (e.g. how much power do you have to resist an effective marketing pitch?); technological determinism (e.g. has your iPhone changed the world on its own?); as well as gender and social class (e.g. what car brands communicate wealth, masculinity, and status?).

By building on our students' insights into consumer culture, we believe that this book represents a distinct pedagogical innovation. While this text is designed to be a useful and comprehensive resource for undergraduate teaching, it does *not* present sociology as a laundry list of fixed ideas, concepts, and thinkers to be "deposited" in the empty heads of students. A critique of the "banking model" of education was famously theorized by Brazilian educational thinker, Paulo Freire, in the late 1960s, and remains highly relevant today. To illustrate, we can apply Freire's words to the traditional sociology approach to pedagogy: "the [sociologist] talks about reality as if it were motionless, static, compartmentalized, and predictable. Or else [the instructor] expounds on a topic completely alien to the existential experience of the students" (Freire 2014 [1968]: 71). Taking inspiration from Freire's critique of traditional education, this book is about using the stuff of everyday life to teach sociology in a way that is directly relevant to students' existential experience. Our thematic focus on consumer culture has the advantage of being deeply interesting to students because it encourages a commitment to understanding the life-world—the trials, tribulations, and pleasures of everyday life.

A focus on consumer culture is not only interesting for students; it is also (we would argue) pedagogically superior to more traditional approaches. By engaging students through their stuff, we seek to move beyond teaching *about* sociology (e.g. simply memorizing the names of scholars and theories), to teaching the *practice* of *sociological thinking*. Rather than simply describing what sociology *is*, this book teaches students what sociological thinking *can do.* We encourage students to think sociologically by showing them how to use a wide range of the discipline's most effective tools—tools that allow them to think critically about knowledge, rigorously evaluate evidence, and reflect on the meaning and structures that shape their lives. Put differently, this book is designed to get students to learn and *apply* sociological concepts and perspectives to the material goods and cultural products that surround them. Our focus on the stuff of everyday life has an added advantage: it sharply illustrates the dynamics of inequality, which are so central to our discipline. Consumer goods like toys, coffee, and iPhones present us with vivid examples of stratified labor systems, life choices, and consumption patterns. Linking sociology with the study of stuff can help students think through and make sense of the vast, multifaceted inequalities that characterize our social world.

THE POTENTIAL AND PROMISE: FLEXIBLE AND VISUAL, CRITICAL, AND ENGAGING

As is now clear, the book's central premise is that we can understand sociology —and sociological thinking—by looking at everyday consumer stuff. While an academic text will never resemble a big-budget action movie or a Mac product launch, we wanted the book to reflect something of the spirit, vitality, and visual appeal of consumer culture itself. For that reason, each chapter begins with an accessible introduction that invites readers to imagine how they (or another student) might fit into the phenomena being discussed. To enhance this invitation, the text is deliberately designed to be visually appealing. Images are not put forward as "filler", but as tools to elicit sociological insight or pose sociological questions. The book as a whole is designed to be colorful, attractive, engaged with various elements of youth culture, and affordable for students.

Most chapters are organized around a common item, like a phone or a car, but some chapters are centered on a larger consumer phenomenon, like shopping, weddings, or sports. A typical chapter begins with a consumer case study to engage and interest the student, and then proceeds to analyze the consumer item using key aspects of a sociological toolkit. Each chapter also profiles a prominent sociological method, and ends with suggestions for "active learning" exercises that encourage students to develop their sociological analysis further—outside the classroom, on the Internet, and through dialogue with fellow students.

A Guide to Sociological Concepts and Methods Covered

While we have deliberately crafted an unorthodox introduction to sociology, we have designed the book to make it as useful as possible for instructors aiming to build core sociological foundations in a single semester. The Guide to Sociological Concepts and Methods Covered on pages ii–iii of the book outlines the key lessons of each chapter as well as the core sociology concepts covered. This guide helps instructors identify the sociological theme, concepts, and method(s) covered in each chapter; it is designed to facilitate an easy transition to a course organized around central sociological subjects like theories of the self, gender, race, and class inequality. Practically speaking, instructors can scan the guide to identify the key ideas covered in each chapter, and then organize the syllabus—as well as individual lectures—accordingly. For students, an extensive glossary/index can be found in the back pages so they can refresh their memory on key sociological concepts as they come across them in various chapters.

How the Book is Organized

The chapters are organized into three sections. After an introductory chapter (chapter 1) that uses the case of jeans to introduce the sociological imagination, **Part I** of the book focuses on the basics of consumption: eating and drinking. These chapters introduce students to the sociological study of culture, norms, and values through the world of food (chapter 2), to theories of labor through the lens of the fast-food worker (chapter 3), and to studies of class and status through the lens of coffee culture (chapter 4). By the end of Part I we hope to have convinced students that everyday consumer items cannot be taken for granted, and hold significant potential for understanding the structure of the social world.

Having made the case for a sociological approach to the stuff of sustenance in Part I, the remaining sections explore how commodities connect to two key social dynamics: fitting into a group (Part II) and standing out from the crowd (Part III). More specifically, in **Part II,** we use the example of shopping (chapter 5) to introduce key sociological ideas about group life and social solidarity. We then explore processes of group membership, exclusion, and inequality using examples of sports (chapter 6), toys (chapter 7), weddings (chapter 8), and phones (chapter 9). Through these examples, we demonstrate how consumer culture marks some groups as more worthy than others, and how social relationships stratified by race, gender, and sexuality are intertwined in our consumer dreams and practices. Part II makes clear that while individuals experience a desire for belonging on a personal level, the forces that enable individual belonging have broader social underpinnings.

In **Part III** we focus on the question of crafting a unique, individual identity—a focus that is kick-started with a chapter on brands and their relationship to sociological theories of the self (chapter 10). From there, we examine how individuals differentiate themselves based on their physical appearance (chapter 11), music (chapter 12), and modes of transport, such as cars (chapter 13). Broadly speaking, the chapters in Part III encourage students to reflect on the choices they make to add style, meaning, and distinction to their lives, while also encouraging reflection on how these lifestyle choices intersect with larger structural forces—such as institutional racism, beauty ideologies, and economic downturns. To supplement the 13 case-study chapters, we have also included a substantive appendix on sociological methods. This appendix uses a case study of advertising to introduce methods of data collection and analysis within sociology, and can be assigned as a chapter in its own right.

THINKING SOCIOLOGICALLY AS A COMPREHENSIVE GOAL

Beyond the thematic focus on consumption, a key feature that sets this book apart from other introductory texts is the three "thinking frames" that unify sociological content across the chapters. From the outset, we made a deliberate decision not to organize chapters around the classic "trifecta" of functionalism, conflict theory, and symbolic interactionism, although these are theoretical perspectives that we do introduce at different points in the book. Talking with colleagues and fellow instructors, it became clear that this "trifecta" did not reflect the way most working sociologists think about the discipline, or the core challenges involved with getting students to think sociologically. We instead designed the book to focus on a set of three core tensions or dualisms that are central to virtually all sociological thinking:

1) the relationship between *material* and *cultural* analyses of social life;
2) the tension between an analysis of social *structure* and individual *agency*; and
3) the different sorts of inquiries and insights made possible by *microsociological* and *macrosociological* research.

By highlighting these thinking frames within each chapter, we encourage students to engage in the practice of *sociological thinking*, rather than passively receiving sociological content. At the end of each chapter, we present a chart that relates the three thinking frames to the sociological case study and invites students to draw additional connections. This may involve reflecting upon the material and cultural dimensions of a commodity like jeans, questioning the extent to which individual consumer actions can promote social change, or investigating the relationship between broad economic patterns and everyday social interactions. These are challenging sociological questions, but the consumer case studies help to ground them in the context of everyday life.

When we have shared the ideas for this book with our colleagues—informally, at conferences, and through formal reviews—we have been encouraged by their enthusiastic responses. It seems that many instructors are ready for something new. While not every one of our classroom lectures is a home run, we are heartened by the positive response of students to this approach. Many of our undergraduates report that they enjoy the process of thinking about sociology by reflecting on the commodities and cultural practices of consumer society. They also tell us that moving from one piece of consumer culture to another each week works to keep things fresh. We hope that this book provides a resource to enliven the sociology classroom, and inspires students to look anew at the stuff of their everyday lives. We also hope that our experiment with reimagining the nature of the introductory sociology textbook is not only pedagogically effective, but also makes for a rewarding and spirited teaching experience.

INSTRUCTOR SUPPORT MATERIAL AVAILABLE WITH OUR BOOK

Ivanka Knezevic, a fellow Instructor in Sociology at the University of Toronto, has worked closely with us to produce a wealth of support material for teachers interested in assigning our book to their students. These include a complete range of test materials, both essay-type and objective, and prepared so they can easily be imported into any learning management system without negatively affecting their format. Other materials include an additional annotated list of web-links (beyond those already in our book), and suggestions for their effective use; a guide to the use of classroom response systems ("clickers") for introductory sociology; unusual PowerPoint slides for each chapter; useful information on how to adapt our book's use to various introductory course syllabi. We are very grateful to Ivanka.

PREFACE: FOR STUDENTS

This is NOT just a book about sociology. It is also not just a book about the stuff of consumer culture (e.g. toys and sneakers and cars and make-up). This is a book about the intersection of these two arenas, as you can see in the diagram below. More specifically, it is about *thinking sociologically* about the stuff of our everyday lives.

Venn Diagram of Sociology and the Stuff of Everyday Life

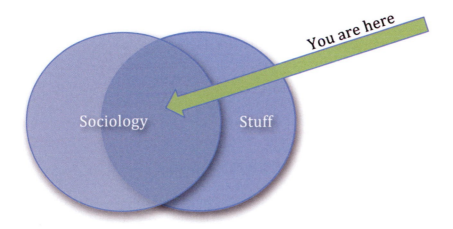

What can you expect in the pages that follow? We think (and hope) that you can expect to be reasonably entertained. Of course, reading sociology is not like the latest Jason Bourne movie or _____ (insert example appropriate to your life). However, we have deliberately written this book so that it will resonate with your everyday experiences in consumer culture. While many of us don't always know what we want to "be" when we grow up, many of us have dreams, or ideas about the next thing we will buy—or the thing we *wish* we could buy, if only we could afford it. This makes intuitive sense. Consumer culture often gives us ideas for short-term gratification ("Hello cheeseburger!"), while larger structural forces can make it difficult to know exactly how we will be making a living in 25 years. We hope to inspire you to think about why, when, or how you developed the consumer dreams and aversions you now possess. At the same time, this book asks questions about who can finance common consumer lifestyles, who is excluded, and who are the people making the stuff more affluent consumers covet and collect. Just as the Disney movie *Toy Story* allowed us to imagine the secret lives of toys when people left the room, we hope that our book will encourage you to imagine the secret lives of commodities. How did all the stuff that surrounds us come to occupy space in our drawers, our homes, and in our collective consciousness? Why do we want the stuff we want, and how does it relate to our sense of self, as well as our role as a member of various social groups like families, communities, ethnic groups, and nations?

In each chapter, you will engage with a particular consumer item or phenomenon. We will ask you to first imagine why this consumer item is important, to think about how it relates to your life, or the lives of people around you. Then we will introduce some key sociological concepts, thinkers, theories, and research methods that allow you to understand this item better, and in the process, understand the social world more deeply. At the end of each chapter, we summarize the case study in relation to three key "thinking frames" that organize our analysis in each chapter. These thinking frames encourage you to explore the same topic from different angles—by focusing on its material or cultural dimensions (material/cultural); by emphasizing individual actors or structural forces (structure/agency); and by studying small-scale or large-scale social processes (micro/macro). At the end of the chapter we will also ask you to extend your knowledge of the consumer phenomenon—and the sociological theory—beyond the text. We provide you with questions to take your analysis outside the pages of this book, finding other examples of this consumer culture in the "real" world of everyday social relationships as well as the virtual or mediated worlds consumed via our televisions, cell phones, or laptops.

Many students have told us that introductory textbooks tend to be boring and out of touch. If you opened this book with that assumption, we hope to prove you wrong. We're not saying that reading this book will be easy: in the pages ahead, we ask you to confront some difficult realities (like persistent racism, sexism, and worker exploitation), and ask you to think through some hard questions. But rather than feeling like a chore, we hope this challenge will provide you with new tools to see the world around you. This is a much more important skill than doing well on a test or passing a course (although those things are important, too). While reading this book, we hope you find yourself bringing a new perspective to everyday life, as you let your sociological imagination run wild. What do we mean by sociological imagination, you ask? You'll have to read the next chapter to find out.

One last thing: When teaching sociology through the lens of consumer "stuff", we have been continually amazed, surprised, shocked, and inspired by the stories that our students tell in class. As you read through this book, you will hear the voices of many of our students as they make their way through a world of exciting consumer goods and limited resources. While we know that you have plenty to do getting through your first sociology class, we invite you to share your stories with us, as well as your suggestions on how to make this book better.

Josée Johnston; josee.johnston@utoronto.ca

Kate Cairns; kate.cairns@rutgers.edu

Shyon Baumann; shyon.baumann@utoronto.ca

ACKNOWLEDGEMENTS

This project was facilitated by the teaching experiences we have had; our students are gratefully acknowledged for sharing their opinions, experiences, and ideas, all of which have made an imprint on this book. Josée would like to acknowledge the contributions of the students who actively participated in the Consumers and Consumption undergraduate seminar at the University of Toronto. All of us want to thank the incredibly smart and effective research assistants we were lucky enough to rely on: Elisha Corrigan, Martin Lukk, and Ali Rodney. As we scrambled to meet our deadlines, these graduate students helped with completing a range of tasks, in many cases better than we could have done ourselves. We received helpful resources from Patricia Arend, Corey Chivers, Nicki Cole, Virginia D'Antonio, Deszeree Thomas, and many of our colleagues in the Consumers and Consumption section of the American Sociological Association. Ivanka Knezevic's work on generating teaching materials is enormously appreciated; we are lucky to be able to draw on her extensive expertise. We are indebted as well to the many reviewers—all introductory sociology instructors—who read the chapters and provided thoughtful and detailed feedback that has made the book better tailored to the needs of a range of instructors. We would like to thank Dean Birkenkamp, Amanda Yee, and many others at Routledge who worked to make this book possible. We are especially thankful for Steve Rutter's advocacy of this project and for his infectious enthusiasm, his smart editorial views, and his seasoned insights.

Lastly, we would like to thank the following fellow teachers of introductory sociology who offered us invaluable feedback on our overall design and individual chapters of this book through multiple drafts.

Michaela DeSoucey	North Carolina State University
Michael Gibson	University of Arizona
Eryn Grucza Viscarra	Georgia State University
Ross Haenfler	University of Mississippi
Judith Halasz	SUNY, New Paltz
Kia Heise	University of Minnesota
Jodi A. Henderson-Ross	University of Akron

Caroline Hodges Persell — New York University
David Karen — Bryn Mawr College
Thomas J. Linneman — College of William and Mary
Melissa MacDonald — American International College
Diane Pike — Augsburg College
Sally Raskoff — Los Angeles Valley College
Rachel Z. Schneider — Ohio State University, Newark
Kyler J. Sherman-Wilkins — The Pennsylvania State University
John Zipp — University of Akron

Chapter 1

A DAY IN THE LIFE OF YOUR JEANS: USING OUR STUFF TO DISCOVER SOCIOLOGY

INTRODUCING KEY CONCEPTS

This introductory chapter uses the case study of blue jeans to introduce the concept of the sociological imagination. *A sociological imagination allows you to connect private troubles to public issues and* social structures. *The overall philosophy of the book is explained: to use stuff from everyday consumer culture to explain key sociological concepts and ways of thinking. We also introduce the concepts of* capitalism *and* consumer culture, *which will be key reference points in the pages ahead. You will learn how the discipline of* sociology *grew up alongside capitalism, and how sociology can help us better understand the ups and downs of our lives within consumer culture. Finally, we introduce three thinking frames that will be used throughout the book, and which highlight three key modes of sociological thinking. Specifically, these frames sensitize us to 1) the* material *and* cultural *elements of social life; 2) the tension between social structures and human* agency; *3) the importance of looking at the social world through small-scale ("*micro*") perspectives as well as large-scale ("*macro*") standpoints. Using these thinking frames, you will learn to think like a sociologist, and approach the commonplace "stuff" in your life with fresh eyes.*

1. INTRODUCTION: SOCIOLOGICAL IMAGINATION AND GLOBAL BLUE JEANS

This may seem like a strange request, but take a moment to look down at your legs. Now look at the legs of the people around you. Chances are that you—or somebody close to you—is wearing a pair of jeans. Around the globe, more than half of the world's people are wearing denim jeans on any given day (Miller 2010: 34). Marketers estimate that on average, humans wear jeans 3.5 days a week, and 62% of people state that they love or enjoy wearing jeans (Miller and Woodward 2012: 4). The average American woman owns eight pairs of jeans, and young girls own an average of 13 pairs (Snyder 2009: 116). Not only are jeans found on billions of bodies around the globe, but they have taken on a special, iconic place in our hearts. In a stylebook devoted to denim, the authors write: "Loving a pair of jeans is like loving a person. It takes time to find the perfect one and requires care and mending to make it last" (Current et al. 2014: 7).

How did denim come to be such a widely accepted and beloved uniform? Our favorite jeans feel personal and unique, especially as they are washed and faded, molded over time to match our body shape. At the same time, jeans are a mass-market good produced by myriad anonymous laborers and shipped from thousands of miles away. These everyday pants are often taken for granted, but when examined closely, jeans raise some interesting questions. For example, how did a piece of clothing that was historically developed to outfit miners, factory workers, and cowboys evolve into a high-fashion item that can be paired with heels or a suit jacket? Why are jeans a wardrobe classic for many, but also a key piece within changing fashion cycles that float in and out of style (e.g. skinny legs, flares, and overalls)? Why are some people content to buy basic, low-budget jeans, while others shell out hundreds of dollars for a pair of distressed designer jeans with holes in them?

To address these jean-related questions, we need more than a keen fashion sense. We need sociology. Sociology helps us find the meaning in the mundane. Rather than dismissing everyday trends like jean wearing as inconsequential, sociologists explore the meanings and motivations behind our daily decisions. Sociology pushes us, and also *trains* us to explore connections between our individual lives and broader social factors—that is, to develop a **sociological imagination***. This term was coined by C. Wright Mills, a 1950s sociologist who had a reputation for being a bit of a badass. (Mills rode a motorcycle, and he probably taught his classes wearing jeans.) For Mills, developing a

---

* **Boldface terms in the text are defined in the glossary/index at the back of the book.**

Variety of Jeans

Despite their origin as the preferred apparel of miners and factory workers, jeans have become a versatile item of clothing available in a wide variety of cuts, dyes, styles, and price points.

Source: http://www.cleanclothes.org/resources/publications/Breathless/view

sociological imagination allows us to see the connections between "private troubles" and "public issues". Without a sociological imagination, we tend to reduce our private issues to *personal* failings and foibles: *I shop too much because I just love new stuff. I am unemployed because I am lazy.* When you have a sociological imagination, you are able to connect personal issues to larger social structures and historical context. You then start to ask questions like, *why* do you feel the way you do about your appearance? How are social groups formed and consolidated through clothing choices? How do the relations of capitalism and globalization shape the choices that are available to us as consumers?

Using our sociological imaginations, we can better appreciate the multiple meanings underlying everyday clothing choices, and also identify the social significance of jean wearing. In one jean-focused study, researchers Daniel Miller and Sophie Woodward spent time with people in London, England, asking questions about their everyday lives and clothing habits (Miller and Woodward 2012). These researchers discovered that jeans play a paradoxical role in many people's lives. Wearing jeans allow people to feel "ordinary"—like an average person who fits in with the crowd. At the same time, jeans are often used to make a person feel special and unique; they might buy a new pair of jeans for a special occasion, or feel proud of their appearance in a particular pair of jeans. In other words, the meaning behind jeans is incredibly versatile, allowing the wearer to feel both part of the group, but also like a unique individual—a finding that goes a long way to explaining jeans' widespread popularity. This finding was especially poignant for people who had immigrated to the United Kingdom (UK), and wrestled to feel at home in a new land. For example, Miller and Woodward talked to a Sri-Lankan born mother and her teenage daughter about their clothing choices. For the mother, wearing fashionable skinny jeans was a way to feel connected to London fashions as well as her teenage daughter's youthful spirit; jeans allowed her to craft a new identity distinct from her traditional upbringing where she was expected to wear a sari (Miller and Woodward 2012: 34–5). Of course, not every immigrant to London wears skinny jeans, and the exceptions can be as revealing as the jean-wearing norm. Another woman in Miller and Woodward's research study, Fatima, eventually stopped wearing jeans after she was harshly criticized by her family (her mother, her brother, and finally her husband) for being "too big", and told "you look really bad in them". These two examples reveal that jeans are a way for people to feel included *and* excluded in social life. Jeans may seem simple and commonplace, but when approached with a sociological imagination, they reveal a great deal about the meanings and power relations underlying everyday life.

The meaning of jean-wearing is not the only interesting factor here: sociology can also help us think about how we come to *own* jeans in the first place. Today, very few people have experience sewing their own jeans, let alone weaving their own cloth. To get jeans, most people need to go shopping. To understand how jeans end up on store shelves requires a look at their complex global backstory. The design process may take place in Italy, the cotton may come from Turkey, the jeans may be assembled in China, and the "distressed" look may be created by hand in a Mexican factory. Jeans are the consummate globetrotters. Cotton thread is sourced from around the world and mixed

LA Jeans

While most jeans are made outside North America in countries like China and Mexico, many brands of more expensive designer jeans are manufactured in the United States. Pictured here are workers inspecting jeans in the quality control room at J Brand jeans factory in downtown Los Angeles.

Source: APimages.com # 653631180108

together to make a consistent product over time; a single foot of thread might contain fiber from the United States, Azerbaijan, India, Turkey, and Pakistan (Snyder 2009: 46). As with other globally produced goods, the trend is for the cheapest jeans to be made in the cheapest labor environment, often in conditions where workers put in long hours and earn very low wages. Premium jeans that cost $200 are more likely to be manufactured in the United States or Japan; in contrast, a pair of moderately priced jeans is more likely to be made in China. One region of China, Guangdong, makes half of the world's jeans, and labor activists have criticized these factories for alarmingly long hours, low wages, and dangerous working conditions (CCC 2013).

Distressed Jeans by Distressed Workers

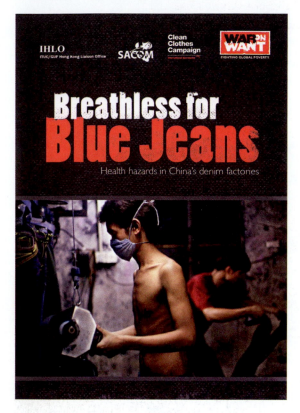

A report on denim manufacturing in China suggests that many factories use a technique of "sandblasting" (firing sand onto denim under high pressure) to create a distressed look, even though most Western brands banned sandblasting because it causes a deadly lung disease called silicosis.

Source: http://www.cleanclothes.org/resources/publications/Breathless/view

Once you have purchased your jeans, you may feel good in them for a while, but eventually, you may wonder if your jeans are looking a little dated. Living in our contemporary consumer culture, we often feel pressure to buy something new—to upgrade our worn-in jeans with a fresh new pair. If your old jeans feel dull, you have options for new jeans that are colored (or white for summer), ripped, skinny, flared, boyfriend-style, made with raw denim, or emblazoned with a high-status logo like Diesel, Nudie or 7 For All Mankind. When you live in a capitalist economy, you are surrounded by opportunities to buy something new, and it is often difficult to be content with your old, familiar stuff. This can be irritating at times—especially if you feel like you are spending money just to stay on top of trends—and create stress for those on a limited budget. At the same time, shopping can sometimes feel intensely meaningful, even liberating. One Italian sociologist who interviewed teenagers in Milan found that people formed an emotional relationship to their jeans; teens talked about loving their jeans, not wanting to throw them out even when they were no longer wearable, as their jeans helped them to feel physically attractive (Sassatelli 2011). From an early age, many of us feel that our stuff says something about who we are and what matters to us. While we go to stores to purchase life's necessities—clothing to cover our body, and food to fuel our actions—most of us don't shop *only* for necessities. We often find ourselves shopping for items that give us pleasure and avenues for self-expression, even though it's hard to pinpoint exactly when or how certain consumer items came to feel pleasurable and satisfying. The norms and desires of consumer culture often get into our heads in subtle, relatively unconscious ways. We may find ourselves buying things we once thought ridiculous, unnecessary, or unfashionable. One student described it to us this way:

Often I am completely unaware of why I like something or why I have grown to like it after having rejected it. For example, I disliked skinny jeans when they first became an important fashion piece, and now I can't imagine my wardrobe without them.

(Diana, Colombian-Canadian)

How can we mock things like skinny (or high-waisted) jeans one day, and then find ourselves thinking of these items as basic necessities the next? More broadly, how do we make sense of shopping decisions that feel personal, but clearly involve forces larger than ourselves?

A Lee is Washed with Your Sweat

Jeans makers can encourage the idea that a pair of jeans is an intensely personal and meaningful item— and that their purchase is an act of self-expression—through marketing. Consider this advertisement for Lee jeans, suggesting an intimate, even biological connection between jeans and wearer.

Source: http://modenews.zalando.fr/a-lee-is-washed-with-your-sweat/

These kinds of questions are the *stuff* that makes up this book. Examining a wide range of "stuff" from consumer culture—from jeans to cars to iPhones to wedding dresses—we use sociological tools to break down and explain key elements of social life. Throughout the book, we show how sociology can help us think critically about the taken-for-granted features of our everyday environment. Instead of assuming that consumer society is a fixed, inevitable, immutable thing, we will visit the "sausage factory" and see how social life is constructed with and *through* our stuff. Sociology seeks to better understand the forces that shape our everyday lives. Sociologists are interested in individuals, but they—*we*—are also interested in how individuals come together: as workers, communities, consumers, and citizens. In the pages that follow, we shed light on how individuals fit into the world of consumer culture and introduce core sociological tools that can help us in this task.

While this book focuses on the everyday stuff of consumer culture (like jeans) to orient our sociological endeavor, we want to be clear that this is not a trivial or superficial pursuit. The relatively "fun", expressive dimensions of consumer culture are deeply enmeshed in serious social problems. Consider the ecological and social exploitation associated with cotton farming, the fiber used to make denim. In developing countries, women mainly pick cotton by hand for low wages; most poor countries that grow cotton have no hope of alleviating poverty by exporting cotton, since the real money is made producing higher-value products, like finished pairs of jeans (Snyder 2009: 41). One ton of high-quality cotton earns a farmer in Azerbaijan about US $300, a price so low that most farmers don't make enough to survive from their land (Snyder 2009: 61, 48). Growing cotton is labor, chemical, and water intensive. For example, even though cotton is grown on a small fraction of the world's arable land (3%), this crop consumes one quarter of the world's pesticides (Snyder 2009: 73). Working with cotton is also dangerous, and carries the risk of byssinosis ("brown lung disease"), a condition caused by inhaling cotton dust and all the things it contains (e.g. pesticides, bacteria, fungi) (Snyder 2009: 63). Once cotton is transformed into jeans, the social problems do not dissipate, especially when we consider the extremely low wages experienced by the 30–40 million people employed in the global garment industry (Snyder 2009: 22, 28). Industry analysts suggest that denim products are consistently contaminated with toxic chemicals—chemicals that come from harmful dyes as well as chemically rich treatments that are used to give jeans a "distressed" look (Snyder 2009: 134–5).

When we turn our analytical lens closer to home, private troubles remain connected to public issues. Consider, for example, the punishing emotional impact for those who struggle to conform to extreme body standards displayed on billboards for designer jeans. Or consider the consequences for people who feel pressured to make consumer purchases they cannot afford. The average indebted person in the US has a $15,600 balance on their credit card (Johnston 2015). While it is tempting to blame individuals for their problems (like credit card debt), a sociological perspective cues us to examine the social factors underlying these trends. For example, consider the recent real-estate crisis; at the peak of the crisis in 2010, one in forty-five properties received a foreclosure filing (RealtyTrac 2010). When we look at the crisis through a sociological lens, we see that many people lost their homes not because of poor consumer choices, but in response to a host of complex, but critical systemic factors, like a poorly regulated mortgage market and reduced regulations on US financial institutions.

Making connections between the "personal" world of individuals' lives, and the "public" world of institutional forces like states, markets, and bureaucracy is not always easy—particularly in a culture that places a strong emphasis on the individual. When people can't pay their mortgage and lose their homes, they typically see their lack of housing as a *personal* failure, and wonder what they could have done differently. Tragically, suicide rates increased along with foreclosure rates during the real-estate crisis (Houle and Light 2014). Indeed, we experience our own lives as deeply personal; we make our own choices, form relationships with others, and negotiate life challenges. When we go shopping, it usually feels like those decisions are ours, and ours alone. As noted sociologist and consumer culture expert Sharon Zukin writes, "there is no central authority compelling us to shop" (2004: 17). Yet shop we do. The sociological imagination doesn't deny the existence of individual choice, but pushes us to look at how outside forces contribute to our situation and life outcomes. This is precisely why we emphasize the term *imagination*— because it takes some creative effort to connect the dots between our personal experiences and the institutional forces like culture, education, mass media, and economy that envelop our daily lives. Sociology pushes us beyond our own individual perspective toward a *systematic* understanding of society. By seeing the world sociologically, we come to see patterns in the way that society is organized. This helps us to understand how individual lives are powerfully shaped by social factors. It also helps us see how simple decisions—like wearing jeans—can be better understood through sociological thinking.

2. HOW WE CAME TO BE A SOCIETY OF SHOPPERS

To more fully appreciate how sociology relates to consumer culture, we need to take a brief trip back in time, and learn a bit about how capitalism, consumerism, and sociology grew up together. In this section, we examine the origins of **consumer culture**, which Roberta Sassatelli defines as "a historical type of society in which the satisfaction of daily need is accomplished through the acquisition and use of 'commodities': goods which are produced for exchange and are on sale on the market" (Sassatelli 2008). Put differently, in a consumer culture, we typically *buy* the stuff we need—like jeans—rather than make it ourselves. While this might seem like an obvious point today, the now common-sense idea of shopping for daily necessities is a relatively recent historical development. For most of human history, people have applied their own labor to get the things they need to survive—their food, clothing, and shelter. These subsistence economies have been the norm throughout human history, and can still be found today in some rural areas in developing countries.

Most readers of this book will *not* be acquainted with a subsistence way of life, but will be deeply familiar with life in a market economy, also known as **capitalism**. As sociologists, we think of capitalism as a core element of **social structure**, which refers to enduring patterns and institutions that organize social life. Many of us take capitalism for granted. It's almost as though we are the fish in an aquarium, and capitalism is the water around us—it is commonsensical, invisible, and feels essential. Yet historically speaking, capitalism is relatively unique. Two of capitalism's most dramatic features have been a shift to **wage labor** as a means of providing for oneself, and the dominance of markets as a primary way of distributing goods in a society. In a capitalist economy, most of the necessities of life are acquired for purchase in markets, and these purchases are usually only possible if we have money obtained by working for a wage. Another prominent feature of a capitalist economy is the predominance of profits and growth; without these two things, a capitalist enterprise, or a capitalist economy, is in crisis. Put in more everyday language, capitalist economies don't like to stand still. They are considered most successful when they are expanding and growing (hence, the fashion cycle encouraging people to expand their wardrobe by purchasing that new pair of jeans).

Although a capitalist way of life feels natural to many of us, thinking like a sociologist means bringing a new perspective to the world in which we live.

In the words of sociologist Peter Berger, we must work to *see the strange in the familiar*. Berger's advice pushes us to ask questions such as the following: why are things organized this way? How did it come to be this way? How might it be different? Bringing our sociological imaginations to the capitalist context that surrounds us can explain *a lot* about why we consume the way we do.

To understand the contemporary capitalist context, it is useful to briefly look back in time to examine how it emerged—and especially, how it grew alongside the expansion of commodity culture. As a social and economic system, the expansion of consumption and capitalism emerged in industrializing England. In the second half of the 17th century, members of the emerging middle class began to accumulate more stuff, namely household items and clothing (Falasca-Zamponi 2010: 8–9). With the advent of the Industrial Revolution in late 18th century England, manufacturing capacity grew, as did the economy's capacity to provide people with consumer goods in the marketplace. By the early 20th century, a system of mass consumption had emerged, which meant virtually all citizens—at least those in wealthy industrialized countries like the United States—came to acquire the stuff of daily life through the marketplace.

Interestingly, the pathways of industrial capitalism emerged alongside sociology as a discipline. Early sociologists like Marx, Durkheim, and Weber

Dying Denim

This 1900s mill was owned by the Cone Mills Corporation of North Carolina, once the world's largest producer of denim. This particular mill was located in North Carolina to be close to the cotton fields, and from 1915 onward made denim for Levi Strauss Corporation. Unable to compete with overseas textiles, Cone Mills filed for bankruptcy in 2003.

Source: https://en.wikipedia.org/wiki/Denim#/media/File:Dyehouse,_White_Oak_Cotton_Mills._Greensboro,_N.C,_by_H.C._White_Co.jpg

(see textbox below) were interested in changing methods of industrial production, as well as the impact of these new economic systems on social cohesion and social strife. Karl Marx (1818–83) recognized the fundamental class division between factory workers (the proletariat) and business owners (the bourgeoisie). Later sociologists followed up on Marx's insights to show how classes were separated not just by their place in the production system, but also by their consumption styles and habits. For example, Marx was alive at the time that Levi's jeans made their first appearance. In the mid-1800s Levi Strauss (an immigrant from Bavaria to the US) developed a product called "waist overalls"—rugged brown work pants that were the progenitor of modern

SOCIOLOGY'S FOUNDERS: CRITICAL COMMENTATORS ON CAPITALIST RELATIONSHIPS

Sociology developed in the midst of industrialization and emerging mass-consumer societies. The earliest sociological thinkers sought to understand the changing nature of industrializing society. Karl Marx (1818–83) is widely considered one of the founders of sociology; his main concern was the exploitation of workers under early capitalism. Marx saw the economy as the driving force of society, and was critical of the vast inequalities between the ruling and working classes. Emile Durkheim (1858–1917) is also considered one of the founders of sociology. Durkheim sought to better understand how large-scale, industrialized, urban societies managed to hold together after the bonds of tradition had been broken. Max Weber (1864–1920) is a third key founder of sociology. His work was preoccupied with the complexity and bureaucracy of industrialized capitalist societies. For example, while mass-produced goods deliver a certain kind of efficiency and uniformity for the consumer, dealing with large-scale bureaucracies can also reduce the "humanity" of the experience (e.g. trying to return something without a receipt at a big box store). While scholars often speak of the founding "fathers" of sociology, it is important to recognize the importance of women's perspectives, and more specifically, feminist perspectives, that emerged alongside the evolution of consumer capitalism in the 18th and 19th centuries. Women of this time period were positioned as "homemakers", and were not thought suited to comment on issues of politics or economics. Even so, various female reformers wrote about the rights of workers, the injustices of slavery, and the rights of women. For example, British sociologist Harriet Martineau (1802–74) campaigned in support of women's rights and is perhaps best-known for her writing on research methodology. She argued that sociological research should include the perspectives of marginalized groups, like women and people of color. In addition, Harriet Beecher Stowe (1811–96) was a strong social critic of slavery, and wrote the bestselling account, *Uncle Tom's Cabin*. Her writing also critiqued the way women were viewed as the "property" of their husbands.

day jeans. These tough denim pants were intended to be long-lasting, and to protect workers from the rigors of hard labor. In contrast, social elites used their consumption habits to distance themselves from any associations with hard labor. One early sociologist, Thorstein Veblen (1857–1929), coined the term **conspicuous consumption** to refer to consumption of high-status, visible luxury goods by wealthy elites to signal their power and distance from the working class—a practice especially common amongst the *nouveau riche* made wealthy through industrialization (1967[1899]). Conspicuous consumption in the late 19th century was an early and important way that people used their stuff to signal their social status to others. Impractical clothing—like elaborate bonnets, high-heeled shoes, or waist-constraining corsets—were useful for visually communicating to others that one didn't have to perform manual labor.

Given the tendency of capitalist economies to grow and expand, it is perhaps not surprising that this economic system has grown into a global

Japanese Burger King

Globalized fast-food brands, concerned with maximizing profit across the many nations in which they operate, often accommodate their restaurants and menus to satisfy particular national consumption habits. Pictured here is an employee at a Burger King in Tokyo holding two special edition Kuro burgers featuring black buns, bamboo charcoal-smoked cheese, and black sauce made from squid ink.

Source: Gettyimages.com # 455631330

system of buying and selling. The period of **globalization**, which is roughly dated from the 1970s onward, is generally understood as a period of heightened global capitalist expansion, as the flow of goods, information, and capital across national borders increased dramatically. Today, most middle-class people around the world are thought to live in a system of globalized consumer cultures where most necessities of life are bought in a market context. Most consumers not only rely on the market for their daily necessities, but these goods originate from all corners of the earth. In addition, a surprising number of commodities look similar across national contexts—think here of the global presence of iPhones, Coca-Cola, Hello Kitty backpacks, and Guess jeans. This is not to say that consumption habits are identical amongst the world's consumers. For one thing, the global economy is characterized by tremendous inequality—the global capitalist class may fly across the world in private jets, while approximately one billion of the world's people live in extreme poverty and worry about getting enough to eat. Even amongst the world's middle classes, people who consume the same commodities may do so in different ways. For example, while Americans commonly view a trip to McDonald's as the route to a super-quick meal, anthropologists who study McDonald's in Asia have suggested that fast food can be viewed as a time to relax, linger, and enjoy a social outing (Watson 2006).

IS HELLO KITTY SLOWLY TAKING OVER THE WORLD?

Though she officially weighs the equivalent of three apples, Hello Kitty has become a heavy hitter in global consumerism. Hello Kitty was created by the Japanese design firm Sanrio in 1974 with her first appearances on stationery and coin purses. Today, she has moved far beyond the coin purse: she is the focus of two Japanese theme parks, has starred in two television series, and even inspired a Hello Kitty maternity hospital in Taiwan. Hello Kitty has a sweet, innocent face, but don't let that fool you—she is a global capitalist powerhouse. Her image appears on tens of thousands of products, generating over $5 billion in annual sales worldwide (Walker 2008). What accounts for Hello Kitty's continued success among an ever-expanding array of consumer goods? Anthropologist Christine R. Yano (2013) places Hello Kitty within the larger spread of Japanese Cute-Cool to other parts of the world, a trend she calls "pink

Hello Kitty

globalization". She is a global symbol of cuteness that transgresses national borders, and bonds girls around the world in a shared culture of consumption and a devotion to cute stuff. Hello Kitty was originally designed to appeal to young girls, but her popularity is remarkably age defying. This stylish kitten has collaborated with high-end fashion firms like Dior, and found a core consumer audience amongst adult women (Kaiser 2009), many of whom see Hello Kitty products as a fun, but rebellious representation of global girl power.

As part of the global expansion of the Hello Kitty brand, in 2014 Sanrio signed an agreement with Major League Baseball (MLB). Here, Hello Kitty prepares to throw the first pitch at a game between the LA Dodgers and Philadelphia Phillies (July 2015). With each of her special MLB appearances, a new special-edition toy was made available for baseball fans.

Source: Gettyimages.com # 480832448

3. THE SOCIOLOGY OF STUFF: THE CHAPTERS AHEAD AND THREE THINKING FRAMES

Just as we examine the sociology of jeans in this introductory chapter, in the chapters that follow, we will apply our sociological imagination to common consumer items that surround us. In each chapter, we have two goals: 1) to encourage reflection and greater understanding of how consumer culture shapes our everyday lives, and 2) to give you a sense of how sociologists *do sociology*. To accomplish this second goal, each chapter provides a concrete example of a professional sociologist and a particular **research method** used in their work. These examples clearly illustrate how sociologists collect data, develop arguments, and back up their claims with evidence.

The chapters of the book are organized into three sections. In the *first* section, our case studies focus on *sustenance*. By this, we mean the stuff of consumer culture that sustains us, like food and drink. These chapters make clear that even the most biologically necessary items, like food, have a deeply social and cultural dimension. While we have a certain amount of control over the consumer items we like and dislike, these chapters demonstrate how our tastes are shaped by a larger social, political, and economic context. Our consumer habits reflect individual desires, but they are also constrained by what stuff is made available in globalized capitalist economies.

In the *second* section of the book, our case studies focus on *fitting in*. In this section, we explore how consumer goods help us form social groups and give us a sense of belonging. To put this in jeans terms, consider how a pair of faded Levi's can make us feel like one of the group—an average American. The first chapter in this section explores how shopping fosters solidarity and social order. Next, we use a case study of professional sports to investigate the formation of group boundaries, with a particular focus on race. We also examine the socialization processes surrounding two specific items: toys and cell phones. The other chapter in this section is devoted to weddings, where we analyze the collectively valued (and expensive) commodities of this celebrated social ritual, like elaborate gowns and diamond rings.

Critique of Ideology Glasses

The 1988 sci-fi horror movie They Live *features a protagonist who discovers a mysterious box containing sunglasses that, when worn, reveal the everyday world in new and shocking ways. As shown in this image from the film, items like city billboards suddenly appear as straightforward commands rather than glossy images of alluring consumer products. The sunglasses function as a metaphorical filter for ideology (see chapter 3) and allow the wearer to more effectively criticize global capitalism. Consider the thinking frames in this book like the glasses from* They Live, *each showing the world through a different tint, revealing new and surprising aspects of our everyday lives as individuals and consumers.*

Source: https://whispersystems.org/blog/they-live/

In the *third* and final section of the book, the case studies focus on *standing out*—the process of crafting a unique identity and sense of self. We examine how we creatively use commodities to express our individuality—that pair of jeans that makes you stand out in the crowd. In these chapters we examine how our sense of self is constrained by larger structural forces that make certain identities more accessible than others. We discuss this dynamic of "standing out" in relation to cases that are central to our sense of self: the way we look, the music we listen to, and the car we drive (or don't drive).

Throughout the following chapters, we challenge you to think sociologically about the consumer stuff at hand. To make this task more concrete, we employ three *thinking frames* that are developed and applied in each chapter. Each thinking frame is like a particular tint of eyeglasses—when you put them on, certain features of the social world will stand out and appear clearer. Together, these frames offer a window into key modes of sociological thinking. Doing sociology is not simply about memorizing a set of sociological "facts", but learning tools and techniques for thinking like a sociologist. Thus, our three thinking frames do *not* present simple rules for how society functions. Instead, each thinking frame represents a key point of tension within sociological inquiry; this is a useful tension, because it highlights different sociological strategies for analyzing a piece of consumer stuff. Be forewarned: when we apply these thinking frames to the world around us, things often appear *more* complex, rather than less. However, the payoff is significant. These thinking frames challenge us to transcend our individual outlooks, and use sociological thinking to appreciate the interrelationship between our daily lives and the broader world around us. Put differently, the thinking frames provide guidance for developing our sociological imaginations, and connecting our private troubles to public issues.

Pac-Man Demonstrates Structure and Agency

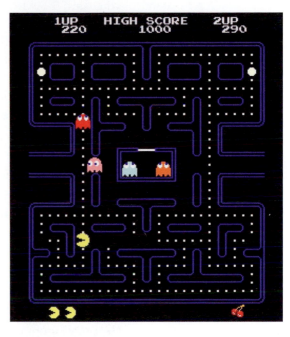

For a simplified, schematic illustration of the tension between structure and agency, consider the world of the two-dimensional arcade game character Pac-Man. Pac-Man's activities take place within a fixed maze (structure) in which the player—and by extension, Pac-Man— nonetheless has free movement (agency). At the same time, Pac-Man's actions are constrained by the location of the dots he must eat to advance and the harmful ghosts he must avoid (structure), forcing him to choose between competing approaches to accomplishing his goal (agency). Finally, every action that Pac-Man takes to eat a pellet changes the pattern of dots remaining and the location of the ghosts, thus determining his subsequent movement—in this way, structure and agency are fundamentally intertwined.

Source: http://www.usgamer.net/articles/other-franchises-that-could-use-the-dragon-quest-xi-treatment

THE EVOLUTION OF JEANS CULTURE: A MATERIAL AND SYMBOLIC STORY

The meaning of a professional woman wearing jeans to work in the United States today is very different from what it would have been 100 years ago. Until the early 1930s, jeans were strongly associated with working-class men. Jeans were not even available for sale in women's sections of department stores—stylish middle-class women wore tailored clothes imported from France, or made from French designs (Comstock 2011). Starting with the Great Depression, the cultural meaning and material landscape of jeans began to change. The regulatory environment worked to encourage American denim production, and the Smoot-Hawley Tariff Act of 1930 protected the denim industry by increasing import duties on foreign goods (Comstock 2011: 28–9). These tariffs increased the price of French clothing, and created space for the emergence of distinctly American fashion. Jeans emerged as a potent symbol of American-made fashion that was forward-thinking, gender-ambiguous, and shockingly modern (Comstock 2011: 28–9). Female Hollywood celebrities embraced jeans as a bold new look, and in 1935, *Vogue* featured "Lady Levi's" in its summer issue; by the end of the 1930s, fashionable women could find jeans on offer in department stores (Comstock 2011: 28).

Jeans wearing only continued to grow in the post-WWII decades, although the meaning of jeans shifted alongside the changing material and historical context. In the 1950s, jeans were seen as the premier leisure pants, and were also a potent and ubiquitous entry point to mass-produced consumer culture. *The New Yorker* magazine described jeans as "the classic of mass production" (in Snyder 2009: 142). In the 1960s, jeans were associated with a long-haired hippy counterculture—a symbol of discontent to straight, buttoned-up corporate culture. By the 1970s, jeans become more respectable, mainstream, and even a symbol of good taste. The concept of "designer" jeans arose in this decade, as Italian designer Elio Fiorucci offered consumers tight-fitting jeans (called "Buffalo 70s") that were highly sought after and imitated by American designers like Gloria Vanderbilt and Calvin Klein. The "casual Friday" trend of the 1980s

The Birth of Designer Jeans

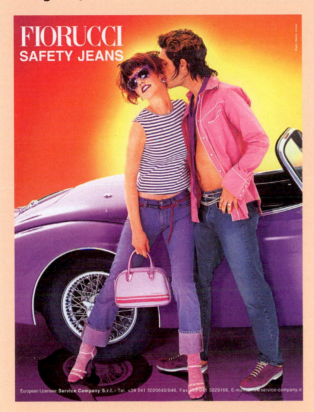

A 1990s advertising campaign for the strength of Fiorucci "Safety" jeans. In the 1970s, the Italian designer Elio Fiorucci introduced "Buffalo 70s", the first "designer" jeans (and arguably, the first skinny jeans). Fiorucci was allegedly inspired by the way wet denim clung to women's bodies at the beach. These jeans were worn by celebrities and spawned a host of imitators.
Source: Alamy EXR0JF

brought denim further into white-collar workplaces (Snyder 2009: 116). More recent decades have brought a renewed interest in multiple kinds of stylistic denim innovations. Today, it seems that there is a pair of jeans for virtually every lifestyle, occasion, budget, body-type, and fashion inspiration, leading some to argue, "we are living in the Golden Age of denim" (Snyder 2009: 116). While most people purchase relatively inexpensive jeans produced by low-wage workers in offshore factories, denim is simultaneously embraced by the world of high fashion. Wealthy consumers can practice conspicuous consumption by purchasing expensive jeans branded from famous design firms like Gucci, Dolce & Gabbana, and Roberto Cavalli.

MATERIAL/CULTURAL

The first thinking frame highlights the dual-sided material *and* cultural nature of social life. Consumer culture is clearly rooted in the world of material goods. It involves raw materials, factories that turn materials into commodities, shipments of commodities to stores and markets, and waste facilities, like landfills, where our discarded belongings spend their final days. For example, our jeans have a material existence—they involve cotton crops grown in fields, textile factories where denim fabric is woven using industrial looms, laborers who stitch jeans together and apply chemicals to create a distressed look, as well as transnational corporations that organize production, market jeans to consumers, and handle retail operations where the jeans are finally sold. While the material element of jeans is undeniable, sociological thinking requires that we also attend to the meanings embedded in this clothing item—that is, the *cultural* dimension of our jeans. Denim is a particularly rich symbolic fabric. In the words of journalist Rachel Snyder, who wrote a book about the denim trade, "No other fabric has held the symbolic fortitude of denim—the rebellion, the antiestablishment rhetoric, the edginess" (2009: 105). Even if we are not particularly interested in rebellious fashion choices, the jeans we purchase and wear are inevitably connected to social systems of meaning, value, and symbolic rituals that are rooted in specific social, historical, and material contexts.

In the material/cultural thinking frame, the central message we want to convey is this: we cannot fully understand the world of consumer stuff without thinking about both its material and cultural significance. The evolution of jeans wearing cannot be understood without appreciating the material context surrounding their rise to fashion prominence, or the rich cultural meanings that they came to embody. This makes sociology different from other disciplines. For example, an economist would typically focus on the economic significance of the jeans industry. An English or film studies professor might study the symbolic role of jeans in classic James Dean films. In contrast, the sociologist is interested in *both* jeans' material and cultural dimensions, as well as how these two dimensions intersect. The sociology of jeans involves the labor conditions of the workers who make and sell them, the impact of jeans manufacturing on the environment, as well as the shifting meanings of jeans in popular culture. Some sociological research will emphasize material analysis in some instances, and cultural analysis at other moments, but both are important in the project of sociological thinking.

In this book, we start with the most obviously material stuff—food and drink—and work towards stuff that is more obviously cultural and social—belonging and self-expression. The early chapters show how seemingly material objects have a cultural dimension, and the latter chapters show how seemingly cultural phenomena (like social media) have material underpinnings (like technological change).

THINKING FRAME #1

STRUCTURE/AGENCY

The second thinking frame represents one of sociology's most deeply rooted and debated topics—the relationship between *structure and agency*. As noted earlier, sociologists use the concept of social structure (or simply "structure") to refer to enduring patterns that organize social life, including things like capitalism and gender inequality. While sociologists are particularly interested in unearthing hidden social patterns, we also recognize the importance of **agency**—that is, the ability of individuals to make decisions and take action within their lives. All actors have some degree of agency, but some are better positioned to act autonomously in the face of structural constraints. Thinking about your **social location** is one way to conceptualize how some groups may be able to exercise agency more freely than others in a given social structure. The term social location refers to one's particular position in a variety of social relations, like racial hierarchies, gender hierarchies, age relations, and the economic system. Although the agency of wealthy White men will still be constrained by structure, they typically face fewer constraints compared to groups disadvantaged by dominant structures, such as poor people who face economic constraints and people of color who face racism. To give an example, a woman from a privileged social location—a woman who is White, thin, heterosexual, educated, and wealthy—may feel like she can choose freely when she visits a high-end fashion boutique. Not only does she have money to pay for a pair of $200 ripped designer jeans, but she also conforms to dominant social standards about who is fashionable and beautiful (Mears 2010). She can fit into tight jeans, she doesn't have to worry about how she will pay for them, and she may not be particularly concerned about how long a pair of ripped jeans will last.

The concept of social location highlights how our identities as individuals, and our *location* within society, reflect the overlapping social groups that we're a part of—our race, gender, class, age, language, education level, religion, sexual orientation, etc. Our social location shapes our perspective on the world, as well as how others view us. Social location also has an important impact on the kind of opportunities and choices that are available to us. For example, the choice to purchase expensive jeans is not available to all consumers, and is certainly not available to most of the low-paid workers who pick cotton or work in manufacturing plants in poor countries. Understanding the significance of social location can help us to see how factors like race, gender, and social class structure our lives in patterned ways. This doesn't mean that these aspects of our social location completely *determine* who we are. We exercise choices in our daily lives that reflect our own personalities and interests. For example, some people may be able to afford

THINKING FRAME #2

expensive jeans, but choose to wear second-hand Levi's purchased at a thrift shop. While our ability to make choices is essential to keep in mind, sociological research can help us understand how our choices and desires are structured by factors beyond our control. The kind of educational opportunities available to us will impact our spending power. Our race will affect whether we've ever been followed around by security in a clothing store. Finally, our race, age, and gender will impact how we see ourselves represented in jeans advertisements in the media landscape, and whether we're represented at all. While we may be able to choose to buy the jeans that make us look our best, we cannot control all the factors that shape our self-image or purchasing power in the broader consumer culture.

Different sociologists emphasize different ends of the structure/agency continuum. Some see agency as heavily constrained by economic and social structures, while others focus on understanding how individuals create the world around them through their everyday actions. Many are somewhere in the middle, attending to how structures constrain human agency, but also how human agency shapes structures. For example, the agency of anti-sweatshop activists in Bangladesh has publicized the low wages and poor safety record in the nation's garment industry, especially after the collapse of the Rana Plaza factory in 2013 which killed more than 1,110 workers and injured twice as many. As a result of this activism, there is increased pressure for global brands to ensure that their clothing is produced in acceptable working conditions using a process that is transparent and accountable. Throughout this book, you will develop your own understanding of the interrelationship between structure and agency. Your position will likely change depending on the issue, but what will remain constant are questions like the following: how much control do we have over our daily tastes and preferences? How much agency do we possess to shape the course of our lives in consumer capitalism? How much of our daily consumption routines are dictated by powerful economic and social structures?

These questions provide the launch pad for each chapter, where we take a seemingly straightforward consumer preference (e.g. for fast food, or cappuccinos, or hip-hop), and explore its material and cultural underpinnings. The overarching goal is to consider how agency is exercised within a particular context that shapes our actions. In each chapter we also explore individual and collective efforts to critique or change some of the most damaging elements of consumer culture (such as fast-food workers protesting to raise the minimum wage, or consumer organizations advocating car-share programs). Through these examples, we consider the subtle differences between individual consumer agency (e.g. choosing a pair of jeans made

THINKING FRAME #2

with 100% organic cotton), and the collective agency that emerges through coordinated efforts in **civil society** (e.g. signing a petition to demand that global jean brands provide decent wages and fair working conditions).

MICRO/MACRO

The third thinking frame—micro/macro—concerns the different scope, or level of analysis applied within sociological research. A **microsociological** approach focuses on social interactions and meaning-making. A research project from this perspective would look at small group settings and face-to-face exchanges, and would attend closely to the following question: how is social life—and social inequality—created through everyday interactions? Think back to the Daniel Miller and Sophie Woodward project on jeans described earlier in this chapter. By hanging out with Londoners and asking them about their clothing, they brought a microsociological approach to jeans, focusing on the meanings they hold for individuals. In contrast, a **macrosociological** approach would widen the analytical lens to examine large collectivities (e.g. how Japanese jean manufacturing competes with American manufacturing), or even entire systems or structures (e.g. how global trade provides a steady flow of cheap commodities, like jeans, to American consumers). Macrosociological perspectives focus on how society works at the institutional, national, and global level. A macrosociological approach should not be seen as antithetical to microsociological perspectives. While spanning different levels of analysis, they are often fruitfully used together to generate greater understanding of a particular problem or issue. Consider the story we shared earlier about jeans' historical evolution from the working man's uniform to a fashionable item that is popular across gender and class divides. Understanding this shift requires a macrosociological analysis of government policy and trade relations as well as a microsociological analysis of consumer meaning-making and self-expression. Like the dynamics of material/cultural and structure/agency, these macro/micro dimensions are deeply intertwined.

The micro/macro thinking frame is particularly useful for sensitizing us to different spatial scales—a point that seems particularly important in the era of **globalization** where people, ideas, and commodities often seem to move seamlessly and quickly across neighborhoods, cities, and national borders. These scales of analysis range from individuals and family members, to small social groups (e.g.

THINKING FRAME #3

friendship and acquaintance networks), to groups of relatively anonymous individuals who share a common interest (e.g. online fan cultures), to large groups of anonymous individuals (e.g. nations), to globally scaled phenomena (e.g. climate change). One particular instance of the micro/macro dialectic that we explore throughout this book is the dynamic between "local" and "global". Thinking of how consumer items are locally received and valued, and how they connect to global flows of commodities and capital, allows us to explore points of similarity and difference, as well as independence and interconnectivity among different places in the world. The local/global dualism also encourages us to think beyond our own geographic perspective and discern issues and patterns that would be otherwise invisible. For instance, examining the relationship between the local and the global allows us to consider how the fast pace of fashion cycles in affluent consumer nations is connected to waste disposal and labor relations in the Global South.

THINKING FRAME #3

We return to these three thinking frames at the end of each chapter throughout the book. The table combines an element of chapter summary with questions to think about as you hone your sociological imagination. In the following table, we reflect upon the sociology of jeans, summarizing key points in this chapter that illustrate the utility of each thinking frame.

THINKING FRAMES

How can each thinking frame help us better understand the sociology of jeans?

Material / Cultural	A pair of jeans is a material item linked to cotton farming, denim factories, and factory workers. At the same time, jeans hold cultural significance; the particular meanings associated with this clothing item have shifted across historical and cultural contexts, as well as for different social groups.
Think about . . .	Do you know where your jeans were made? Can you trace the path they traveled from cotton field to retail outlet? What do your jeans say about who you are? Are there styles of jeans that you would never wear because you associate them with a particular "look", identity, or social group?

Structure / Agency	Our individual consumer choices are shaped by structural constraints—such as how much money we possess, and how (dis)advantaged we are within relations of social inequality. At the same time, consumers also possess agency. Opportunities for exercising agency are shaped by our social location.
Think about . . .	What clothing stores do you feel most comfortable in? How might this be shaped by your social location? Have you ever been made to feel out of place in a retail environment because of your gender, age, class, or race?

Micro / Macro	A microsociological study of jeans could investigate the meanings people associate with specific brands. To study jeans at a macro level, we might ask questions about how clothing corporations promote consumer identities, the sustainability of high-consumption lifestyles, or how jean culture has been globalized.
Think about . . .	Think about the last pair of jeans you bought. What social meanings do you think are conveyed when you wear these jeans? (e.g. that you are a soccer mom? A hip-hop fan? A sexually attractive 20-year-old?) Now think about the macro implications of this pair of jeans, and all the other jeans made in the same factory. Which nations were implicated in the production process of these jeans? What regulatory frameworks governed the wages and safety conditions of the workers who made these jeans?

ACTIVE LEARNING

Online

Calculate your consumption footprint:
Use an online ecological footprint calculator to learn about the larger material impact of your consumption choices. Go to: http://footprintnetwork.org/en/index.php/GFN/page/calculators/

Live in Levi's:

Watch the "Live in Levi's" film available on YouTube: https://www.youtube.com/watch?v=ZB7AAQcBB_E. How does this film balance a perspective on jeans as both a humble, everyday item, and a piece of clothing that makes people seem cool, unique, and distinct? How does this film portray jeans as both an intimate, personal commodity, and an item that has a global reach? Do you think the film provides a positive perspective on the Levi's brand? Why or why not?

Discussion/Reflection

The first thing I bought was . . . :

When sociologist Sharon Zukin (2004) interviewed people for her book on shopping, she found that many people remembered their first purchase. Think about the first thing you remember buying. What was it? Pokémon cards? A t-shirt featuring your favorite sports team? Think back to the experience of that first memorable purchase: How did you feel buying it? How did you come to have the money to buy it? How long were you satisfied with this item? Next, think about this experience using a bit of sociological imagination, to consider the social forces surrounding this individual purchase. What social pressures made you think that this was a good purchase? How was this shaped by your social location (e.g. gender, age, class), family structure, or the mass media?

Thinking about a commodity's "backstory":

When you buy a coveted consumer item (e.g. that new pair of jeans), how often do you think about the economic structures, labor, and natural resources that went into its construction? Would this awareness make you feel differently about your purchase?

Sociology Outside the Classroom

Personal consumption journal:

Record your purchases for a day, or even better, for a week. Write down when you bought the item, where it was from, and how you felt making this purchase (e.g. Was it stressful? Annoying? Pleasurable? Uneventful?). Make note of anything you consumed that you produced yourself. Think about how each commodity you buy connects you to others. How does it involve social and economic relationships?

PART I

Surviving (and Thriving) in Consumer Culture

Chapter 2

YOU ARE WHAT YOU EAT: CULTURE, NORMS, AND VALUES

INTRODUCING KEY CONCEPTS

In every culture, people have to eat and drink to survive. Making food choices is particularly complex in contemporary consumer culture, where we are surrounded by food basics like rice, milk, and chicken, as well as branded food delights like "Blazing Buffalo Rush" Doritos, XXX Açai-Blueberry-Pomegranate Vitamin Water, and Frosted Red Velvet Pop Tarts. In this chapter, we will examine how the everyday practice of eating and drinking is profoundly social and sociological. Using food as a focal point allows us to understand different theoretical perspectives within sociology: Marxism and commodity fetishism, *Durkheim's perspective on food as* totem, *and* feminist *perspectives on foodwork in the home. By seeing food as more than a biological necessity, you will also come to see how food is a form of* culture. *We explore how our food choices and tastes relate to collective* norms *and* values, *how departures from collective norms and values result in deviance, and how such judgments illustrate contrasting concepts of* ethnocentrism *and* cultural relativism.

1. INTRODUCTION: HOW FOOD IS SOCIOLOGICAL

At first glance, the topic of food might not seem very sociological. After all, food is a biological necessity. At a very basic level, we eat to survive. Even so, *what* we eat and *how* we eat it varies tremendously around the world, revealing vast differences in the food that is available, the rituals that surround eating, and the meanings attached to the foods we consume. In some parts of the world, eating bugs is a common practice, while in others it's a reason to demand your money back at a restaurant! Indeed, what is deemed inedible in one cultural context may be revered as a delicacy in another. Consider the following tasty treats from around the world:

Escargot: A delicacy for thousands of years in the Mediterranean, escargot, or snails, are now primarily associated with French cuisine and commonly enjoyed in their shells with butter and garlic. An estimated 40,000 tons of escargot are eaten in France each year; at about 50,000 snails per ton, that's 2 billion snails.

Spiders: Thought to have become common under food shortages during the Khmer Rouge's regime, catching and eating spiders has now become a local subsistence and tourist activity in Cambodia. While vendors sell deep-fried spiders as a snack to travelers in Cambodian cities, spiders are also believed to have medicinal properties, enhanced by serving them with rice wine.

Pufferfish: Daredevil foodies who like to take a walk on the wild side can try pufferfish, a Japanese delicacy. The skin and organs of a pufferfish contain a toxin that can cause paralysis, asphyxiation, and even death when ingested. Only licensed and trained personnel can prepare the fish for consumption.

Horsemeat: When horsemeat was discovered in meatballs sold at Ikea in thirteen European countries in 2013, it became another anger-inducing tale in a long line of food labeling controversies. Many societies harbor a taboo against the human consumption of horsemeat, but these taboos are far from universal. Although horsemeat cannot be legally sold for human consumption in the United States, it *is* commonly eaten in countries like France, Italy and Argentina, and enjoys some recent popularity due to its low fat content.

Nose to tail eating: It's not always what you're eating that's unusual but what part of it you're eating. Take warm pig's head, crispy ear salad, and duck's neck terrine, for instance. Such dishes are increasingly making it onto the menu of

Eating Horse

A butcher prepares a piece of horsemeat in a Parisian "boucherie chevaline" (horse butcher shop).

Source: Gettyimages.com # 162360713

Fried Spiders

A vendor offers fried tarantulas, marinated in oil and garlic, for sale in Phnom Penh, Cambodia.

Source: Gettyimages.com # 71780782

prestigious restaurants interested in nose to tail eating—that is, eating every part of an animal. Nose to tail eating is about chefs showing their skills, but it's also about reducing waste and showing respect for the animals—by eating (or at least, not wasting) every part of them.

Not only do eating practices vary tremendously across time, space, and cultural context, but they are also closely tied to our identities. As the 19th century French food writer, Brillat-Savarin, famously wrote, "Tell me what you eat, and I will tell you who you are." This often comes through when we discuss food with our students. For example, a charismatic Chinese-Canadian student, Liz, came to one of our classes wearing a t-shirt with a stylized hamburger on the front—a shirt she said she bought despite her friends' objections. For Liz, eating fast food is not just a convenient choice, but a choice that speaks to the essence of who she is. In the following passage that Liz posted on her blog, she describes not just a love of fast food, but a connection between hamburgers and her sense of self:

> Although many of my friends did not like the [hamburger] shirt as much as I did, I still went ahead and bought it because I felt like it represented my love for fast food. To me, the burger is the ultimate symbol of being able to indulge in whatever I want, whenever I want, and however I want.

The burger can be customized in so many ways (for instance, I always eat mine without onions) that it not only stands for how versatile one food item can be, but it also reflects how broad my palate is. If we are what we eat, then I am certainly a burger: fun and delightful!

(Liz, Chinese-Canadian)

Liz clearly has a taste for hamburgers, but her taste preferences speak to broader sociological processes that relate to the place of the individual in mass consumption societies. In other words, food offers a kind of window into ourselves and our position in a broader social context. Food scholar Warren Belasco captures the social importance of food when he writes: "Food is the first of the essentials of life, the world's largest industry, our most frequently indulged pleasure, the core of our most intimate social relationships" (2008: 1). Belasco's words bring us back to the thinking frames that we laid out in the first chapter—material/cultural, structure/agency, micro/macro—each of which can help us think sociologically about the topic of food.

So, while food can teach us about ourselves, we are not just talking about personal culinary discoveries. Thinking about food offers multiple opportunities for thinking sociologically. For one thing, food is inseparable from the material context of the environment and the cultural context of human life. Every time we eat something we are eating a piece of the material world, as well as a piece of our **culture**. In addition, studying food sociologically can also help us to understand social and ecological problems associated with our systems of production and consumption.

Returning to the example of the hamburger, let's put our sociological imaginations to work. At the same time that this food is a symbol of Liz's "fun and delightful" personality and a larger culture of consumer choice, it is also connected to some deeply troubling social and ecological processes. Consider the material dimension of this commodity: where did Liz's burger come from? Many hamburgers are the result of industrial livestock production. Often called factory farming, industrial livestock operations are associated with a range of concerns, such as environmental degradation caused by manure run-off into waterways, as well as the ethical implications of raising animals in confined operations. Food scholar and activist Raj Patel (2009) argues that given its far-reaching environmental impact, the cost of a hamburger is actually much greater than the few dollars we pay for a fast-food burger. *New York Times* food journalist Mark Bittman (2014) did his own investigation of the "true cost" of a burger, and found that if the price took into account the environmental costs of carbon generation (linked to industry beef production and associated with climate change) as well as the health costs of obesity (linked to the fast-food industry), the average hamburger would be much more expensive.

In addition to environmental and animal welfare issues, industrial meat production has come under public scrutiny for a host of human health concerns, such as the impact of antibiotics and hormones on children's physical development, and the threat of bacteria like E. coli. While media attention has generally focused on health risks to consumers, it's important

The Food Bank Challenge

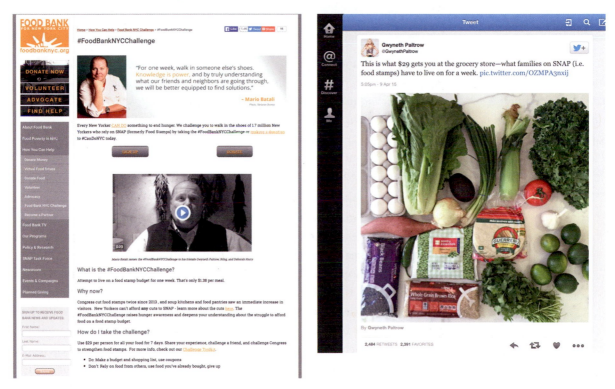

Food banks—like the New York City Food Bank—try to get people to appreciate the challenge of living on a very low income by challenging people to live on the resources of a typical food bank recipient (go to foodbanknyc.org). The NYC Food Bank challenge in 2014 asked participants to buy all of their meals for one week for $29. Celebrities like Gwyneth Paltrow took up the challenge of living on such limited resources; her food photo was widely discussed in social media for not containing enough calories (and containing an unusual number of limes).

Sources: (*left*) http://www.foodbanknyc.org/how-you-can-help/food-bank-nyc-challenge; (*right*) http://goop.com/my-29-food-stamp-challenge-and-the-recipes-brouhaha-that-ensued/

Hungry Planet

In their critically acclaimed book Hungry Planet: What the World Eats, *photojournalist Peter Menzel and author Faith D'Aluisio showcase the diversity of food habits globally. Here, we see a family's weekly food consumption in an Andean village in Ecuador (left) and in an American suburb (right). What key differences do you notice? What factors do you think might shape these different family diets?*

Source: http://time.com/8515/hungry-planet-what-the-world-eats/. Two photos taken from the book, *Hungry Planet*. (http://menzelphoto.photoshelter.com/gallery-image/Hungry-Planet-Family-Food-Portraits/G0000zmg WvU6SiKM/I0000k1asqBIfJec/C0000k7JgEHhEq0w)

to consider the many workers who handle the meat in a hamburger before it reaches our plates—both on farms and at meat-packing plants. These workers may also face health risks, in addition to potentially unsafe and exploitative working conditions (an issue we explore in greater detail in the next chapter). Finally, there is the issue of hunger, and the challenge of feeding a growing population. While some have argued in support of industrial meat production as a strategy for combating world hunger, others argue that this same land could sustain even more people if it were used to grow grains and vegetables. Clearly, the sociology of the hamburger is a complex issue.

More broadly, thinking sociologically about food draws our attention to vast levels of inequality at a local and global scale. An estimated 842 million people worldwide struggle with chronic hunger and malnutrition, 827 million of whom live in the Global South (FAO, IFAD, and WFP 2013). But the issue of food insecurity—that is, not having consistent access to affordable, healthy, culturally appropriate food—is also a serious social problem within the world's richest countries. In our own research, we have spoken with women in Canada about the challenge of feeding themselves and their families in the context of poverty (Cairns and Johnston 2015). For these women, food was a constant source of stress in their lives, and many felt guilty about the restricted diet they were able to provide for their children. Viewing these feelings of stress and guilt through a sociological lens, we can see that the seemingly "private trouble" of food insecurity is most certainly a "public issue".

Throughout this chapter, we will explore a range of sociological tools that can help us gain new perspectives on our everyday eating practices. In doing so, we will pay particular attention to sociological approaches to culture. While our tastes have an obviously individual dimension (e.g. I love olives, but you think they are disgusting), our tastes are powerfully shaped by the culture in which we live.

2. THEORIZING FOOD

Not all sociologists think about food in the same way. That is, there are multiple **theoretical perspectives** that can inform our understanding of food's sociological significance. Theoretical perspectives offer different ways of approaching the same empirical issue—think of them almost as tinted, or specialized glasses. When you employ a particular theoretical perspective, it will bring a different facet of a problem or phenomenon into focus. Theoretical perspectives are *not* like political parties, where you are either a member of one or another. In our work as sociologists, we use theoretical perspectives in a relatively flexible way, applying the one that seems like the best "fit" for the particular problem or issue we are studying. Some theoretical perspectives focus on the micro dimensions of everyday interaction, while others center on the macro, "big picture" questions of how society works. Some theoretical perspectives focus on how society manages to function as a cohesive whole, while others focus on understanding social conflicts between groups of people. You will be exposed to different theoretical perspectives throughout this book, but in this chapter, we introduce three key perspectives that help us understand food as a sociological topic: Marxism and the related concept of commodity fetishism, Durkheim's perspective on food as totem, and feminist perspectives on foodwork in the home.

2.1. Marx: Food as "Fetish"

Marxist theoretical perspectives focus on conflict, and more specifically, the class conflict that occurs in capitalist societies. A key concept here is **commodity fetishism**, which is particularly useful for understanding our relationship to food. By "fetish", Marx was not talking about somebody's sexual proclivities, like a foot fetish. Instead, Marx was recounting how the commodity *form* is fetishized—focused on so strongly that other aspects of social context are ignored. Commodity fetishism obscures the true social relationships involved in making a product. For example, the labor that goes into turning a living, breathing chicken into a chicken nugget is invisible to the casual eater. From a Marxist perspective, the sometimes exploitative and alienating interactions between workers and employers are not generally known to consumers purchasing products. Because of commodity fetishism, these interactions (and exploitations) are routinely concealed, and the value of the commodity is not connected to the labor that went into its production. Put differently, when the chicken nugget is "fetishized", you the consumer don't see or appreciate all the forms of work that went into putting it on your plate. Marxist perspectives have traditionally emphasized the obfuscation of labor relations in the production process (e.g. the experiences of workers employed at the chicken nugget factory), but they have also pointed out how elements of nature are obscured through capitalist processes (e.g. the treatment of chickens, the environmental pollution associated with factory farming, or even the fact that the nugget is made with animal flesh).

To what extent is the truth about our food concealed from us through capitalist relationships and commodity fetishism? There is a lot of evidence to support the Marxist perspective. As the food journalist Michael Pollan notes with incredulity, we have gotten "to a point where we need investigative journalists to tell us where our food comes from" (as in Belasco 2008: 6). We do seem quite naïve, as a society, about where our food comes from, and the conditions under which it is produced.

This disconnect with our food source is a product of global capitalism, but isn't a completely new phenomenon. In fact, commodity fetishism has been with us since the beginning of capitalism (at least). Belasco notes that as far back as 1701, the East India Trading Company boasted the following in its advertisements: "We taste the spices of Arabia yet never feel the scorching sun which brings them forth." These words still seem true today. Chocolate is an obvious example—a product marketed as a luxury and mythologized in children's literature and movies, like *Charlie and the Chocolate Factory*. Yet, the reality is that many workers in the West African cocoa industry are children, and a significant percentage of those children are enslaved. Researchers studying this industry note that most of us who have eaten chocolate have eaten the product of slaves and of child-workers, but this isn't something that most chocolate consumers are aware of, or like to think

The Food (Exploitation) We Eat

The International Labor Rights Forum has a campaign devoted to issues of child labor in cocoa production. Visit their page to learn more, and find out about campaigns to address these issues: http://www.laborrights.org/industries/cocoa.

Source: http://www.laborrights.org/industries/cocoa

Three girls in New York City celebrate the unveiling of the world's largest Hershey's Kisses chocolate, weighing in at over 6000 pounds. Because it takes 500 cacao beans to produce 1 pound of chocolate, it would have taken over 3 million cacao beans from more than 3000 trees, picked and carried by plantation workers, to produce this single giant chocolate (International Cocoa Initiative 2014).

Source: Gettyimages.com # 2351455

about. Cocoa agriculture in Ghana and Côte d'Ivoire accounts for 60% of global production, and a Tulane University study projected that 1.8 million children in these two countries alone engage in cocoa-related activities, some carrying heavy loads, using machetes, and spraying chemicals (often unprotected) ("Oversight . . . " 2011; "ILO-IPEC . . . " 2012).

2.2. Durkheim: Food as Totem

In contrast to Marxist theoretical perspectives and their emphasis on capitalist conflict and exploitation, the Durkheimian tradition tends to focus on understanding how society comes together to function as a cohesive whole. Put simply, a Durkheimian perspective emphasizes how food brings us together, and acts as a kind of "totem" creating a sense of social cohesion. Durkheim's concept of the totem was derived from the indigenous practice of creating and celebrating a plant or animal form. According to Durkheim, this form actually represents the group itself, and belongs to the realm of the "sacred" (as opposed to the realm of everyday, profane social life). Reflecting on the role of religion, Durkheim made a useful distinction between two realms of social life: the sacred and the profane (the ordinary). Totemic objects belong to the sacred realm of social life. When the group worships the sacred totem, the group is in essence, worshiping itself, and generating a sense of social cohesion in the process. The totemic principle highlights how culture unifies people though specific revered objects.

What objects bring people together in collective worship today? Some have suggested that the TV is a contemporary totemic object, bringing families and friends together in a shared ritual. But we can also see food as a totem—an object that represents society, an object that we worship, and an object that creates social cohesion. Consider the example of the Thanksgiving turkey. For many North Americans, this meal symbolizes the values of family, tradition, and national identity. Preparing and eating a Thanksgiving turkey is a powerful representation of coming together to give thanks for what one has, and what a nation can provide (Johnston, Baumann, and Cairns 2010). A lot of meaning, memory, and group membership can be packed into a simple, roasted piece of poultry.

Group identities are often signaled by specific food totems, and these identities can exist at various scales. At a local level, for example, one might feel part of the group by coming together to enjoy a local specialty—gumbo in New Orleans, or the specific BBQ styles found in different regions of the United States. National food identities are particularly powerful and contentious, especially since food totems can travel across global borders in surprising and unpredictable ways. For example, the food that many Mexicans feel represents their national identity is not the same as what most Americans think of as "Mexican food". As Jeffrey Pilcher writes in his book, *Planet Taco: A Global History of Mexican Food*, "For Mexicans, the fast-food taco must seem like a funhouse mirror, distorting their cuisine beyond all recognition" (2012: 5). Put differently, food totems can help people gain a sense of themselves, but these food totems—like tacos—can also be used to shape perceptions of groups held by outsiders. As Pilcher notes, "People use food to think about others, and popular views of the taco as cheap, hot and potentially dangerous have reinforced racist images of Mexico as a land of tequila, migrants, and tourists' diarrhea" (2012: 16–17).

2.3. Feminism: Food as a Women's Issue

Bringing food to the table in a capitalist economy generally requires paid labor (e.g. the work of farm laborers, factory workers, grocery cashiers), but food is also the focus of significant *unpaid* labor. As **feminist** sociologists have long pointed out, unpaid foodwork in the home has historically been performed by women. Think back to your own childhood: who was primarily responsible for making grocery lists, going shopping, cooking dinners, and packing lunches? Whether it was a mother, grandmother, sister, or nanny, for most of us, that person was a woman. One important factor shaping the gendered division of food labor is the longstanding cultural association between food, care, and **femininity** (Cairns and Johnston 2015). In the words of feminist sociologist Marjorie DeVault, "by feeding the family, a woman conducts herself as recognizably womanly" (1991: 118). (For more on DeVault's research, see Sociologists in Action: Qualitative Interviewing.)

In a contemporary Western context, the idea of foodwork as "women's work" might seem old-fashioned, yet sociological research indicates that women still perform the vast majority of domestic labor, including food labor (Lachance-Grzela and Bouchard 2010). American journalist Emily Matchar reports that "women cook 78 percent of all home dinners, spend nearly three times as many hours on food related tasks as men, and make 93 percent of the food purchases" (2013: 26). These findings are corroborated by multiple academic studies that find similar levels of inequality in women's and men's time spent on foodwork (see, e.g., Craig and Baxter 2016 or Castellano 2015). How is it that women still continue to shoulder so much of the foodwork burden? Canadian sociologist Brenda Beagan (2008) and her colleagues conducted a study exploring how women, men, and teenagers described the division of foodwork in their family. Interestingly, the vast majority of the people they interviewed rejected the idea that foodwork is "women's work". However, participants drew upon other rationales to explain why the woman in their house tended to take the lead when it came to food. For instance, some said that women had higher food standards, were more concerned about health, or were just generally more knowledgeable and skilled in the kitchen. In the words of one woman they interviewed: "It's just easier for me to do it" (Beagan et al. 2006: 653). These kinds of implicit ideas about women's connection to food can uphold gendered inequities in food labor—that is, they can make it seem natural that women continue to do most of the foodwork.

SOCIOLOGISTS IN ACTION: QUALITATIVE INTERVIEWING

One way sociologists explore people's experiences and understandings of their social worlds is by talking to them about their lives—a technique called **qualitative interviewing**. This research method was aptly deployed by feminist sociologist Marjorie DeVault (1991) in her classic book *Feeding the Family*. During the 1980s, DeVault interviewed women and men from 30 Chicago households about food in their homes. Her research revealed the "invisible work of feeding" (56) that is crucial to the everyday maintenance of the family, yet seldom recognized as such (e.g. the mental work of planning a meal while taking family members' taste preferences and nutritional needs into consideration). Significantly, DeVault found that this work of caring for others through food was an important source of identity for many of the women in her study, even as it also contributed to their oppression. DeVault interviewed a relatively small group of women, so her research was not intended to shed light on the experience of all women. Even so, these detailed conversations helped scholars better understand how inequalities between men and women are reproduced, and how feeding others served as a vital expression of a woman's femininity.

3. FOOD RULES: CULTURE, NORMS, AND DEVIANCE

The British sociologist Raymond Williams famously wrote that "culture is one of the two or three most complicated words in the English language" (1983: 87). Indeed, culture is one of those words that we use all the time in everyday communication to refer to very different things—our ethnic background is our "culture", a famous work of art is "culture", and we also talk about the "culture" of a workplace or even the "culture" of an entire nation. From a sociological perspective, we can think of **culture** as systems of meaning that are shared by members of a group. Culture includes both material and non-material elements. For instance, the food you ate for lunch is an aspect of material culture, but the manner in which you ate it—e.g. with utensils, chop sticks, or with your hands; alone or with friends?—are shaped by the norms, values and symbols that make up non-material culture.

Norms refer to informal, but widely accepted ways of doing things, which guide our everyday behavior. Because norms are so ingrained in social life, they are often invisible to us—that is, until they are broken. As an illustration, just think back to the last time someone butted in front of you while you were waiting in line. From a sociological perspective, not waiting in line can be considered an act of **deviance**—a violation of a social norm. To be clear, the sociological definition of deviance does not carry the same negative connotations commonly associated with this term. Deviance is not necessarily criminal or evil. Deviance can provoke moral outrage, but it can also provoke shock, laughter or mockery. Deviance simply refers to the violation of social norms, whether they are informal expectations about proper behavior (like waiting in line at the grocery store), or collective rules that are formalized within institutions (like laws against shoplifting). Just as norms vary from one culture to the next, so too do understandings of deviance.

For example, consider the issue of whether eating dog meat is "deviant". Historically, eating dogs has been far from deviant. Archeological evidence suggests that dogs have been consumed since ancient times, and dog consumption has been documented in 13th and 17th century England, 14th century China, and 18th century France and Germanic countries (Podberscek 2009: 616). Today, in cultures where dogs are seen as household members, eating dog meat is viewed as deviant and provokes strong emotions. Interestingly, in cultures where dogs are viewed as vermin—as in India or the Middle East—dog-eating is also viewed as deviant, comparable to eating a rat in the United States. However, in cultures around the world where dogs are conceptualized as a food animal, eating dog meat is not deviant (Herzog 2010: 186–7). For example, dog meat is eaten in Cameroon, Ghana, China, Cambodia, Thailand, Vietnam, and South Korea. However, it is important to note that norms not only vary cross-culturally, but also change over time. For example, attitudes towards eating dog have shifted in recent years in South Korea so that most people (55%) now disapprove of using dogs as human food (Podberscek 2009: 625). Interestingly, however, eating dog is not straightforwardly deviant, as most South Koreans do not support an outright ban on dog consumption (Podberscek 2009: 626). From the perspective of South Korean culture, Western campaigns to present dog eating as "deviant" may be seen as an attack on Koreans' cultural heritage, as well as hypocritical given the millions of pets that are abandoned and euthanized each year in the United States (2 million cats and 2–3 million dogs are euthanized in the US annually) (Podberscek 2009: 626, 629; Herzog 2010: 6, 9).

Dog Eating Protest

Activists around a particular cause often try to effect change by organizing public protests to spread awareness about what they see as problematic social norms. Pictured here are activists for PETA (People for the Ethical Treatment of Animals) operating a mock dog meat shop during a protest in India. The protest uses an existing understanding of dogs as pets and household members to argue that if you would not eat your dog, you should also not eat other animals like chickens and goats.

Source: APimages.com # 299576778482

Norms exert such a powerful force on our lives that breaking them can generate moral outrage—as the case of dog consumption suggests—or simply draw the attention of those around us. In a well-known episode of the much-loved television show *Seinfeld*, the character Elaine observed her boss eating a Snickers bar with a knife and fork. This act of deviance then became the focus of the entire half-hour episode. Have you ever been unsure of the appropriate norms to follow in a particular food context? If you made the wrong move, you might have noticed some funny looks or stifled laughter from your dinner mates. These sorts of sideways glances serve as social **sanctions**—informal signals that you have deviated from the norm, and that work to encourage social conformity.

Another key aspect of non-material culture is **values**: beliefs held by individuals or groups about what is right and wrong, important and unimportant, desirable and undesirable. Values often inform social norms, and guide us in our actions, interactions, and decision-making. We can also think about potential values that are left out of public debates about food. For instance, some food activists argue that a society that values *equality* would work to prioritize universal access to healthy food (as opposed to profit and consumer choice), regardless of how much money one has. We can think of many core values linked to food, such as health, tradition, and family—values that may come into conflict with each other. In one research project we were involved with, an interview with a Pakistani family that immigrated to Canada clearly showed the tension between food traditions and North American ideals of "health". In this family, the mother took great pride in her ability to make healthy home-cooked Pakistani meals from scratch, and she encouraged her son to eat at home because she believed he was "obese" from eating Western food at his university campus. The son culturally identified with his family's Pakistani food, which he saw as part of his ethnic heritage, but he also responded that his mother's cooking was "oily", meat-focused, and "not all healthy" (Beagan et al. 2015: 119, 194).

3.1. Ethnocentrism and Cultural Relativism

Given that norms, deviance, and values are always defined within the context of a particular culture, it becomes clear that our ideas of "good" or acceptable food are highly relative, and not necessarily connected to the inherent property of the food itself. For example, many consider dogs "too smart" to eat, but scientists have shown that pigs are also highly intelligent and sentient beings (Angier 2009). As sociologists, we must strive toward **cultural relativism**: that is, understanding an individual's beliefs, behavior, feelings, and worldview in relation to his or her culture. Think back to the different food rituals discussed throughout this chapter, such as the French tradition of eating snails (escargot), the South Korean tradition of eating dog, and the American devotion to BBQ (often made with pig meat). A food choice that might seem unappealing from our own perspective can be a delicious and meaningful symbol for someone raised in a different cultural context.

In contrast to this commitment to cultural relativism, people often see their own culture as "normal", and thus inherently superior. Within sociology, this sense of superiority about one's own culture is referred to as **ethnocentrism**. We can see this in the following story told to us by Sabrina, a 22-year-old South

Asian-Canadian woman who described a particularly memorable school lunchtime:

> Once when I was in second grade it was lunchtime and as all the other kids were eating their white bread sandwiches with the crusts cut off, I was eating what my mom packed which was *rajma*, kidney beans and rice (my favorite). One of the older kids, a lunchroom supervisor, noticed what I was eating and started to make fun of me! And then his friend joined in! It made me feel sad and so embarrassed that I immediately stopped bringing what my mom had made, and instead started eating white bread sandwiches too.

Sabrina's story reveals food's powerful cultural significance. The jokes and laughter of the lunchroom supervisor and his friends provide a clear example of ethnocentrism, as Sabrina's lunch differed from the foods they had been raised to view as "normal". Their laughter could be interpreted as a social sanction: by laughing, the boys signaled that Sabrina's lunch constituted a form of deviance, and thus worked to encourage conformity to the dominant social norms within this setting. Sabrina's story illustrates how acts of deviance are often met with mechanisms of **social control**: the process of regulating individuals' behavior to ensure that it conforms to group expectations. As a social sanction, the boys' laughter and singling out of Sabrina's meal prompted her to adhere to the social norms of the lunchroom. Whether or not they were aware of it, the boys were engaging in a form of social control.

As sociologists, it's important to examine how these kinds of small-scale interactions, or **microsociological** processes, are shaped by broader **macrosociological** dynamics. Within a particular school, city, or country, some individuals have the privilege of sharing cultural practices with the dominant group. Thinking sociologically can help us to examine the relationship between everyday cultural practices—like Sabrina's bringing a South-Asian lunch or like the group disapproval expressed by the older kids—and broader patterns of social inequality. To do so, sociologists ask questions like the following: Which norms and values are accepted as the shared cultural standard? Whose culture is privileged as "normal"? Whose culture is marginalized as deviant?

Recall that as sociologists, we must work to *see the strange in the familiar*, which means bringing a critical eye to norms that might otherwise be invisible to us. In the final section, we briefly look at two different approaches to the sociological study of food.

4. FOOD AS A SOCIOLOGICAL RESEARCH TOPIC

Food is a great topic for showing the diverse ways that sociologists approach their subject matter. Here, we will explore how food can be studied from a microsociological and a macrosociological perspective. We also demonstrate how food sociology can have a **normative** approach.

Recall from chapter 1 that a microsociological approach explores patterns of thought, behavior, meanings, and interaction in small-scale social groups and settings. This was the approach taken by Ferne Edwards and Dave Mercer in their **ethnographic** research with "freegans" in Australia (2012; also see Barnard 2011). The word "freegan" is taken from the words "vegan" and "free", and freegans are particularly concerned about issues of food waste (e.g. supermarkets tossing out food that is perfectly safe to eat, but has an expiry date that has passed). It is estimated that one out of four calories of food produced globally is lost or wasted, and in North America, most of this waste occurs at the consumption stage (Lipinski et al. 2013). The freegans studied by Edwards and Mercer were involved with two major food waste activities: dumpster diving and making free meals in the activist "food not bombs" soup kitchen. By spending time with freegans, the researchers were able to identify interesting and often surprising details about this **subculture**. (As discussed in chapter 12, a subculture is a smaller cultural group with its own norms, values, symbols, and styles that distinguish it from the larger culture.) Interestingly, most freegan dumpster divers are not poor, but are relatively educated, middle-class-origin men who are deeply concerned about environmental issues of food waste. Part of what freegans enjoy about dumpster diving is the "element of surprise"—not knowing what one will find in a dumpster—and being delighted to come across items like "200 boxes of Ferrero Rocher chocolate" (Edwards and Mercer 2012: 182). Also somewhat surprising is the fact that the dumpster divers that Edwards and Mercer studied rarely became sick from eating dumpster food; part of this related to their vegetarian and/or vegan diet (thus avoiding the risks associated with decaying meat), the careful process with which they filtered through edible and inedible food, and the large quantity of unspoiled supermarket food they were able to access in dumpsters. By taking a microsociological approach, Edwards and Mercer shed light on freegans' motivations, perspectives, and experiences, generating insight into shared norms and values within this subculture.

Disco Soup

One group working in food activism combines a passion for reducing food waste with disco music. Pictured here are volunteers at a New York City "Disco Soup" event, where volunteers cook soup made from discarded food that would otherwise be wasted—while playing disco music.

Source: APimages.com # 841125465450

In contrast to the microsociological perspective achieved by hanging out with freegans, a macrosociological approach draws our attention to key elements of the food system. For example, Tony Winson's book *The Industrial Diet* (2013) studies the evolution of mass-produced food, and documents how it has negatively impacted population health. By studying the large-scale systems through which food is produced and marketed as a commodity, Winson shows how a tremendous amount of the food industry is controlled by a handful of corporations, and how these companies aggressively market "pseudo foods", the term Winson gives to un-nutritious foods that are a key part of our high-fat, -salt, -sugar diet (e.g. ice-cream, chips, fruit drinks, cookies, sugared cereals, soda). *The Industrial Diet* shows how pseudo foods dominate supermarket shelves as well as other food environments (e.g. school cafeterias, hospitals, convenience stores) and ultimately, Winson argues that this industrial diet compromises the health of billions of people on the planet.

Clearly, food is an important topic for microsociological and macro-sociological empirical research—for understanding what is eaten, how different foods are valued, the meanings associated with food consumption, and powerful systems of food production. We use the term **empirical** to describe scholarship that aims to document what *is,* without saying anything about what *ought to be*. In contrast to a purely empirical focus, food can be studied with a **normative** approach that goes beyond "fact finding" to say something about how the world of food production and consumption *should* be organized. A normative approach to sociology is often associated with a famous Karl Marx quotation: "The philosophers have only interpreted the world, in various ways. The point, however, is to change it." Correspondingly, food scholarship with a normative perspective is keen to identify social and ecological injustices (e.g. hunger, malnutrition, ecological devastation), as well as find ways to address these issues. A normative approach to food doesn't just consider what a person or group *likes to eat*, or finds convenient to eat, it also asks about our responsibility—as consumers, citizens, and as a social collective. Belasco describes our responsibility to the food system this way:

> Being responsible means being aware of one's place in the food chain—and of the enormous impact we have on nature, animals, other people, and the distribution of power and resources all over the globe . . . In eating even the simplest dish we join a chain of events linking people and places across the world and across time, too—past and future . . . Having a sense of responsibility entails both remembering how the food got to you (the past) and anticipating the consequences down the line (the future).
>
> (2008: 9)

Viewed sociologically, responsibility is not just something that falls on the shoulders of individual consumers; rather, it is a social process that must be carefully studied. As Belasco states, "ultimately, assigning responsibility is a political process, for it entails sorting out the separate duties of individual consumers, food providers, and government" (10). In terms of *doing sociology*, a normative approach to food studies that considers "responsibility" means two things. First, the professional sociologist and the sociology student must think about their own perspective on issues of food justice, inequality and sustainability, and reflect on what questions will shed light on these issues. Second, it means that food sociologists must pay attention to efforts to struggle for greater food justice. Historically and cross-culturally, food has been a lightning rod for social protest. Today is no exception, and one doesn't have to look very hard to find evidence of food-centered discontent—from demonstrations in the Global South over high food prices (Lagi et al. 2011; Lowrie 2011), to freegan dumpster-diving to protest food waste (Edwards and Mercer 2012), to rising consumer interest in "ethical" foods that are sustainably and humanely produced (Johnston, Szabo, and Rodney 2011).

THINKING FRAMES

How can each thinking frame help us ponder the sociology of food?

Material / Cultural	Food is a material good that is necessary for our survival and is enmeshed within capitalist economies. Food is also a cultural symbol inscribed with rich personal and collective significance.
Think about . . .	What norms and values do you associate with food? How is your food culture shaped and constrained by the material elements of the food system—e.g. the foods available at the local supermarket, or the foods that you can afford?

Structure / Agency	Everyday we make multiple decisions about food: what to buy, cook, eat, and not eat. These everyday food decisions reflect our agency, but the food choices available to us are shaped by structural forces. The industrial food system involves practices of growing, harvesting, packaging, transporting, and marketing foods that are often invisible to consumers, and yet have a powerful influence over the choices we make.
Think about . . .	How are people's food habits and preferences shaped by their food environment that surrounds them (e.g. the relative presence or absence of fast-food restaurants)? How do your daily food habits compare to what you are told to eat by government food guides? Or by food advertisers?

Micro / Macro	A microsociological approach can reveal food meanings, interpersonal dynamics, and rituals within a specific cultural context. Macrosociological approaches are useful for understanding broader food system issues, such as the industrial processes that lead certain products—and not others—to end up on supermarket shelves.
Think about . . .	How do the norms of mealtime differ in different places and in different dining contexts—e.g. eating at home, at McDonald's, at a fancy restaurant, or in a different country? How could state policies be designed to encourage people to cook and eat differently?

ACTIVE LEARNING

Online

Active Learning

The true cost of a burger:
Prominent chef and food writer Mark Bittman writes on the hidden costs that are obscured within the industrial food system (*New York Times*, July 15, 2014). Consider the theoretical perspectives discussed in this chapter; which perspective do you think Bittman is coming from? Do you think the price we pay for a burger should more accurately reflect these hidden costs? http://www.nytimes.com/2014/07/16/opinion/the-true-cost-of-a-burger.html?hp&action=click&pgtype=Homepage&module=c-column-top-span-region&region=c-column-top-span-region&WT.nav=c-column-top-span-region&_r=1

Inside the refrigerator:
Photographer Mark Menjivar allows us to peek into the refrigerators of various homes throughout the United States. Here, he speaks with journalist Lynne Rossetto Kasper about the project. As you read, see if you can identify connections to at least three different key terms introduced in this chapter. http://www.splendidtable.org/story/photographer-takes-voyeuristic-peek-inside-refrigerators

The future of food:
The *National Geographic* profiles various sociological issues surrounding food, including agriculture, hunger, health, waste, and environmental degradation. Which of these issues do you see as the most pressing concern within the food system? http://food.nationalgeographic.com/

Discussion/Reflection

Your daily diet:
Think about your diet and write down all the food you eat on a particular day. How would you describe your diet at an **empirical** level? How would you evaluate it at a **normative** level? What kinds of responsibilities do you have, and do you think other actors have, that shape your individual choices?

Contrasting Durkheimian and Marxist perspectives:
Think of a food that serves as a totem in your own life. What rituals surround this food, and what meaning does it hold for your sense of belonging to a particular social group? Now consider this same food through a Marxist lens of commodity fetishism. If you pulled back the curtain of this commodity, what material contexts, relationships, and practices might you find that have been concealed?

Sociology Outside the Classroom

Breaking the norm:
One of the best ways to illuminate the power of social norms is to break them—that is, to perform a small act of deviance. In this group activity, one of you will violate a minor norm related to food and eating, and the others will observe the social response. Afterwards, write a description of what happened, including the setting, the norm violation, and the reactions of others. Did people respond as you'd expected? What sanctions did you encounter? Can you think of a different context (e.g. culture, age, place, etc.) where this act would be considered more acceptable?

Chapter 3

FAST-FOOD BLUES: WORK IN A GLOBAL ECONOMY

INTRODUCING KEY CONCEPTS

In this chapter, we shift away from the perspective of the consumer to look at the people who work in the global food economy. Through an in-depth look at the fast-food industry, we explore sociological approaches to work, with a particular focus on concepts of *wage labor*, *alienation*, *class*, *ideology*, and *hegemony*. Profiling the research method of *ethnography*, we consider how macrosociological processes like the rise of *transnational corporations* shape everyday experiences and interactions among workers. We also discuss the theory of *McDonaldization*, which extends Weber's famous writings on the *iron cage* of bureaucracy and presents the fast-food icon as a model for rational, efficient, predictable workplaces. Finally, we highlight some key challenges facing workers, particularly as they struggle to improve working conditions in the fast-food industry.

1. INTRODUCTION: DO YOU WANT FRIES WITH THAT?

Many of us have a love–hate relationship with fast food. You may love the convenience and low price of a drive-through meal, but wonder why the food is so cheap. Or perhaps you embrace the opportunity to satisfy a salt craving, but recoil at the idea of "pink slime" (see photo below) being added to hamburger products. Maybe you are a person who loves to eat a fast-food burrito, but later worries about the calories, salt, or fat you have ingested. Clearly, many consumers feel conflicted about eating fast food. However, consumption of fast food is only growing, especially as fast-food brands spread around the world. McDonald's retains its title as the most globally recognized fast-food brand with 18,710 restaurants worldwide; other firms in the "top 10" global fast-food brands include KFC, Subway, and Pizza Hut (Tice 2013). Besides the traditional fast-food giants like McDonald's, up-market "fast casual" success stories like Chipotle and Shake Shack are growing in popularity, featuring a more expensive product that may offer "natural" meat and tastier toppings (Surowiecki 2015).

There are many elements of fast food that concern us as consumers, but what about those working on the other side of the fast-food counter? In recent years, fast food has entered the media spotlight not only as a consumer good, but also as a key site of labor unrest. The fast-food industry employs millions globally, and some of those employees are speaking up about the troubling conditions in which they work—conditions that some of you may have experienced firsthand. From the long shifts and unpredictable schedules, to the low wages and lack of job security, fast-food workers have plenty to complain about. For example, a 2014 *New York Times* feature called "Working Anything But 9 to 5" profiled the life of Jannette Navarro, a single mother struggling to make ends meet through food service work (Kantor 2014). While leaving a job at KFC to work at Starbucks gave Ms. Navarro a slight increase in wages, the erratic schedule made for frequent parenting crises. She sometimes received only a day's notice before her next shift, and was constantly struggling to find last-minute childcare for her son. Navarro's story provides a glimpse into the lived experience of a work life that is all too common in the fast-food industry—a US industry where work is organized around the ideal of efficiency, where the median wage is $8.69 an hour, where only 13% of fast-food jobs provide benefits, and where only 28% of fast-food workers attain full-time hours (Allegretto et al. 2013). In addition to insufficient hours and low pay, schedules are frequently generated by a software system designed to

Pink Slime

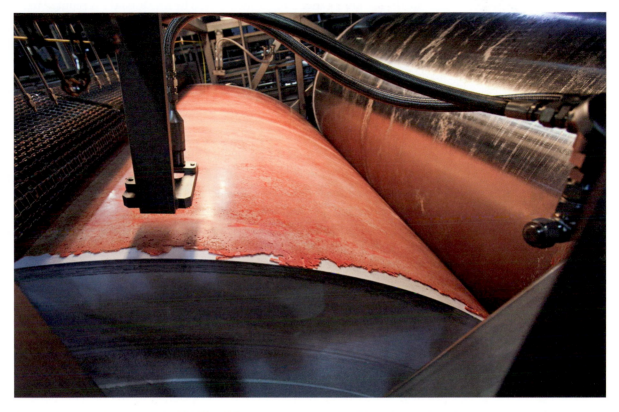

The industry refers to "pink slime" as "finely textured beef"; although it looks like pink toothpaste, it is really ground-up beef trimmings treated with ammonia hydroxide to kill off E. coli and other harmful bacteria. The story of "pink slime" was covered by ABC News in 2012, which reported that it was present in 70% of American ground beef; images of pink slime subsequently went viral.

Source: APimages.com # 120329070656

maximize the corporation's financial gain. Scheduling is not simply an inconvenience for workers, but an important factor in corporate profitability (Kantor 2014). One journalist described the situation he observed in a New York City McDonald's this way:

> Most of the workers here make minimum wage, which is eight dollars an hour in New York City, and receive no benefits . . . Exacerbating the problem of low pay in an expensive city, nearly everyone is effectively part-time, getting fewer than forty hours of work a week. And none of the

employees seem to know, from week to week, when, exactly, they will work. The crew-scheduling software used by McDonald's is reputed to be sophisticated, but to the workers it seems mindless and opaque.

(Finnegan 2014)

While these kinds of labor struggles may be experienced as private troubles to be negotiated on an individual level—like the question of who will look after your toddler when you are called in for a shift—we can use our sociological imaginations to understand worker struggles as a public issue. Indeed, activists have worked to do just that. In November 2012, workers walked off the job in 40 fast-food outlets in New York City, participated in marches, and made clear their demands: an industry-wide raise to $15/hour and the right to form a union (Finnegan 2014). Building on the momentum of this one-day walkout, the summer of 2013 saw one-day walkouts and marches in sixty cities throughout the US. In 2014, the movement went global; in May of that year, fast-food workers staged protests in 230 cities around the world (Tasch and Nathan 2014; Finnegan 2014). In July of 2014, fast-food workers gathered in Chicago to discuss the campaign. In her keynote address, the president of the Service Employees International Union, Mary Kay Henry, drew attention to the vast inequalities within the fast-food industry, describing fast food as an industry where "a selfish few at the top are using their power to hold down

Fight for 15 Protests

Fast-food workers draw attention to low wages and poor working conditions in this highly profitable industry.

Sources: (*left*) GM1EA5F1RQP01 Reuters, (*right*) Gettyimages.com # 488583819

wages, no matter how much that hurts families and communities across the country" (Henry quoted in Greenhouse 2014). By 2015, the "Fight for $15" had grown to become the "largest protest by low-wage workers in US history" (Greenhouse and Kasperkevic 2015). How can sociological thinking help us to understand this struggle, and the labor conditions from which it emerges?

2. WORKING IN A GLOBAL FOOD ECONOMY

In the previous chapter, we explored some of the unpaid labor that surrounds the food we eat, like planning dinners, buying groceries, and packing lunches. In this chapter, we focus on the paid work that goes into our food, with a particular focus on the fast-food industry. A sociological approach to fast food must go beyond the moment of purchase and consumption to consider the various forms of labor that contribute to each meal. By deploying our three thinking frames, we can begin to see the relationship between the micro interactions that take place over the fast-food counter, and the macro-sociological forces that structure work in the global food economy.

To begin, it's useful to take a brief historical look at the concept of "work". For most of human history, people obtained the essentials of life (e.g. food, shelter, clothing) from their own labor, or the labors of those who lived and worked close to them. With the arrival of **capitalism** (see chapter 1), many people's relationship to work changed profoundly. Instead of working for themselves, and making or bartering for the necessities of life, more people began to work for a wage, which they then used to purchase everyday items like food, shelter, and clothing. Today, wage labor is the norm for most adults in industrialized economies (with a few exceptions, like stay-at-home parents, or the ultra-rich who live off their wealth and investments). While we may harbor a fantasy of growing our own food or sewing our own clothes, most of us need a job to stay alive and to participate in the consumer economy. While paid employment is crucial for most people's survival, work also generates much more than a paycheck. Work is an important aspect of people's identity (e.g. the sense of self you get as a lawyer, or a police officer, or a fashion designer), as well as a key source of social relationships. Depending on the work we do, our job may generate tremendous personal meaning, as well as feelings of accomplishment, pride, and pleasure. Of course, work can also generate feelings of resentment, alienation, exploitation, and boredom. In this chapter we explore some of the origins of these feelings, connecting private "troubles" of the workplace to the public issues of labor in a capitalist economy.

One of the most influential sociological approaches to work has been Karl Marx's writings on capitalism, class, and wage labor. As you may recall from previous chapters, Marx was concerned about the inequalities engendered by a capitalist economy. His analysis focused on two social **classes**: the workers (whom he called the *proletariat*) and the owners of the means of production (whom Marx called the *bourgeoisie* or capitalists). Marx argued that in an economic system where workers do not own or control the fruits of their own labor, they are *alienated* from their work, since this work is the source of profits for the capitalist class. The Marxist concept of **alienation** refers to the feeling of estrangement often associated with work under capitalist conditions. According to Marx, workers in capitalist systems perform creatively unful-filling work, with little control over how their work is conducted or the things they produce. Consequently, workers are alienated from the work process, the products of their work, other workers, and their own nature as creative beings. If you've ever worked an eight-hour shift making burgers and smiling at customers, you may have experienced this sense of alienation firsthand. Not only did you have little control over the conditions of this work—e.g. the timing of your shift, what you wore, the way you prepared the food or interacted with coworkers—but you also didn't get to take home the burgers at the end of the day. Instead, Marx would say that you were forced to sell your labor power for a wage—what sociologists call **wage labor**. Within this capitalist system, your work generates revenue for the owners (i.e. the franchise or corporation), who then pay you a small proportion of this revenue in your paycheck. Indeed, the fast-food industry provides a particularly glaring illustration of the class inequality that Marx described. According to the activist group Fast Food Forward, fast-food workers in New York City make an average salary of $11,000 a year, whereas fast-food CEO's can make as much as $25,000 in a *single day* (fastfoodforward.org). Marx contrasted this capitalist division of labor with relations of production in traditional societies, where peasants possessed greater autonomy in their work, and were directly rewarded by the fruits of their labor.

In the last chapter, we introduced Marx's concept of **commodity fetish-ism**, which draws our attention to the relations and conditions of produc-tion that are often invisible when the final product appears on a store shelf. This key insight suggests that thinking sociologically about the work of fast food goes beyond the labor performed in the service industry—i.e. beyond the smiling employee who hands us our fries—to examine the steps that bring the food to the restaurant. In *Every Twelve Seconds: Industrialized Slaughter and the Politics of Sight*, Timothy Pachirat (2011) helps us see how a hamburger starts out as an animal. Working as an employee in a slaughterhouse, Pachirat carried out an **ethnography** (see the Sociologists in Action textbox) of industrial slaughterhouse labor—a key component in the commodity chain of fast-food production. A PhD student at the time of his research, Pachirat describes how his own **social location** (see chapter 1) allowed him to pose as a plant worker in rural Kansas. In his words, "my brown skin, upbringing in Thailand, and prior experience with manual labor mapped nicely onto the slaughterhouse managers' conceptions of who should be working in their plant" (Pachirat quoted in McWilliams 2012). His book provides a firsthand account of the gruelling work of industrial slaughter—the sights, sounds, and smells of hanging livers in industrial freezers, guiding cattle to the "kill floor", or completing the act of slaughter itself, all under the watchful gaze of the plant supervisors. Pachirat builds on this experience to develop a broader sociological argument about the way such disturbing labor practices are hidden from view, allowing the public to avoid confronting the sometimes violent realities behind our food, especially our animal-based meals.

A key factor contributing to these hidden forms of labor has been the rise of **transnational corporations (TNCs)**, which operate across national boundaries and are arguably the most powerful actors in global food **commodity chains**. (A commodity chain is the path that a commodity takes from its conception and design, to its manufacturing, retailing, and consumption, to its final end as a waste product.) Only three companies control most of the global frozen French fry market (Guptill et al. 2013: 123), and four companies control over 80% of beef packing in the US (Carolan 2012: 43). This pattern is repeated throughout the food system: only a handful of TNCs control most of the global trade in grains, cocoa, seeds, coffee, tea, and the agro-chemicals used by farmers. Within this corporatized global food economy, the class inequality that Marx described now operates at a transnational scale. A transnational capitalist class moves seamlessly across international borders, and often shares more similarities than differences— even when they hold different passports (Sklair 2001). At a global scale, workers are much more divided than transnational capitalists, and more vulnerable when they travel abroad to live and work. For example, an estimated 50% of US farmworkers are undocumented migrants, and 80% of them speak Spanish as a first language (Guptill et al. 2013: 115). While these undocumented migrants may find work in the US, they do so without legal rights and recourse when they find themselves exploited. What this trend speaks to is a larger division of labor between the **Global North** and **Global South**; these terms are used to differentiate countries of relative industrialization, development and wealth in the global economy. Global North countries (like the US or Japan) are relatively rich and powerful, whereas countries in the Global South (like Brazil or India) have large poor populations and less clout in the international system. Since the time of colonialism, the Global South produced export crops (e.g. cocoa, coffee, sugar) and cheap labor to the Global North. In turn, many countries in the Global North transform commodities from the Global South into higher value, manufactured items—like roasted coffee or chocolate bars. The worker in the cocoa fields is alienated in multiple dimensions; he or she may not control the cocoa trees in the fields of West Africa, but they also don't control the trade in international cocoa or the manufacturing and retailing of chocolate products.

While capitalist market forces and transnational corporations exert a powerful force in the global food system, sociological research has shown that national borders remain an important factor shaping labor conditions. Put simply, the state is an important actor regulating and shaping how global markets work, and how workers are treated. For example, the state sets minimum wage laws, and regulates standards for worker safety, vacation time, sick-leave, and parental leave. This helps explain why fast-food workers in different state settings can have better working conditions. For example, a McDonald's worker in Denmark earns more than $20/hour and belongs to a union; notably, the price of a Big Mac in Denmark is only 35 cents more than the US (Finnegan 2014). The US fast-food industry—which is generally regarded as highly profitable—is being subsidized by the state. A 2013 study found that 52% of fast-food workers in the US receive some kind of public assistance (e.g. Medicaid, food stamps), and these programs cost the state (and taxpayers) an estimated $7 billion annually (Allegretto et al. 2013).

We can see these connections between state policies and worker experiences in the production of a single food commodity. Carolina Bank Muñoz (2008) studied two tortilla factories owned by the same transnational corporation but located on different sides of the US/Mexican border. Her book, *Transnational Tortillas*, demonstrates the important role of the state in shaping labor dynamics on the shop floor. This is evident in the strategies that managers use to divide, and ultimately control, their workers. In the US plant, Bank Muñoz found that managers focused on migration status, providing perks and rewards to documented workers, while disparaging undocumented workers through demeaning work assignments and threats of deportation. Bank Muñoz argues that this "migration regime" of shop-floor politics emerged in the context of the US's strict immigration laws. By contrast, the Mexican managers focused on gender and race, privileging men over women, and pitting light-skinned and dark-skinned female workers against each other. Bank Muñoz situates this "gender regime" in the context of Mexican economic policy, which has allowed this particular corporation to dominate the tortilla industry, leaving workers with limited alternatives and a union that is closely aligned with management. Bank Muñoz's research contributes to sociological understandings of work in the global economy by demonstrating the continued significance of state policy and national labor markets, even in an industry dominated by transnational corporations.

To return to the subject of fast-food workers, how do we position these jobs within the larger economic landscape? Is making French fries necessarily a bad job? One thing to note is that fast-food jobs reflect a growing gap between relatively poor employees and relatively affluent CEOs (CEO stands for Chief Executive Officer). Michael Norton and Sorapop Kiatpongsan studied social understandings of the pay gap between workers and CEOs in 40 countries around the world. The average person in the study estimated that the CEO/worker pay ratio was about 10:1, and wished that it was about 5:1—a finding that the authors interpreted as a high degree of consensus on the importance of wage equity (Norton and Kiatpongsan, forthcoming). Within the countries studied, the CEO/worker pay gap was much, much more significant than most people estimated. It was most significant in the US, where the average CEO makes 354 times more than the average employee; next on the list was Switzerland, where the CEO/worker pay ratio was 148:1. The fast-food industry has the highest CEO/worker pay discrepancy of any sector of the US economy, clocking in at $1200 CEO dollars for every $1 earned by a worker. This means the average take-home pay for a fast-food CEO is almost twenty-four million dollars a year (Finnegan 2014).

How do we explain the massive inequality that we see among workers on a global scale? Sometimes this

Food Stamps

This image depicts a food stamp from 1939—the year that food stamps were first introduced in the United States. Policy-makers then—and now—believed that food assistance could effectively channel agricultural surpluses to hungry Americans. In 2008 the federal food stamp program was renamed the Supplemental Nutrition Assistance Program (SNAP). The majority of SNAP recipients are children, the elderly, and disabled individuals. SNAP benefits are no longer physical "stamps", but are delivered on electronic payment cards using the Electronic Benefit Transfer (EBT) system. A growing number of farmers' markets are set up to accept EBT cards.

Source: https://commons.wikimedia.org/wiki/File:First_food_stamps.jpg

SOCIOLOGISTS IN ACTION: ETHNOGRAPHY

In the sociological research method of **ethnography**, the researcher is immersed in a particular social context for an extended period of time, in order to observe and document the complexities of everyday life. This research method informs Seth Holmes's (2013) book *Fresh Fruit, Broken Bodies*, which explores the relationship between immigration, work, racism, and health. Drawing upon a year and a half of ethnographic research, Holmes documents the experiences of indigenous Mexican migrants working on farms in the Pacific Northwest. Through his study, we can see that fast food is not the only food industry with dubious labor practices. Holmes's research reveals how the fresh fruits and vegetables that nourish the health of many Americans and Canadians may come at the expense of the health and well-being of Latin American farm workers, who experience the dangers of border-crossing, the physical pain and health risks of days spent kneeling in pesticide-ridden strawberry fields, and the daily reality of cramped and squalid living quarters. His interviews with farm owners, local residents, and public health officials document the racism that contributes to these exploitative work conditions, including ideas about Mexican and indigenous workers as being "naturally" suited to grueling physical labor. Such racist beliefs naturalize the tremendous stress on workers' bodies, and sometimes lead medical professionals to trivialize the injury and illness that so many experience as a result of this work. Yet, Holmes shows how these health impacts are clearly shaped by structural forces. He argues that global trade policies like the North American Free Trade Agreement have caused many indigenous Mexicans to lose their family farms, creating a context where they are forced to migrate to the US for farming jobs that are low-paid and potentially exploitative. Thus, while Holmes' research focuses on the micro level of lived experiences of work and migration, his ethnographic account sheds light on the interconnections of politics, economics, and health in the global food system.

inequality is explained as a result of increased demand for high-skilled "knowledge workers", like those employed in the technological or financial industry. However, economic sociologist Matt Vidal argues that contemporary income inequality is not only due to a rise in highly skilled jobs, but also due to the economy's increasing tendency to produce "bad jobs" (2013: 70). Examining shifts from the 1960s to 2005, Vidal finds that "the economy used to provide decent pay for low-skill jobs in a way that it no longer does" (71). Instead of being marginal jobs, low-wage positions now account for "three out of five jobs generated" between 2009 and 2012 (Allegretto et al. 2013: 4). In the words of journalist, William Finnegan: "Particularly since the onset of the global recession of 2009, McJobs are often the only jobs available" (Finnegan 2014). The groups most likely to work these jobs tend to be those who are already disadvantaged. For example, "more than two out of five front-line fast-food workers are African American (23 percent) or Latino (20 percent), and 73 percent of workers are women" (Allegretto et al. 2013: 10).

Vidal points to a number of factors that have contributed to this shift towards McJobs, including increased international competition, the out-sourcing of labor overseas, a rise in part-time and temporary employment, and a decline in the power of unions. Food service employees comprise a substantial core of these low-paying jobs: "After the corporate restructuring of the 1970s and '80s, the core of the now-internationalized and reconfigured domestic economy was service-based—among the 10 largest employers in 2005 were Walmart, UPS, McDonalds, Yum! Brands (Taco Bell, KFC, and Pizza Hut), Kroger and Home Depot" (Vidal 2013: 72). Sometimes the low pay of these jobs—especially for fast-food workers—is justified by the logic that these jobs are held by teenagers who live at home. However, over two-thirds of fast-food workers are over the age of 20, 68% are the main earners in their families, and more than one-quarter are parents (Allegretto et al. 2013). The median age of a McDonald's employee is 28 years old, and more than a quarter of McDonald's employees have children (Finnegan 2014). Given these structural shifts toward low-wage employment, it appears that rectifying massive economic inequalities requires more than improving the education level of prospective workers. Instead, Vidal argues that we need to connect low-skill work to a "living wage" (2013: 72). A living wage allows workers to meet the basic needs associated with a decent life in their particular geographic location, and avoid the poverty levels that are associated with low-wage work. Put simply, current fast-food wages are generally not enough to allow people to escape poverty (Allegretto et al. 2013: 4).

McJobs

Low-wage McJobs are especially common in the food service industry and likely to be occupied by people from disadvantaged groups. Although such work generally does not provide a living wage, many employees in these positions are parents or their family's primary earner.
Source: Gettyimages.com # 525063314

Given the serious inequality and poverty facing low-wage workers in the fast-food industry, you might be asking, why don't workers resist and fight back against exploitation? This question has preoccupied scholars since the time of Karl Marx, who suggested that the growing gap between the proletariat and bourgeoisie would eventually lead to social revolution. One factor explaining the relative acceptance of the status quo is the importance of commonly held *ideas*, or what sociologists call **ideology**. The concept of ideology is used in two distinct ways in sociology. First, an ideology can refer to a set of ideas or beliefs, like the ideology of a political party. We can think of this as a power-neutral conception of ideology, which is similar to the notion of a worldview. The second understanding of ideology draws from the Marxist sociological tradition, and makes an explicit link between ideology and the power held and used by the capitalist class. From a Marxist perspective, ideology refers to a set of ideas that are used to justify inequality or exploitation, and ultimately sustain domination. You can recognize an ideology when it "makes inequality appear to be the inevitable outcome of the economic elite's superior talent and effort" (Kincheloe 2002: 45).

Closely related to ideology is the concept of **hegemony**, developed by the Marxist Italian scholar, Antonio Gramsci (1891–1937). Gramsci was interested in the role of ideas in political and economic domination. That is, why do people consent to the rule of others? Gramsci suggested that this is rooted in the process of hegemony, in which the views and interests of the ruling class take on a common-sense appearance and seem like natural truths. For example, we might accept the idea that fast-food CEOs "naturally" deserve to make far more money than fast-food employees. The belief that we live in an equal, meritocratic society where people earn what they deserve has become common sense—that is, it has become **hegemonic**. Thinking sociologically, we can see how the ideal of meritocracy operates ideologically when it obscures the fact that many people become wealthy through inherited wealth and privilege—simply being born into the right family and having access to certain kinds of opportunities. On the other hand, many people are born into conditions of poverty that can be difficult to break through, even when they are talented and work exceptionally hard. Recall from the first chapter that a key part of sociological thinking is *making the familiar strange*. By highlighting the ideological dimension of seemingly common-sense ideas, sociologists can expose the connection between cultural understandings and material inequalities.

For the American sociologist Joe Kincheloe (2002), fast food is an important sociological topic precisely because it contains a core ideological dimension. Focusing on the case study of McDonald's, Kincheloe argues that the firm is not simply a seller of hamburgers, but is a cultural pedagogue, teaching consumers important ideological lessons about how society can and should work, and positioning itself as the embodiment of "democracy and egalitarianism" (2002: 53). By employing effective ideological messages, a corporation like McDonald's can exercise a kind of "soft" power that advances its economic interests, while detracting attention from its social and ecological problems. As a corporate pedagogue, McDonald's teaches consumers multiple lessons: that free enterprise produces "freedom and satisfaction for consumer citizens", that family meals bring people together, that fast food is fun and wholesome, that McDonald's founder Ray Croc was a capitalist genius, that McDonald's brings freedom and consumer choice to diners around the world, and perhaps even that French fries are part of a healthy meal (2002: 49–50). It is not that these lessons don't contain some truth. Ideology is not about perpetuating complete falsehoods, or brainwashing people. Instead, we can see how certain messages operate ideologically when they diminish public

Big Sugary Drink Ban

Standing next to a display demonstrating the amounts of sugar in different soft drink sizes, the New York City Health Commissioner makes a case for a ban on the sale of large sugary drinks in New York restaurants, delis, and movie theaters in 2012. The proposed ban was ultimately rejected in 2014, when a court ruled that the city's Board of Health was exceeding its scope of authority in making the proposal.

Source: APimages.com # 120531128904

No More Big Soda?

A protestor criticizes Bloomberg's proposed ban on large soda drinks during the Million Big Gulp March protest in New York City on July 9, 2012.

Source: Gettyimages.com #148084592

awareness of other issues in the fast-food industry—issues like labor exploitation, health degradation, and environmental destruction. Also, we want to explicitly acknowledge what many of you are thinking—that fast food often tastes good, and feels like a pleasurable indulgence. Ideology doesn't deny pleasure. Instead, it's precisely through its pleasurable dimensions that firms like McDonald's exercise their cultural power (Kincheloe 2002: 10).

When thinking about ideology sociologically, it's important to understand that ideologies are not static, but are constantly being reshaped and contested. Thus, ideology itself is less of a "thing", and more of a process. Corporate critics of globalized fast-food systems have emerged, they sometimes change public opinion (and public policy), and sometimes, they are discredited. Various voices have critiqued McDonald's for its low-quality burgers, its impact on human health, and its tendency to homogenize culture around the world, a critique that's sometimes referred to as cultural imperialism. In the words of a Brazilian school teacher who spoke with Kincheloe: "The danger of McDonald's imperialism is that it teaches children to devalue Brazilian things and to believe that the U.S. is superior to all of us poor South Americans" (2002: 35). Kincheloe argues that a key corporate tendency is to "depoliticize the public", and discredit dissenting voices "in areas such as labor, environmental politics, racial and gender justice, child advocacy, nutrition, or critical pedagogy" (2002: 52). An important ideological strategy to discredit critiques of the fast-food industry is to paint critics as elitist, no-fun purists who want to deny the pleasure of burgers and fries to the common person. Indeed, Kincheloe reports that the McDonald's employees themselves tend to "associate political criticism of the company with disdain for them and their low-status position" (2002: 43). The tendency to associate a fast-food critique with cultural elitism came out clearly when former NYC mayor Michael Bloomberg tried to ban the sale of soda drinks over the size of 16 ounces. Opposition to this public health initiative was heavily financed by the powerful National Restaurant Association (an association representing nearly half a million restaurants, but thought to be dominated by fast-food chains). However, the protest was often portrayed in the popular media as a grassroots movement of everyday people standing up for their right to drink a large soda; meanwhile, the corporate interest of fast-food companies wanting to *sell* large sodas was diminished from view. This is ideology at work.

3. THE COSTS OF FAST FOOD: MCDONALDIZATION AND THE IRON CAGE

Like the other topics explored throughout this book, the sociology of fast food isn't just about understanding the fast-food industry—although that's certainly an important topic of study. In addition to shedding light on this powerful industry, the political economy of fast food can help us to think sociologically about broader institutional processes that organize our lives. The sociologist George Ritzer developed the term **McDonaldization** to explain widespread changes in the way goods and services are delivered. Ritzer argued that the McDonald's service system—with its emphasis on efficiency, predictability, calculability and control—represents a large-scale change in how social institutions operate. McDonaldization is not just about what happens at McDonald's, but can be thought of as a paradigm of contemporary institutional

Global Starbucks

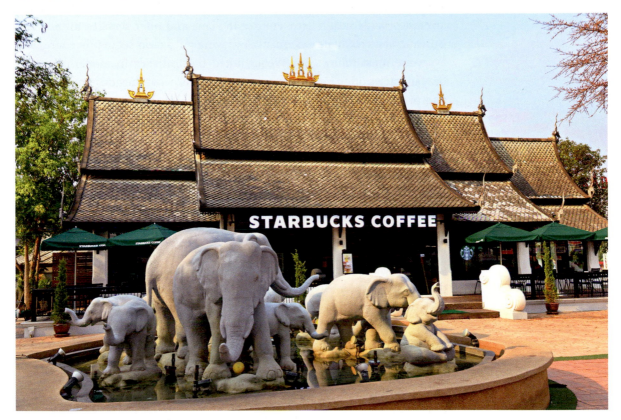

The process of McDonaldization allows chains like Starbucks to offer customers a predictable product, atmosphere, and purchasing ritual at its locations around the world, such as this Starbucks coffee shop in Chiang Mai, Thailand.

Source: 387045229 Shutterstock

processes—a kind of model for doing business that many other firms have adopted. To develop this theory, Ritzer built upon sociologist Max Weber's (1930) writings on the rise of bureaucratic rationality within early capitalism. In this section, we'll introduce Weber's foundational ideas about rationalization, and then discuss how Ritzer extended these ideas to conceptualize McDonaldization.

As you may recall from the introductory chapter, the German sociologist Max Weber is considered one of the founders of the discipline. One of his key contributions to sociological thinking was an analysis of institutional processes. While Marx focused on the power held by those who owned the means of production, Weber observed the growing power of **bureaucracy**—the administrative bodies that emerged to do things like collect taxes, organize armies, provide health care, enforce the law, and offer services to the poor. Bureaucracies facilitate governance by laying out a clear set of procedures that everyone must follow. But Weber noted that officials in modern, rational bureaucracies often have little or no power over what they do, since the rules and procedures of bureaucracies take on a life of their own. These bureaucracies can restrict the agency of those who work in them, as employees must respond first and foremost to bureaucratic imperatives; put simply, they are compelled to follow the "rules". Weber conceptualized these bureaucratic restrictions as an "**iron cage**" within which individuals in modern societies must live and work. If you've ever experienced a frustrating bureaucratic chain of regulations—perhaps when requesting a change in course schedule at your university—you have struggled within the iron cage of bureaucracy. While Weber drew attention to the sense of disenchantment that can arise when navigating large bureaucracies, he argued that the iron cage is the price that must be paid for living in a highly complex and technologically advanced society. For this reason, Weber argued that bureaucratic rationality was a necessary constraint to individual freedom.

Weber's model for rationalization was 19th century German bureaucracy. He observed how bureaucracies were able to attain a high degree of efficiency through functionally differentiated, hierarchical systems based on rules or laws. After World War II, the same principles of efficiency began to gain traction within sectors outside state bureaucracy—most notably in fast-food restaurants and other spaces of consumption. Rationalization meant that post-war consumers had more access to a greater variety of goods than ever before. They could also expect more consistency, lower costs, and in some cases, a higher level of quality from their purchases.

George Ritzer's McDonaldization thesis extends Weber's theory of rationalization to help explain 21st century capitalism. Ritzer takes the fast-food restaurant as the paradigm of contemporary rationalization, and argues that rationalization now extends into more sectors of society than Weber ever imagined. He defines McDonaldization as a "process whereby the principles of the fast-food restaurant are coming to dominate more and more sectors of American society as well as the rest of the world" (Ritzer 2002: 7). McDonaldization consists of four key dimensions: *efficiency, calculability, predictability, and control*.

First, McDonaldization emphasizes *efficiency*, and the effort to discover the best possible means to whatever end is desired. Consider the production of your fast-food burger, which is prepared, and sometimes even cooked, in an assembly-line fashion, just as in traditional factory work. Customers also expect to acquire and consume their meals efficiently; think of how impatient you can become if you sense it is taking too long to deliver your food, especially when you are hungry. We have become so accustomed to the norm of efficiency that we may become frustrated with other customers if we feel they are being *inefficient* when placing their order. The drive-through window is the consummate means for customers to obtain, and employees to dole out, meals with maximum efficiency. Ritzer's point is not just that efficiency is emphasized within McDonald's, but that McDonald's pioneered ways of maximizing efficiency, and that we come to expect the same degree of efficiency in other outlets of consumer culture. Studying the efficiencies of Starbucks as a globalized corporate chain, Bryant Simon argues that Starbucks has been effectively McDonaldized, even though it aggressively tried to sell itself as an authentic and personalized experience: "as Starbucks grew, it became more like McDonald's every day, turning consumption, work, and management into a series of predictable centrally controlled routines" (2009: 71). The global growth of Starbucks speaks volumes about the importance of McDonaldization for corporate expansion. These principles have since been broadly applied, so that businesses that don't live up to these efficiency standards may find it difficult to survive in the global marketplace.

The second dimension of McDonaldization is *calculability*, which refers to efforts to measure all elements in the production process. To return to the topic of labor, consider how various activities performed by fast-food employees are under strict time regulations. This emphasis on speed may adversely affect the quality of work, and can make employees feel dissatisfied with their jobs. When McDonald's in Florida introduced a 1-minute drive-through guarantee in 2014, the corporation came under fire by worker activists who criticized the promotion for placing additional strain on employees who were already overworked and underpaid. In response, McDonald's stated that "The 60-second guarantee promotion is reinforcing a standard we've had for many years regarding timing from the 'cash' window to the 'food present' window" (quoted in Tuttle 2014). Of course, such calculating techniques can also provoke resistance. For example, drive-through employees may ask customers to back up before pulling forward in an attempt to reset the timer sensors, making it appear as though they are serving more people in less time.

Workers aren't the only ones subject to calculation; as consumers, the time you spend eating is also closely monitored. The fast-food environment is designed to get you in and out in 20 minutes, so that you don't slow down the speed of business. And of course, calculability applies to the product being sold. Ideally, the quantity should be standardized, and consistent in terms of its size and weight. Think of the uproar that might ensue if customers discovered their Egg Mcmuffins weren't the same size! Finally, there is the popular idea that bigger is better—both in terms of value to the consumer, and profits for the firm. This is exemplified in the film *Supersize Me*, where the director, Morgan Spurlock, eats exclusively from McDonald's for 30 days. Spurlock suggests that "supersized" meals are presented as better value, but are designed to increase profit margins for McDonald's, while ultimately making Americans unhealthy, encouraging them to eat more food than they would normally consume.

A third and closely related feature of McDonaldization is *predictability*: ensuring that the settings, procedure, and production in a McDonaldized system are consistent across time and place. Part of the reason why people love McDonald's and other chains like Starbucks is because they are predictable. The fast-food outlet provides "a ritual experience" (Fantasia 1995: 221), and one with ample emotional rewards, especially for people who find themselves in a strange or unfamiliar setting. In the words of one businesswoman, "as a frequent traveler, I am always happy to find a Starbucks and have a familiar place to order my coffee . . . I have been happy to find them internationally, in the most unexpected towns in Europe" (Simon 2009: 64). The predictability of fast food applies not only to the product and the planned atmosphere, but also to the labor process. In *Fast Food, Fast Talk*, Robin Leidner (1993: 23) analyzes McDonald's as an exemplar in "the routinization of service work": employees are expected to greet customers in a predictable manner, wearing set uniforms, using specialized terminology, and following interactional scripts. A rigid work environment not only undermines workers' autonomy, but also raises questions about personal identity. As Leidner asks, "what does participation in routinized interaction do to [workers'] sense of self?" (1993: 12). Regardless of the answer, Ritzer argues that "the success of the McDonald's model suggests that many people have come to prefer a world in which there are no surprises" (2013: 14).

The fourth and final element of McDonaldization is *control*. Here, Ritzer draws attention to the way that workers are controlled through technology, as the use of machines can save both labor and time spent on production. Thinking back to the beginning of the chapter, consider the story of Jannette Navarro, whose entire life was subject to the output of a computerized scheduling program, which allocated employees' shifts in ways designed to maximize profits. Such technologies are also used to prompt workers to perform their specified routines, typically using a system of timers and blinking

Automated McDonald's

New technologies like touchscreen self-service kiosks—pictured here in a Manchester, UK McDonald's restaurant—offer the potential to increase efficiency, replace human labor, and further standardize the customer's ordering experience.

Source: Gettyimages.com # 483624436

lights to orchestrate when a particular procedure will be performed. While a good deal of technology is used by employees, the integration of technology is often intended to *replace* labor power; as Kincheloe puts it, these spaces are "labor-proofed" (2002: 70). For example, to prevent workers from burning or under-cooking French fries, timers are installed to ensure that the fries are automatically lifted out of hot oil at precisely the right moment. Soft-drink dispensers pour out regular, medium, and large drinks automatically. Little or no cooking skills are required, since the food arrives already "cut, diced, sliced, molded, and fused by automatic technologies" (Kincheloe 2002: 70). Codified routines make it easy to train new employees, deal with high staff turnover, and keep labor costs low. They have also contributed to a firm's ability to supply a standardized product over time and across multiple outlets. The enlistment of customers as active participants, from the beginning of the dining experience through to the process of bussing their own tables, also contributes to the overall efficiency of the operation. When you go out for fast food, you follow a fairly predictable routine: you stand in line, you order your food (you can't ask for many exceptions or substitutes), you eat, and you leave quickly.

While McDonaldization consists of these four defining elements— efficiency, predictability, calculability and control—Ritzer also highlights a fifth element that is an outcome of McDonaldizing processes: what he calls

Food Container Waste

Although an efficient way to package and sell food, take-out containers, including pizza boxes and Styrofoam containers, constitute a substantial and environmentally degrading volume of waste produced as a result of fast-food operations.

Source: Gettyimages.com # 457939105

the *irrationality of rationality*. To be clear, Ritzer does not propose that predictability and efficiency are inherently bad or harmful. Instead, he argues that McDonaldized systems come to take on a life of their own—just like Weber's iron cage—and he suggests that this hyper-rationality can lead to irrational outcomes. Thinking sociologically about the McDonaldized ideal of efficiency, we might ask *efficient for whom*? What is efficient from the perspective of the fast-food industry—which is always concerned about its bottom line—may be inefficient and irrational from a long-term perspective concerned with health, sustainability, and workers' dignity. Here, it's helpful to think back to the hidden costs of the hamburger discussed in the previous chapter. A fast-food industry that is organized around principles that are designed to maximize profit can lead to worker exploitation, not to mention extensive environmental degradation—just consider the amount of waste generated by the highly efficient production of take-out meals. In sum, while McDonaldization can produce positive results—like standardized, predictable products delivered in an efficient manner—it can also produce irrational outcomes for the larger society, especially over a longer time frame. While the McDonald's meal may be predictable and efficient, the ultimate cost of this highly rationalized process may be very great for both society and the environment.

4. WORKER RESISTANCE IN THE FAST-FOOD INDUSTRY

After reviewing the many negative issues facing laborers in the fast-food industry, it's useful to return to the growing movement to organize fast-food workers. What challenges do they face in the years ahead, and how likely is it that they will win their key demands—a $15 minimum wage and the right to unionize?

In general, labor union participation rates have been on the decline. Less than 7% of private sector workers in the US are union members—the lowest rate in a century. The US rate of private sector unionization is lower than many other Western countries; it is less than half the levels of private sector unionization in the UK (14.4%), Canada (16.4%), and Ireland (16.6%), and considerably lower than Sweden's 65% (Fulton 2013; Bureau of Labor Statistics 2015: 1; Department for Business Innovation and Skills 2014: 5; Galameau and Sohn 2013: 4; Walsh 2015: 5).

Unions are easier to organize in a large factory setting, and in part, the declining union participation rates in the United States and other industrialized

Unionization in Western Countries

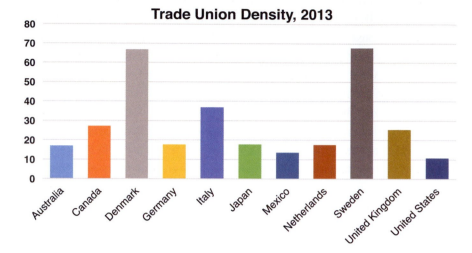

Fast-food workers face challenges in improving their working conditions, yet the rate of labor union participation in several Western countries is in decline.

Source: OECD Stat. 2015. "Trade Union Density." https://stats.oecd.org/Index.aspx?DataSetCode=UN_DEN

countries reflect the decline of the manufacturing base, and the rise of low-pay service sector jobs. Service sector jobs are often more difficult to unionize because work settings are small, employees often work part-time, and the threat of retaliation is high. Nevertheless, some service sector unions have made some gains. For example, the Service Employees International Union (SEIU) includes over 2 million members across Canada, the United States, and Puerto Rico. The SEIU has worked hard to attain representation for health care workers and janitors, two groups that often work in isolated conditions, and has been a key voice of support for fast-food workers who are organizing around the "Fight for $15" (which is the name for the struggle to gain a $15 minimum wage).

The fast-food drive for unionization, at least in North America, is clearly an uphill battle. Organizing each individual fast-food restaurant is particularly daunting in a context where employees who participate in union efforts risk getting fired (Finnegan 2014). Given that context, the fact that fast-food workers have organized nationally, sparked protests globally, and broadly publicized their demand for a union and a higher minimum wage, are notable achievements. While fast-food labor organizing is clearly important as an economic issue, it is also important culturally. (Remember that one of our sociological thinking frames draws attention to the relationship between material and cultural processes.) As workers draw public attention to the issue of service sector employment, they may challenge some of the hegemonic messages that underpin a capitalist economy (e.g. working hard brings wealth, whereas poverty results from laziness). The growing divide between rich and poor was a key feature of the Occupy movement in 2011, which drew global attention to the accumulation of wealth amongst the world's richest 1%. The "Fight for $15" movement shares this theme, drawing attention to the struggle to make ends meet on eight dollars an hour, without full-time hours or benefits. The movement has already made significant achievements. At the time of writing this book, Seattle, California, and New York had already passed laws indicating that they would raise the minimum wage to $15 over the next few years. By the time you are reading this, other cities and states may have followed suit. Although the fast-food industry is organized according to a large-scale corporate logic of McDonaldization, these labor movements show that workers organizing collectively can fight against the disadvantages of working in an "iron cage" of corporate bureaucracy.

The Occupy movement and the Fight for 15 movement are examples of a kind of collective activity that sociologists call **social movements**. Social movements are groups of people and the activities they undertake to work together to make a particular social change. Movements can be any size, from limited (think about getting a neighborhood park cleaned up), to global (the Occupy movement spread to dozens of countries on six continents). The social change desired can be specific (protecting whales), or general (social justice); it can entail a legislative change, raised consciousness, a business decision, a policy change, a directed expenditure of public or private resources, or people's individual choices.

Sociologists have developed a great deal of knowledge about the mechanics of social movements—how they emerge, how they function, and the factors that contribute toward social movement success and failure. The concept of **resource mobilization** is useful for understanding how it is that social movements can get started and build in size. Social movements must be able to recruit resources of people and money to their cause, as well as build the organizational capacity to manage those resources (McCarthy and Zald 1977). This concept for analyzing social movement shifts the analytical focus away from the nature of the desired social change or the alleged deviance of the movement or its members. Instead, it emphasizes that social movements are like other kinds of organizations; access to and management of resources are rational goals that social movements must achieve for success. In the case of Fight for 15, this social movement has been able to draw on the resources and experience of a number of labor unions that help organize fast-food workers, solicit research and draw public attention to issues facing low-wage workers, and mobilize other local-level organizations that were seeking the same or similar goals. The evolution of the social movement from fragmented local groups to a US-wide movement involved developing an organization that could coordinate communications between movement members nationally, as well as present a unified identity to the public through an Internet and social media presence and a central press office for the media to relay the movement's messages. Resource mobilization also helps us to picture how social movements evolve from a shared idea through various stages of organizational development to fully formed social movement organizations. When movements involve the management of enough people and resources, they require a bureaucratic organizational form, and the workings of the organization can in time function just like other bureaucracies we are familiar with, like universities or corporations.

A parallel process to organizational changes are the ideological refinements that a movement engages in as it grows. Most social movements have variation in the exact goals that their diverse members think are most important. For example, in the case of Fight for 15, some members emphasize the goal of a $15 minimum wage for fast-food workers, while other members think the extension of that wage to all service workers is more important, while still others think that the formation of a labor union for fast-food workers is key. A social movement must carefully decide on what its core goals are, and just as importantly they must decide on the **framing** of those goals. By framing we mean the identification of a particular social problem and the justification for why the proposed goals are the right solution to that problem. Having the right framing can influence the legitimacy of a social movement in the eyes of the public.

The **political process model** is a complementary way of studying social movements. Rather than focus on how movements mobilize resources, the political process model includes an emphasis on understanding how opportunities in the broader political environment can help or hinder a movement to achieve its goals (McAdam 2010). The goals of social movements can vary in the extent to which they are easily aligned with other ideas in the wider society, and other kinds of social change can make the movement's goals more or less easy to legitimize to the public or to decision-makers. In the case of Fight for 15, the recent activities of the Occupy movement had directed the public's attention toward economic inequalities. Moreover, the actual amount of wage inequality and wealth inequality were widely reported in the media to be at all-time highs. While some actors were extremely (and visibly) wealthy, employment was sluggish and the economy struggled to recover from recessionary conditions. These conditions gave the movement moral legitimacy, and helped frame service sector working conditions as a legitimate **social problem**. Fight for 15's successes in various jurisdictions in raising the minimum wage must be seen within the context of the political opportunities of the time.

THINKING FRAMES

How can each thinking frame help us ponder the sociology of fast food?

Material / Cultural	The service sector economy—embodied in the case of fast food—involves a labor system that is low in pay and highly rationalized, or "McDonaldized". The material inequities of capitalist labor markets may be "softened" by the ideological messages of fast-food corporations (e.g. "I'm lovin' it").
Think about . . .	Does working in certain low-wage settings feel better (less exploitative) when there are positive feelings associated with the employer? (e.g. working for a firm with a "cool", high-status brand, like Hollister or Coach or Abercrombie and Fitch?)

Structure / Agency	Globalized fast-food corporations continually seek the lowest labor costs and the most rationalized, predictable labor settings. At the same time, laborers are working together to try to challenge exploitative corporate practices that lead to poverty wages.
Think about . . .	How much agency (and power) do workers hold vis-à-vis fast-food corporations? How do individual fast-food workers express their dissatisfaction with their jobs and their employer? How do workers collectively work to change their employment situation?

Micro / Macro	At a macro level, the fast-food sector reflects structural shifts toward "McJobs", a term used to describe low-wage work in a service economy. At a micro level, fast-food workers are trained to perform routinized practices that reflect processes of McDonaldization.
Think about . . .	How might a tough job market (e.g. lots of McJobs, but not enough well-paying careers) shape micro-level interactions between employees and customers in retail and fast-food settings? How would employee morale be impacted? Customer service?

Active Learning

ACTIVE LEARNING

Online

A spy in the slaughterhouse:
Read this interview with Timothy Pachirat to learn more about his ethnographic research at an industrial slaughterhouse in Kansas.

McWilliams, James. 2012. "A Spy in the Slaughterhouse." *The Atlantic*, 5 June 2012. Accessed 28 June 2014. www.theatlantic.com/national/archive/2012/06/a-spy-in-the-slaughterhouse/258110/

Walmarts of higher ed?
In this article in the *Atlantic*, Timothy Pratt explores the concern that a university education is becoming increasingly organized around market principles—a shift that some suggest is creating "Walmarts of higher education".

Pratt, Timothy. 2013. "We are creating Walmarts of higher education." *The Atlantic*, 26 December 2013. Accessed 21 June 2014. www.theatlantic.com/education/archive/2013/12/we-are-creating-walmarts-of-higher-education/282619/

Discussion/Reflection

McDonald's global menu:
McDonald's is the world's biggest and most globally expansive fast-food brand. A key component of McDonald's success around the world is its ability to adapt

to local markets, while still serving a relatively standardized and predictable product. For example, Chinese McDonald's offer the "Rice McWrap", while Italian McDonald's serve a calzone called the Pizzarotto. Have you experienced or read about other examples of McDonald's shifting global menu? How does the cultural impact of McDonald's shift in different geographic contexts? What ideological messages about McDonald's (and America) do you think are conveyed through the global spread of McDonald's?

Corporate ideologies:
Pick a corporate brand that you connect with or that seems meaningful in the lives of those around you. Discuss how this corporation might serve as a cultural pedagogue, teaching consumers specific lessons about their lives, consumption habits, and the role of free enterprise. How might some of these messages be considered *ideological*, especially in regard to how the firm pays its workers? Have any of these ideological messages reached the level of hegemony—that is, come to be seen as common sense?

Fight for $15:
What do you think about the fast-food campaign demands for a $15-hour minimum wage and the right to unionize? (http://fastfoodforward.org/). What factors might encourage (or discourage) the unionization of fast-food workers?

McDonald's U?
In *The McDonaldization of Higher Education,* edited by Dennis Hayes and Robin Wynyard (2002), sociologists explore how Ritzer's theory can be applied to the context of postsecondary education. Is your own college or university a McDonaldized institution? Working in groups, rate your school on a scale of 1–10 with regard to each of the four dimensions of McDonaldization (i.e. efficiency, calculability, predictability, control). Come up with specific examples that illustrate the degree to which this institution fits the characteristic in question (Caronna 2010).

Critiquing fast food:
Is it possible to critique McDonald's, or fast food, without being a cultural elitist?

Sociology Outside the Classroom

Fast-food wages:

Research the average wage for fast-food workers in your state or province. Do you think you could cover your living expenses on this wage? Could you support a family on this wage?

Fast-food labor:

Interview someone who works in the fast-food industry. You might want to ask what factors led them to this job, what their typical workday entails, and how they feel about their job. After the interview, see if you can draw connections between their personal work experiences and some of the sociological concepts discussed in this chapter, such as alienation, ideology, and McDonaldization.

Chapter 4

COFFEE: CLASS, DISTINCTION, AND "GOOD" TASTE

INTRODUCING KEY CONCEPTS

This chapter explores how our consumer tastes connect to our social class. *We discuss how visible and demonstrative consumption habits—*conspicuous consumption*—distinguish some groups from others. We also identify the differences between Bourdieu's concepts of* economic, cultural, *and* social capital. *The case of coffee, and coffee shops more specifically, is used to examine the sociological concepts of* public space *and* third place. *Finally, we explain coffee's connection to globalized* commodity chains, *and describe how a $4 beverage is connected to poverty and hardship for coffee growers and laborers.*

1. INTRODUCTION: CONSUMING THE PERFECT COFFEE . . .

For many people, drinking a daily cup of coffee feels more like a biological necessity than a sociological phenomenon. This routine was aptly described to us by Melissa, a White undergraduate student:

> Up until about six months ago, every morning, like many of us, I would start my day with a cup of coffee. It wouldn't matter how much sleep I had, how I was feeling, or how soon I needed to be up and moving to start whatever responsibilities I had planned to accomplish for the day. In my mind, my day could not start until after that ten minutes of me alone, with no distractions, just sipping on my coffee. This was my morning routine for a good ten years. A routine that became so embedded that it occurred without much thought. Until one morning, it occurred to me, like an epiphany, I really don't like the taste of coffee. In fact, I've never liked the taste of coffee. It isn't refreshing. It leaves this awful aftertaste that often leads to that dreaded, unpleasant coffee-breath and it stains your teeth. So, I began to question, why the hell have I been drinking it so mindlessly all these years?

Many would disagree with Melissa's negative assessment of coffee's taste, and would passionately defend their morning cup of coffee as one of life's greatest taste pleasures. But why exactly was Melissa drinking coffee every morning for ten years? Especially if she didn't particularly enjoy the taste of it?

In this chapter, we use the case of coffee consumption to examine the social aspects of our tastes. When we say that somebody has "good taste", we are usually implying that they have "class", that they can consume in a high-status way. At least implicitly, we recognize that our tastes are not simply biological, but also profoundly social. Whether or not you drink or enjoy coffee seems like an individual taste preference, but it turns out to be a remarkably social phenomenon. A morning cup of coffee is not just a mundane habit, but also speaks volumes about how social classes consume differently, and distinguish themselves from one another. Throughout this chapter, we explore how our everyday consumption patterns are not simply related to our own personal and idiosyncratic taste preferences, but are shaped by factors like social class. Before we examine the cultural and class dimensions of our coffee habits, we'll start by looking at how sociologists conceptualize the connection between consumption and class.

2. HOW CONSUMPTION CONVEYS CLASS AND STATUS

Sociologists have long observed that people in different social **classes** not only do different kinds of work in the capitalist economy (as we saw in our previous chapter on fast food), but also *consume* different kinds of things in different ways. Sociologists have many ways of understanding and measuring social class. When sociologists want to study social class, it is most often conceptualized as a combination of education, income, and occupation. These factors play a large role in determining how much power and authority we have relative to other people who are participating in the economy. Put simply, people in higher classes often have more power to control their lives. Importantly, our own class position as adults is strongly influenced by our parents' class position, although of course people sometimes end up in a different class position from their parents, a process called **social mobility**.

While class position is typically understood in sociology as determined by people's roles as workers or producers, it has become common for sociologists to note how class identities—that is, how people understand their own class position—are also shaped by **consumption** (Bauman 2007). Different classes consume differently. Partly, this has to do with the fact that we often consume items not just for utilitarian ends, but also to send a message to others about who we are, where we think we belong, and how we think we are different from others. The term **conspicuous consumption** was coined by sociologist Thorstein Veblen (1857–1929) in the late 19th century to describe the ways social elites purchase and display high-status items to distinguish themselves as socially superior and to demonstrate their high **status**—the amount of respect, deference, or prestige a person commands. In Veblen's words, "the consumption of . . . excellent goods is an evidence of wealth, it becomes honorific; and conversely, the failure to consume in due quantity and quality becomes a mark of inferiority and demerit" (1967: 75). Veblen's writing also identified how high-status consumption items tended to "trickle down" to lower classes, creating a competitive cycle of consumption. More recently, economist Robert Frank (2011) has termed this phenomenon an "expenditure cascade": when people at the top of the class hierarchy spend more on a given item (like a cup of coffee), it can lead to an expansion of expectations and expenditures by those lower down the socio-economic totem pole. This phenomenon helps shed light on why lower and middle income people (often inadvertently) may come to desire high-status items (e.g. designer shoes and purses, luxury cars, expensive baby strollers). Once coveted

One and Only Wu Tang Album

In 2015, the acclaimed American hip-hop group Wu-Tang Clan, pictured performing here, created a limited edition album: only a single copy was made and auctioned to the highest bidder. In what appears to be an extraordinary act of conspicuous consumption, the single copy of the album was purchased for $2 million by the controversial American pharmaceuticals entrepreneur Martin Shkreli, who expressed no immediate plans to listen to it.

Source: Gettyimages.com # 489825618

consumer items are too widely consumed, however, upper classes move on to other conspicuous consumption items to maintain their high status.

Veblen wrote about conspicuous consumption in the last few decades of the 19th century, providing some useful historical context on contemporary consumption patterns. This was an era that Mark Twain referred to as the "gilded age", a time when a certain portion of the American population became fabulously wealthy through industrialization. These wealthy families often purchased ostentatious clothes, furniture, and tableware (china, glassware, linens) to symbolize the family's economic success. Tableware became impossibly elaborate, with a fork for every conceivable dish. There were literally *hundreds* of forks designed and sold for eating specific items like toast, pickles, tomatoes, oysters, ice-cream, and even soup. While not everybody could afford such an elaborate set of forks, people from varying social classes felt compelled to buy the best sets they could afford, and to learn the newly expanding rules of table etiquette. Food writer Darra Goldstein notes how people developed "fork anxiety" when faced with the elaborate tableware settings, a nervousness made worse by the fact that there was a small and ever-changing list of foods that could be acceptably eaten by hand (e.g. taking a sugar cube with your hands was gauche, but eating an olive with your hands was the sign of a true gentleman/woman) (B. Wilson 2012: 188–9). The expanding silverware trend was socially competitive, long-lasting, and so excessive that in 1925, the US government's Secretary of Commerce, Herbert Hoover, stepped in to decree that American silver services should contain no more than 55 different, distinct pieces (Goldstein 2006: iv).

Oyster Forks

A set of silver Chrysanthemum oyster forks dated from 1880–91 manufactured by Tiffany and Co. NYC.

Source: https://collection.cooperhewitt.org/objects/18706037/

While few people today own, or even know about, an ice-cream fork, knowing "what fork to use" remains a symbol of one's cultural sophistication and class upbringing. A major stream of sociology takes up Veblen's investigation of classed consumption habits and examines how consumption works to shape social class boundaries—that is, to align us with certain kinds of people and mark distance from others. For example, Juliet Schor's research makes clear that contemporary shoppers continue to "upscale" their consumption, attempting to use their purchases to emulate the lives of social elites. This phenomenon is referred to as **upscale emulation** (Schor 1998; 1999). Schor (1999) argues that today's consumption—what she calls the **new consumerism**—is not just about "keeping up with the Joneses", but also about purchasing (or aspiring towards) the goods displayed by celebrities, actors, musicians, and models—whose lives are prominently featured on television and in magazines. Schor also contends that the surge of upscale consumption (e.g. diamonds of a carat or more, SUVs, plastic surgery) came at a historical moment when wealth was shifting to the top 20% of the population. Those "at the top" consumed in flashy ways, while those at the bottom increasingly compared themselves to the richest Americans. The result is a persistent, and troubling "aspirational gap: with desires persistently outrunning incomes" (Schor 1999: 3; also Frank 2011).

For Schor and other sociologists who study social class and consumption, it is important not just to examine the economic dimension of inequality, but also its cultural and social dimension. Of course, consumption practices are also material practices; you need money to be able to consume high-status goods, like a luxury vehicle or a 2-carat diamond engagement ring. However, in the gilded age—and even more so today in the age of credit cards—people can consume beyond their means to achieve a sense of elevated status. Lower- or middle-class consumers can also display a familiarity with high-status consumer items, like designer purses (even if they end up purchasing a fake), that allow them to behave like social elites. At the same time, people of great wealth can conceal or minimize their economic resources by consuming modestly. For example, Warren Buffett—one of the richest people on earth, worth around $70 billion—is famous for a low-budget lifestyle that involves driving himself to work, and living in the original house he bought in the 1950s. Closer to home, some wealthy college students may buy second-hand clothes and get excited about finding vintage household items in thrift shops. Put differently, high-status consumption and wealth are related, but that relationship is culturally complex. The challenge for sociologists is to better understand how culture and consumption work together to construct classed identities and naturalize social inequality.

One sociologist who has delivered great insight into the study of class, consumption, and status is the French sociologist Pierre Bourdieu (1930–2002). One of Bourdieu's (1984) key insights was that class inequalities are reproduced over time through consumption habits, and that consumption is a key way that elites attain a kind of status or distinction. For example, a middle-class child's status is not simply related to her parents' income, but also to the fact that her family upbringing and education encourage consumption and lifestyle habits that reproduce her class advantages later in life—e.g. dining etiquette, piano lessons, art appreciation. Interviewing for a job, for example, the middle-class person may know how to speak about a new art exhibit, or display a high degree of comfort and familiarity at a fancy restaurant. This may not only impress her potential bosses, but also make them feel like she fits in, giving her an advantage over an applicant from a lower-class upbringing who may not have had as much exposure to these settings. This familiarity with middle-class consumption habits creates a sense of belonging that makes it more difficult for disadvantaged groups to "break in" to elite social circles. Crucially, these tastes are generally recognized as nothing more than an individual's "good taste", rather than mechanisms for legitimizing class position. Thus, Bourdieu's work helps us to see how cultural tastes both reflect and reinforce social inequalities.

It's helpful to develop a sociological vocabulary for the difference between simply having money and having knowledge about how to consume in a high-status way—a way that affords maximum social status. Bourdieu (1986) usefully differentiated between three forms of capital: **economic**, **social**, and **cultural**. These different forms of capital can be exchanged for one another, but you can be rich in one form of capital while lacking in another form. The meaning of economic capital is straightforward; it refers to the amount of money you possess, and is a basic way that we can understand inequality. Some groups have more economic capital, and some groups have less. Social capital refers to the value that comes from your social relationships and networks; if you know a lot of people, and those people can help you out in life (e.g. helping you get a job, providing stock market tips), you have plenty of social capital.

Cultural capital is a concept of key importance for understanding consumption. It refers to the kinds of knowledge and skills that are highly valued within a particular culture, and thus provide social advantages. Bourdieu (1986) identified 3 types of cultural capital: 1) the cultural capital that is *embodied* in our tastes and self-presentation, like modes of speech and body language; 2) cultural capital that is *objectified* in our possessions, such as books, clothing, or works of art; and 3) cultural capital that is *institutionalized*, such as the capital that you will gain by having a university or college education. Seen through everyday examples, having cultural capital can mean things like having a degree from an Ivy League school (institutionalized cultural capital), being able to comfortably navigate an elaborate table setting in an expensive restaurant (embodied cultural capital), or owning a piece of original artwork (objectified cultural capital). Having ample cultural capital means knowing *how* to consume like a social elite. Having this kind of knowledge and experience not only confers status on an individual, but is also used to transmit advantages within the family. Parents with high cultural capital are able to share this resource with their children, often without being aware of doing so. For example, parents may not explicitly think of their kids' piano lessons or trips to the museum as strategic efforts to maintain their family's class privilege, and yet, these activities serve to foster cultural capital within their children.

In addition to the social reproduction of class advantage within the family, Bourdieu was particularly interested in the role of cultural capital within education. He argued that schooling sustains social inequality by favoring middle-class cultural practices over those associated with a working-class upbringing. Middle-class children come to school with certain forms of cultural capital that are valued within the school—particular speech patterns, demeanors, tastes, and so on—giving these children an advantage relative to their peers. For example, a child who has been exposed to artwork and piano lessons at home, may feel more comfortable discussing her opinions on art and music in class, and will better convey an impression of being a "smart student" to the teacher. Thus, middle-class norms become an important source of privilege for children because they are granted greater legitimacy within the institution of schooling (Bourdieu 1974). In this way, the cultural capital transmitted within the family is validated by the education system, further reproducing relations of class privilege.

Elite groups typically have all three kinds of capital—economic, social, and cultural capital—but some groups may have more of one kind of capital than

Celebrities on Instagram

Given the popularity of social media platforms like Instagram and Snapchat among wealthy celebrities—like recording artists Jay-Z and DJ Khaled, pictured here—audiences have increasingly easy and rapid access to elite consumption habits (as well as enhanced information about how to emulate them).

Source: Gettymages.com #504951960

SOCIOLOGISTS IN ACTION: SURVEY RESEARCH

A large part of Bourdieu's famous work, *Distinction*, relies on surveys of French consumers from the 1960s. **Surveys** are a key method used within large-scale **quantitative** research. While qualitative methods like interviewing and ethnography (discussed in chapters 2 and 3) facilitate in-depth understandings within particular cultural contexts, surveys allow sociologists to explore wider social trends. Since researchers cannot possibly survey every single person in the population they want to study, surveys are administered to a **sample**, or subset, of a wider population. For instance, if you were interested in exploring coffee preferences among students at your school, your research population would include the entire student body, but your research sample would include a subset of these students whom you would ask to complete the survey. In Bourdieu's survey research, over 1200 respondents answered a range of questions regarding their taste preferences (J. Lane 2000). Through statistical analysis of the survey results, Bourdieu was able to demonstrate the close link between class background and cultural tastes, revealing striking classed consumption patterns within French society. While surveys may provide less detailed information about individual experiences and specific cultural contexts, a key strength of survey research is the ability to generalize a study's findings to a wider population.

another. For example, a newly rich Texas oil-tycoon may be flustered at a fancy French restaurant, and only want to eat plain old steak; he has economic capital, but not cultural capital. On the other hand, a 25-year-old hipster may have low economic capital because she works in a low-paying retail job, yet possess abundant cultural capital: she may struggle to scrape together her rent money, but possess a graduate degree in creative writing and know how to appreciate a piece of aged French cheese. Consuming high-status items is certainly easier if you have economic capital (e.g. especially when it comes to *owning* fine art, or high-status items like a Bentley or a Rolex), but it is possible to possess bounteous cultural capital and be perennially short on cash. In those situations, consuming high-status, but relatively low-budget items, can be an important way to compensate for your lack of money. This is exactly where the gourmet coffee trend comes in.

3. COFFEE CONSUMPTION AND SOCIAL STATUS

As recently as a few decades ago, coffee meant one thing and one thing only to most Americans—a brown, mildly flavored drink made with supermarket grinds that often came in a vacuum packed can. People drank coffee as part of their breakfast or workplace rituals, but it wasn't an item that made them feel particularly special or unique. Today, going out for a coffee can mean *many* things—a regular drip coffee, a sweetened icy drink with whipped cream, a tiny cup of espresso, or a foamy chai latte. The coffee consumption experience also varies widely, from a quick order at a drive-through window, to a social date with a friend, or a quiet afternoon of studying. Coffee has become much more than a simple drink; it is also a way to express social status and cultural capital.

How did coffee come to play this role? A big part of the change can be attributed to Starbucks, a corporate coffee retailer that dramatically changed North American coffee culture. Coffee scholars Benoit Daviron and Stefano Ponte talk about the "Starbucks factor" to refer to the significant impact this single firm has had on the industry (2005: 77). Starbucks emerged out of Seattle in the 1970s, and initially sold itself as a place where connoisseurs could go to buy coffee, and the uninitiated could go to learn about it. Put differently, Starbucks was a place that traded not just in coffee, but in cultural capital— knowledge of how to identify a single-origin, high-quality coffee roast, how to grind beans, and how to distinguish yourself from mass-market coffee consumers (Daviron and Ponte 2005: 142, 151). When Starbucks moved into a phase of aggressive corporate expansion in the late 1980s and early 1990s, it appeared to deliberately follow a Veblenian strategy of conspicuous consumption (Simon 2009: 34). As Starbucks scholar Bryant Simon writes, "Starbucks went right to the center of worlds of wealth, higher education, and creative professional work" (2009: 35). New locations were strategically placed in areas where high-status people lived and shopped, so that it was hard for somebody "with an Ivy League degree, a passport filled with stamps from foreign countries, and annual incomes over $80,000 not to trip over one of [Starbucks'] logoed outlets" (Simon 2009: 34). Having a trademark white and green cup became a status symbol—a sign that you knew how to consume good coffee, you knew the coffee employee was called a "barista", and you knew how to order in Starbucks-specific language (e.g. a "tall", not a "small"). Consuming an everyday "luxury" like Starbucks became a known sign of good taste and sophistication. You might not have the economic capital to acquire large-scale

The Evolution of Coffee Culture

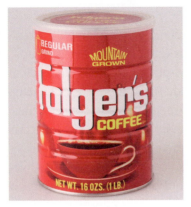

Pictured here is a can of Folgers ground coffee from the 1970s. Until relatively recently, most North Americans associated coffee exclusively with this kind of product, consumed during breakfast or at the workplace without much contemplation. Today, the drink can take many forms as well as signal status.

Source: Alamy B7GAMD

Today, coffee connoisseurs have come a long way from instant coffee. This photo depicts Blue Bottle's elaborate "siphon" coffee system, which draws from a traditional Japanese method of making coffee.

Source: Blue Bottle Moments https://www.flickr.com/photos/50979393@N00/14860545918

luxuries like a fancy car, or a vacation home, but those with cultural capital could signal their status and good taste by buying coffee at Starbucks. In Simon's research, one New York City junior executive admitted to buying a Starbucks coffee at the start of the week, and then refilling the cup with cheap homebrew before he left the house each day (2009: 43).

The high-status connotations of Starbucks (and similar chains) can still be seen in everyday attitudes. One of our students, Melissa, whom we introduced at the beginning of this chapter, told us that in her social circles, "people want to be seen sipping a cup with that infamous logo because it makes them feel a heightened, more superior form of identity . . . like they are 'better' for choosing Starbucks over McDonald's." Sociologists studying coffee consumption have made similar findings. Canadian sociologist Sonia Bookman (2013) interviewed people who went to upscale chains like Starbucks, as well as those who drank coffee at Tim Horton's, a low-brow Canadian chain comparable to Dunkin' Donuts. She found a clear class divide, where Starbucks was associated with high-status ideals of sophistication and refinement, and Tim Horton's was viewed as a pragmatic choice for "ordinary" folks who want a no-fuss cup of coffee. Bookman's interviewees didn't

CAFFEINE AS AN ACCEPTABLE ADDICTION

In chapter 2, we introduced the concept of **deviance**: a violation of social norms. While many chemical addictions are viewed as deviant—like addictions to illegal drugs or alcohol—an addiction to coffee is generally socially accepted. The different social evaluations ascribed to a caffeine addiction and, say, an addiction to cocaine, bring to light the power of social norms in defining what constitutes deviance. One kind of coffee consumption that has historically been seen as deviant is feeding coffee to kids. The conventional wisdom on this point is that coffee consumption stunts children's growth. However, the only research to back up this claim was generated by an advertising campaign by the Postum company in 1933 to help promote sales of its non-caffeinated hot drink; no research since that time has shown that caffeine stunts growth. Nevertheless, this message has endured, largely because it draws on hegemonic ideas about children as a vulnerable consumer population that is in need of protection. To read more about the history of the "stunting growth" coffee myth, visit the following website: http://www.smithsonianmag.com/science-nature/its-a-myth-theres-no-evidence-that-coffee-stunts-kids-growth-180948068/?no-ist

explicitly mention social class, but they drew class boundaries between different types of consumers based on their coffee preferences. Bookman argues that brands are a key way for contemporary individuals to enact their class identities, even if they don't overtly use the language of class. In her words, "brands are used as a means to co-construct notions of class—ways of being, acting or feeling, whether working or middle class—in more implicit, complex ways" (2013: 414). In keeping with Bryant Simon's research, Bookman found that the mostly middle-class and upper-middle-class Starbucks customers positioned themselves as coffee connoisseurs who possessed a refined knowledge that informed their cultivated tastes. By contrast, the predominantly working-class and lower-middle-class Tim Horton's consumers rejected the pretension of Starbucks, and took pride in a coffee experience that was low maintenance and affordable. In one of Bookman's research subjects' words, "I in fact avoid Starbucks . . . because it is too much aesthetics and it is too expensive, and I don't like that people sit there all day" (2013: 419). Thus,

Starbucks: A Global Coffee Giant

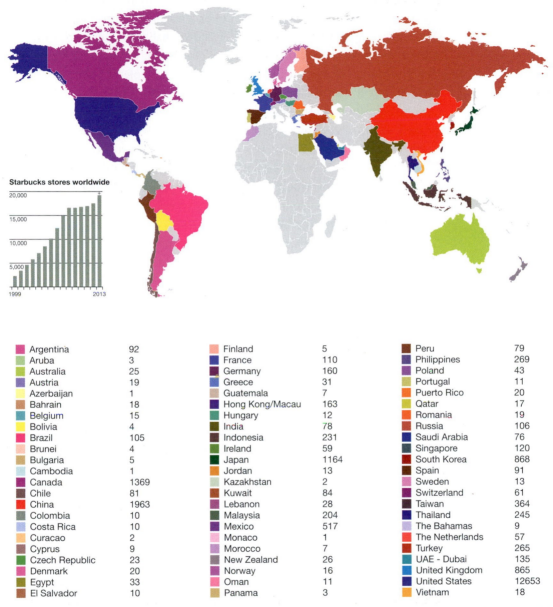

Starbucks stores worldwide

Argentina	92	Finland	5	Peru	79
Aruba	3	France	110	Philippines	269
Australia	25	Germany	160	Poland	43
Austria	19	Greece	31	Portugal	11
Azerbaijan	1	Guatemala	7	Puerto Rico	20
Bahrain	18	Hong Kong/Macau	163	Qatar	17
Belgium	15	Hungary	12	Romania	19
Bolivia	4	India	78	Russia	106
Brazil	105	Indonesia	231	Saudi Arabia	76
Brunei	4	Ireland	59	Singapore	120
Bulgaria	5	Japan	1164	South Korea	868
Cambodia	1	Jordan	13	Spain	91
Canada	1369	Kazakhstan	2	Sweden	13
Chile	81	Kuwait	84	Switzerland	61
China	1963	Lebanon	28	Taiwan	364
Colombia	10	Malaysia	204	Thailand	245
Costa Rica	10	Mexico	517	The Bahamas	9
Curacao	2	Monaco	1	The Netherlands	57
Cyprus	9	Morocco	7	Turkey	265
Czech Republic	23	New Zealand	26	UAE - Dubai	135
Denmark	20	Norway	16	United Kingdom	865
Egypt	33	Oman	11	United States	12653
El Salvador	10	Panama	3	Vietnam	18

This map published by the Washington Post charts the tremendous growth of Starbucks around the world. To read more about Starbucks' global expansion (and to find out which country has the highest number of Starbucks per capita) read the feature published by the global news website Quartz: http://qz.com/ 208457/a-cartographic-guide-to-starbucks-global-domination/

Source: http://www.washingtonpost.com/apps/g/page/world/a-coffee-giants-global-footprint/514/

Bookman's research illustrates how working-class consumers may challenge the cultural evaluations of the middle class, even as many middle-class people accept the idea that drinking upscale coffee is a sign of cultural sophistication. More generally, the example of coffee shows that taste hierarchies are not natural or universal, and may develop differently for different social classes.

The Starbucks story teaches us a lot about the role of coffee as a status symbol, but it also demonstrates the cyclical nature of status trends and upscale emulation. Starbucks' symbolic status as the coffee of upscale people peaked in the 1990s, and began to fade with market saturation and mass-market expansion. As Simon writes, "Starbucks has grown so rapidly and spread so far, so fast, that it has replaced McDonald's as the symbol for many of the newest and most troubling wave of homogenization" (2009: 76). Indeed, Starbucks went from having 165 stores in 1992, to 7500 outlets in 2004 (Simon 2009: 45; Daviron and Ponte 2005: 78).

In the late 1990s, critics began to point out that the corporation acted like a "bottom-feeder" in the coffee market, purchasing cheap, low-quality beans (Simon 2009: 45). Starbucks also began to introduce practices of standardization that led to the impression that it was more interested in corporate expansion than selling delicious coffee for aficionados (Patterson, Scott, and Uncles 2010). Automatic machines eliminated the high skill required of well-trained baristas, so that quickly trained employees could make espresso-based drinks with the touch of a button. The de-skilling process "resulted in a loss of 'theatre' for people wanting to see their coffee made that way and has also had implications for taste" (Patterson et al. 2010: 45). Long-lasting, pre-ground, pre-roasted coffee was shipped to locations in vacuum-packed bags, contra the coffee aficionada insistence that coffee should be ground fresh before brewing, and beans should be consumed within 15 days of roasting (Simon 2009: 45; Daviron and Ponte 2005: 149). Starbucks also introduced a range of flavored drinks like Frappuccinos that were heavy on cream and sugar, and light on coffee flavor (Simon 2009: 49). These drinks were important for bringing in teenage customers who weren't crazy about the taste of coffee. However, the success of their blended, frozen drinks diluted the impression that Starbucks was a serious place for coffee aficionados. The amount of cultural capital required of Starbucks consumers declined, especially as more people got the knack for their unusual drink lingo, and the status acquired by going there dropped accordingly. Discerning coffee customers gained more status by finding independent coffee shops that promised greater authenticity, and more commitment to a "true" coffee product. These are places where you can't order a strawberry flavored milkshake and where pulling the perfect espresso shot is seen as an art form. Independent coffee houses may refuse to sell decaffeinated espresso beans or insist on selling *only* fair-trade coffee. These establishments position themselves as unique, coffee-focused specialists in opposition to Starbucks' homogenized, watered-down coffee offerings. In Daviron and Ponte's words, "by becoming another large corporation and providing a homogenized retail experience with a consistent but not exceptionally good product, Starbucks has in many ways become the opposite of what independent coffee houses perceive themselves to be" (2005: 79; also Ruzich 2008: 439).

While Starbucks' role as a status symbol has declined, what it continues to offer is a predictable, clean place for people to meet, work, and take a break. Starbucks cafés look remarkably similar wherever you find them, and that familiarity is reassuring for people—even if it is not particularly cool or cutting edge (recall from last chapter that predictability is a key feature of McDonaldization). As Simon writes, "a high-priced cup of coffee is the price of admission to this clean, predictable place" (2009: 70). While Starbucks prides itself on its predictability, we can debate the extent to which Starbucks (or other chains) offer a kind of **public space**—an open, social space where everyone is welcome, like a public park or library. In an obvious way, Starbucks is *not* a public space. It is a privately owned and operated business. If you make a scene, or stage a protest, or if you are obviously homeless, chances are you will be asked to leave. To sit in a comfy chair and use the washroom, you need to pay the price of admission: a relatively expensive cup of coffee. At the same time that Starbucks is obviously a private business, people use Starbucks in ways that resemble a public park or library—they hang out and read a book, they check email, they use it as a meeting place, and they linger over extended conversations with friends. How then do we conceptualize the ways that coffee chains like Starbucks are used as a kind of "quasi-public" space in everyday life?

Sociologist Ray Oldenburg developed the concept of **third place** (1989) to describe spaces where people can get together to meet and talk, and contrasted them with the "first place" of a private home, and the "second place" of a workplace. According to Oldenburg and other theorists of public spaces, the benefit of third places—like barbershops, coffee shops, or public squares— is that they offer a place for people to hang out in a realm outside their private home, discuss ideas with others outside the influence of the state, and come into contact with people they might not meet otherwise. This was a key part of traditional, 18th century English coffee houses, where men from different social classes came together to learn about the news and debate politics (Cowan

2005). Writing about urban mixing in places like Philadelphia's historic Reading Terminal Market, urban sociologist Elijah Anderson argues that these experiences can be "profoundly humanizing", as people "have a chance to mix, observe one another, and become better acquainted with people they otherwise seldom observe up close" (2004: 28), especially those from different racial and ethnic groups.

So does Starbucks serve the role of "third place"? The evidence here is mixed. On the one hand, some people—maybe even you, dear reader—have personal experiences of Starbucks as a place where they chat with strangers, and meet people they wouldn't otherwise interact with. Starbucks' customer policy is to let you stay as long as you like, once you have bought your drink of choice. Starbucks' CEO, Howard Schultz, discusses Oldenburg's concept of a "third place" in his biography of the company, writing that "[o]nce we understood the powerful need for a Third Place, we were able to respond by building larger stores, with more seating" (1997: 121). Not surprisingly, some of Starbucks' advertising plays on the third place concept, as in the print ad which states, "There's home. There's work. And there's Starbucks".

Starbucks Advertisement

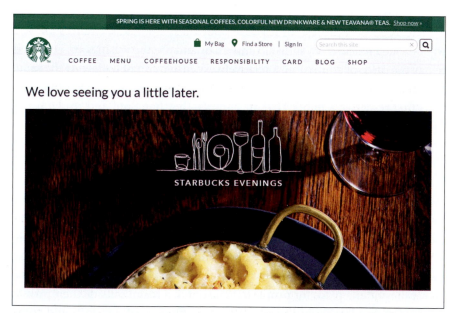

Does Starbucks meet the standards for the sociological concept of a "third place"?

Source: https://www.pinterest.com/ajpolston/starbucks/

While the idea of Starbucks as a "third place" resonates with understandings of the chain as a safe, predictable, and comfortable setting, there are signs that caution us against applying the "third place" label too enthusiastically. Bryant Simon's ethnographic experiences in Starbucks suggest that people commonly use Starbucks as a "second place" for working: lawyers make calls, salespeople check their email, students read their textbooks. Some of Simon's New York city interviewees talk about Starbucks as a cheap way of renting office space with strong coffee and a clean restroom (which seems especially economical in expensive urban settings), a trend which has emerged alongside telecommuting and flexible work schedules. Simon's study of day-to-day life in Starbucks also suggests that by and large, people don't go to Starbucks to chat with strangers, but more often to talk with people they already know, or go there to be "alone in public" (2009: 115). Simon describes going there repeatedly in order to deliberately make conversation with strangers, and finding that process awkward, uncomfortable, and in violation of the perceived norm—to not bother people who are comfortably reading or working on their own (2009: 100). This leads him to conclude that Starbucks "simulates" the ideal of a coffeehouse, but doesn't produce genuinely open social interaction required of a third place (2009: 119):

> Under Starbucks' reign, the coffeehouse has become something to consume more than an actual public gathering place. You rent out space for work or a meeting or pay for a chair for twenty minutes of relaxation, or maybe you use it as a place to show off your good taste . . . at a real third place, you participate by talking and listening; you don't just sit there, and it isn't just about you.

4. THE PARADOX OF THE $4 CAPPUCCINO

Besides teaching us about classed consumption habits, the case of coffee is instructive for teaching us about the material inequities of **globalization** and global **commodity chains**. Roughly 90% of the world's coffee is grown in the **Global South**, and most of that coffee is consumed in the affluent countries of the **Global North**. (Only Brazil and Ethiopia have significant markets for domestic coffee consumption) (Daviron and Ponte 2005: 50, 59). Many consumers in Global North countries have gotten used to the high price of specialty coffee beverages at chains like Starbucks. They begrudgingly, but commonly, shell out $4 or $5 for a mochachino or a vanilla latte. The popularity of these chains begs the question of who benefits from these high-priced drinks. The 20–25 million peasants who grow coffee in developing economies? The more than 50 countries in the Global South that grow and export coffee? These are not insignificant economic questions. For much of the post-WWII period, coffee has been one of the most valuable globally traded commodities, second only to oil. Each year, more than $80 billion of coffee is traded globally (Sharf 2014).

Scholars who study the production end of the coffee business point to the low prices that coffee farmers and laborers continue to receive, despite the success of upscale coffee retailers and the increased profit margins for coffee roasters. The "coffee paradox" refers to the gap between the "coffee boom" in consuming countries and a "coffee crisis" in producing countries (Daviron and Ponte 2005: xvi). In the words of coffee scholars, Daviron and Ponte (2005: 79):

> What difference does it make to a smallholder [small coffee grower] if a consumer can buy a "double-tall decaf latte" for US$4, or if specialty beans are sold at US$12 per pound in the US if he/she gets less than 50 cents for the same quantity of coffee?

A key reason behind the coffee paradox is the fact that coffee farmers and laborers have little control over most stages of the commodity chain beyond immediate production: they don't own roasting facilities which transform fresh green beans into toasty brown beans, they find it difficult if not impossible to sell their coffee directly to consumers in the Global North, and they participate little in the governance of globalized coffee commodity chains (Daviron and Ponte 2005). Also significantly, producers in the Global South don't own the retail chains that cater to upscale coffee tastes in the Global North. Economic analysts note how these chains add a lot of economic value (also known as mark-up) to the product through its symbolic, emotional, and in-person attributes. When consumers pay for an expensive latte, they are not just paying for the drink, but they are also paying for the comfy couch, the high-priced real-estate, and the expensive espresso machine. None of the profit from these investments goes back to the coffee farmer. This suggests that inflated coffee prices in cafés have little impact on the day-to-day struggles of coffee farmers. Indeed, coffee prices on international markets experienced record lows in the 2000s. Many countries in the Global South were encouraged to grow coffee for export, and over-supply became a serious problem. In 2002 the world market (inflation-adjusted) price of coffee was just 14% of what it had been in 1980 (Weis 2007: 123). Unfortunately, coffee seems to be another

Coffee Shop Interiors

Coffee growers rarely benefit from the high-priced drinks sold at coffee shops in the Global North. Consumers do not just pay the production costs when they buy an expensive coffee drink but also for such aspects of the consumption experience as the lighting, music, and furniture inside the café.

Source: Gettyimages.com # 506055488

case in which a raw resource is exported from the Global South to the Global North under economic terms that do little to diminish poverty (Jaffee 2007).

With globalization processes, the commodity of coffee—as well as information about coffee production—moves from the Global South to the Global North. Because of transnational activist efforts on behalf of impoverished coffee producers, consumers in the Global North are becoming aware of the inequalities of coffee commodity chains. Increasingly, consumers are interested in **ethical consumption** options—coffee that they can feel good about drinking, because it is seen to "do good". Ethical consumption can lead

The Fairtrade Label

Arabica coffee bearing the FAIRTRADE Max Havelaar label, used to denote a product's fairtrade status in Belgium, France, the Netherlands, and Switzerland. Max Havelaar was the first Fairtrade label, started by a Dutch development agency in 1988. More recent fairtrade labeling efforts include the creation of Fairtrade International's certification mark (the blue, green, and black logo) in 2002, signifying that all of the ingredients in a product that one can source are fair trade.

Source: Gettyimages.com # 169371268

consumers to participate in consumer boycotts. A consumer boycott involves deliberately not purchasing a product to make a statement about the company and its social, political, or environmental policies. For example, the Organic Consumers Association (OCA) has a longstanding campaign urging consumers to boycott Starbucks (OCA 2014). The OCA hopes that a consumer boycott will push Starbucks to stop selling genetically engineered products and non-organic milk from factory farms, and to instead sell drinks made with organic milk and ethically sourced coffee products (ibid.).

Besides boycotting products that they don't support, another consumer option is to "buycott", which involves deliberately channeling your purchasing power towards products that you support for social, political, or environmental reasons. One major buycott option for coffee consumers is to purchase fair-trade coffee. Fair-trade systems of certification guarantee premium, stable prices for producers, and historically have supported small, cooperative operations (Jaffee 2007; Cole and Brown 2014). Fair-trade schemes are designed to ensure that coffee farmers are paid an amount for their crop that allows them to maintain a decent standard of living, and also to promote basic needs in the community, like clean water and education. Coffee was the first fair-trade certified product, although now consumers can buy other fair-trade goods like bananas, tea, sugar, and chocolate—all goods that were a key part of the agricultural exploitation strategies of colonialism. Fair-trade products were once hard-to-find specialty items, but now can be picked up in places like Costco and Target. Indeed, all of Dunkin' Donuts espresso beverages are made with certified fair-trade coffee. Fair-trade has certainly channeled more resources to coffee growers in the Global South, with an estimated $61 million in premiums flowing from the US to coffee cooperatives since 1998 (Cole and Brown 2014: 52).

While many agree that fair-trade coffee is a good place to start addressing the inequalities of coffee commodity chains, the movement is not without its critics. One concern is that by allying itself with major corporations and becoming more mainstream, the fair-trade movement's social-justice

Prominent Fair-trade Products

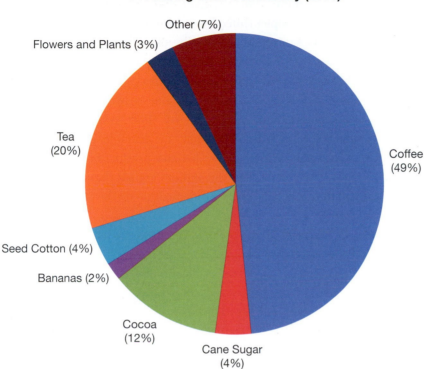

**Percentage of all Fairtrade Farmers and Workers
Producing each Commodity (2013)**

- Other (7%)
- Flowers and Plants (3%)
- Tea (20%)
- Seed Cotton (4%)
- Bananas (2%)
- Cocoa (12%)
- Cane Sugar (4%)
- Coffee (49%)

Source: Fairtrade International. 2014. *Monitoring the Scope and Benefits of Fairtrade: Sixth Edition 2014.* http://www.fairtrade.net/impact-and-research.html (page 23).

motivations have been diluted. Critics point out that major coffee retailers, like Starbucks, sell only a small amount of fair-trade coffee (about 8% of their total sales), even though they use the fair-trade logo enthusiastically to promote themselves as a socially responsible coffee retailer (Simon 2007; Jaffee 2007: 16). In general, supply outstrips demand for fair-trade coffee in the global marketplace, so that only about 20% of it can be sold at the fair-trade price (Cole and Brown 2014: 53). Indeed, certified fair-trade coffee comprises only about 5% of the American coffee market (Fair Trade USA 2013).

A second critique of fair trade questions the efficacy of a market-based strategy for changing the massive inequalities between the Global North and the Global South. The promise of fair trade is that wealthy consumers can act in the marketplace—"voting" with their dollar to purchase a more equitable product that addresses poverty and inequality. Some scholars of globalized capitalism argue, however, that market mechanisms like fair trade are a very minor, inadequate response, and that greater justice in the global economy requires major changes implemented by states and international institutions (e.g. World Trade Organization) pushed by civil society (Jaffee 2007: 35). Leaders of the Nicaragua Association of Rural Workers described fair trade as a "drop in the bucket" of the coffee market, and a program that cannot help people who don't own their own land (Cole and Brown 2014: 53). Even on their own terms, fair-trade projects often fall short. A study of fair-trade bananas grown in the Dominican Republic, for example, documented how most farmers engaged with fair-trade banana production had very little knowledge of fair-trade principles; the authors argued that the certification system even had the potential to *increase* inequalities on the ground (Getz and Shreck 2006: 498–9).

A final, more recent critique involves the move by the major American fair-trade body—Fair Trade USA—to allow large coffee plantations to sell fair-trade coffee. Traditionally, fair-trade certification for coffee was only possible for small growers and worker-owned cooperatives. Indeed, much coffee production in the Global South is produced on small plots by small producers. However, Fair Trade USA made the decision to allow large plantations to sell fair-trade coffee in 2012—a move that sparked major criticism, and forced the US organization to break from the international fair-trade certifying umbrella organization, Fairtrade International (Cole and Brown 2014: 52). Cole and Brown report that "[t]he majority of the voices we have heard from within the fair-trade movement are disappointed at the concentration of power within Fair Trade USA. It doesn't seem, well, fair" (2014: 54). As public awareness of these issues grows, consumer confidence in the fair-trade label may falter. When you buy a cup of fair-trade coffee in the United States, your coffee may have been produced by a small, worker-owned cooperative, but it may also have come from a large corporate plantation. So while a fair-trade coffee purchase probably provides more resources to coffee farmers than conventional coffee, this ethical certification system does not completely reveal, or ameliorate the complex material relations embedded in global commodity chains.

THINKING FRAMES

How can each thinking frame help us ponder the sociology of coffee?

Material / Cultural	Social class is not only an economic category, but also has a cultural dimension that is expressed through consumption. Knowing how to consume like an elite can be a source of social status—a form of what Pierre Bourdieu calls cultural capital.
Think about . . .	How do the goods we consume allow us to draw social boundaries, aligning us with certain kinds of people and distinguishing ourselves from others? What commodities are particularly useful for drawing boundaries?

Structure / Agency	Consumers have agency to choose what kind of coffee satisfies our cravings, but we have limited agency to give workers a greater share of the purchase price of our drink. Fair trade is one project that tries to address this structure/agency tension.
Think about . . .	How much agency do consumers hold vis-à-vis corporations? Can individuals meaningfully challenge global inequalities through ethical consumption, by buying fair-trade products, or participating in a consumer boycott?

Micro / Macro	The popularity of the $4 coffee has both micro and macro implications: as a source of status display for privileged consumers, and as a reflection of massive inequalities sustained through trade relations between the Global North and Global South.
Think about . . .	How do high-status consumption trends in the Global North relate to labor conditions in the Global South? What happens when consumers want high-status goods for the cheapest possible price? (Possible examples to consider: SUVs, diamond rings, and tropical beach vacations.)

Active Learning

ACTIVE LEARNING

Online

$7 coffee?
Watch this Jimmy Kimmel clip about the introduction of a $7 cup of coffee at Starbucks. How do the people drinking the coffee display their social status as they experience the coffee? Did the ending of the video surprise you? If so, why? https://www.youtube.com/watch?v=HxlGI4OzeBk

Fair trade, ethical consumption, and corporate public relations:
Look at the website, http://fairworldproject.org/ which seeks to protect the fair-trade label from being diluted, misrepresented, and misused. Now look at the website of a major corporate coffee or chocolate producer (e.g. Hershey's or Starbucks). Can you identify what strategies they use to promote themselves as a socially responsible corporation? What claims seem substantiated, and what claims seem more ornamental?

The significance of your coffee order?
Watch this clip from the Tom Hanks movie, "You've Got Mail": http://www.youtube.com/watch?v=hZ7lFV9Z2hk. In it, Tom Hanks's character delivers the following pronouncement: "The whole purpose of places like Starbucks is for people with no decision-making ability whatsoever to make six decisions just to buy one cup of coffee. Short. Tall. Light. Dark. Caf. Decaf. Low-fat. Non-fat. Etc. So for people who don't know what the hell they're doing, or who on earth they are, can, for $2.95, get not just a cup of coffee, but an absolute defining sense of self." Do you agree? Disagree? Does something as seemingly mundane as a coffee order provide people with a defining sense of self?

Discussion/Reflection

Third place:
Is Starbucks a "third place"? What is a genuine third place—a place where access is relatively open, and where strangers can have conversations and casual encounters? Brainstorm with your classmates to think of examples of "third places" where you come into contact and talk with people you don't know.

Boycotts and buycotts:

Working with your classmates, make a list of contemporary boycotts and buycotts. Which strategy do you think is more effective? Do you think that corporations worry about how their brand image is impacted by a consumer boycott?

Sociology Outside the Classroom

Coffee shop ethnography:

Go to a coffee shop and hang out. Observe people's coming and going. Do strangers talk to each other? How friendly does the space feel? Do some people seem more welcome than others? What groups of people does this coffee shop seem to cater to in terms of age, class, race, or other social factors?

Consuming status:

Take note of the kind of things people eat and drink in publicly visible ways— on television, in advertisements, at restaurants, and at social events. What foods and drinks seem associated with high status? What foods and drinks seem less prestigious? What social clues help signal high and low status?

PART II

Fitting In: Being Part of the Group

Chapter 5

SHOPPING LESSONS: CONSUMING SOCIAL ORDER

INTRODUCING KEY CONCEPTS

This chapter examines a key activity in consumer culture: *shopping*. After learning a bit about the history of shopping, we look at the broader social context that shapes our individual desires, motivations, and values. This topic raises questions of consumer *agency*: are we consumer dupes manipulated by corporations to buy brand-name products, or are we consumer heroes who have full sovereignty over decision-making? We also examine the role shopping and consumer culture play in establishing *social order*, drawing from sociological concepts like *social solidarity* and *anomie*. Shopping offers insight into how we come to feel part of social groups, as well as the isolation that can accompany our modern emphasis on *individualism*. We may shop to feel a connection with others, but at the same time, shopping may exacerbate feelings of isolation. For that reason, some scholars see shopping as a *social problem*.

1. INTRODUCTION: WHY SHOPPING MATTERS

A key part of what consumers do in a consumer culture is go shopping. At first glance, the idea of shopping seems obvious and intuitive. You go to the store, choose what you want, hand over your money, and go home with your stuff. But from a sociological perspective, shopping presents a bit of a puzzle. One the one hand, shopping is a major leisure activity enjoyed by millions of people. As many of our students tell us, shopping is fun; it's a release from boredom and stress, a way to treat and express oneself, and an easy way to experience or acquire something new. Consumers frequently relish making choices in the store or shopping online, and use shopping as an opportunity to bond with others (e.g. a day at the mall with friends, mother–daughter shopping trips). While consumers have numerous happy associations with shopping, it also has a number of negative associations. When some people think about shopping, they think about drudgery, standing in line, credit card debt, social pressure, financial stress, and the hectic crowds of a Black Friday sale. Consumers sometimes feel as though they can't control their shopping habits and unwittingly go into debt. Others feel as though they can't afford to buy the things they want and deserve, and experience a shopping trip as an exercise in frustration. Still others like to shop for new things, but worry about the excess stuff in their lives (e.g. How to store it all? Does most of it end up in landfill?).

Sociologist Christine Williams aptly summarizes a central shopping paradox: "shopping can be both a pleasurable distraction and a laborious chore, a means to express my individuality and to forge bonds with others, an activity at once discretionary and mandatory, highly personal and inherently social" (2006: 13). Our goal in this chapter is to use sociology to shed light on the shopping paradox: how one seemingly straightforward activity can be simultaneously liberating and punishing, fun and hellish, expressive and conformist. At the same time, by studying shopping we can better understand how we form social groups and social bonds in contemporary society, and what happens when those groups and bonds weaken. Before proceeding, we want to make clear that our intention is to neither disparage nor romanticize shopping. Sociologically, our goal is to *understand*, and this requires a certain amount of empathy and critique. Sociologist, Sharon Zukin writes,

A shopper's life isn't easy. Our choices of stores, and choices of products, often contradict our ideals . . . This doesn't mean we should either

Black Friday

Customers at an Ohio Walmart jockey for discounted videogames on Black Friday, 2011. Black Friday is a day of discount shopping that kicks off the Christmas holiday shopping season, and follows the American Thanksgiving holiday. In 2008, Jdimytai Damour, a temporary Walmart employee, was trampled to death in Valley Stream, New York, as a crowd of 2000 shoppers broke down the doors to gain access to the store on Black Friday just prior to the 5 a.m. opening.

Source: Gettyimages.com # 134072180

demonize shopping or give it up. Not when it gives us pleasure, sharpens our sense of value, and creates a public space like the farmers' market . . . *we can only develop that critical consciousness if we understand why, and how, we shop.*

(2004: 276–7, emphasis ours)

It is this kind of critical consciousness about consumer culture that we hope to inspire and develop among readers of this book.

In the first part of the chapter, we consider how we came to live in a land of big box stores and ubiquitous brands. This brief history of shopping sheds light on shopping's social significance, which goes beyond simply acquiring the goods we need to survive. Shopping is also deeply aspirational, allowing us to pursue the fantasy of an idealized life. In the next section of the chapter, we examine some of the complex meanings and motivations that underlie our shopping decisions. We also discuss how to conceptualize consumer agency, which is often framed as a debate between consumer dupes and consumer heroes. After that, we relate shopping to the theme of "fitting in" using Emile Durkheim's sociological concepts of solidarity and anomie. Shopping can be a way in which people deal with the anxieties of modern life, including feelings of detachment as well as a desire for belonging. Put differently, shopping can be a kind of social glue that pulls us together and fosters a sense of "we"-ness. However, shopping can also be a compensatory mechanism: we may shop in an attempt to inject a greater sense of community, creativity, and control into modern lives that feel isolated and lonely.

Before proceeding, an important point to keep in mind is the distinction between consumption and shopping. Shopping is best understood as a sub-category of consumption. As a social category, consumption is much broader than shopping, and can include acquiring and consuming goods through myriad non-market means. Consumption is also common to both pre-modern and capitalist societies; it can involve eating vegetables from a backyard garden, trading music with a friend, or wearing a sweater that someone knitted for you. Shopping, in contrast, refers to a specific way of acquiring goods through the marketplace. We normally think of shopping as the practice of buying things in person in a store or through an e-commerce website.

2. SHOPPING: A BRIEF HISTORY

Shopping in some form undoubtedly dates back to ancient times. In pre-modern cultures, people met up in marketplaces to trade and barter goods. However, the history of shopping as we know it—as an activity where we attain virtually all of life's essentials through the marketplace—emerged alongside the rise of **capitalism**. As we discussed in the first chapter, the development of capitalist markets meant that people gradually moved from making most of their daily life goods, to buying them in exchange for money. This trajectory has continued until the present day. Most of us would have a hard time producing most of our everyday essentials, like clothing, shelter, or food. Instead of making these basic life goods, we go out and shop for them.

Some of the earliest modern shopping spaces to attract scholarly attention were the 1800s Paris Arcades. Housed in multiple buildings and decorated with

A Consumer's Guide to Shopping History

	• **A Consumer's Guide to Shopping History**
1400s–1900s	• The mass consumption of goods like fur, tobacco, opium, coffee, and tea propels exploration, trade, the Industrial Revolution, and colonialism in Asia, Africa, and the Americas.
1796	• The UK's first department store, Harding, Howell & Co's Grand Fashionable Magazine, opens in London, with four departments: furs and fans, millinery, haberdashery, and jewelry and clocks.
1820s +	• The majority of the Paris arcades are constructed.
1834	• Soon-to-be iconic British department store Harrods is founded as a wholesale grocery store.
1846	• A. T. Stewart opens America's first department store, a four-story marble building in New York known as the "Marble Palace".
1852	• France's first department store, Le Bon Marché, opens in Paris. It is one of the earliest stores to feature fixed prices and allow customers to browse without buying.
1879	• The first Woolworth's, a precursor to the modern dollar store, opens in New York.
1903	• Ehrich Brothers Emporium, a New York department store, holds the first known American fashion show, to attract middle-class female customers.
1950s/1960s	• Philadelphia Police begin to refer to the day after Thanksgiving as "Black Friday", owing to all the shopping mayhem they encounter.
1955	• The first Dollar General store opens in Springfield, Kentucky; it later becomes one of America's largest and most successful dollar store chains.
1956	• Architect Victor Gruen designs the Southdale Mall in Edina, Minnesota, America's first indoor, fully enclosed, climate-controlled mall.
1962	• On July 2, Sam Walton opens the first Walmart store in Rogers, Arkansas.
1971	• On August 15, America goes off the gold standard; with money no longer tied to a commodity, economic growth comes to further rely on manufacturing and consumption.
1988	• Walmart opens its first Supercenter in Washington, Missouri, adding diverse supermarket items to its existing product range.
1992	• On August 11, The Mall of America opens its doors in Minnesota, becoming a model for combining shopping and other entertainment attractions, and the largest mall in the US.
2008	• On November 4, The Dubai Mall opens; with over 1200 shops, it is the world's largest shopping mall.
2011	• Walmart comes to own more than 10,000 retail units globally when it acquires South African retailer MassMart.

The Paris Arcades

The Modern Mall

The Festival Walk Commercial Centre in Hong Kong features globally recognizable retailers, including Juicy Couture, Brooks Brothers, French Connection, Lancôme, Tommy Hilfiger, and COACH.

Source: Gettyimages.com # 523027387

The Galerie Vivienne in 1905. Built in 1823, its mosaic floors and glass roof make it an iconic Paris arcade. It is currently host to high-end fashion boutiques, gourmet grocers, book shops, tea rooms, and more.

Source: Wikimedia Commons: Galerie Vivienne— interior, 1905 https://commons.wikimedia.org/wiki/ File:Galerie_Vivienne_-_interior,_1905.jpg

ornate iron columns, the Arcades were topped with a glass roof, allowing shoppers to travel between shops in a seamless fashion. The Arcades can be seen as an early form of a shopping mall, and signify the emergence of modern consumer society. In sociological terms, the Arcades were significant as a site where affluent consumers could purchase luxury products, and where the less fortunate could window shop and be socialized into an emerging consumer culture (Gunn 2002). One of the first scholars to theorize this new shopping space was Walter Benjamin, who wrote *The Arcades Project* (1927–40). Benjamin described the Arcades as "temples of commodity capital", alluring in the way they invested commodities with longing and desire, but also threatening in the way that political consciousness could become buried in consumer fantasies (Gunn 2002: 268). He also emphasized how this prototypical shopping space blurred the boundaries between public and private life, consumption and leisure (Buse et al. 2005; Hayward 2007).

What Benjamin's account highlighted—and what remains true today—is that shopping is not just a utilitarian act, but is a kind of dreamlike experience that can engage us on a creative, emotional level. Beyond satisfying basic needs, shopping often involves an element of fantasy—envisioning what your life could become, if only you possessed commodity X, Y, or Z.

The creation of middle-class, idealized consumption spaces was epitomized in the early department stores of the 19th century, which ushered in the form of mass urban consumption that we know today. One of the world's first department stores, the Bon Marché department store opened in Paris in 1852, and can still be visited today. Its focus on luxury was a model that soon spread to the US, and by 1873 many similar stores could be found in the "Ladies' Mile" section of Manhattan. In 1917, the world's largest department store was built in Chicago, boasting an impressive twenty stories. This was soon surpassed by Macy's, which covered an entire city block at its 1924 NYC location.

The department store was significant not only for its size, but also because these shopping spaces offered a drastically new and exciting consumer experience. Prior to this, shopping meant asking a clerk to retrieve a specific item from behind the counter. Now, goods were on open display for customers to peruse, touch, and ogle. With fixed department store prices, haggling was not required or even allowed. Consumers—especially middle-class women— were encouraged to browse, or "window shop", in order to develop desires, rather than just acquire what they needed and immediately leave the store. Department stores worked to make dreams of luxury available to regular people, especially since these stores were often located in city centers close to mass transit lines (Leach 1993). As with the Paris Arcades, the department store was not just about meeting basic needs, but delivering fantasy and spectacle, an out-of-the-ordinary experience. Zukin (2004: 19–20) writes:

> plate glass, electric lights, and atrium construction made stores seem bigger and more spectacular. Elevators and escalators expanded shoppers' perceptions of moving rapidly through space and time. A profusion of goods, brought from everywhere and piled in luxurious displays, made "just looking" at merchandise a popular pastime, both within the store and on the streets, even when stores weren't open for business.

As department stores transformed the middle-class shopping outing into a more leisurely and desirous experience, women were the clear targets for these stores. While men's work in the paid labor force was valorized, women became "experts in consumption", as their work of "making a home" required them to purchase an array of goods in the marketplace (Slater 1997: 56–67). Early department stores provided a space for women—especially White middle-class women—to enjoy themselves in a public space that was safe and socially sanctioned (Zukin 2004). These stores had tea rooms, fashion shows, and restrooms with areas to relax and freshen up. With supervised play areas for children, women were invited into a temporary escape from childcare duties (Cook 2003). At the same time that shopping became a feminine-coded domain of expertise and experience, women's consumption in these public shopping spaces was also seen as a threat, with women shoppers seen as irrational, easily seduced, and even hysterical (Slater 1997: 57). Social anxieties emerged around the idea of shopping addicts abandoning their children and husbands to satisfy their lust for new goods (Slater 1997: 75). Writing in the late 19th century, French author Émile Zola explored retailers' attitudes towards women in his novel *Au Bonheur des Dames* (The Ladies' Paradise). In the novel, the fictional store owner Octave Mouret explains how women are conceptualized as weak-willed targets:

> Woman was what the shops were fighting over when they competed, it was woman whom they ensnared with the constant trap of their bargains, after stunning her with their displays. They had aroused new desires in her flesh, they were a huge temptation to which she must fatally succumb, first of all giving in to the purchases of a good housewife, then seduced by vanity and finally consumed.
>
> (Zola 1883: 75)

Women continued to be targeted as primary shoppers, but physical shopping spaces transformed over time. While downtown department stores were essential to the history of North American shopping, they came to face stiff competition from enclosed suburban malls in the years following World War II. During this time, many middle-class, predominantly White families moved to the suburbs. Department stores followed, and took up a central spot anchoring newly built suburban shopping malls, where they were initially charged little or no rent (Short 2007; Wiedenhoft 2007). In 1960s and 1970s shopping malls, consumers encountered specialized brands that conveyed a sense of individuality and personality, exclusivity and luxury. A desire for designer labels, like Calvin Klein jeans, replaced satisfaction with more generic products. Today, a trip to the mall in multiple nations

Sears Closures

US department stores have experienced dwindling profits in the face of competition from online retailers and specialty big box stores, leading to the closure of department stores around the country, like this Sears location in Pennsylvania.

Source: APimages.com # 733208117589

demonstrates the ubiquity of iconic stores—like The Gap, Victoria's Secret, Williams & Sonoma—each with its own specific cultural and lifestyle associations. As people developed their own personal relationships and loyalties to specific brands, the multi-purpose department store became less significant—culturally and financially—and business commentators began to muse about the "death" of the department store. With the popularity of online shopping and specialty big box stores threatening its hold on the middle classes, Sears, one of America's oldest and most ubiquitous retailers, endured its fourth year of falling profits in 2014. In response to low profits, Sears Holdings Corporation closed and sold off around 1800 Kmart and Sears stores between 2009 and 2014, closing 234 locations in 2014 alone (Chapman 2015).

Another key milestone in the history of shopping involves the rise of big box stores like Bed, Bath and Beyond, Best Buy, and Home Depot. Big box stores are freestanding spaces that specialize in selling large quantities of a

IS THE MALL OPEN TO EVERYONE?

A shopping mall is technically a privately owned corporate space. However, as a shopper you may feel like you are in a **public space**, a place where people mill about, where you may run into friends, and where you can feel part of something even amidst large numbers of strangers. For this reason, we can think of a mall as a kind of quasi-public space, recognizing how the space is used, but acknowledging the legality of private corporate ownership. Of course, as we explored in chapter 4's discussion of coffee shops, not everybody is equally welcome or comfortable in shopping spaces. In the United States, Blacks were often not allowed to try on clothing in department stores prior to the Civil Rights movement (Zukin 2007). While institutional racism is no longer explicitly tolerated, research shows how even today Blacks with high incomes experience significant racism while shopping in high-end department stores (Pittman 2012), and that experiences of retail racism may drive some Black consumers to shop online (Ekpo 2014). These sorts of exclusions are heightened for youth. The shopping mall is one of the few spaces available for young people to hang out, and yet teens are often viewed with suspicion and made to feel unwelcome in retail environments (Matthews et al. 2000), especially working-class youth of color (Chin 2001). These exclusions are also evident for retail workers at the mall. One American study found that Black and Latino retail workers are more likely to live below the poverty line than their White counterparts, less likely to be placed in supervisory roles, and earn only 75% of what Whites earn for the same work (Ruetschlin and Asante-Muhammad 2015). These findings lead the study authors to suggest that the retail sector plays a major role in perpetuating racial inequalities in the United States (ibid.).

specific category of merchandise—like toys or pet food—at low prices. Big box stores work to monopolize a specific type of goods, often at the expense of both local retail stores and department stores. For this reason, they are sometimes dubbed "category killers" because they make it difficult, if not impossible, to compete in the category they occupy (Spector 2005). According to Spector (2005: 11–29), the modern big box store was institutionalized by

Charles Lazarus, the founder of Toys R Us. Department stores dominated the market for toys until this category killer was established. Today, very few department stores maintain a toy section. A similar pattern can be seen in other markets, including home furnishings, home goods, and electronics, leading to steady decreases in the number and diversity of department stores' departments. Ultimately, big box stores have built their success on the convenience and low prices made possible by self-service, a warehouse-like setting, and product specialization.

While big box stores are relatively new, modern consumers have long looked for a good deal. The early 20th century five-and-dime store, like Woolworth's, represented a space where the rich and the poor could buy goods that were reasonably priced—for either a nickel or a dime. The modern-day five-and-dime is seen in the rise of dollar stores (Woloson 2012) and discount department stores like Walmart—places where almost everyone can afford to buy something. This opportunity is especially relevant in a contemporary context with heightened inequality and large numbers of people living in poverty (Laird 2009), even though low wages in the retail sector arguably worsen this poverty. In this context of heightened social inequality, it's perhaps no surprise that Walmart has seen such remarkable growth. Walmart's success has been controversial, especially its strategy of keeping prices low by squeezing wages down for workers at various points in the commodity chain (Lichtenstein 2010; Haiven 2013). (Here, think back to low-income workers' fight for a living wage, discussed in chapter 3.) Walmart's role as a fast-growing capitalist success story, however, is uncontroversial (see Walmart 2014). Today, Walmart is the biggest private employer in the world with 11,495 locations ("Our Locations" 2015), and members of its founding family (the Waltons) appear at various top spots in the Fortune 500 list of the world's billionaires (Forbes 2015).

While we often associate shopping with a physical, "bricks and mortar" shopping space, many of us now buy goods online. This phenomenon is not altogether new, since mail order catalogues were an important shopping source for rural people in the US and Europe from the 1870s onward (Zukin 2007). Today, with the connections made possible through the Internet and global financial channels, shopping has taken on a more long-distance nature than ever before. Amazon.com, for example, earned $62 billion in 2012. Online retailing is gaining ground throughout the world, raising questions about Amazon's monopoly position in various national markets. While online shopping is a major trend, physical shopping spaces are still significant—as economic engines of growth and as symbols of prosperity. Empty storefronts

Gentrified Times Square

One of New York's most iconic sights, Times Square demonstrates the characteristics of gentrification processes by blending tourism, shopping, and entertainment in a single space.

Source: Gettyimages.com # 472361084

represent a potent symbol of urban decay, and store closings can generate feelings of despair about urban life and communities. On the other hand, shopping spaces can also serve as a symbol of urban rejuvenation. The transformation of New York City documented by Sharon Zukin (2004) tells a story of suburban flight from the city followed by urban renewal and **gentrification**, exemplified by the regenerative branding (or what some call "mall-ification" or "Disney-fication") of Times Square. Gentrification processes frequently establish a link between shopping spaces, leisure, and tourism. While this influx of business can boost the local economy, it may come at a significant social cost. Gentrification is a process in which the increase in prices and rents makes it difficult for lower-income residents to stay in the neighborhood. As a result, longstanding residents are often pushed out of newly gentrified spaces that cater to the taste preferences and budgets of middle- and upper-income inhabitants.

Although shopping spaces have changed considerably over the last several hundred years, one thing that has remained relatively constant in recent history is the belief in shopping as a social good—as both an indicator and a driver of collective prosperity. From the 1930s onwards, a dominant economic policy of Keynesianism (based on the ideas of economist John Maynard Keynes) suggested that shopping and spending—rather than saving—was a boon to the economy since it pumps in dollars to help avoid recession. In the 1960s, shopping took on a renewed importance, as many industrialized economies began to outsource factory work, giving new weight to the idea of consumption as a catalyst for both domestic and global economic growth (Zukin 2004: 15). One of the most striking illustrations of this belief in shopping as a barometer of collective well-being occurred on the day after the September 11, 2001 attack on the World Trade Center, when then President George W. Bush told the public to "go shopping" and return to "life as usual" (Grewal 2005: 218). Even though some were appalled at Bush's suggestion, the idea of "going shopping" after a terrorist event speaks to the central place this activity plays in our collective conscience and in the broader economy. In the next section, we explore how shopping can play a unifying role, creating a sense of solidarity and group cohesion in a complex and often alienating modern world.

3. SHOPPING MOTIVATIONS AND VALUES, COMPARISON AND CHOICE

The brief history of shopping outlined above raises the question of consumer motivation: is shopping *always*, or even *mostly*, about a simple cost–benefit calculation of getting the greatest value for the best price? The story of the Paris Arcades, department stores, and designer boutiques all suggest that shopping is about much more than prices. Consumers want to get a good deal, but they also go shopping to experience something new and pleasurable. Shopping is a way to gain a reprieve from the humdrum of everyday working lives, and try out different lifestyles. In this way, going shopping is not simply about the mundane, but can also involve a collective search for the sacred in social life, reflecting our deepest values and desires. In this section, we look at the complex and multifaceted nature of consumer shopping motivations.

For some kinds of shopping, saving money is the main story. You go to buy a mop, for example, and you choose the cheapest one that will still do a good enough job cleaning the floor. The standard economist's story of shopping—sometimes called the utility maximization model of social behavior—is well equipped to study these kinds of transactions. This approach emphasizes the rational exchange of money for well-priced items in the shopping process. Social scientists from different fields refer to this as a rational choice model of human behavior; it assumes that actors are rational, and behave purposively, acting to achieve a desired result (e.g. you spend the least amount of money to buy a functional mop). The rational choice model of behavior often has great predictive power: shoppers often *do* pick the lowest priced product (Williams 2004: 11). Partly for that reason, the shopping landscape has become dominated by big box stores and discount super-centers. These spaces allow shoppers to get a better bang for their buck, and are particularly popular in recessionary times when money is tight (Osborne and Kunz 2011: 24–5).

While getting a good deal is important, low prices do not *always* predict what consumers buy. A sociological perspective on shopping takes us beyond low prices to ask a broader question: what do we *value* when we go shopping? For many consumer goods—like a car or an outfit for a special occasion—we balance a complex calculation of emotional, habitual, cultural, social, *and* economic considerations before we make a purchase. We often value products and shopping experiences that make us feel fashionable, allow us to express care for others, and communicate a desirable sense of self to the outside world. Sometimes we value getting the best deal, but sometimes we are drawn to high-priced brands and specialty stores where goods have a special allure. In part, this is because consumption is powerfully linked to our identity—the story we tell about who we are, both to others and to ourselves (a topic we explore more closely in chapter 10). But consumption is not just about the individual. Shopping is also intertwined with intimate relationships and social belonging; it is this collective element that is the focus of the remainder of this chapter.

Consumers are often motivated to buy certain products to fit in with a particular social group. In comparison to previous eras, where people may have primarily identified themselves with their religion or their occupation, today people often develop a sense of belonging based on how they shop and what they buy (Bauman 2007; Miller 1995: 17). Most people like getting a good deal, and some people pride themselves on their ability to save money by comparison shopping. At the same time, not everybody wants to signal membership in a cultural grouping of "cheapskates" or budget shoppers—groups that are frequently **stigmatized** in a culture that disparages poverty and admires luxury, opulence, and celebrity lifestyles (Ashworth et al. 2005; Sandlin et al. 2011). For example, a Google image search for "Walmart shopper" reveals an offensive set of images that reflect racist, **classist**, sexist, and fat-phobic stereotypes. High-priced shopping places and prestigious brands allow consumers to draw lines of inclusion and exclusion, demarcating themselves as members of high-status social groups, and perhaps conveying a desire for, or an experience of, upward **social mobility**.

As we learned in chapter 4, consumption standards and desires are not always connected to economic realities. Consumer culture scholar Juliet Schor (1998) argues that that the 1980s and 1990s ushered in a period of **new consumerism**, where income inequality worsened at the exact moment when Americans' consumer reference group went upscale. People increasingly desired upscale goods possessed by the top economic tier—elites whose incomes vastly exceed those of average Americans. Economically, the **upscale emulation** trend contributed to increasing levels of indebtedness and decreased savings, as consumer desires exceeded incomes. Culturally, the new consumerism trend worked to reinforce an association between having "good taste" and consuming like a social elite—buying marble countertops instead of cheaper laminate countertops, SUVs instead of compact cars, all-inclusive beach holidays instead of visiting family. Overall, Schor's research suggests that shopping is deeply social and relational: we compare ourselves and our possessions to the people we see around us—in person or on the screen—and this can have the effect of ratcheting up the pressure to consume. As Schor writes, the problem with the socially competitive dynamic of consumption is its persistence:

> If we aped the guy in the corner office once and that was the end of it, it would be a relatively minor issue. The difficulty is the dynamic aspect of keeping up: the emulation process never ends. Growth is built into the very structure of our economy [and] consumers have not escaped this escalation mentality.
>
> (1998: 98)

So how much power do we have to jump off the competitive treadmill of consumption? How difficult is it to resist buying a new cell phone and to ignore the constant marketing message to shop "till you drop"? To take the bus instead of drive, or to hold back from leasing a car you can't afford? These questions bring up important debates surrounding the question of consumer agency. Sociologically, we see this as an example of a classic structure–agency tension. For consumer culture scholars, this is often described as a debate between a vision of consumer dupes on the one hand, and consumer heroes on the other. Looking first at the consumer dupe end of the spectrum we find a view where structure trumps agency, and consumer culture is seen as a manipulative force that encourages reckless spending. More common amongst Marxists, globalization critics, and environmentalists, this perspective tends to have an impoverished view of human motivations. Instead of delving into the social, relational, or cultural reasons why people consume, the consumer dupe approach takes a macro perspective that emphasizes the downsides of overspending, the deleterious environmental aspects of consumer culture, or the exploitation that occurs along global commodity chains.

On the consumer hero end of the spectrum, there are those who see consumption as a form of expression and meaning, while depicting consumers as free agents. Consumer heroes are seen as exercising agency by selecting and *transforming* the goods they purchase. Shoppers choose what they want, and the market works to serve their needs. This relates to the **consumer sovereignty** thesis, which suggests that consumer demand drives the social good, because consumers are autonomous actors who send messages to companies to produce things they want to buy, promoting a kind of virtuous, self-satisfying circle. The consumer sovereignty perspective often relies on a rational-choice model of human behavior. As Schor notes, these rational-choice consumers "act to maximize their own well-being", and they are not seen as beings who act "capriciously, compulsively, or self-destructively" (1999: 4). Common among marketing professionals, advertising agents, CEOs, and some feminists and cultural studies scholars, the consumer hero side of the spectrum depicts consumer culture as a pleasurable form of choice, and even a marker of political freedom. These perspectives also emphasize the creative ways that consumer culture can be manipulated, transformed, and used in unexpected ways (e.g. vandalizing a billboard to critique the company's message).

A strong version of either perspective—consumer heroes or consumer dupes—is sociologically flawed. While there is much truth to be found in both perspectives, extreme versions tend to produce moralizing rhetoric rather than critical analysis. A sociological perspective can help us avoid this tendency, and develop a nuanced vision of shopping that transcends the assumption that "we have absolute freedom and choice", or "we are totally manipulated by the capitalist overlords". To do so requires attention to both micro and macro perspectives on our shopping habits. A sociological perspective must take seriously the *multiple* motivations for shopping—economic, emotional, cultural, and social. Consumers are certainly capable of making "rational" choices, but we are also complex beings with feelings, impulses, and habits that shape our choices. Our consumer preferences and values are dynamic, shifting, and emerge in a social world—not a bubble of cost–benefit analyses. A sociological perspective also moves beyond an individualistic approach to consumer choice, and fully considers the social and relational nature of consumption and the related tendency for competitive consumption dynamics—as documented in Schor's important work on the "new consumerism" (1999). Even if you are an incredibly strong-willed person and believe that you are "above" the influence of marketing campaigns, social relationships and cultural dynamics inevitably shape your values and visions of the good life. These values and visions will in turn influence how, when, and why we shop. The promise of sociology is to reveal these often hidden connections between the self and society. In the final section of the chapter, we use classic sociological concepts from Emile Durkheim to explore the relationship between shopping and social belonging.

4. SHOPPING, SOCIAL ORDER, AND SOLIDARITY

Does shopping create a society of antagonistic individuals fighting over the last item on the shelf on Black Friday? Or, are we actually *united* by shopping, bonded together by a shared love of bargains, cool new gadgets, and trusted brands? How does consumer culture—and shopping specifically—contribute to **social order**? When sociologists talk about social order, they are referring to the degree of stability, order, and cohesion in society (as opposed to chaos, warfare, and conflict). Different sociological traditions approach the topic of social order differently. A Weberian or Marxist approach is most likely to emphasize the creation of social order through power, domination, and hegemony (see chapter 3). In the remainder of this chapter, we focus on an approach to social order influenced by Emile Durkheim. Durkheimian approaches tend to focus on the importance of shared values and norms that integrate society, and allow it to gel as a whole. For Durkheim and those following in his wake, the question of shared values was critical to understanding the creation (and breakdown) of social order in the modern world. Sometimes, these approaches are described as part of the broad sociological tradition of **functionalism** because they emphasize how various elements of society—like family, law, and religious values—are necessary for the functioning and stability of society as a whole. Below, we explore some central Durkheimian concepts for understanding social order, and then relate them specifically to consumer culture.

4.1. A Durkheimian Approach to Social Order and Solidarity

As we note above, shopping can help integrate us into groups and form bonds with others. We shop not as isolated individuals, but as members of society who share common social obligations (e.g. buying gifts for loved ones) and social norms (e.g. lining up at the checkout), and we inevitably make social comparisons about our purchases (e.g. is your car more expensive than your best friend's car?). Sometimes, shopping can create a sense of connection, as when we bond over a shared consumer experience. Think of the common sense of frustration at a long grocery store line-up, or conversely, the sense of excitement that is shared when people bond over the release of cutting-edge technologies.

Having a sense of "we-ness" or connection with others is what sociologists refer to as **social solidarity**. A society with strong social solidarity is a society with cohesive norms regulating action, a strong sense of shared values, intense and frequent interactions between group members, a sense of "unity", and minimal conflict (Hornsby 2007). Durkheim believed that societies with strong social solidarity were likely to have lower suicide rates (Durkheim 1970 [1897]). Why? Because individuals who are well integrated into a larger social group were less likely to feel the despair and isolation that can lead somebody to take their own life. At the time of his writing, Durkheim was arguing against psychological approaches to society that focused on individual motivations for social action (e.g. explaining suicide by individual factors, instead of *social* factors). Instead of focusing on individual impulses, Durkheim believed that sociologists needed to study **social facts**. Social facts are entities that are external to the individual (e.g. laws, collective norms, social expectations), but nonetheless govern their actions. Social facts confirm that there is an external "society" that exists above and beyond the individual psyche. For example, laws prohibiting shoplifting can be viewed as a social fact. They are an element of society that exists independently of your individual thoughts, but also influence and shape your actions. If you *do* decide to pocket an item in a store, you will do so in a larger social context that morally condemns this behavior, penalizes you if you are caught, and shapes your feelings of risk around this action.

iPhone Customers Waiting in Line

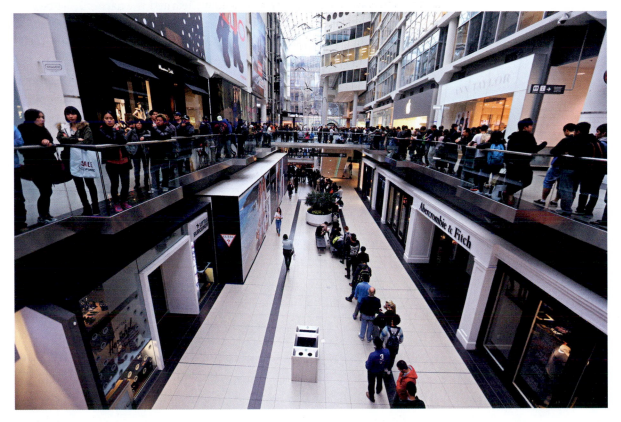

Hundreds of shoppers, some having camped out for days, gather in Toronto's Eaton Centre shopping mall for the launch of the iPhone 6 and iPhone 6 Plus in 2014. The line started at the Apple store, and was so long that it stretched across multiple levels of the mall.

Source: Gettyimages.com # 455917576

Durkheim referred to the social facts of shared values as the **collective conscience**. We commonly think of a "conscience" as something that belongs to an individual. Durkheim talked about a *collective* conscience to draw attention to the external normative order that exists outside of individuals and regulates their behavior. The collective conscience may feel especially tangible to us when we gather in large groups—for religious gatherings, a music concert, or in a large auditorium to watch a sporting event. In these settings, we may feel a powerful sense of the "we" that is greater than our individual thoughts and feelings, and unites around a common purpose (e.g. praising God, appreciating music, cheering for the home team). The central focus of these gatherings (such as a musical group or a sports team) can serve as sacred **totems** in secular modern life. As we learned in chapter 2, Durkheim used the concept of a totem to refer to an object that the group worshiped (formally through religious practices, or informally in secular societies), and which gave the group a kind of shared purpose and sense of solidarity. The American author and satirist Jen Lancaster jokingly writes, "I still believe in the Holy Trinity, except now it's Target, Trader Joe's, and IKEA" (Lancaster 2007: 29). In this quote, she cheekily suggests that sacred religious iconography faces competition from other shared symbols and beliefs in consumer culture— like a love for affordable Ikea furniture, Trader Joe's delicious product lines, and Target's stylish but affordable red-dot products. Quasi-sacred consumer

Star Wars Social Solidarity

The celebration of a beloved TV, film, or book series, as seen at this Star Wars celebration in California, can be a powerful source of social solidarity made possible by consumption.

Source: Gettyimages.com # 469983972

totems constitute a concrete way to represent the interests of the group, especially the group's desire for unity, social cohesion, and agreement on core values—like the value of reliable products that don't break the bank.

To understand the nature of modern totems in consumer culture, we need to reflect a bit on how society has evolved and changed. To explain social order, Durkheim drew a contrast between pre-modern "traditional" societies and modern industrialized societies (1964 [1893]). Recall from chapter 2 that many early sociologists wrote in the context of 19th century industrialization, and sought to understand the rapidly changing society around them. Durkheim argued that traditional societies had a kind of **mechanical solidarity** that came relatively naturally in small group settings with a religiously oriented common culture. Because most people in this setting shared a similar kind of life, it was relatively easy to generate shared values and norms. The collective conscience was a powerful unifying force, and there was little sense of an individual identity. Instead of seeing themselves as unique individuals, in this pre-modern context people might instead see themselves as members of a family, a clan, a warrior group, or a village.

With the advent of modern, industrial life, society became more complex, and the power of mechanical solidarity waned. The existence of multiple political viewpoints, different ethnic/racial groups, and specialized occupations demands a more complex form of social solidarity—one that could offer a feeling of unity in a social context with a specialized division of labor, diminished religiosity, and heightened individualism. Put differently, Durkheim was interested in the puzzle of how modern society holds together with so many interdependent elements, and with people playing so many different social roles. He used the term **organic solidarity** to refer to the kind of solidarity that emerges in a modern social context. To understand organic solidarity, we need to understand the complex division of labor in modern society (Durkheim 1964 [1893]: 226). With industrialization, people shifted away from subsistence labor on the family farm to take on specialized jobs as blacksmiths, factory workers, bakers, bankers, and store clerks. With a more complex division of labor, it becomes more difficult to find common values, since people's lives are characterized by a greater sense of difference from one another. Bankers, bartenders, and ballet dancers live very different lives, and may not share much in common. As a result, Durkheim (1964 [1893]) suggested that modern culture gave rise to **anomie**, which can be understood as a "lack or ineffectiveness of normative regulation in society" (Deflem 2007). Anomie occurs when social solidarity breaks down due to a decline in the strength of shared social norms. Durkheim was concerned that the lack of shared meaning in modern life could result in a feeling of emptiness. Without a strong sense of social bonds tying people together, he worried that social order would break down, leading people to choose illegitimate or illegal pathways to achieve their goals (Deflem 2007). While Durkheim worried about anomie, he also believed that modern society's complex division of labor could itself foster social cohesion, as members of society had become increasingly dependent on each other. The sense of interdependence that follows from a complex division of labor is what Durkheim understood as organic solidarity. Sociologists who follow in Durkheim's footsteps and take a functionalist approach to society have likened organic solidarity to the human body: just like the body, society is a complex system of interdependent parts that must work together in order to continue functioning as a whole.

While sociologists have critiqued functionalist ideas as overly deterministic, many of Durkheim's central ideas have a lot of staying power. In a modern society where people have different ethnicities, religions, and a diverse range of occupations and incomes, shared norms and values are harder to identify than in traditional societies. As a result, the collective conscience in modern life is relatively fraught, and behavior is often difficult to regulate. Social solidarity is challenging to achieve in a heterogeneous society, even though our complex division of labor makes us reliant on one another to sustain our way of life (e.g. keeping fresh food in the stores, making sure that power flows into our homes, collecting taxes so that the garbage is regularly picked up). Paradoxically, Durkheim suggested that one of the few commonly held values in modern societies was **individualism**—a belief in the importance and primacy of the individual. As such, an emphasis on the individual was central to the collective consciousness that allowed organic solidarity to take hold. In a way, individualism can be seen as the flipside of anomie. We may be united by a common belief in individualism, but our reliance on individualism as a central social norm can lead us to feel isolated and alone. The shared modern value of individualism is key to fully appreciating the ways that consumer culture—and shopping—helps shape a shared collective consciousness in contemporary society.

4.2. Consumer Culture and Social Solidarity: Bonding Through Brands

Durkheim wrote about organic solidarity and the collective conscience over a century ago, but these ideas can provide insight into contemporary consumer culture, and the challenge of building social solidarity in our complex modern world. One connection is the enduring value of individualism. Shopping feeds off our modern cultural valorization of the individual, and it in turn, fuels our individualism, suggesting that we can use consumer products to forge a unique individual identity (Zukin 2004: 34). (This is a theme we explore more in chapter 9.)

Beyond individualism, consumer culture itself can provide a basis for organic solidarity by creating common goods, brands, and experiences that strengthen our sense of "we-ness", or bonds of social solidarity. At a societal level, we achieve a sense of solidarity around our everyday shopping practices, common brands, and shared affection for shopping itself. Put differently, a belief in consumer values, as well as a common consumer culture, can help maintain and form bonds of solidarity. For example, when consumers come together to admire or even love certain shared consumer items (e.g. Ray Bans, Air Jordans, iPhones), it can create a sense of group identity. Shared consumer symbols and brands serve as a kind of commodity "glue" that holds us together as a society, and gives us a sense of common values. Searching for common values in modern cultures may be more challenging than it is in traditional societies, but that doesn't mean we give up the search. Shopping itself can be a way that we seek common values—to be part of something larger than ourselves.

Sociologists note that through the act of shopping, people seek out community—a way to form bonds with others—as in the example of teens who spend the afternoon at the mall, or car enthusiasts who go to an auto show together. While shopping has an individualistic component (explored further in chapter 10), it is also a group activity, a way to be out in public, to socialize, to take part in group culture. Sociologist Sharon Zukin defends the idea of shopping as a "cultural activity", writing that shopping is a common way that "we satisfy our need to socialize—to feel we are part of public life" (2004: 7). Recall from our discussion of Durkheim in chapter 2 that when a group worships a sacred totemic object, its members are creating a sense of a group that is worthy, and worth belonging to. Bringing the idea of the totem to the modern world, sociologist Marshall Sahlins (1976: 180) argued that contemporary societies use manufactured consumer goods (rather than the natural items used in traditional societies) as sacred totemic objects that are central to our social classification schemas. In particular, Sahlins suggested that specific kinds of clothing can be used to create a sense of group membership and solidarity within and across multiple cultural categories, such as men versus women, young versus old, and blue-collar versus white-collar. As we discuss in chapter 10, the consumer objects we wear and the brands we

SOCIOLOGISTS IN ACTION: FOCUS GROUPS

To what extent can our relationship to consumer goods bring us together around a shared collective conscience? **Focus groups** provide a useful research method for exploring this question, using group conversation to collect data on collective thought processes. In a focus group, a small number of people (e.g. 4–6) are brought to together to have a conversation about a specific topic that is focused by a moderator. The researcher uses the group conversation to collect data on individuals' perspectives, but crucially, they also study the group conversation itself, and how it reflects social debates, collective values, and group meaning-making. Besides being used by sociologists, focus groups are also a common method used by marketers to gain a better understanding of how consumers understand and relate to their brands.

Sociologist Judith Taylor and colleagues (2014) used focus groups to study how young feminist-identified women of different racial backgrounds reacted to the Dove "Campaign for Real Beauty"—a multi-year, multi-media promotion that sought to increase sales of Dove products by disseminating critical messages around narrow beauty ideals (in the form of print ads, bill boards, viral videos, and programs to enhance girls' self-esteem) (see: http://www.dove.us/Social-Mission/campaign-for-real-beauty.aspx). In conversations about the Dove campaign, many women initially expressed a shared sense of solidarity with the brand. They reflected positively on the first time they encountered the campaign, and appeared grateful that the Dove campaign had broadened public images of beauty appearing on billboards and bus shelters. However, as the group conversations progressed, the conversations frequently became more critical of Dove, as participants asked questions about the narrowness of beauty images depicted (e.g. focusing on White and light-skinned women, excluding women with fat rolls, women of color, and women wearing a hijab), and critiqued Dove for reinforcing the idea that women's appearance is the central measure of their social worth. By using a focus group approach, the researchers were able to learn from individual women in the group, but also from their spirited group conversations. In these conversations, women debated how much social change could be expected from a capitalist corporation, discussed their own responsibility for reshaping consumer culture, and reflected on the role that beauty should play in women's lives. While women in the focus groups did not agree on all of these issues, the researchers found that the Dove brand and its "Real Beauty" campaign provided a compelling focal point for discussion about issues and values close to their hearts. Not all the brand associations were positive, but it was undeniable that the Dove campaign figured prominently in the collective conscience of these young women—even for those who bonded over shared feelings of resistance to this corporate initiative.

endorse say a great deal about our individual sense of style, as well as our group membership. Owning specific kinds of clothing can work to mark one as an insider or an outsider in social groups. For example, wearing a preppy Lacoste polo shirt to a death metal concert would clearly mark one as an outsider. Indeed, even *rejecting* consumer labels can serve as a way to establish group identity, as documented by a researcher studying devout Muslim women's condemnation of Western brands as "infidel brands" (e.g. Nike, Polo, Burberry) in squatter neighborhoods of Istanbul (Izberk-Bilgin 2012).

One compelling example of a contemporary consumer totem that both marks and solidifies group membership is the Harley Davidson motorcycle. In an ethnographic study of Harley Davidson enthusiasts, researchers revealed the significance of this iconic motorcycle for solidifying bonds of group membership, solidarity, and "we-ness" (Schouten and McAlexander 1995). In this group, it was considered a violation to touch another rider's bike without their express permission, reflecting the Harley's sacred quality (Schouten and McAlexander 1995: 51). Given the bike's totemic status, it is not surprising that the researchers weren't accepted into the group until they owned their own Harleys. Borrowing a motor-bike and hanging out at events (e.g. club meetings, bike rallies) was insufficient to completely understand the bikers, as the researchers explain:

What was missing methodologically . . . was an empathic sense of a biker's identity, psyche, and social interactions in the context of everyday life. To fill this gap we each bought Harleys and made them our primary means of transportation. Furthermore, we purchased appropriate riding clothing and wore it whenever we rode (which meant living out significant portions of our work and leisure lives in jeans, black boots, and black leather jackets).

(1995: 46)

It was only when the researchers themselves owned the branded totemic item—Harley Davidson bikes and clothing—that they could gain full access to the group, and appreciate the collective identity that defined this branded biker subculture. From there, they found that the totemic Harley was associated with key shared values including a belief in freedom (as symbolized by the iconic eagle with outstretched wings), American patriotism (symbolized by the ubiquity of the American flag), and machismo. While Harley culture is characterized by numerous internal subcultures and divisions (e.g. lesbian riders, Mom & Pop riders, rich urban poseurs), overall, the researchers established that Harley culture was united by a fierce sense of loyalty and brotherhood, as well as a shared sense of being an "outsider" in relation to mainstream society (1995: 51). Interestingly, the ethnographers also observed a contradiction within Harley Davidson bike culture: while a key value of the bikers was "freedom", members also "commonly choose, in joining formal organizations, to accept rigid new structures, new codes of conduct, new pressures to conform, and new sources of authority" (1995: 52). Put simply, even in an "outlaw", "outsider" biker culture, there are bonds of social solidarity and shared values that govern behavior and create social order.

While case studies like the Harley Davidson example point to feelings of belonging that may be generated through our shopping choices, other scholars suggest that consumer culture can weaken group ties and diminish social solidarity. Critical perspectives on consumer culture point out that shopping may serve as compensation for modern life's loss of meaning and fractured emotional connections. The concept of anomie can help us to understand why shopping might appeal to people who lack social connections: if you feel isolated and lack a sense of purpose, going shopping may be a way to try to counterbalance those feelings, to provide a sense of purpose in your life, and feel connected to the larger group. While this compensatory strategy has a certain logic to it, it's not clear that shopping can meaningfully address structural issues of anomie. Sometimes, anomie itself is evident in shopping practices; with a paucity of normative regulation, shopping habits become deviant (e.g. overspending, shoplifting, hoarding). The anonymity of the Internet and the absence of social cues from retail staff and other customers may lower online shoppers' inhibitions and encourage compulsive shopping habits (Rose and Dhandayudhan 2013: 87). Loneliness is not only a risk factor for over-spending, but individuals may seek to hide compulsive shopping and hoarding behaviors from others, fearing what they might think, thereby furthering a cycle of social isolation (Sohn and Choi 2014: 251).

Consumer choices may promise a meaningful identity project, but they may not always deliver these promises in the long term. In this way, "shopping [can be seen as] a kind of empty compensation" for modern anomie, a point made especially forcefully by those who see "consumerism as inherently opposed to the achievement of fulfilling social relationships and meaningful lives" (Williams 2006: 15; also R. Lane 2000). Some scholarship looks to shed light on the connections between consumer culture and feelings of social connectedness. While studying happiness is notoriously difficult (e.g. how do you define happiness cross-culturally?), some scholarship suggests that more materialist societies are not necessarily happier ones. Across advanced market democracies, Robert E. Lane (2000: 4) notes a trend of "growing unhappiness and depression, interpersonal and institutional distrust, and weakened companionship", with self-reported levels of happiness in the United States falling, despite gains in real income, throughout the second half of the

Brand Tattoos

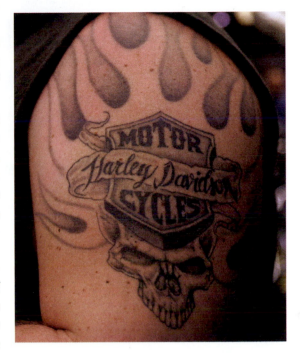

Tattoos can be a way to communicate a more durable commitment to a particular brand, like Harley Davidson motorcycles. As is the case with branded clothes, certain kinds of tattoos can also indicate a person's belonging to a social group.

Source: Gettyimages.com # 112928028

20th century. Why? Like Juliet Schor, Lane suggests that consumer culture puts individuals on a "hedonic treadmill", where desires, standards, and expectations escalate as rapidly as one's achievements, leaving individuals in a state of constantly striving for material ends (R. Lane 2000: 76).

The connection between consumer culture and well-being continues to be of significant interest to scholars who seek to empirically study this relationship (rather than make moralizing statements about the emptiness of consumer culture). For example, an article by Rik Pieters (2013) used a **longitudinal** study of 2500 Dutch consumers surveyed over six years to study the connection between shopping, materialism, social connections and loneliness. In this study, loneliness was understood as the feeling of being isolated from others, and materialism was connected to people's desire to

Hoarding

US documentary television shows like Hoarders *have recently brought greater attention to people who engage in compulsive hoarding and deviant shopping behaviors.*

Source: Gettyimages.com # 165451884

acquire and possess material possessions (2013: 615). Pieters wanted to investigate the possibility that loneliness leads to more materialism (as people buy things to compensate for a lack of social relationships); conversely, he was also interested in whether materialism leads to more loneliness (as people prioritized acquiring things over valuing relationships). This longitudinal study found that higher levels of materialism did increase loneliness over time, *and* higher levels of loneliness also led to increased materialism. In other words, materialistic people became lonelier over time (perhaps because they valued acquiring stuff over building relationships), and lonely people tended to shop as a way of compensating for their loneliness. This research suggests that shopping cannot resolve the modern dilemmas of social solidarity. Also, loneliness—a feeling which is connected to modern life's lack of rich social connections and a heightened challenge of social solidarity—can actively push people towards compensatory shopping strategies. In some instances, our consumer choices can give us a sense of group belonging and meaning (say, for example, in a group of Harley Davidson enthusiasts), but in other instances, our consumption may actually be contributing to the modern problem of anomie.

4.3 Is Shopping a Social Problem?

Reflecting upon this discussion of solidarity, social order, and consumer culture might lead one to ask the question: is shopping a social problem? A social problem is an important, but slippery concept in sociology. What is a problem for some groups is not a problem for others. For example, some might think that homelessness constitutes a social problem that should be addressed collectively (e.g. through greater state-subsidized affordable housing), while others might suggest that individuals are responsible for their own living situation. The concept of a social problem is useful for sociologists because it draws attention to how our understanding of collective problems is socially defined, and reveals the political implications of this process. Powerful groups often have a greater say in determining which social issues are defined as problematic in the mass media, and what kind of solutions are presented as viable and reasonable to state actors.

Although sociologists generally agree that social problems are socially defined and linked to power relations, scholars may disagree on what counts as a social problem. The question of whether shopping constitutes a social problem depends on the perspective that you bring to the issue. (Recall from chapter 2 that a theoretical perspective is like a pair of tinted glasses that color your perception of an issue in a particular way.) From the perspective of an economist interested in growth, shopping is not a problem—it builds the national economy and creates jobs. From an environmental perspective, shopping *is* a problem because it involves resource- and waste-intensive lifestyles that are ecologically unsustainable. A psychologist might see shopping as a social problem because of its connection to feelings of loneliness and social isolation. A Marxist sociologist might see shopping as a way that hegemony is achieved—that is, a way that the interests of powerful groups come to be accepted as common sense—and therefore a social problem. From a Durkheimian perspective, the question of whether shopping constitutes a social problem is not clear-cut. On the one hand, shopping can contribute to a sense of anomie and isolation; on the other, consumer choices and brand culture can address these very problems by providing a shared consumer experience that contributes to a shared collective conscience, as well as totems that are fodder for social solidarity. Each of these perspectives offers important insights into the social significance of our consumer lives.

It is impossible to pin down the "truth" of shopping to a single sociological story. Rather, as we have explored throughout this chapter, shopping is both an expression of, and a response to, the social facts at play in a particular place and time. We frequently encounter stories that construct our shopping habits as a problem—stories of vanity and superficial ideals, financial stress and credit card debt, waste and environmental degradation. In this chapter, we have explored a Durkheimian perspective that focuses on the relationship between shopping and social solidarity, consumer choice and the collective conscience. In the remaining chapters in this section, we continue to examine the role of consumption within processes of "fitting in"—dynamics of group membership, belonging, inclusion, exclusion—and turning an individual into a member of society.

THINKING FRAMES

How can each thinking frame help us ponder the sociology of shopping?

Material / Cultural	Consumer culture theorists have highlighted the aspirational nature of shopping, where the value of material goods extends beyond their utilitarian purpose and into the realm of fantasy and desire. A Durkheimian approach to shopping emphasizes the role of culture in maintaining social order, wherein shared norms and values provide a sense of collective conscience.
Think about . . .	What are some key shared values that relate to shopping in consumer culture (e.g. love of the new, a belief that more stuff equals a better life)? How are these social values functional from an economic perspective that sees consumer demand as a positive force growing the economy?

Structure / Agency	Scholarly accounts of shopping often fall into polarizing perspectives: the consumer "hero" who exercises free choice through her purchases vs. the consumer "dupe" who is entirely manipulated by market forces. Sociological analysis must avoid these extremes in order to investigate the complex interplay between structure and agency.
Think about . . .	When you buy something or simply desire a product, how are you *both* an active consumer hero, and a consumer dupe influenced by social and economic forces larger than your individual conscience?

Micro / Macro	A brief look at the history of shopping reveals the interplay of macro and micro forces, as broad shifts in the organization of society (e.g. industrialization, globalization) are negotiated through everyday purchases. A microsociological approach to shopping extends beyond the motivations of individual consumers to consider shopping's relational significance, fostering social bonds and furthering feelings of "we-ness".
Think about . . .	Imagine somebody buying a Hello Kitty pencil case for her niece. How is this purchase simultaneously related to the "macro" and the "micro" of the global consumer economy? What macro-economic patterns and micro-meanings are involved?

ACTIVE LEARNING

Active Learning

Online

The Story of Stuff:
Watch the short documentary, *The Story of Stuff*. Do you think the creators of this video see shopping as a social problem? Why or why not? What is the central theoretical perspective they are taking in this documentary? What social values around shopping are they critiquing, and why? What theoretical perspectives on shopping are absent from the *Story of Stuff* perspective?
http://storyofstuff.org/movies/story-of-stuff/

Discussion/Reflection

Shopping for "we-ness":
Can you think of a time that you purchased something because you wanted to fit in with a group? How did this item convey your membership in a group? Did this purchase end up satisfying your desire for belonging?

Anomie or social solidarity?
Do you see shopping as a reflection of anomie? Or is it a tool to create social solidarity, and address the modern problem of anomie? Find examples that support both perspectives, and then discuss which perspective seems more convincing.

The macro and the micro stories of our stuff:
Think about a product that is important to you (e.g. a piece of clothing, a car, a phone). Can you describe this object in a way that connects the product to a specific macrosociological context of production, *and* a set of micro-sociological meanings and values? Put differently, tell a story about this item that describes the macro context that allowed this product to be produced, as well as the micro context that gave this product meaning in your social world.

Sociology Outside the Classroom

Mini focus group:
Conduct a mini focus group analysis with a group of friends or your family members. Present the group with a product, as well as an advertisement for that product. (The conversation will be livelier if you bring in a product with a clear connection to social belonging, like a brand-name piece of clothing.) Ask them to discuss what they like and dislike about the product and brand. How are emotions, ideas, and feelings about the product shaped by group discussion about the product? Do focus group participants tend to agree or disagree about the product? How do these agreements or disagreements speak to the relative success or failure of the product's marketing? How do participants' responses vary by aspects of their social location, such as age or gender?

Watch the shopping network:
Over the course of a week, regularly watch and analyze the products and marketing techniques of the home shopping network. What messages do the

salespeople send about the role of products in constructing one's lifestyle and identity? Do they treat consumers as heroes or dupes? Does home shopping make the act of buying stuff less of a social activity? Does this kind of shopping seem to isolate people or provide a kind of virtual community?

A televised history of shopping:
Two recent British costume dramas *Mr. Selfridge* (based on the rise of Selfridge's department store in England) and *The Paradise* (based on Zola's novel *Au Bonheur des Dames*) depict the advent of department stores in the 19th and early 20th centuries. Watch these television shows, thinking about the history of shopping presented in this chapter. How do these television shows depict gender, class, and the role of spectacle and innovation in the rise of the department store?

Chapter 6

GET IN THE GAME: RACE, MERIT, AND GROUP BOUNDARIES

INTRODUCING KEY CONCEPTS

Billions of people around the world love to play sports, watch professional athletes compete, and adorn themselves with team logos. Sports are not only fun to watch and play, but can help us better understand how social groups and social boundaries are formed. Knowing about and talking about sports provides a form of bridging *and* bonding social capital, *allowing us to make friends and connections at school and at work. Being a sports fan also fosters a sense of belonging, generating bonding* rituals *as well as* in-group *and* out-group *distinctions. Sports can be used to engender projects of cultural* assimilation *and create forms of* imagined communities *that link us to fans in distant locations whom we will never know personally. The study of sports is a particularly useful lens for understanding race, and allows us to debunk popular* essentialist *ideas about the certain "natural" physical talents of racial groups. Sociologists typically view race from a* social constructionist *perspective that presents racial categories as social creations rather than objective biological categories. This approach sheds light on the social nature of* racism *and* racial segregation *in the case of sports and more broadly. Studying the sports world also illuminates social ideals of meritocratic fair play—and our aversion to cheaters. We discuss the* sanctions *that cheaters face when their* deviance *is discovered, as well as the ways that sports can help us understand processes of* social control.

1. INTRODUCTION: WHO ARE YOU ROOTING FOR?

Most sports are based on the idea of a relatively straightforward game—shooting a ball in a net, racing a horse around a track, chasing a puck with a hockey stick, running a race to see who is fastest. While these games seem simple, the world of sports is anything but trivial or inconsequential. Sports loom large in society, and many of you reading this book probably consider yourself a fan or sports enthusiast. Perhaps you are wearing a jersey or a cap with your favorite sports team's logo. Maybe you watch your favorite teams on TV in the evenings, or stream highlights on your phone as you ride the bus to campus. Many readers likely have fond memories of playing sports as a kid, or still play pick-up games with friends on the weekends. For the fan, the importance of sports is self-evident. Even for those of you who don't identify as fans, the world of sports pervades our everyday social lives. Myriad sports stars have become household names and celebrities—Serena Williams, Kobe Bryant, Tom Brady, Usain Bolt. The contemporary sports landscape is expansive and varied, including major league sports, global spectacles like the Olympics, college sports (officially classified as amateur but generating billions of dollars in revenue), as well as a diversity of locally organized athletics such as community leagues, clubs, and athletic facilities. Like many aspects of our social worlds, the contemporary sports landscape may seem obvious and natural. People *like* sports, so it's no wonder a massive industry has developed around athletic competition. But our sociological imaginations push us to dig deeper, in order to see the *strangeness* in the seemingly familiar activities of playing a sport, watching sports on TV, or buying sports paraphernalia. As we do so, it becomes clear that the sports landscape as it exists today represents a fascinating evolution from decades past, in terms of which sports are popular, how they are organized, who is playing them, and how they become consumer goods.

Consider the case of professional basketball. Invented near the end of the 19th century, basketball was quickly increasing in popularity throughout the United States in the early decades of the 1900s. As an indoor sport, it could be played throughout winter months. With increasing popularity in schools and colleges, amateur and professional leagues soon developed, making basketball a spectator sport. Among the early participants were a socio-economically marginalized ethnic group who happened to be disproportionately successful. At the time, explanations for their success pointed to stereotypes of the group's "typical" way of thinking—tricky and scheming—and to their physical stature.

Boston Celtics Team Portrait

In 1948 the Boston Celtics fielded an all-White basketball team. In this picture, we see how sports can reflect aspects of the broader society such as racial inequality.

Source: Gettyimages.ca Editorial # 80920993

Such rationalizations for athletic success might sound familiar, but it might surprise you to learn that the ethnic group in question was Jews. At that point in history, Jewish Americans were socio-economically disadvantaged, and it is this particular point of social context that helps us to understand the group's success on the court. Jews were more likely to take up basketball in part because it was more available to them than other sports. Compared to hockey or football, basketball required less investment from the individual players in terms of equipment, and less investment from the community in terms of space. At the time, Jews were concentrated in poor, urban areas: open fields were less available to them. However, the conventional wisdom on Jewish success in basketball pointed not to social context, but instead to essentialist understandings of Jews as an ethnic group. Sociologists use the term **essentialism** to refer to the (false) belief that members of a particular social group share innate and universal qualities. In the early years of professional basketball, the focus on innate ethnic differences went so far as to point to Jews' average shorter stature at the time as an advantage in the game because it provided balance and speed (Leonard 2015).

Today, the social group predominantly associated with basketball has shifted. As a group, African Americans are disproportionately successful at professional basketball. As sociologists, we can detect similarities between the social contexts of American Jews in the early 1900s and African Americans today that are relevant to understanding differentials in participation in basketball. But rather than looking to social factors, the link between a particular social group and a particular sport is commonly perceived as innate or "natural". As Miller (2015) has documented, for many decades African Americans' athletic successes have been explained through a lens that focuses on genetic racial differences, with basketball being a prime example. A sociological perspective challenges such essentialist thinking. What our historical example shows is that explanations of racial differences that seem scientific or perhaps like common sense are often based on flawed understandings—not only of racial differences but of the very concept of race itself.

In this chapter we'll use the world of sports to illuminate many core sociological concepts relating to race and the formation of social groups. Sports form an enormously popular industry whose appeal cuts across age, race, class, gender, and geographical boundaries. People connect to sports in many ways: as a consumer item, as a social activity, as a mechanism to express group membership, as part of a healthy lifestyle, and more. Importantly, sports also often express many of society's core values concerning talent, effort, competition, and merit. In this way, they can help sociologists to understand fundamental aspects of society and social relationships.

2. SPORTS TEAMS, GROUP MEMBERSHIP, AND BOUNDARY WORK

As sociologists such as Bonnie Erickson (1996) have shown, talking about sports provides a way for people to interact with a wide range of others, whether it be coworkers, friends and family, or neighbors and acquaintances. Sports knowledge, even superficial knowledge, can act as a basis for social encounters that generate **social capital**, to maintain or sometimes enhance social relationships and bonds. Like talking about the weather, sports can be invoked fairly reliably as a kind of common ground, especially when interacting with people whose **social location** differs from one's own.

Sociologists are not only interested in the formation of social bonds, but also social boundaries. As discussed in chapter 4, **symbolic boundaries** demarcate who belongs to what group—who is an insider and an outsider. Possessing a degree of knowledge about sports is a way to affirm or signify membership in society—you are supposed to know who your local teams are and how they are doing. Sports can serve as a form of what Robert Putnam (2000) has termed **bridging social capital**, fostering connections among people who are socially distant. When meeting someone with whom you share little in common, you might attempt to break the ice by asking, "Hey, did you see the game last night?" In this scenario, the seemingly shared world of sports offers a way to forge bonds across social difference.

In addition to providing a sort of bridge to reach those who are different from us, sports can also serve as a form of **bonding social capital**, allowing people who are already socially tied to reinforce their sense of identity and group belonging. A quintessential example might be the kind of support for high school football depicted in the television series *Friday Night Lights*. In this show, a Texan town came together as a community in order to support its team, and all the ups and downs of the team's performance were subject to intense scrutiny. The team functioned as a focal point for the expression of the community's group identity and group boundaries. Of course, group boundaries are not only about inclusion, but also *exclusion*; boundaries reinforce a sense of difference from those who are not "one of us". In the case of high school football, the group boundaries correspond closely with residential location—the community being reinforced is the town, while other towns are reinforced as outside the local community. On the football field, these boundaries are made explicit, as fans are seated in opposing stands with their team names clearly displayed on either side of the scoreboard. But the process of drawing social boundaries is not limited to athletic competition. Consider other realms of social life where we derive a sense of group membership by distinguishing ourselves from others, whether that is based on our tastes (e.g. Starbucks versus Dunkin' Donuts), our beliefs (e.g. liberals versus conservatives), or various aspects of our social location (e.g. class, ethnicity, religion). In this way, the world of sports shines a light on more subtle social processes.

Men Bowling in a Bowling Alley

In the 1950s and 1960s, local bowling leagues were very popular. This sport in particular brought together in a social setting people who might not otherwise get to know each other, contributing toward a community's social capital.

Source: Gettyimages.ca Editorial # 50776404

We can extend this sociological lens on sports from the local to the national scale. As the most watched sporting event in the United States, the Super Bowl is a massive spectacle designed to keep the attention of as broad and diverse an audience as possible. Super Bowl Sunday approaches the status of a national holiday, and attending a Super Bowl party can be seen as an especially American **ritual**, one that also happens to be popular in Canada. Sociologists use the concept of ritual to refer to an event or cultural practice that serves to affirm group membership or shared values. The Super Bowl can be seen as a sporting ritual that reaffirms the boundaries of the nation. To understand this process, it's helpful to refer to Benedict Anderson's (1983)

Denver Broncos Entrance to Super Bowl 50

An occasion like the Super Bowl calls for a grand entrance. This pageantry is a testament to the emotional investment that fans make in supporting their teams.

Source: https://commons.wikimedia.org/wiki/File:Denver_Broncos_Entrance_Super_Bowl_50.jpg

classic book describing the nation as an **imagined community**. While small communities can affirm their membership through face-to-face interactions, large communities, like nations, must be imagined by their members, as most will never encounter one another in person. Membership in this imagined community is facilitated through shared symbols (like the American flag) and smaller-scale rituals that occur nationwide (like 4th of July or Thanksgiving celebrations). Mass media are a key channel through which the nation's symbols are transmitted and shared. In this way the Super Bowl broadcast—including not only the singing of the national anthem, but also the mega-star half-time show and innovative commercials—contributes to a sense of national belonging. Watching this spectacle in living rooms and bars throughout the country, Americans connect with geographically distant others who share membership in this imagined community.

The connection between sports and national identity extends well beyond football and well beyond the case of the United States. The most popular sporting event globally is the FIFA World Cup of Soccer. There are literally billions of fans who feel intensely connected to the fortunes of their nation's soccer team—or shall we say, "football", as the sport is known outside of Canada and the US. A similar dynamic takes place in the Olympics, where countries from around the world send their top athletes to compete on the global stage, proudly displaying their nation's flag on their jerseys, helmets, or swimsuits. The dramatic and strongly hyped opening ceremony involves the introduction of each nation's team and creates an opportunity for each nation's audience to emotionally bond with their athletes at the start of competition. Because Olympic events are organized as explicitly international competitions, they provide a particularly stark example of reinforcing group boundaries at the level of the nation.

Success at the Olympics is a huge source of national pride, so much so that many nations invest tens of millions or even hundreds of millions of dollars annually in support for athletes, training centers, and related costs. Nations negotiate their respective identities in part through international sports competitions. When we root for "our" athletes in the Olympics, we might ask ourselves: what makes them "ours"? They are "ours" in a way that relies upon and also reinforces our membership in a national community. While reinforcing national boundaries, such global sporting events incur social costs at a local level that can have devastating effects for marginalized groups. In their research with street youth in Vancouver and London, Jacqueline Kennelly and Paul Watt (2011) found that a successful bid to host the Olympics can intensify practices of surveillance, criminalization, and displacement among local homeless populations. So the image of national pride and global unity associated with events like the World Cup and the Olympics can obscure the damage wrought by such global spectacles at the local level.

The association between athletics and nationalism also emerges in the realm of immigration, as playing a cherished sport is commonly seen as a way to integrate newcomers into society. This is often framed in a positive light, as seen in a news story depicting refugees in Sweden playing bandy (a variant on hockey popular in Scandinavia) as part of their new Swedish lives (Isley 2016). The power of sports to integrate newcomers is linked to their *cultural* significance as a national pastime (e.g. what could be more American than playing baseball? Or more Canadian than playing hockey?), and to their *social* significance as a site for building relationships with others. While there are surely positive experiences facilitated through sport in the context of immigration, it's important to bring a critical perspective to these feel-good stories. As many scholars have shown, sport has historically served as a tool to assimilate immigrants to an American way of life (Iber et al. 2011). The concept of **assimilation** refers to the process through which members of an ethnic **minority group** shed their own distinct culture and assume the cultural practices of the dominant group. (Note that in sociology, the term minority group refers to groups who are subordinated within a particular society, not necessarily groups who are smaller in number.) While the project of assimilation through sport may be depicted as one of inclusion, the flipside of this process is a potential loss or devaluing of immigrants' cultural practices and ethnic identities. In sociological terms, we can question whether the cultural assimilation of immigrants via sports is as welcoming as cultural *integration* would be, where immigrants' own sports traditions are not lost in their new country, but instead contribute to an evolving sports repertoire. Beyond assimilating newcomers within the US, Gerald Gems (2012) argues that sports have played a key role in the broader project of American imperialism. Bringing sports like baseball to other areas of the world has been seen as a way to instill uniquely American values in colonial contexts.

The implications of social boundaries drawn through sports are heightened for the athletes themselves, especially in the case of team sports. In order to perform well, team members must be socially cohesive—they need to feel like they are working as a group, not just as individuals. In this way sports can facilitate group membership directly and intensively. Many parents enroll their children in organized sports in order to develop their capacities as "team players". But the kinds of group membership fostered through sports can become complicated when we consider the multifaceted nature of our identities. On the one hand, baseball players may recognize other athletes with similar talents as sharing a fundamental characteristic as team members. On the other hand, not everybody feels equally comfortable on a team. Group membership is evaluated based on a number of criteria, including skill level as well as multiple aspects of social location (e.g. ethnicity, age, etc.). Even different ways of playing a game can be a barrier to social cohesion. In the context of sports, gender and race have both been used to delineate group boundaries—to figure out lines of being in the group or off the team. Historically, these boundaries were reified through formal segregation; this history helps to provide context for the organization of sports today.

The separation of women's sports and men's sports is fairly pervasive. By the teenage years, boys and girls tend to play in separate leagues for virtually all sports. That separation continues, and we see separate professional sports leagues for men and women, and separate competitions at the Olympics. To be sure, there are average physical differences between the sexes, and so separation in sports has a logical justification. However, in terms of our discussion of group membership, sports are a key way that we socialize gender differences, far beyond what would be expected from average group differences in athletics (Hartmann 2003). When we enrol young children in gender-segregated sports leagues, we communicate the message that boys and girls are fundamentally different from each other. This division promotes what sociologists call the **gender binary**, an idea that we'll examine more closely in the next chapter's discussion of gender socialization.

While it is true that at the very elite levels men and women perform differently, it is also true that cross-gender team membership would face an enormous hurdle regarding group identity. The sports team is a strongly gendered group boundary, and also a site of gender inequality. Across virtually all professional sports leagues, men's teams are given significantly more attention, prestige, and resources than women's teams. During the time that we were writing this book, numerous gendered sports controversies surfaced in the media. At a major professional tennis tournament in March 2016, the CEO and tournament director, Raymond Moore, controversially stated that female players "ride on the coat-tails of the men", and added "If I was a lady player, I'd go down every night on my knees and thank God that Roger Federer and Rafa Nadal were born, because they have carried this sport" (Lombardo 2016). (Moore soon resigned from his position.) In another gender-sports controversy, five members of the US Women's soccer team filed a wage-discrimination complaint with the Equal Employment Opportunity Commission, pointing to the vastly unequal salaries of men and women players. Star player Carli Lloyd highlighted the size of this disparity in a *New York Times* op-ed, writing: "The men get almost $69,000 for making a World Cup roster. As women, we get $15,000 for making the World Cup team" (Lloyd 2016). This discrepancy is clearly linked to a broader system of **patriarchy** in which women and femininity are valued less than men and masculinity (see chapter 7), but it is also justified by the drawing of group boundaries to suggest that male and female players are fundamentally different from each other.

As our introductory example in this chapter shows, sports history provides a compelling case study for understanding how group boundaries are drawn along racial lines. Just as with gender, race was historically a basis for segregation in sports. The cases are not completely parallel as this division reflected broader patterns of racial segregation in society. However, thinking sociologically, we can see this as another instance of reinforcing group membership through the creation of social boundaries. The racial divisions reinforced through sport provide a historically significant example of how people use identity markers to create **in-group/out-group distinctions**.

While sports are no longer explicitly segregated along racial lines, the connection between sports, race, and group boundaries persists. Consider common athletic stereotypes that link a particular race or ethnicity with a particular sport. For example, hockey and golf are often seen as White people's sports. Common stereotypes suggest that Black people are good at basketball, that Brazilians are good at soccer, and that Chinese people are good at table tennis. These stereotypes are connected to facts that are subject to misinterpretation. It is true that most NBA players are African American, and it is true that Brazil has won more World Cup titles than any other country, and it is true that the majority of Olympic medals in table tennis have gone to China. But the expansion of these associations into racial or ethnic generalizations is a slip in logic. If we look more closely at Chinese Olympic medals, we can see the case of table tennis as part of a wider trend in Chinese Olympic success; China has been at or near the top of the total medal count at the summer Olympics for the past two decades. Chinese athletes are broadly successful. At the same time, China's Olympic success at table tennis is undoubtedly facilitated by the popularity of table tennis as a sport there, providing a large pool of potential athletes to train and groom. Our key point here is that there is nothing inherent to Chinese ethnicity or biology that can explain the country's success at the sport. And yet, these kinds of essentialist explanations for athletic success among racial and ethnic groups have been around a long time and still enjoy some currency (despite a total lack of scientific support) today. The sports of swimming and skiing are typically seen as "White people's sports". But a comparison of the Olympic medals of Australia and Norway is instructive here: Australia does disproportionately well in swimming events at the summer Olympics, and Norway does disproportionately well in skiing events. Rather than a story of essential racial characteristics, this discrepancy in Olympic success is related to the conditions under which opportunities to develop talent in these sports vary across the two countries. Australia's climate and geography facilitate the use of swimming pools, while Norwegian sports culture is oriented towards exploiting the access to many winter sports opportunities.

A "Miracle on Ice"

A still from the American–Soviet men's hockey game at the 1980 Winter Olympic Games in Lake Placid, New York. Set against the backdrop of the Cold War, the underdog American team beat the Soviet team, four-time-consecutive winners of the gold medal, by a score of 4 to 3, and then beat Finland in the finals to win the gold medal. The American team went on to visit the White House, tour the country, and appear on the cover of Wheaties boxes and magazines, and reunited to light the Olympic torch at the 2002 Winter Olympics in Salt Lake City. Dubbed a "miracle on ice", the win became a point of considerable national pride, and was selected by Sports Illustrated *as the greatest sports moment of the 20th century.*

Source: Gettyimages.ca Editorial # 515124974

3. ATHLETICISM AND THE SOCIAL CONSTRUCTION OF RACE

Although we could focus on many different aspects of a person's background to understand their success at a sport, race frequently pops up as a seemingly straightforward "explanation" or a "reason". In the words of the 1992 movie starring Wesley Snipes and Woody Harrelson, "White men can't jump". The perceived connection between race and athleticism comes from the common idea that race is rooted in our biology, and that members of different racial groups have a fundamentally different genetic makeup. When we think this way, a slippery and problematic concept like race seems simple and natural, even though sociological research shows that race is anything but simple or natural. While many people think of race as a straightforward category based on physical appearance, in fact, the very idea of race is *socially* constructed (rather than being based on a pure biological category). **Social constructionism** is a vitally important concept in our sociological toolkit, and has special utility for studies of race. To say that race is socially constructed means that this seemingly natural category has actually been created by society. Yes, physical attributes like skin color and facial features vary across groups. However, social constructionism asks us to be skeptical of the idea that our physical differences position us in distinct, exclusive categories associated with particular traits and status. It suggests that race is less about biology, and much more about social processes of in-group and out-group distinctions. After all, there is huge variation among people who are said to belong to the same "race", but this diversity is minimized in the way people think about racial groups.

The very notion of classifying people into "races" is not as straightforward as it may seem, and has shifted significantly over time. For example, in the first half of the 19th century, Irish immigrants in the US were thought of as "Black" rather than "White" given their inferior social standing as low-wage laborers. It took a deliberate and violent social process of aligning themselves against African Americans to achieve status as "Whites" (Ignatiev 1995). This is an example of what sociologist Vilna Bashi Treitler calls an "ethnic project". As she explains, "in specific historical moments various outside groups undertook concerted social action (namely, an 'ethnic project') to foster a perception of themselves as 'different' from the bottom and 'similar' to the top of [the] racial hierarchy" (2013: 4). Today, the classification of "Black" doesn't include Irish Americans, but it remains primarily cultural rather than physical or biological. For example, somebody born of a White mother and a

2010 Census Questions on Race and Ethnicity

→ **NOTE: Please answer BOTH Question 8 about Hispanic origin and Question 9 about race. For this census, Hispanic origins are not races.**

8. Is Person 1 of Hispanic, Latino, or Spanish origin?

☐ **No,** not of Hispanic, Latino, or Spanish origin

☐ Yes, Mexican, Mexican Am., Chicano

☐ Yes, Puerto Rican

☐ Yes, Cuban

☐ Yes, another Hispanic, Latino, or Spanish origin — *Print origin, for example, Argentinean, Colombian, Dominican, Nicaraguan, Salvadoran, Spaniard, and so on.* ⬊

[   ]

9. What is Person 1's race? *Mark* ☒ *one or more boxes.*

☐ White

☐ Black, African Am., or Negro

☐ American Indian or Alaska Native — *Print name of enrolled or principal tribe.* ⬊

[   ]

☐ Asian Indian   ☐ Japanese   ☐ Native Hawaiian
☐ Chinese   ☐ Korean   ☐ Guamanian or Chamorro
☐ Filipino   ☐ Vietnamese   ☐ Samoan
☐ Other Asian — *Print race, for example, Hmong, Laotian, Thai, Pakistani, Cambodian, and so on.* ⬊   ☐ Other Pacific Islander — *Print race, for example, Fijian, Tongan, and so on.* ⬊

[   ]

☐ Some other race — *Print race.* ⬊

[   ]

→ **If more people were counted in Question 1, continue with Person 2.**

The first US census in 1790 featured 3 categories for denoting race and ethnicity: free White males and females, all other free persons, and slaves. The 2010 census asked two questions pertaining to race and ethnicity, encompassing 19 different options. These bureaucratic procedures for measuring race reflect predominant perceptions of racial categories, but also are powerful ways that these perceptions can become solidified and reproduced.

Source: http://www.pewresearch.org/fact-tank/2014/03/14/u-s-census-looking-at-big-changes-in-how-it-asks-about-race-and-ethnicity/

Black father would widely be considered Black, even though their family background is equal parts Black and White. This cultural norm is rooted in racist social practices of slave-owning American history, where the "one-drop" rule dictated that anybody with a Black ancestor would be considered Black, and therefore a slave (Omi and Winant 2014). On the other hand, if you are African American with very light skin, people might assume that you are White, putting you in the position of having to explicitly claim your Black identity. Clearly, race is much more complicated than skin color. When discussing race in our classes, students frequently describe the impossible task of trying to fit their complex racial identities into the neat and tidy categories presented on various institutional forms. Indeed, the racial classifications on the American census have changed significantly over time—a clear demonstration of the fact that these categories are social constructs, and thus subject to change.

To say that race is socially constructed means that racial categories are the product of social understandings, rather than a natural "fact". However, that doesn't deny the impact of race—and **racism**—in our lives. The sociological study of racism includes not only interpersonal racial bias and discrimination, but also the vast racial inequalities embedded in the organization of society, including racial disparities in housing, education, health, and incarceration (see chapter 12 for more on institutional racism). The idea of race has very powerful outcomes; socially constructed racial categories influence our identities, opportunities, constraints, and life outcomes. Speaking to the experience of growing up as an African American, one of our students wrote: "As a child you are taught to see the world differently, because the world sees you differently." For example, research conducted by sociologist Michael Gaddis demonstrated that White job applicants were likely to receive more interest from employers and for higher-ranked jobs than Black applicants, even when they both had Ivy League degrees (Gaddis 2014). In a White-dominant corporate culture, racism is not just about one person being denied a job, but the structural tendency for a category of people—Blacks—facing systematic discrimination in the job market.

The social construction of race has powerfully shaped the historical development of professional sports. Consider the case of baseball, the professional sports league with the longest organizational history. In the early decades of the 1900s, professional baseball engaged in **racial segregation**—the practice of physically and culturally separating people by perceived racial identity in order to maintain racial hierarchy. At this time in the United States, racial segregation was legal and sometimes even encouraged through racist laws in housing, transportation, and education. Laws enforcing racial segregation were known as "Jim Crow" laws, and they persisted in the US until the civil rights movement of the 1960s (the term "Jim Crow" was a pejorative term historically applied to African Americans). For example, between 1934 and 1968, the Federal Housing Administration permitted overt racism through the practice of "redlining", which promoted residential segregation by barring

Experience of Neighborhood Diversity by Race

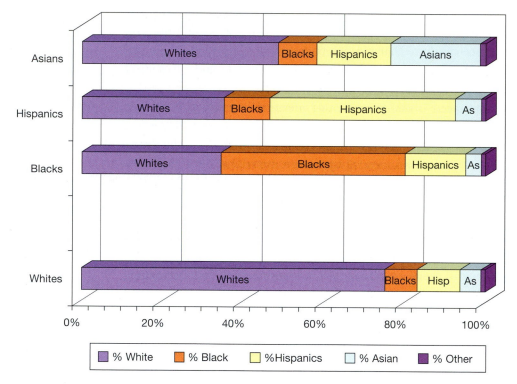

Drawing on 2010 census data for 367 metropolitan areas in the US, this graph shows the level of neighborhood diversity an average member of each racial group might experience. For instance, we see that the average Hispanic American lives in a neighborhood that is 35% White, 11% Black, 46% Hispanic, and 7% Asian. We also see that both Black and Hispanic Americans tend to live in neighborhoods with higher levels of minority representation than White or Asian Americans. In contrast, White people tend to live in predominantly White neighborhoods, and experience lower levels of residential diversity than any other racial group.

Source: John R. Logan and Brian Stults. 2011. "The Persistence of Segregation in the Metropolis: New Findings from the 2010 Census." Census Brief prepared for Project US2010. http://www.s4.brown.edu/us2010/Data/Report/report2.pdf

African Americans from taking out loans in particular areas (Lipsitz 2011). While this practice was outlawed with the Fair Housing Act of 1968, we continue to see the effects of this history in the racial segregation of many US cities today.

It was within the social context of an overtly segregated America that professional baseball emerged. In these early years, the league was under the control of team owners who may have loved the sport but were also aiming to turn a profit. Whatever their own views on race, they were beholden to the beliefs of their players and fans; the predominant view at this time was that White players should not play alongside Black players, and that White fans would not support Black players. The racial segregation of professional baseball was a ubiquitous practice without ever being a formal policy. Using the case of baseball history, we see a profound and large-scale illustration of how racial boundaries are drawn through sports.

The historic refusal of White Major League Baseball to field Black players is a quintessential example of **racial discrimination**. On its own, the term discrimination refers to the application of standards to make choices. We discriminate when we choose to buy one brand of jeans over another brand, or when we decide to eat vegetables instead of candy. There is nothing wrong with making choices that are discriminatory so long as they are based on reasonable standards. By contrast, racial discrimination involves differential

Jesse Owens

Jesse Owens prepares to run the 200-meter race at the 1936 Olympics in Berlin, where he won four gold medals. Owens was credited with challenging the ideology of Aryan supremacy in Nazi Germany, particularly as espoused by the German press, who dubbed him and other Black athletes from America as the "Black auxiliaries". Back home, Owens, the son of a sharecropper and grandson of slaves, had long faced discrimination under Jim Crow laws. While attending Ohio State University, he set track and field records and became the first Black man to be elected captain of an Ohio State varsity team. However, segregation laws barred him from living on campus and staying in the same accommodation as the rest of the team when traveling. After the 1936 Olympic Games, Owens felt snubbed by President Roosevelt, who neither invited him to the White House nor acknowledged his accomplishments, because of his race.

Source: https://commons.wikimedia.org/wiki/File:Jesse_Owens3.jpg

treatment on the basis of race, such as deciding whether or not to employ someone as a baseball player. This form of discrimination is very clearly not reasonable; rather, it is a longstanding and continued source of racial injustice. Choices about hiring baseball players should have been based on athletic talent, not race. However, during the early years of Major League Baseball, racially discriminatory hiring practices were perfectly legal; it wasn't until civil rights legislation was enacted in the 1960s that racial discrimination was legally prohibited in America. Legal protection against racial discrimination is an important tool for promoting equality in multiracial societies, and goes hand in hand with laws that protect a longer list of minority groups, including groups bounded by religion, ethnicity, national origin, sexual orientation, age, ability, and sex. At the same time, laws can only do so much, as racial discrimination is not always detectable as a motive for behavior.

In 1947, Jackie Robinson broke the color barrier in Major League Baseball when he began playing for the Brooklyn Dodgers. As seen in the movie *42*, Robinson encountered significant hostility upon entering the league, as racist fans, players, and owners attempted to preserve the Majors as a White league. Despite this persistent racism, Robinson's entry was the beginning of a historic shift, and teams in both the National League and the American League slowly

SOCIOLOGISTS IN ACTION: FIELD EXPERIMENTS

Racial discrimination is difficult to observe and to measure, in part because it is widely known to be socially unacceptable. People do not label their own discriminatory attitudes and behaviors as such, sometimes not even admitting it to themselves! Behaviors that can be based on unobservable and multiple motivations and beliefs present a challenge to sociologists. When an employer turns an applicant down for a job, how do we know if that is a straightforward process of finding the best applicant or a case of racial discrimination? Field experiments provide a method for untangling these potentially confounding factors. Field experiments are experimentally designed studies that happen "in the field", or within the actual social world rather than in an artificial social setting like a laboratory. The real-world setting adds to researchers' confidence that the study represents typical social behavior, rather than what people do when they know they are being observed by researchers. The experimental design refers to the classic scientific strategy of comparing two outcomes: one where there was a condition of interest present, and another where that condition was absent. This arrangement allows researchers to isolate the effect of the one condition of interest on an outcome. Typically, participants are assigned to one of two groups (or more if it is a complex experiment), and one group receives the experimental condition while the other group does not. Then, both groups are assessed on a particular outcome. Crucially, the experimental design must be unknown to the participants of the experiment, because an understanding of the purpose of the experiment might cause people to change their behaviors in ways that affect the results.

An excellent example of this method is provided by Devah Pager, Bruce Western, and Bart Bonikowski's paper "Discrimination in a Low-Wage Labor Market: A Field Experiment". In this study, the researchers wanted to better understand the reasons for racial group differences in employment. Unemployment rates have differed between racial groups for many decades. But we know very little about how employers make hiring decisions, including "how race influences employers' perceptions of job candidate quality and desirability" (Pager, Western, and Bonikowski 2009: 778). The researchers hired research assistants who posed as job applicants. These "testers" were young men, one White, one Black, and one Latino. The testers were selected to be as similar as possible in every way except race. They were given fake résumés that were also as similar as possible in terms of credentials. The jobs applied for were all low-level entry jobs, which involved mostly showing up in person and filling out an application on the spot. Employers were therefore able to observe the race of the applicants. The researchers measured how initial callbacks and job offers differed according to the race of the testers. They found that White testers were most likely to receive callbacks and job offers. Latino testers were much less likely to receive callbacks and job offers than White testers, and Black testers were significantly less likely to receive callbacks and job offers than Latino testers. The field experiment method was analytically powerful in allowing the researchers to show that employers' decisions were often racially discriminatory.

integrated over the following years. In order to earn the chance to be drafted, Black players had to be exceptionally talented, but these talented examples paved the way for recognition and acceptance of further Black players. In hindsight it is possible to link the gradual integration of Black Americans in baseball to broader social forces dampening overt forms of racism.

Today professional baseball has a long history of cherished Black baseball stars. However, as a recent *USA Today* story reported, only 7.8% of Major League Baseball players are Black, down from as many as 19% in earlier decades (Nightengale 2015). This is an interesting contrast with the National Basketball Association, where over 75% of players are Black, despite the fact that the NBA started as an all-White league. What can we learn about the sociology of race from these discrepant rates of inclusion across sports and time periods? Does the very high rate of participation in basketball mean that African Americans are "natural athletes"? If that were true, then why would their participation in baseball be so low? Does it mean that they lack the skills for baseball? If that were true, then why would their participation rates in earlier decades be much higher than their proportion in the American population and then sink below proportional representation today? The answer is that the link between sports and race is dependent on social factors, *not* inherent racial difference. While the exact nature of the social factors behind these rates of inclusion is hard to pin down, only social factors change with the magnitude and the speed to account for these percentages. The kinds of social factors that are likely involved are those that influence young players' likelihood of trying a particular sport, practicing regularly, and eventually training within elite athletic settings. As mentioned in the introduction, basketball requires fewer individual and community resources compared to the equipment and large, open field required for baseball. To the extent that residential segregation by race persists and can even deepen in some locations, young Black athletes will have different rates of professional success in basketball versus baseball. In contrast to sociological explanations, explanations about race and innate racial differences are simply unable to account for the complex and historically variable patterns of sports participation that we see.

In addition to structural factors like residential segregation and economic inequality, the link between race and sport is culturally reinforced through racial stereotypes. Historically, Whites drew upon ideas of racial difference to explain the achievements of Black athletes. Patrick Miller (2015) writes that in the early 1900s such explanations were upheld by bogus theories that positioned Blacks as physically advantaged in some sports (due to apparent differences in anatomy and physiology), but intellectually and culturally inferior. This "scientific racism" provided a justification for African Americans' athletic success that worked to uphold Whites' privileged position within the racial hierarchy. As Miller writes, "Western discourse of racial difference carefully juxtaposed Black athletic achievement . . . to the supposed intellectual disabilities or cultural shortcomings of African Americans" (2015: 73). While theories of innate racial difference have now been fully discredited, assumptions about the "natural" athleticism of Blacks persist. In an ethnographic study of physical education classes in two American high schools, Azzarito and Harrison (2008) found that White boys drew upon the idea of Blacks' "natural" physical superiority to explain their athletic success. Such explanations not only reinforce racial boundaries, but also undermine the efforts and achievements of Black athletes by positioning their success as the natural outcome of biology. As Azzarito and Harrison write, "Blacks' success in sports, in discourses of race, is rarely attributed to hard work, technique, or intellectual strategy" (2008: 352).

A key source for perpetuating such racial stereotypes is the representation of sport in mass media. While media and sports scholars have criticized racial stereotypes, athletes themselves have also made this critique. At a 2014 press conference, NFL player Richard Sherman criticized the use of the term "thug" to describe him on social media following the Super Bowl. "The reason it bothers me is because it seems like it's an accepted way of calling somebody the N-word now," Sherman said (quoted in Wilson 2014). Sherman's assessment draws attention to how the language used to describe athletes can perpetuate racial stereotypes—and in doing so, perpetuate racism. In 2016, the Carolina Panthers' Cam Newton spoke to the heightened scrutiny he received as a Black quarterback. "I'm an African-American quarterback. That may scare a lot of people," Newton told reporters, "Because they haven't seen nothing that they can compare me to" (quoted in Gibbs 2016). The position of quarterback is associated with intelligence, strategy, and leadership, and as Azzarito and Harrison note above, these traits are rarely attributed to Black athletes. The NFL saw its first Black quarterback in 1968 when Marlin Briscoe briefly occupied the position for the Denver Broncos, before being moved to wide receiver. In a 2016 interview, Briscoe reflects on how the position of quarterback was long associated with Whiteness. "They denied access to that position to the Black man, because it was held in such high esteem," he said, "because it was a position of power on the football field" (quoted in Gibbs 2016). Briscoe's incisive critique highlights how racial stereotypes on and off the football field are not only about *difference*, but also about *inequality*. As we noted at the beginning of this section, the social construction of race works to preserve a racial hierarchy that advantages some groups and disadvantages others.

Sports are often seen as the epitome of meritocracy—a system where people get ahead based on their talents and achievements. On an apparently "equal playing field", the very best athletes rise to the top. However, in this section we've shown how the ideal of meritocracy can work ideologically to mask persistent social inequalities like racism and sexism; these inequalities significantly tilt the playing field, and make some athletes more likely to succeed than others. In the next section, we examine another aspect of professional sports where we must confront our ideals of meritocracy and fairness in athletic competition: the question of who defines the rules of the game, and what happens when we break them.

4. CHEATERS AND LIARS OR STRATEGIC ACTORS? DEVIANCE IN THE WORLD OF SPORT

When we say that people have to "play by the rules of the game", we use a sports analogy that can apply to anything in life. Just as every sport has rules that define how to play and what is allowed, our behavior in everyday life is similarly governed by rules of various kinds. Some of these rules are informal and ambiguous, while others are more formal and clear. In sociological terms, this is the difference between social **norms** and **laws**. As discussed in chapter 2, social norms are the "unwritten rules" of daily life. For example, in Canada and the United States it is a norm to leave a tip in a restaurant of 15–20%. In contrast to social norms, laws are codified, meaning that they are written in precise language and approved by a governing authority. While there is no law saying what percentage your tip must be, there is a law that says you have to pay for what you order and eat. In both cases, paying your bill and leaving a tip means that you are playing by the rules of the game of eating in a restaurant. Crucially, breaking the social norm can be punished only informally. If you don't leave a tip, the wait staff will be disappointed and probably less enthusiastic the next time you visit. In contrast, breaking the law can lead to a formal form of punishment and a criminal charge.

How does the world of sports connect to social norms and laws? As most fans know, each sport has its own set of rules—both formal and informal. For this reason, sports present an ideal microcosm for exploring the sociological concept of **deviance**. Introduced in chapter 2, the concept of deviance refers to the violation of social norms. The sociological study of deviance explores questions about how we come to collectively define and manage the rules that govern everyday life—from informal expectations to formal laws—and what happens when people break them. Just as in the rest of life, athletic conduct is governed by both unofficial norms and official rules. Informal norms in sports overlap a great deal with the norms that apply in social life in general. Think, for example, of how norms about gender shape behavior. In the same way that there is a norm against men crying in general, male athletes are normally not supposed to cry from an injury or a loss in sports. To suggest that this is a norm does not mean that it *never* happens, only that it is relatively socially unacceptable. Another example is the norm against bragging: bragging about one's successes is generally not considered socially acceptable in everyday life; similarly, an athlete who brags about a win may be seen as a "poor sport". But sporting norms can also differ from those in the rest of society. Consider, for example, norms about aggression. Behaving aggressively is quite normal for many sports, like football, in a way that would not be socially acceptable outside of that social setting.

There is less overlap between the rules that govern athletic competition and the laws that govern collective society. As competitive games, sports must follow rules that structure participation uniquely for those games. For example, in basketball a player must dribble the ball in order to move; moving the pivot foot or taking three or more steps without dribbling is a violation called "traveling". It seems simple enough, but in the official NBA rulebook (a 67-page document for 2015–16!), traveling is defined through Section XIII with eight different articles that describe the precise rules that must be followed when receiving the ball, pivoting, stepping, and releasing the ball. If a player fails to conform to these rules, they can incur a penalty. If this seems legalistic, that's because it is. It's not just basketball; all professional sports have rulebooks that look a lot like actual laws. In fact, the preface to the NFL's official rulebook includes a sentence that highlights this similarity: "Where the word 'illegal' appears in this rule book, it is an institutional term of art pertaining strictly to actions that violate NFL playing rules."

Rules in sports get broken often—just think of how frequently a player is called offside in soccer or hockey. When such rules are broken, players face a clearly defined penalty. Whether it means losing possession of the ball or spending time in the penalty box, these **sanctions** provide a mechanism for encouraging athletes to play by the rules. In a simple way, the punishments are designed to make rule-breaking undesirable by making the costs outweigh the benefits. Of course, when athletes break rules it is often a more complicated situation than a simple cost–benefit calculation. Not every infraction of the rules is intentional, and not every infraction is detected and punished. Referees' judgment is fallible, and their view of the game is unavoidably partial. Even with these limitations, penalties in sports are intended to be a tool for achieving a degree of **social control**—the regulation of people's behavior so that it conforms to group expectations. Within sociology, the concepts of deviance and social control go hand in hand; acts of deviance are met with various forms of social control that encourage us to follow the rules. Just like norms, forms of social control vary in severity. Players may receive a disapproving look from other players if they violate a norm like spitting on the court during a tennis match, but they will face much more serious consequences if they violate the norm of fixing a match in exchange for a bribe (match fixing is discussed more fully below). The case of sports provides an especially clear example of deviance and punishment because the rules and penalties of the game are so clearly defined. However, in the broader society, crime and punishment are typically a lot "messier". Unlike being offside in soccer, people break laws in society for much more complicated reasons and in a wider variety of social contexts.

Although we have discussed norms and laws as separate things (i.e. informal vs. formal rules), in fact there can be some blurriness between these categories. Take, for example, the case of "excessive celebration" in the NFL. Under Rule 12 on "Player Conduct", section 3 pertains to "Unsportsmanlike Conduct". Here, the rulebook provides a multi-part description of the kinds of celebrations that are deemed illegal, grouped together under the heading of "Taunting". These rules have evolved over time in response to players' increasingly elaborate celebratory actions, particularly following touchdowns. While these are "laws" within the context of the NFL, they are based on norms about "sportsmanship" and the League's perceptions of dignity. Part of the motivation for the rules is to maintain a connection with fans' expectations about personal modesty and being a "good winner". If players' celebrations conflict with fans' preferences, the league might lose some of its audience. There is a connection, then, between NFL rules and the broader social norms that underpin them. However, the fuzziness of the rules underscores the point that norms are inherently ambiguous. Despite the specific language of the NFL rules, it is impossible to specify in all cases which actions constitute "excessive" celebration or "taunting". The range of possible ways to celebrate after a touchdown is enormous. Furthermore, the League is not seeking to enforce a total ban on celebrations. For example, spiking the ball after a touchdown is not illegal.

The rules about excessive celebration illustrate the challenge of specifying exactly what actions constitute a "crime". Here, we see how deviance itself is socially constructed. The prohibition on excessive celebration is intended to constrain behavior that is unsportsmanlike and inappropriate. But who is to say which actions should be labeled this way? That is, how do we decide when a player's celebratory expression moves from "appropriate" to "excessive"? This is precisely the question explored in a *New York Times Magazine* article called "The Unbearable Whiteness of Baseball". Journalist Jay Kang (2016) described the controversy surrounding Toronto Blue Jays player José Bautista, who flipped his bat into the air after hitting a home run in a 2015 playoff game. Some claimed that Bautista's bat flip was too showy and undignified—behavior that

José Bautista's Bat Flip

When Toronto Blue Jay José Bautista hit a three-run home run to put his team in the lead in the seventh inning of a playoff game against the Texas Rangers, he spontaneously flipped his bat in the air, a common celebratory action in many baseball traditions outside of North America. However, his bat flip was criticized by some other MLB players and some media commentators as inappropriate. Whether this action was deviant depends on which tradition is your reference point.

Source: Gettyimages.ca Editorial # 492830780

was not suitable for the Major Leagues. As Kang reports, Bautista reacted to the criticism by pointing out "the bad faith of the media toward Latino players", whose celebratory expressions are frequently framed as "unsportsmanlike". In his own written response to this debate, Bautista reflected upon his personal relationship to baseball growing up in the Dominican Republic. In this context, Bautista wrote, baseball is not a "country club game", but instead was "packed with emotion" (Bautista 2015). To see the expression of such emotion as "inappropriate" on the field relies upon the social norms established by a particular White Anglo Saxon Protestant cultural tradition. In other words, the social construction of some celebratory styles as deviant fails to recognize the contemporary diversity of Major League Baseball (Kang 2016).

While major sporting events are big news, perhaps the most attention is garnered by stories of wrongdoing in sports: cheating and fraud are spectacles in their own right. One form of cheating that has made headlines for decades is the use of performance enhancing drugs, also known as doping. In general, professional sports have banned the use of these drugs by athletes. This ban is based on the belief that such drugs distort athletic performance: rather than a show of talent and training, the performance of athletes on drugs reflects a scientific intervention that is not authentic. At the same time, many of these drugs can have serious health consequences and even cause premature death. The ban, therefore, protects the athletes, as well as aims to maintain a level playing field. The use of performance enhancing drugs clearly constitutes a crime in the sports context.

One of the biggest doping scandals in recent memory involved Lance Armstrong, the American cyclist who won his sport's crowning title, the Tour de France, a record seven consecutive times from 1999 to 2005. Armstrong had in the mid-1990s successfully survived cancer, and so was an especially sympathetic character for the public to embrace as an icon of grit and perseverance. When he was found in 2012 to be guilty of the doping accusations and had his titles stripped, it was a media spectacle of a magnitude beyond any of his cycling wins. In early 2016, former world #1 ranked tennis player Maria Sharapova admitted to taking a banned performance enhancing drug. Because she was at the time a huge sports celebrity, her infraction was a highly visible news story beyond sports reporting.

While the rules on performance enhancing drugs are clear, a different perspective questions whether doping really does constitute cheating. An article in *Forbes Magazine* (Hartung 2016) raised this question, noting that the use of performance enhancing drugs is so widespread that it could plausibly be considered the norm. Moreover, what counts as a performance enhancing drug is constantly evolving. The drug that Maria Sharapova got caught taking had been added to the list of banned substances only months before she was charged with taking it. What's more, the concept of enhancing performance is deeply embedded in sports culture, where athletic performance is enhanced in countless different ways, many of them technologically based. Why are drugs so different? Shouldn't it be a choice left to the athletes? Questions like these again point to the socially constructed nature of this form of deviance.

Of course, cheating can come in many different forms. Another important kind of cheating that has happened in professional sports is called match fixing. In professional sports, there is a lot at stake in terms of prize money, but the gambling that happens alongside professional sports involves even bigger amounts of cash. If someone can predict the outcome of a contest, that person stands to benefit a great deal by placing the right bets. For that reason, athletes and referees are sometimes offered bribes in exchange for "fixing" the outcome of the game (i.e. causing a loss that appears natural). There has been a long history of this kind of cheating, with examples coming from boxing, baseball, soccer, cricket, and other professional sports. Cases of match fixing are generally major media scandals, just like other cases of cheating in sports, such as 2015's "deflate-gate," where the New England Patriots were accused of underinflating the ball to make it easier to throw and catch.

Why does cheating in sports command so much attention? The answer probably has to do with the popularity of sports in general, and with the fascination the public has with cheating and wrongdoing by high-profile people of all types—politicians, Wall Street executives, celebrities, and also star athletes. But the contradiction between cheating on the one hand, and sports as a "true" test of talent and effort on the other also surely fuels this interest. In this contradiction we can see how cheating violates our expectations for athletes, and thus also helps make transparent the meaning of sports as ritualized competition. When athletes' wrongdoing is revealed, we feel betrayed because it means that the contests we felt so strongly about were never the legitimate competitions we thought they were. Crucially, it is also bad for business, because it risks weakening fans' emotional connection to the game and their sports heroes.

5. SPORTS AS A BUSINESS: CONSTRUCTING POPULAR HEROES

As our discussion of cheating makes clear, professional sports generate massive revenues. There is a tension, here, though, as sports are simultaneously big business but in a way, belong to all of us. No one owns the exclusive rights to any athletic pursuit. Any group of people can organize themselves into a sports league and run with it. In elementary and high schools, sports are part of the curriculum and can also serve as important co-curricular activities and events for older students. Sports are thoroughly integrated into many realms of society and so can come to feel like a natural part of our cultural heritage.

But it is also true that most people engage with sports as *consumers*, which is a key part of what makes sports big business. As fans, we pay ticket prices for professional sports that run from reasonable to astronomical, and we also adorn ourselves with jerseys, hats, and other forms of branded sporting wear. Television broadcast rights for professional and amateur sporting events are worth billions of dollars. Nations spend billions hosting the Olympics and spectators spend vast sums of money to travel around the globe to see the competition in person. As a result of our collective enthusiasm towards sports as a consumer item, many of the world's most famous and popular celebrities are athletes. They can achieve not just local success, but truly global stardom.

While it might seem natural that sports are a popular consumer item, in fact, as with any industry, the products we consume are created through a carefully honed process. The sports matches that we enjoy exist in their current forms after a process of tinkering over time to be maximally appealing to audiences. They also reflect investments in long-term systems for cultivating athletic talent.

While sports stars are associated with fame and fortune, we are commonly told that some of the world's top athletes came from the humblest of origins. NBA fans will surely know that superstar LeBron James grew up poor in a single-parented household in Akron, Ohio. Indeed, the narrative of sports as a way out of poverty is a powerful myth that reinforces the ideology of meritocracy (discussed in chapter 3)—the belief that we live in a fair society where success is awarded on the basis of individual effort and talent. In *Game On: The All American Race to Make Champions of our Children*, Tom Farrey (2008) visits fields, courts, and rinks across the United States to investigate the intense efforts to turn children into future star athletes. While the dream of an athletic scholarship looms large for many struggling families seeking opportunities for their kids, the idea that sports offer a ticket out of poverty is largely a myth. Instead, Farrey shows that opportunity often goes to those with resources—kids who can afford the best equipment and top training, and who can travel across the country to the tournaments where they are likely to be scouted. Contrary to the notion that "the poor benefit the most from college sports", Farrey argues that "rich kids are far likelier to get roster spots" (2008: 147).

Michael Jordan and the Air Jordan Brand

Michael Jordan addressing the media at an Air Jordan launch in 2009. In 1984, after being chosen third by the Chicago Bulls in the NBA Draft, Jordan signed a five-year endorsement deal with Nike worth an estimated $2.5 million. The first of his signature shoe line, the Air Jordan I, was released in 1985 and became the most expensive basketball sneaker available at the time, retailing for $65. These shoes introduced a trend of distinctive, collectible basketball shoes. Fast forward over three decades: a culture of "sneakerheads" (sneaker collectors) becomes firmly established and the 30th version (Jordans XXX) was released in 2016, retailing for $200.

Source: Gettyimages.ca Editorial # 84353885

In fact, sociological research suggests that sports may reinforce social inequalities rather than helping to overcome them. Hilary Levey Friedman (2013) shows how middle- and upper-middle-class parents use sports to provide their children with a competitive edge in the future. She notes that "certain sports, such as squash and fencing, are especially helpful, as they signal elite status in the college admissions process" (2013: 46). Building upon Bourdieu's concept of **cultural capital** (discussed in chapter 4), Friedman suggests that privileged parents view sports as a way to foster what she calls "Competitive Kid Capital". This form of capital refers to the skills and traits children acquire through competition, such as the desire to win and the ability to perform under pressure and within time constraints. Parents in Friedman's study viewed the development of these traits as key to their children's futures, setting them up for success in college and the professional world. Contrary to the meritocratic vision of athletics as a realm where individuals succeed based solely on their effort and talent, organized sports appear to be another realm where already advantaged groups garner additional resources that reproduce privilege.

For the incredibly few athletes who secure elite training opportunities that lead to professional sports opportunities, the payoff can be enormous. Although not always true historically, today many professional athletes are exceptionally well compensated in professional leagues like the NBA, NHL, and NFL. Still, inequality is a key theme in the sports world. Although some athletes are paid handsomely for their talent, others survive on very little—female athletes get paid less than men, amateur athletes don't get paid at all, and many athletes training for the Olympics live below the poverty line. Olympic weightlifter, Sarah Robles, was thought of as the strongest woman in America (she could lift more than 568lbs) and qualified for the Summer Olympics in London; meanwhile, she was living on $400 a month. Or consider the case of college athletes. While the National College Athletic Association (NCAA) brings in a billion dollars annually in revenue and its top coaches earn million-dollar salaries, the association has resisted giving players a salary beyond providing a college education. (The NCAA began to allow small annual stipends of $2000–$5000 for players in 2015.) The issue of impoverished college athletes working to generate billions for the NCAA has mobilized the National College Players Association, which is working to become the first union representing college athletes. Even within the elite group of professional football, baseball, and hockey players, there is an incredible range of salaries. For example, ESPN reports that in the NBA in 2015, Kobe Bryant made $25 million with the Los Angeles Lakers, while over half of all players made less than $3 million. Not only that, but commercial endorsements accrue disproportionately to the most famous players. In the case of Bryant, Forbes reports that upon his retirement in 2016, his lifetime salary and endorsements amounted to $680 million.

While the benefits to the individual athletes can be great, the professional leagues, teams, and universities that employ and sponsor athletes also garner significant financial rewards. In addition to providing the conditions for

The 50 Most Valuable Sports Teams in the World

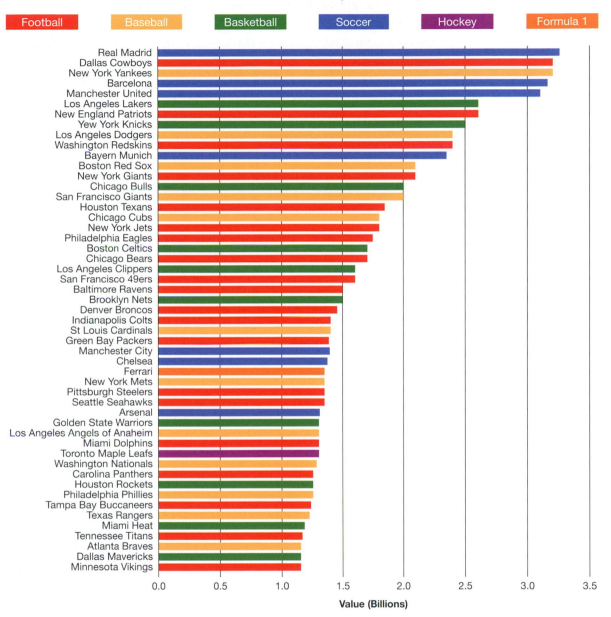

The World's Most Valuable Sports Teams 2015

Football | Baseball | Basketball | Soccer | Hockey | Formula 1

Real Madrid
Dallas Cowboys
New York Yankees
Barcelona
Manchester United
Los Angeles Lakers
New England Patriots
Yew York Knicks
Los Angeles Dodgers
Washington Redskins
Bayern Munich
Boston Red Sox
New York Giants
Chicago Bulls
San Francisco Giants
Houston Texans
Chicago Cubs
New York Jets
Philadelphia Eagles
Boston Celtics
Chicago Bears
Los Angeles Clippers
San Francisco 49ers
Baltimore Ravens
Brooklyn Nets
Denver Broncos
Indianapolis Colts
St Louis Cardinals
Green Bay Packers
Manchester City
Chelsea
Ferrari
New York Mets
Pittsburgh Steelers
Seattle Seahawks
Arsenal
Golden State Warriors
Los Angeles Angels of Anaheim
Miami Dolphins
Toronto Maple Leafs
Washington Nationals
Carolina Panthers
Houston Rockets
Philadelphia Phillies
Tampa Bay Buccaneers
Texas Rangers
Miami Heat
Tennessee Titans
Atlanta Braves
Dallas Mavericks
Minnesota Vikings

Value (Billions)

According to data compiled by Forbes Magazine, Real Madrid is the most valuable team in the world. In general, the value of teams is increasing, with one of the key reasons being the ability of teams to sell broadcast rights to television broadcasters who are looking for exclusive content that audiences are willing to pay a premium to see.

Source: http://www.visualcapitalist.com/50-most-valuable-sports-teams-in-the-world/

maximizing athletic success, sports leagues provide the conditions for maximizing profits. Athletes' images are carefully controlled and managed, as are the images of the teams they play on. In short, professional sports rely on careful branding. Individual athletes are promoted as quasi-brands, just as teams are promoted as literal brands. Major league sports devote a great deal of effort towards protecting their copyrights over the broadcasting of games and the trademarks of their team names and logos. There are good reasons for this. When teams are valued, the evaluation looks at both the revenues the teams pull in as well as the team's brand equity—its recognition and reception among audiences. For example, when *Forbes* evaluates the New York Yankees as the most valuable team in Major League Baseball, that evaluation is based not only on the revenue generated by stadium attendance and broadcast rights, but also on the ability of the Yankees' brand to facilitate other business relationships. The team's name and logo, as with any major corporation, represent a long-term effort to build brand equity.

Understanding the economic forces behind team names and logos helps shed light on the controversy over the use of Native American names and images by teams. On the one hand, names and logos for teams such as the Washington Redskins, the Chicago Blackhawks, and the Cleveland Indians have been criticized as insensitive at best and outright racist and degrading at worst. Vocal Native American critics have argued that these names and images reproduce negative stereotypes about indigenous people as primitive and savage. The use of such names for sports teams is clearly rooted in a colonial history where the European-origin majority oppressed the Native population. The continued use of Native American symbols in this way contributes to the perpetuation of this unequal power dynamic. On the other hand, defenders of these team names and logos argue that they are not offensive, and the teams themselves are working hard to keep them. Businesses are usually averse to controversy, so why are these sports teams working so hard to maintain names and logos that are controversial? The answer lies in the recognition that sports are an industry like other industries, and teams are like any other corporation: they invest in developing their brands and they do not want to lose the value they have built. Despite the fact that such names and logos clearly rely upon harmful racial stereotypes, many fans have developed a connection to these teams as they are, and the teams fear losing their fan base—or, their consumer base—if they were to change their names. These names and logos have brand equity, in the hundreds of millions of dollars, and their owners are more concerned with protecting their investments than in heeding arguments about the promotion of racial inequality.

When we think about sports logos and racial stereotypes, it is clear that sports are never just a simple game, but are a reflection of many of society's most important issues. Our discussion has revealed that group boundaries, racism, and deviance are only a few of the sociological topics that can be revealed through the lens of sports. The metaphor of an "equal playing field" is incredibly powerful, and is commonly used in non-sporting contexts to evoke our meritocratic ideals. Still, this chapter has shown that sports are clearly shaped by broader systems of inequality, especially economic disparities, gender inequality and racial injustice. At the same time, sports also generate feelings of connectedness and build a sense of imagined community. Many people feel more strongly about sports than about virtually anything else: they are a consumer item that can evoke incredibly strong passions as well as billion-dollar revenue streams.

THINKING FRAMES

How can each thinking frame help us ponder the sociology of sports?

Material / Cultural	Sports are a great way to get exercise and to be outside. There are positive health and social benefits that accompany sports participation. At the same time that sports have material benefits, sports also have cultural value; athletic skill is highly prized and can provide people with status and popularity.
Think about . . .	Do you or people you know play sports? How do you or they explain the decision to participate? What kind of material/physical benefits or cultural status is at stake?

Structure / Agency	The popularity of particular sports varies across different societies. While any given individual can have a preference for watching or playing a particular sport, that preference will be affected by the broader pattern of preferences within that individual's culture.
Think about . . .	What is your favorite sport(s)? How many different social factors can you identify that have shaped your love of this sport? (e.g., educational institutions, national sport culture, mass-media)

Micro / Macro	At a micro level, we know that people tend to join groups, like sports teams, with other people who are similar to themselves. At the same time, a macro perspective reveals that many of the most popular sports are broadly popular across many different demographic groups.
Think about . . .	Have you ever played sports with people of different demographic groups? What micro and macro factors influenced who you did or did not play with?

Active Learning

ACTIVE LEARNING

Online

Mapping racial segregation:
"The Racial Dot Map" (created by Dustin Cable at the University of Virginia) uses a dot for every person in the US coded by race (e.g. blue dots represent Whites, green dots represent African Americans). Explore the map to see how cities and regions can vary in their levels of racial diversity and racial segregation. http://www.coopercenter.org/demographics/Racial-Dot-Map

Constructing racial categories:
One way to see the social construction of race is through the racial categories presented on the census. Visit Racebox.org to see images of the American census from 1790 to 2010. What key changes do you notice? How might these be linked to shifts in race relations at particular moments in American history? http://racebox.org/

Who really wins and loses at the World Cup?
Global sporting events are celebrated as a source of national pride, as the world's top athletes fight for their countries. However, such global sporting spectacles incur significant social costs, which are often borne at the expense of a country's most marginalized groups. In this clip, late night host John Oliver pulls back the curtain of the FIFA World Cup. https://www.youtube.com/watch?v=DlJEt2KU33I

Discussion/Reflection

High-school heroes?

What sports were emphasized when you were in high school? Were sports optional or mandatory? Were there social boundaries between athletes and people who were not into sports?

Sports on the silver screen:

Remember the Titans, *42*, and *Race* are three movies that have dealt explicitly with the issues of racism and sports. How much public awareness is there about the history of racism in sports? Does Hollywood do a good job of reflecting the realities of race relations in sports?

Sociology Outside the Classroom

Sports inequalities:

Which athletes are venerated and which athletes live in relative obscurity? Carry out research to create a short profile of two athletes who live (or lived) very different lives. Find one that is celebrated, well-paid, and receives major endorsements. Find another athlete that lives relatively anonymously and with few resources or product endorsements. How can you account for the differences between the lives of these two athletes?

Sports, violence, and deviance:

While aggression is often valorized in a sporting context, excessive violence or aggression can be considered deviant. For example, Mike Tyson had a celebrated boxing career and is regarded by some as the best heavyweight boxer of all time. At the same time, Tyson was nicknamed the "baddest man on the planet"; he was convicted of rape (and spent three years in prison), and was disqualified from a match for biting off a piece of his opponent's ear. Thinking about other examples from professional sports or your own experience playing sports, identify an example where violence and aggression broke a social norm and came to be considered deviant. Why did this instance cross the line of acceptable aggression, and what was the sanction imposed on this player?

Chapter 7

BARBIES AND MONSTER TRUCKS: SOCIALIZATION AND "DOING GENDER"

INTRODUCING KEY CONCEPTS

This chapter uses the case of toys to explore **socialization**: *the lifelong process of learning the norms of a particular society. We focus here on* **gender** *socialization, but also briefly examine socialization processes related to* **class**, **race** *and* **social stratification**. *The bifurcated world of gendered toys allows us to introduce sociological concepts of* **sex**, **gender**, **gender roles**, **gender identity**, **doing gender**, **sexism**, *and* **patriarchy**. *We also consider kids' desire for toys: Are kids' consumer desires driven by the quest for group belonging or social distinction (or both)? A toy box can tell us a lot about how childhood is viewed and experienced, and also reveal hegemonic ideals of gender and parenting in consumer culture.*

1. INTRODUCTION: IS IT "NATURAL" FOR GIRLS TO PLAY WITH DOLLS AND BOYS TO DRIVE TOY TRUCKS?

Do kids naturally gravitate towards certain toys? Is it inevitable that boys play with trucks and toy guns, while girls dress like princesses and set up plastic tea sets to serve snacks to their dolls? Consider the following blog post by a White undergraduate, Amy. Here, she reflects on a shopping trip with her friend and her friend's infant daughter, Zoe:

> At two months, the three of us were shopping through the baby department of a Sears, when I saw this adorable stuffed hippo . . . I immediately picked up the hippo and displayed it to Zoe through her stroller, playfully rubbing its nose on her cheeks. She began to smile and blink with each little nuzzle of the hippo's soft face. "Aww," I proclaimed, "I'm going to buy it for her." To which her mother replied, "But it's blue. You should get her the pink elephant, instead." I could not help but laugh as I asked her whether she actually believed her two-month-old had developed such a color preference. Not sensing my sarcastic tone, she announced, very proudly, that she knew without doubt that her daughter was a "girly girl". "At two months?" I gasped. "How can you know at two months?" "A mother just knows," she replied. Not a mother myself and therefore nowhere near an expert on rearing children, and very aware of how sensitive parents are to questions/criticism of their parenting methods, I refrained from pointing out how flawed I found her pre-conceived beliefs of her daughter to be, and how potentially hindering they could be as well. I simply said, "Well, I think Zoe likes the little blue hippo, I want to get it for her," and off to the checkout counter I went . . . Zoe, now a little over three, is the quintessential "girly girl". My friend was right. Her daughter would grow up to prefer dolls to trucks and pink frills to denim overalls.

Amy's story reveals the tension between believing children can be "anything they want to be", and the well-worn, predictable paths that children's play often seems to take. Indeed, when sociologist Christine Williams went undercover and worked in a toy store, she was struck by the extent of gender conformity in this setting. Most people—both parents and kids—gravitated to the gender appropriate aisle when selecting toys, and rarely strayed from this path during their shopping trips (Williams 2006: 172). As a feminist sociologist, Williams

Gendered Toy Aisles

Retailers commonly organize their product selection in gendered ways. What gendered patterns can you observe in these two images from a toy store in France?

Sources: (*left*) Gettyimages.com # 134283077; (*right*) Gettyimages.com # 134283051

found this pattern disturbing; yet, she writes that "over time, working in the toy stores, I found my personal resistance [to gendered toys] weakening . . . [since] resistance seemed pointless" (2006: 169, 172). Indeed, Zoe's transformation into a "girly girl" doesn't seem surprising, given her mother's commitment to pink toys at two months of age.

Reflecting upon this story, you might think, "Of course. It's just natural that girls and boys like different things." However, a look across cultural and historical contexts reveals wide variation in the kind of toys that are associated with boys and girls, and that kids themselves desire. For instance, you might be surprised to learn that the color pink was once associated with boys. A 1914 article in the American newspaper the *Sunday Sentinel* advised "Use pink for the boy and blue for the girl, if you are a follower of convention" (quoted in Frassanito and Pettorini 2008: 881). This historical contrast illustrates an important sociological lesson: no color is inherently gendered. Our ideas about what is suitable for boys or for girls is **socially constructed** (see chapter 6 for a discussion of social construction). How do these socially constructed understandings shape children's sense of who they are and who they can (or should) become? As sociologists, we are interested in the social factors that shape gendered toys and gendered identities. In this chapter, we unpack some of the socialization processes that help transform babies into pink princesses and action heroes.

Blue Boys and Pink Girls

These photos are part of "The Pink and Blue Project", by South Korean photographer JeongMee Yoon. The exhibit was inspired by her five-year-old daughter's seemingly obsessive love for the color pink. You can view the rest of the images on her website: www.jeongmeeyoon.com

Source: http://www.jeongmeeyoon.com/aw_pinkblue.htm

2. SOCIALIZING GIRLS AND BOYS: HOW TOYS TEACH US TO "DO GENDER"

In everyday language, people often use the terms "sex" and "gender" as though they were interchangeable, but sociologists make an important distinction between them. The term **sex** refers to biological characteristics that are commonly characterized as male or female—things like anatomy, chromosomes, and hormones. At birth, we tend to categorize infants according to these two sex categories. Importantly, though, not everyone fits into the male/female binary. Roughly one in every 1500 to 2000 people are **intersex**, meaning they don't fit within the two-sex model of categorizing bodies as either male or female (Intersex Society of North America 2008). For example, someone might be born with external sexual anatomy that is usually categorized as female and internal reproductive anatomy that is usually categorized as male. So even biological sex—something we tend to think of as totally "natural" and clear-cut—is more complex and varied than we commonly think.

While sex is a biological concept, **gender** refers to the social characteristics —feelings, behaviors, attitudes—associated with masculinity and femininity in a given culture. For example, common gender characteristics associated with femininity in Western society include care, emotional intelligence, and a concern for physical attractiveness. Common gender traits associated with masculinity involve strength, vigor, and emotional control. Gender is socially constructed: we can think of gender traits as being roughly linked together in an ideational package of femininity and masculinity. Being biologically female or male does not dictate that you will possess any or all characteristics of femininity or masculinity. Gender simply means that these traits are socially associated with being a "woman" or a "man" (or "girl" or "boy") in a given culture and historical time period. While gender refers to socially constructed ideas about masculinity and femininity, your **gender identity** refers to how you identify as an individual. This can involve a straightforward association with feminine traits or masculine traits, or—as is the case for many of us— some combination of both. For example, you might be a woman who considers herself tough and assertive (traits commonly associated with masculinity), and yet also embrace styles of self-presentation that are seen as quite feminine (e.g. makeup and high heels). Similarly, you might be a man who enjoys car culture and new technological gadgets (cultural traits associated with masculinity), but also love watching romantic comedies (associated with femininity). The way we live gender identities is often more multifaceted and nuanced than the seemingly straightforward binary categories of "masculine" and "feminine".

We may also find that our gender identity does not align with the biological sex we were assigned at birth, as is the case for **transgender** people. The term **cisgender** refers to individuals whose gender identity matches the cultural expectation for their biological sex: so if you were designated male at birth and you identify as a man, you are cisgender. The variation of gender identities that actually exist in the world problematizes the common assumption of the **gender binary**: the false idea that all people fit neatly into one of two sex/gender categories: male/masculine and female/feminine. Many of you reading this book probably feel like you don't perfectly reflect the stereotypical man or woman. And yet, the **ideology** (see chapter 3) of the gender binary persists as a powerful idea organizing the social world. This is because we learn dominant social expectations about gender throughout our lives, and these provide a framework for understanding the world and our place within it. Learning the ideology of the gender binary, and the socially constructed expectations about masculinity and femininity that go along with it, are central to the process of **socialization**. Just as biological sex doesn't always fit neatly into the categories of male and female, the same goes for gender: many of us identify and express ourselves in ways that do not neatly correspond with "masculine" or "feminine" expectations.

Socialization refers to the learning that takes place to prepare humans to function in their social worlds. Through socialization, individuals learn the **norms** of a particular social context, and acquire the skills that allow them to live together in large groups. This learning comes from **agents of socialization**—people and institutions that convey important lessons about fitting into social life. In our early years, the primary agent of socialization is often our families, where we learn lessons about everything from the etiquette of saying "please" and "thank you", to the cultural rituals associated with our ethnic heritage, to moral questions about what is right and wrong. As we grow older, many other agents of socialization enter into the mix, including school, media, peers, and religious institutions. While these kinds of lessons can be particularly profound for children, the process of socialization takes place throughout the life course: social life is continually evolving, and our roles change as we get older. For instance, think about the process of adjusting to your new role as a university or college student, or on the job at a new workplace. In each of these social settings, you had to learn all kinds of subtle cues about what was expected of you in order to fit in—how to dress, what to say (and not to say) to whom, etc. These lessons are rarely explicit. Often, they are things we pick up simply through observing and interacting with those around us.

A key part of the socialization process for children is learning to recognize and eventually take up **gender roles**. By gender roles, we mean the social norms and behaviors that are considered appropriate for women and men in a particular cultural and historical context. Think back to your own childhood. Did anyone ever tell you to "sit like a lady" as a girl? Or to "toughen up" and hold back tears as a boy? Often, these messages are conveyed in more subtle ways, such as colors used to decorate your room, the different chores assigned to you and your siblings (e.g. washing the dishes versus cutting the lawn), or the adjectives used to praise you (e.g. "pretty" and "nice", or "smart" and "strong"). Historically, feminine gender roles in North America have emphasized activities related to nurturing, caregiving, and other private-sphere roles. In contrast, historically masculine gender roles have emphasized power, breadwinning and public-sphere roles. Of course, gender roles vary across cultural and historical context, as is clear from the fact that over 70% of American women with children under 18 years of age have paid employment outside the home (US Bureau of Labor Statistics 2014). Nevertheless, the ideology of the gender binary persists, and the "ideal man" continues to be associated

Masculinizing the Feminine: Zit Camo

When companies attempt to sell products typically associated with women—like beauty and skincare products—to men, they often market them in stereotypically masculine ways to comply with dominant gender expectations. For example, consider the marketing for this pimple concealer for men, called "Zit Camouflage". The product is available in three shades: "pale ale", "medium lager", and "amber ale", referring to varieties of beer.

Source: Website screen capture: http://www.theyhatepimples.com/ (10/2/2016)

with power, wealth, stoicism, and career success, while the "ideal woman" is associated with care, nurturance, emotional engagement, and physical attractiveness. Even if most people in our lives do not fit these narrow parameters, images of masculinity and femininity are a powerful force within our ongoing socialization, particularly as they are idealized within media and popular culture—including toys.

Some sociologists argue that we shouldn't think of gender as a set of static roles we take on, but as a set of practices we continually perform in everyday life; from this perspective, gender is less something that we intrinsically are, and more something that we do. The concept of **doing gender** was developed by sociologists Candace West and Don Zimmerman, who emphasized how we perform gender in everyday life (West and Zimmerman 1987). Because we tend to talk about gender as something that we intrinsically have, or that we simply are, the idea of doing gender can seem strange at first. But when you reflect upon all the subtle ways in which we present ourselves as gendered beings—through the way we sit, walk, talk, dress, relate to others—it becomes clear that we are actively doing gender in our lives on a daily basis without even knowing it. Through the process of gender socialization, ways of doing gender come to feel natural to us. A key part of this process involves lessons about how not to do gender—that is, learning when we are not properly conforming to gender expectations. The concept of **gender policing** draws attention to how our ways of doing gender are managed and regulated by others. This can range from a subtle look of disapproval, to playful teasing, or explicit instructions to "act like a lady" or to "man up". While gender policing can be harsh and uncomfortable (such as excluding a tomboy from the "popular" girls' group or calling a boy a "fag"), some gender policing is motivated by efforts to help others fit in. For instance, imagine that your daughter paints her younger brother's nails on the weekend, and he gets excited to show his friends in kindergarten on Monday. Even if you personally don't mind your son's sparkly purple nails, you might worry that he'll be teased by others, and thus tell him that nail polish is not suitable for a boy at school. Even those who reject rigid gender roles can end up policing the masculinities and femininities of those around them simply because doing gender is so central to collective ways of fitting in.

Playing with toys is a key part of gender socialization in childhood, as we are invited through play to do gender in particular ways. Toys communicate powerful messages to children about what is expected of them. Historian Gary Cross notes that "playthings have across time and space introduced the young to the tools, experiences, and even emotional lives of their parents" (2002: 125). Put differently, toys teach children implicit lessons about the future gender roles they are encouraged to adopt—such as the skilled masculine engineer (e.g. toy train) and the nurturing feminine caregiver (e.g. toy kitchen), or the tough masculine competitor (e.g. toy dart gun) and the glamorous feminine beauty (e.g. toy makeup kit).

At first glance, these gendered toy preferences might seem like simple common sense: boys like trucks and toy guns, and girls like dolls and playing house. But sociological research reveals that toy preferences are not biologically inevitable, but rather deeply social. Sociologist Elizabeth Sweet's research shows significant historical variation in the gendered nature of toys and toy advertising, suggesting that these patterns are far from natural. By studying how toys were advertised in the Sears catalogue, Sweet made several fascinating findings. In brief, she found that toy advertisements were fairly gender neutral at the turn of the 20th century. From 1920 to the 1960s, toy ads became increasingly gendered—mainly to prepare girls for domesticity (e.g. tea-sets) and to prepare boys for work in the industrial economy (e.g. construction sets). Similarly, Cross describes how electric trains and chemistry sets "introduced boys to dreams of adult success and power. They were to train boys for manhood through the machines of men, since play anticipated the future" (2002: 128). The gender contrast in toys at this time was striking: "While boys' toys glorified technology and machines, companion and baby dolls taught girls to act out personal relationships and keep up with fashion trends" (Cross 2002: 128). However, Sweet notes that during these decades (1920–1960s), at least half of the toys available were *not* gender specific. Additionally, she documented how the gender divide in toy advertising diminished significantly in the 1970s. This is likely not a coincidence, since the 1970s was a key historical decade for women, as the feminist movement generated a broad push for gender equality. Sweet (2014) found that in this time period only 2% of toys were gender specific, and it was common for advertisements to depict toys in gender non-conforming ways. Boys were shown playing in toy kitchens, and girls were shown wearing blue jeans and building Lego.

However, by the 1990s, the gender-neutral trend was on the downswing, facilitated in part by the deregulation of children's television programming in 1984. This shift allowed toy companies to make TV shows that were basically extended toy commercials—things like Transformers, Care Bears, and Hot Wheels. At the same time, targeting boys and girls separately allowed for greater market segmentation, and thus increased sales. In the current era, Sweet reports that it is difficult to find any toy that is not marketed in a gender-specific way; even things like glue-stick or pens are often sold with a "boy's" and "girl's" version (Let Toys Be Toys 2015). You might be surprised to learn that rigid gender stereotypes are more prevalent in toy advertising today than they were 40 years ago, since we often assume that we are gradually progressing toward greater gender equality. This historical research challenges the notion that gendered toy advertisements simply respond to children's preferences; in fact, these preferences are socially engineered in ways that both reflect and reinforce dominant gender expectations. If kids "naturally" gravitated toward gendered toys, why would marketers go to such great efforts to enforce these divisions in their advertisements?

Gender Neutral Lego Campaign, Early 1980s

In the 1970s and early 1980s, toys like Lego were marketed in relatively gender-neutral ways—in contrast to contemporary marketing campaigns which are much more gender segregated.

Source: http://thesocietypages.org/socimages/2012/05/08/part-i-historical-perspective-on-the-lego-gender-gap/

It is clear that toys are differently gendered in different historical periods; the question you may be asking yourself is, "Who cares? So girls like Barbies and boys like Monster Trucks. Is this a problem?" Well, as noted earlier in the chapter, one way to think about the significance of gendered toy advertisements is their role in the process of socialization. Thinking sociologically, we can see toys as socially loaded and highly meaningful objects. Marketers appeal to children not simply as kids, but as girls and boys, inviting them to express different interests and pursue different activities that develop different types of skills. Think for a moment about what commonly distinguishes a "girl toy" from a "boy toy". First, you might think of the difference in colors (e.g. pink and purple vs. red and blue), or activity (e.g. dress-up vs. construction). But if you probe a bit further, you'll see key differences in the kinds of traits and skills that gendered toys promote in children's play. Many toys targeted to boys emphasize power and aggression (such as toy guns or action figures), while others encourage them to build and problem solve (such as model airplanes and science kits). By contrast, toys targeting girls often emphasize either caring for others (e.g. dolls, toy strollers, kitchen sets) or beauty and romance (e.g. princess costumes and toy makeup). In Williams's words, "the toy store provides a window into the socialization of the next generation of consumers" (2006: 8). And the toy store window reveals these socialization processes to be deeply gendered.

British education scholar Becky Francis (2010) shows the power of these gendered socialization messages in her research exploring the learning facilitated through toys. Francis asked the parents of more than 60 three- to five-year-olds what they perceived to be their child's favorite toy. She found that parents' choices for boys' favorite toys involved action, construction, and machinery, while girls were associated with dolls and perceived "feminine" interests, such as hairdressing. Reflecting upon this research, she states: "The very clear message seems to be that boys should be making things, using their hands and solving problems, and girls should be caring and nurturing" (Francis, quoted in Lepkowska 2008). Francis is quick to point out that her study focused on parents' perceptions of children's favorite toys, not children's own perspectives. Thus, she notes that "It is likely that many of the boys in the study sleep with a teddy, but this was not noted by parents as a favorite toy" (Francis, quoted in Lepkowska 2008). As an education scholar, Francis links the gender differences apparent in parents' toy perceptions to the kinds of capacities fostered through children's play. In addition to conveying the message that boys and girls are fundamentally different (reinforcing the ideology of the gender binary), gendered toys tend to position boys as active, creative leaders; by contrast, the toys targeted toward girls emphasize caregiving and personal appearance. As sociologists, it is important to reflect critically on the larger, long-term implications of these stark differences in childhood play by putting our sociological imaginations to work.

Significantly, the socialization facilitated through toys not only emphasizes gender difference, but also perpetuates gender inequality. Watching a series of toy commercials, it is not difficult to see how they reinforce the gender **stereotypes** described above. These stereotypes present an extremely narrow range of options for what it means to be a girl or a boy, and thus constrain the ways of doing masculinity and femininity available to children. Beyond

Gendered Market Segmentation: Bic for Her

An advertisement for Bic for Her, a line of pens marketed specifically to women. Notably, the advertisement presents the pens primarily as an accessory rather than a writing utensil, as something that brings "a touch of personality and a pop of color" to the user's day. Today, gendered marketing practices are used to sell a variety of products not limited to toys.

Source: http://www.katelacey.com/recent/ (Direct link: http://41.media.tumblr.com/cd 1c3f2fc8ef931a2c403c2d01d3dcec/tumblr_n2adt1 KXrq1qzl13eo1_1280.jpg)

limiting childhood play to such rigid boxes, these stereotypes reinforce gender norms that are not valued equally in society. In this way, we can say that toys contribute to **patriarchy**. Patriarchy is a system of inequality that privileges masculinity (and boys/men) and disadvantages femininity (and girls/women) in areas like property-holding, wealth, and leadership positions. In a patriarchal society, men hold disproportionate social, economic, and political power.

Many, if not most societies around the world, including North American society, have degrees of patriarchy. This means that traits associated with masculinity are valued more highly than those associated with femininity, and men tend to have more power and authority than women. Women and femininity may be valued in their own way—as when people love their mothers—but feminine traits are collectively devalued, and women hold less political power, authority, and wealth. **Sexism** is the term used to describe a belief system (backed by patriarchal power) that favors masculinity (and men/boys) over femininity (and women/girls). We can see clear evidence of patriarchy and sexism in the realm of work. Caring professions are financially undervalued (England et al. 2002), while leadership and competition is viewed more positively and more economically remunerated (Fitzsimmons et al. 2014). (Today, less than 5% of the CEOs of Fortune 500 companies are women; Fairchild 2014.) The gender socialization promoted through toys encourages boys to develop skills and adopt traits that are socially rewarded and associated with power; conversely, toys targeting girls encourage them to adopt traits that are less valued and involve putting the needs of others first. Indeed, Williams argues that a key lesson that kids learn in the toy store is that "shopping is mothers' work, part of a system of care work that women do for their families" (2006: 147). Besides the fact that Williams mainly observed women buying gifts and toys for children, she argued that the lesson of femininity and care was reinforced by the toys purchased: "Mom and daughter bought 'baby items' to care for other family members, real or imagined, while the son purchased vehicles evocative of masculine independence" (2006: 147).

While children clearly learn powerful lessons about patriarchy and sexism through their toys, it is important to recognize that socialization is not a unidirectional process where children simply internalize the gendered messages that they receive from adults. Rather, as we noted earlier, socialization occurs throughout our entire lives, and children are active agents in this process. For example, Williams's toy store research makes clear that socialization is not simply about parents "molding" passive children, but is an interactive process in which children are key participants, voicing demands and resisting parental directives. In her words,

> Adults and children are often locked in battle over the norms and values
> of shopping—evident in the number of temper tantrums I witnessed at
> the checkout line. Adults try to teach children a set of ideal norms
> regarding consumerism, while children struggle to satisfy their own sense
> of what is good and valuable.
>
> (2006: 144)

What's more, children do not always accept the gender expectations that they encounter in the world of toys. As social agents in their own right, children actively interpret, negotiate, and sometimes resist the gendered messages that are communicated through various agents of socialization, such as parents and media. Consider the example of Riley, a young girl who gained Internet fame when a video went viral showing her passionately critiquing the gender stereotypes on display at her local toy store (www.youtube.com/watch?v=-CU040Hqbas). Riley is not alone in her frustration. In 2012, eighth grader McKenna Pope started a petition calling on the toy company Hasbro to stop marketing the Easy Bake Oven exclusively to girls. McKenna's younger brother had expressed interest in the cooking set, but said he couldn't play with it since it only came in pink and purple. Her campaign gained massive public support, and eventually led to the sale of a silver and black Easy Bake Oven in 2013. Of course, it is not only famous kids like Riley and McKenna who are challenging the gendered messages conveyed through toys. Children all over are making various meanings out of the advertising and toys that they encounter, and are responding to them in different, creative ways.

Kids may not always want what their parents offer, but as the ones who largely control household spending, parents clearly have a big influence over what toys enter the home. In our teaching, when we ask students to reflect upon a time when they experienced gender policing as a child, the most vivid examples often revolve around toys. One student discussed how he dreamed of having an Easy Bake Oven when he was young, but (much like McKenna Pope's brother described above) he never asked for one because he knew that the request would lead to refusal and ridicule. Another student recalled the day that his dad came home and found him playing with his sister's Barbies. He could clearly remember his father's horror at this gender transgression, scolding him that dolls were for girls. The dad then went straight out and bought a set of toy trucks to provide a "gender appropriate" activity for his son.

Why do adults participate in this kind of highly gendered toy schema? Christine Williams suggests that parents select toys that fulfill their own

Child Activist McKenna Pope

McKenna Pope, pictured here behind her younger brother Gavyn, was 13 when she successfully petitioned the toy company Hasbro to produce an Easy Bake Oven in more gender-neutral colors. In 2013, McKenna spoke at the TEDYouth conference, encouraging children and teenagers to engage in activism and take action in response to issues facing their lives.

Source: APImages.com # 236118070419

idealized gender fantasies, and thus extend the promise of these fantasies to their children. This brings us back to idealized notions of masculinity and femininity discussed earlier. Even if regular women don't actually resemble Barbie, and most men are not as strong as the Hulk, these figures embody powerful gender ideals. Reflecting upon parents' motivations, Williams suggests that "even if they don't conform, or didn't conform in their youth, many want and expect children to have the opportunity to experience conventional gender socialization. In this way, they can share an idealized gender as part of their fantasy life" (2006: 174). Put differently, when parents police their kids' gender socialization through their toy purchases, they may have their children's best interests at heart: the world of toys presents an opportunity to live out dominant gender fantasies, and thus to reap the rewards of masculine and feminine ideals.

2.1. Rich Kids and Poor Kids: Toys and Social Class

While the gender expectations promoted through toys are particularly glaring, these are not the only socialization processes at work in the toy industry. Drawing upon her research working in toy stores, Williams concludes that these spaces are ones where "the social inequalities of shopping are . . . taught to children" (2006: 4). Thus, toys are also tied up in processes of class socialization. Williams argues that "the lessons learned in the toy store have repercussions throughout society. How we shop is shaped by and contributes to social inequality" (2006: 138).

Recall from chapter 4 that while class inequality has an important material dimension in terms of economic capital, class also has a cultural dimension that is expressed and reinforced through consumption practices. Here, we return to Bourdieu's concept of **cultural capital**, referring to culturally valued forms of knowledge and experiences that provide access to social status. Williams suggests that by carefully selecting the "right" consumer items, toy consumers can convert economic capital into displays of class status. She describes how middle-class parents approached toy shopping as an opportunity to "cultivate sophisticated tastes in their children, providing them with all-important cultural capital they need to succeed in a class-stratified society" (2006: 150). Williams's toy store observations are in keeping with sociologist Annette Lareau's (2003) study of classed parenting styles. By studying White and Black parents and children from different class backgrounds, Lareau identified two different classed parenting styles: "concerted cultivation" and "natural growth". In a "concerted cultivation" parenting style, middle-class parents (White and Black) deliberately mold children through controlled interventions to enhance their cognitive and social skills and improve their performance, while fostering a sense of individualism and entitlement. In a "natural growth" parenting style, working-class parents (both White and Black) put children more squarely in charge of their own leisure, and have more faith that children will develop "naturally" without costly interventions or putting pressure on children to perform.

Lareau's study of parenting concludes that "concerted cultivation" both feeds middle-class children's sense of entitlement, and offers them a form of class advantage—a finding that resonates with Christine Williams's toy store observations. For example, Williams observed that books are an especially popular consumer choice among middle-class consumers interested in concerted cultivation. Williams overheard one woman in the toy store assuring her friend that she exclusively purchased books for her grandchildren (2006: 165). Williams concludes that when middle-class parents engage in concerted cultivation, "playtime is perceived as an opportunity for children to acquire talents and dispositions valued by adults" (164). Put bluntly, a concerted cultivation approach to toy consumption socializes children to perform, to get ahead, to learn, and to be sophisticated cultural consumers. By contrast, a more working-class approach to toy shopping that Williams observed in the toy store was more in keeping with the "natural growth" approach to parenting described by Lareau. These kids tended to have more autonomy in their purchases, were observed shopping alone more frequently, and were more likely to receive toys that were simply fun—and didn't come packaged alongside claims about their educational or cultural value (William 2006: 165). Both Williams's toy store ethnography and Lareau's research on parenting suggests that toys are important not just for gender socialization, but to socialize children to fit into a position in the class hierarchy.

Allison Pugh's research with children and parents in Oakland, California also reveals important class differences in the way parents mediated children's consumption. She found that upper-income parents were conscious of demonstrating restraint in the face of consumer demands, a practice Pugh terms "symbolic deprivation". During interviews, many affluent parents insisted that they did not buy much for their children, despite the widespread prevalence of Sony PlayStations, $100 American Girl dolls, and $500 birthday parties. In these affluent households, parents established allowances and rules (e.g. limiting television and gaming) in order to socialize children's self-control and consumer restraint. For middle-class parents, "symbolic deprivation" was a strategy to manage their own ambivalent relationship to consumer culture, which was viewed as a troubling but inescapable component of children's lives.

By contrast, low-income parents in Pugh's research negotiated a different set of challenges in providing for their children. In poor families, the emphasis was not on modeling restraint, but on demonstrating that they were buying enough for their children. These parents saved up in order to provide the key consumer items necessary for kids to fit in among their peers—a consumption pattern that Pugh calls "symbolic indulgence". While affluent parents were careful to demonstrate that they weren't overindulging their children's consumer desires, Pugh describes how low-income parents wanted to demonstrate that they were doing enough, and "viewed provisioning unequivocally as the sign of a good parent" (2009: 122). However, within the context of limited economic capital, buying that coveted videogame can come at a significant price. While parents worked extremely hard to provide their children with the key items needed to fit in, such purchases sometimes threatened the family's financial stability. Contrary to the notion that parents were thoughtlessly fulfilling children's materialistic demands, the study draws attention to the symbolic value of consumption practices that communicate care and facilitate children's sense of belonging. While parents from different income brackets exercise different consumer strategies that reflect different access to various resources, nobody in Pugh's study was able to live outside of children's consumer culture; almost all parents wanted to help their kids acquire the consumer items that helped them fit in.

Both Pugh's and Williams's studies show how toys socialize children to understand their role in **social stratification**, that is, systems of inequality that organize society, and position different categories of people in different tiers of value and importance. Toy stores themselves are deeply unequal places that reproduce stratification along intersecting lines of gender, race, and social class. For example, while working in toy stores, Williams noticed a particular way that middle-class White people, especially middle-class White women, related to retail staff, often expecting staff to wait on them like personal valets (2006: 154). As an employee, she learned to not ask, "Is there anything else?", because there was always something else, and the White customer would rarely "dismiss" her. As White middle-class children observe their privileged parents interacting with store employees in this way, they learn to see themselves as particular kinds of people who are entitled to a particular kind of consumer experience—one that relies upon service from other people (who are often women of color) (Williams 2006: 153). Williams argues that in the toy store, these White children learn a lesson "about the importance of controlling service workers and demanding their attention" (2006: 154).

Toy stores deliver other lessons about race. These lessons are conveyed through the sea of mostly White dolls on the shelves (see textbox below), and also in the relative status assigned to stores located in different neighborhoods. Williams worked at two different stores during her study: "Toy Warehouse" and "Diamond Toys" (she assigned **pseudonyms** for these stores, which is a term for fake names that researchers create in order to protect the confidentiality of their participants). Toy Warehouse was a big box store located in a redevelopment zone of big box stores on the outskirts of a poor urban neighborhood. Toy Warehouse employees referred to this location as "the hood", and described it as being located "in the middle of a ghetto" (2006: 9). Working at this store, Williams was one of four White female employees in a staff of 70; other employees were Latino/a, African American, and Asian American. In contrast, Diamond Toys was located in a more upscale neighborhood, where only three African Americans were employed (Williams 2006: 9). While the toys were remarkably similar at both locations, the prices at Diamond Toys were higher, and perceptions of each store were very different: Toy Warehouse was a low-status store, while Diamond Toys felt "special", worthy of a visit by tourists, even "inspiring reverence and awe" akin to Disneyland (2006: 163). Williams writes, "Buying at Diamond Toys offered proof of one's cultural refinement . . . Shopping at the Toy Warehouse, in

Class Socialization at FAO Schwarz

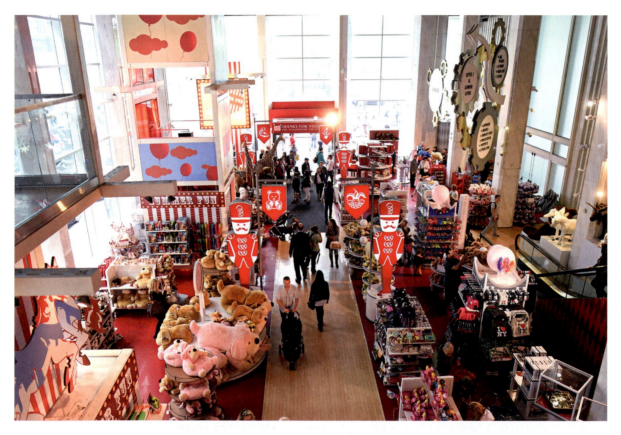

FAO Schwarz is one of America's best known high-end toy retailers. The brand is known for its expensive and unique selection of toys, including a nearly $1500 Etch-A-Sketch made with over 10,000 Swarovski crystals, featured in its 2011 holiday catalog. In 2015, FAO Schwarz closed its iconic flagship store on New York City's Fifth Avenue, pictured here, due to rising rent costs.

Source: Gettyimages.com # 473910194

DOLLS, RACE, AND AGENCY IN CHILDREN'S PLAY

In addition to perpetuating gender stereotypes, toys also reinforce racial inequalities. The most obvious example of this is the fact White children encounter many more dolls and action figures that look like them. While many have called for greater racial diversity in the toy industry (Harris and Vega 2014), Elizabeth Chin's (1999) research contributes a different perspective: the experiences of poor and working-class Black girls who played with the exclusively White dolls that were available to them. Through play, these girls creatively adapted their White dolls to fit within their own social worlds, often by styling their hair. As Chin writes, the girls "worked on their dolls materially and symbolically, blurring racial absolutes by putting their hair into distinctively African American styles using beads, braids and foil" (1999: 306). Chin's study highlights the valuable insights that can be derived through research with children. While the dominant whiteness of the toy industry is clearly a problem, this does not mean that children are passively accepting these racial messages; rather, children actively create meaning through play. For the poor and working-class girls of color in Chin's study, the range of toys available to them was particularly limited—a reflection of how their socialization experiences are constrained by structural inequalities. Yet, these girls clearly exercise agency as they creatively and collaboratively adapt these White dolls to more closely reflect their lived experiences—an insight that we could only discover through research with children.

contrast, conveyed no such superior status" (2006: 140). Reflecting on the difference in value assigned to these two toy stores, Williams argues that this status hierarchy works to legitimize and normalize inequality by "making it seem that shoppers at Diamond Toys simply have better 'taste' than shoppers at the Toy Warehouse, when really they have more privilege (due to class and race inequality)" (2006: 140). Thus it is not only toys themselves that convey socialization messages to children; the spaces where toys are purchased (and the interactions with those who work there) are also loaded with sociological meaning that both reflect, and reproduce, class and racial inequality.

3. UNDERSTANDING KIDS' DESIRE FOR TOYS: DYNAMICS OF INCLUSION AND EXCLUSION

Our casual observations in the toy store may give the impression that toy sales are simply a reflection of kids' incessant desire for more stuff—cue image of a toddler throwing a tantrum because his parent has placed a coveted item back on the store shelf. However, thinking sociologically we can see how individual toy purchases—and the adult–child negotiations that surround them—are embedded within structural forces.

Several interrelated phenomena in the toy industry are worth briefly noting: increased outsourcing of production, falling prices, and changing marketing and consumption patterns. The American toy industry has long had a global element. Even the iconic Barbie was manufactured in Japan from its beginnings in the 1950s to take advantage of low labor costs. (Barbies have since been manufactured in Hong Kong, the Philippines, Malaysia, Indonesia, and China; Oppenheimer 2009: 30.) Today, most of the world's toys are produced in China, a country with massive manufacturing capacity that rests on long hours and low pay. (The Chinese legal monthly minimum wage is around US$176; "Seven Countries" 2011.) Low-cost offshore production enables companies to keep toy prices down. Today, toys are relatively cheap for North American kids, with consumer prices falling around 50% between 1993 and 2005 (Schor 2005b: 314).

There is a dark side to cheap toys. Pressure to keep prices low, combined with the ease of shifting manufacturing to cheaper jurisdictions, places tremendous pressure on producers in the Global South to cut corners in working conditions, product safety, and environmental standards. In 2007, for example, Mattel and its subsidiary Fisher-Price had to recall 19 million toys made in Asian factories, because of choking hazards and high levels of lead in the paint (Roloff and Aßländer 2010: 525). Sociologist Beryl Langer highlights the perversity of a "multi-billion-dollar global industry promoting itself as fostering and serving the 'true essence of childhood'", while it in turn relies on the low-paid work of young people (2002: 74). A critical look at this global commodity chain reveals how

the toys that "enchant" the children of the affluent are made in the Enterprise Processing Zones of countries like China, Thailand and the Philippines, where young women little more than children themselves work for low wages in factories which also serve as dormitories and, on occasion, death traps.

(Langer 2002: 74)

In this low-price environment, purchasing power and consumer demand grow, contributing to what sociologist Juliet Schor (2005: 311) labels "excess consumption" with significant environmental consequences. This includes rapidly acquiring and throwing away consumer goods (e.g. Happy Meal toys) and purchasing multiple versions of the same product (e.g. why buy one Furby when you can buy multiple Furbies that communicate with each other!). Of course, this is not the experience of *every* child; even in the wealthy countries of the Global North, children living in poverty may have few or no toys at all, as family resources are devoted to food and other necessities. Another additional force contributes to toy consumption: aggressive marketing and advertisements (Schor 2005a). Until the mid-20th century, advertising for children's toys primarily targeted parents as the purchaser (Buckingham 2011: 73). Today, marketers increasingly see children as savvy consumers with both their own money and significant influence over parents' spending decisions. The increase in what Sutherland and Thompson (2001) call "kidfluence" means that marketers target children in their advertising, a move that has helped further boost toy sales.

Overall, it is important to connect the micro interactions among parents, children, and toy store employees to the macro dynamics of labor, trade, and marketing within global commodity chains. Children's consumption expectations in affluent countries can only exist in a global labor context where toys can be cheaply manufactured and shipped around the world.

While our sociological imaginations lead us to contextualize individual toy purchases within this massive industry, it is equally important to recognize that kids aren't simply "victims" of capitalist toy culture. The "hero"/"dupe" dichotomy discussed in chapter 5 assumes particular force in the context of childhood, where hegemonic ideas about childhood innocence mean that the young consumer is often

SF "Happy Meal Ban"

Cheap toys can be an effective way for marketers to make fast-food meals more appealing to children. In 2011, San Francisco become one of the first US cities to ban fast-food restaurants from giving away free toys with children's meals that do not meet nutritional standards. To comply with the law, McDonald's restaurants in San Francisco began charging customers an additional 10 cents to receive a toy with their Happy Meal.

Source: APimages.com # 110726129932

imagined to be exceptionally vulnerable to capitalist manipulation. While traditional conceptions of socialization tended to position children as passive receivers of culture, scholars of childhood have made the important contribution of highlighting children's agency vis-à-vis the market and consumer culture (Cook 2010). As social actors in their own right, kids are not simply "dupes" of capitalist structures; at the same time, they don't fully control, or dictate the culture they are born into, and their choices are often closely monitored and regulated by adults. Just like adults, children's agency is constrained by structural forces, including the age-based authority relations that surround their social location as children.

Another important scholarly contribution in studies of children's consumption has been to challenge the assumption that childhood can exist entirely separate from consumer culture, and thus remain untainted by the corrupting influence of market forces. Rather, as Dan Cook (2010) argues, children's lives are thoroughly enmeshed in consumer culture even before birth. The cultural rituals of throwing a baby shower or designing a nursery are materialized through consumption practices that anticipate the baby's arrival and welcome them into the world of consumer goods. Consumer culture is a world that is impossible for children to avoid, and as we have shown throughout this chapter, forms an important part of the socialization process.

It is now well established that marketers relentlessly target children, but how do children interpret and respond to these messages? The sociologist Allison Pugh (2009), discussed above, set out to answer this question. She spent three years hanging out with both poor and affluent kids in Oakland, California. Based on this research, Pugh argues that children's desire for toys and other consumer goods is part of a deeply held need for belonging. She suggests that children's relationship to consumption is central to their everyday negotiations in a social world where they navigate their relative worth and sense of belonging and dignity among their peers. Pugh's research makes the important point that socialization is not simply about messages that are communicated from adults to children—or conversely, from children to adults—but also occurs among peers within children's culture (a world that adults are often oblivious to). Children at the schools she studied used consumer goods to forge and maintain friendships, and to establish their membership within particular social groups. Fitting in was not simply about having the most stuff, but was also achieved by demonstrating knowledge of key consumer items—as seen in the case of a boy who had few toys but gained credibility through his expert understanding of Magic cards (Pugh 2009: 57–8). By observing children's social interactions, Pugh identified various practices that children performed to secure their place within the group. These include such things as the importance of "claiming" symbolically valued items (establishing authoritative knowledge of an item, even if they didn't actually own it), and the "bridging labor" required to fit in with their peers when resources were lacking (2009: 67). As Pugh notes, bridging labor allows poor children to "portray [a] deficit as an asset" (2009: 67). For instance, one girl who was aware of how her father's blue-collar job differed from the professional careers of her friends' parents suggested that his work installing driveways put him in contact with various pop culture celebrities.

While differential access to economic resources clearly shaped kids' relationship to consumer culture, a striking finding in Pugh's research was the fact that kids from vastly different class backgrounds were united through shared consumer fantasies. It was common for wealthy and poor kids to express remarkably similar desires for key commodities like brand-name clothing, collectible cards (e.g. Pokémon), and of course, videogames. The specific items varied in ways that reflected price differences (e.g. expensive American Girl dolls vs. more affordable Bratz dolls) (2009: 62), but there was a common repertoire of consumer stuff that kids from different backgrounds related to and desired.

While Pugh's research emphasizes the significance of toys and other consumer goods for children's *belonging*, there is a flipside to this story—status seeking and distinction. Sociologists who study the formation of social boundaries remind us that efforts to "fit in" often involve processes of exclusion—that is, we establish our own membership within the group by distancing ourselves from those who are outside of it. Thus, at the same time that consumer goods can facilitate children's sense of belonging, they can simultaneously be used to establish status as markers of distinction among peers. The question of whether toys are primarily about belonging or distinction highlights the way that different sociological perspectives allow us to see the same set of social processes in a different light: on the one hand, a Durkheimian emphasis on social solidarity (discussed in the previous chapter), and on the other, a Bourdieusian emphasis on social status (discussed in chapter 4). While these perspectives may seem contradictory, we can draw useful insights from both of them to see belonging and distinction as interrelated processes in children's peer cultures—and in social life more broadly. At the same time that a child may long for a pair of Air Jordans in order to fit in with others, this coveted item may also serve as a status symbol that establishes one's place among the popular kids, and thus signals distance from those lower down in the social hierarchy.

SOCIOLOGISTS IN ACTION: DO VIDEOGAMES SOCIALIZE VIOLENT BEHAVIOR?

If toys and other elements of children's culture are important agents of socialization, then should we be concerned about the kinds of messages conveyed through the videogames kids play? This question has inspired significant debate, as powerful corporations, concerned parents, young gamers, and a host of others weigh in with competing views. From a sociological perspective, the question of whether videogames promote violent behavior poses an interesting methodological challenge: how do we accurately research the impact of violent videogames on our complex, multifaceted social lives? Some scholars have expressed concern that videogames glorify violence and socialize children (particularly boys) to take on the persona of a violent actor through first-person shooter games. Until 2013, the official position of the American Psychological Association (APA) was that scholarly research demonstrated a link between videogames and aggression. However, some academics have challenged the connection between videogames and violence, noting the multiple socialization influences at play and the methodological difficulties of establishing this connection.

The debate surrounding videogame violence draws our attention to a mode of analysis that examines the relationship between two factors: an **independent variable** and a **dependent variable**. If we were to hypothesize that playing videogames increases violent behavior, then the independent variable would be playing videogames, and the dependent variable would be violent behavior. Examining the relationship between two variables, it is crucial to ensure that any relationship found is not actually the result of other, unmeasured or unknown factors—and this is where the challenge comes in. Even in the context of laboratory research, it is impossible to extract a gamer from the broader social context, such as family upbringing, other media influences, peer networks, and a range of other factors. Of course, experiments are not the only way to examine the potential connection between videogames and violent behavior. For example, survey research has also identified a **correlation** (or relationship) between self-reported levels of aggression and videogame play (Willoughby et al. 2012: 1055). However, it is important to remember that correlation does not necessarily mean **causation**. That is, two factors can be related to each other without one clearly causing the other. For example, people who are already prone to aggression may be more attracted to violent videogames, so it would then be inaccurate to say that the videogames cause violence. (In this case, playing videogames becomes the dependent variable, and the independent variable is a disposition towards violence.) In addition, there are broader societal patterns that challenge the claim that videogames cause violence. While violent videogames are more popular than ever, the rates of actual violent crime in North America are down (Ward 2011). Given these complicating issues, in 2013 the APA began reviewing their position on videogames and violence, due to a lack of clear scholarly consensus. The case of videogames and violence illustrates the complexity of socialization. As sociologists, it is difficult to identify a straightforward "cause" and "effect" relationship in the context of socialization. Nonetheless, we can seek to better understand that complex set of factors that come together in the making of individuals and societies.

Toys have long played an ambivalent role in our culture. On one hand, they have served as a vehicle for parents' hopes and aspirations. Toys have been celebrated for their educational value, and as a means of training children for adult life. Toys also serve as a domain for children's freedom and imagination, and a site in which we invest nostalgia for childhood innocence. For all of these reasons, many of us recall our own childhood toys with fondness and vivid memories. We may gain pleasure in giving children access to toys that we think are cute, educational, or just plain fun. On the other hand, toys serve as a key site for our fears regarding the commercialization of childhood and the commodification of play. Many people shake their heads at the number of toys possessed by kids in wealthy parts of the globe, worry about the millions of plastic toys that end up in landfills, or look aghast when they hear that the average American child receives about 70 new toys a year (Schor 2005b: 314). Sociologists note that toys can be used as a substitute for spending quality time

Spurious Correlations

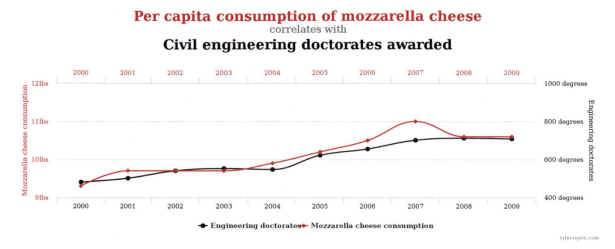

The statistical principle that "correlation does not imply causation" was the subject of a recent viral website titled Spurious Correlations, which collected meme-like graphs of highly correlated but often comically unrelated variables. Pictured here is a graph plotting data for US per capita consumption of mozzarella cheese per pound and the number of civil engineering doctorates awarded in the US; the variables are shown to be highly correlated but one is not caused by the other. The website was created by law student Tyler Vigen and has since been published as a coffee table book by the same title.

Source: http://tylervigen.com/spurious-correlations

with children, and that working women alleviate their maternal guilt by buying more stuff (Williams 2006: 167; Schor 2005a: 302).

Toys not only serve as a window into our ambivalent relationship with consumer culture; the research presented in this chapter also suggests that toys are an important mode of socialization. Children learn about gender expectations in a toy store, alongside lessons of racial inequality and class marginalization. As with the other consumer items explored in this book, the topic of toys is sociologically rich, a source of pleasurable and sometimes painful memories, but also a jumping-off point for analyzing poverty, racism, and sexism.

THINKING FRAMES

How can each thinking frame help us ponder the sociology of toys?

Material / Cultural	Consumer goods—like toys—communicate powerful messages about fitting into society (including gender expectations), and thus are key to processes of socialization. Studying toys can help us understand how inequalities come to be normalized and taken for granted. The cultural symbolism of toys is not created out of thin air, but is connected to the economy of globalized toy production, as well as a broader material system of social stratification.
Think about . . .	Can you see varying cultural ideals of masculinity and femininity by looking at different toys across different cultures and time frames? (e.g. think about the toys your parents might have played with, and compare them to the toys you played with, and commercials you see for toys today.)

Structure / Agency	Socialization is not simply about transmitting culture to the next generation; this is an interactive and lifelong process in which children are active participants. Socialization is also shaped by structural inequality, as seen in classed differences in the ways parents negotiate children's consumer desires.
Think about . . .	How much choice do children have in the toys available to them? What are the key factors shaping children's desire for toys? How might children resist or reinterpret the dominant messages of consumer culture in their play?

Micro / Macro	We can learn valuable sociological lessons by situating the micro interactions among parents, children, and toy store employees in relation to macro dynamics of labor and trade within global commodity chains. We can also learn about kids' toy culture by doing research with children, instead of simply studying parents, toy commercials, or toy production.
Think about . . .	How do you think children's lives in affluent countries are shaped by a macro context where toys are relatively cheap and available? How does this context shape micro interactions of play, and social pressure to possess new toys and acquire new things?

Active Learning

ACTIVE LEARNING

Online

Kids as change agents:
Watch 13-year-old McKenna Pope's TEDYouth Talk called: "Want to be an activist? Start with your toys." What does McKenna's story tell us about children's agency within consumer culture? https://www.ted.com/talks/mckenna_pope_want_to_be_an_activist_start_with_your_toys?language=en

Let Toys Be Toys:
Visit the website for the UK organization "Let Toys Be Toys" (http://www.lettoysbetoys.org.uk). Check out some of their recent campaigns to promote gender neutrality and equity in toy advertising. Do you think that these campaigns will have an impact? Can you think of similar initiatives that you might promote in your local community? How would you extend this conversation to include other social issues, such as race or disability?

Discussion/Reflection

Your first toy:
What is the first significant toy you remember having? Using the insights you gained from this chapter, can you identify whether this toy taught you about your gender? What examples of gender policing can you remember from your early experiences with toys?

Toys and inequality:

Do you think there is a link between the gender segregation of toys and gender inequality? In other words, how might toys contribute to the roles and responsibilities (and inequalities) children face later in life?

Toy advertising:

Do you think there should be stricter regulations on the ways toys are marketed to children? How is toy marketing regulated differently in different parts of the world?

Sociology Outside the Classroom

Toy store observation:

On your own or in a group, visit a local toy store and take note of the ways that toys are gendered. How are the toys organized? How can you tell a toy is targeted toward boys or girls? Are any toys gender-neutral?[1]

Game of life:

What socialization messages are communicated through popular board games? Play your favorite board game with a group of friends and see if you can identify all of the messages this game conveys about how to fit into society. E.g. what are some of the central norms and values emphasized within Monopoly? Or Settlers of Catan?

---

1 The idea for this activity is drawn from Betsy Lucal's contribution to *Sociology for Active Learning*, edited by Kathleen McKinney, Barbara S. Heyl 2009, Sage.

Chapter 8

DREAMING OF A WHITE WEDDING: MARRIAGE, FAMILY, AND HETERONORMATIVITY

INTRODUCING KEY CONCEPTS

Weddings are both a massive industry, and a powerful ritual. In this chapter, we use the case study of weddings to think sociologically about the family. We focus in particular on the "white wedding" phenomenon of big dresses, bridesmaids, multi-leveled wedding cakes, and luxury honeymoons. The popularity of white weddings—and the related growth of a billion-dollar wedding industry—suggests a vital connection between our romantic ideals, prevalent understandings of masculinity and femininity, and escalating consumption standards. Studying wedding rituals also allows us to explore key concepts in the sociology of the family: marriage, romantic love, the nuclear family, social reproduction, the second shift and heteronormativity. We investigate changing norms around marriage, including the legalization of gay marriage. We also consider how the white wedding operates ideologically to obscure inequalities related to gender, sexuality, class, and race.

1. INTRODUCTION: THE DREAM OF MARRIAGE, OR THE DREAM OF A *WEDDING*?

Many people assume that they will one day get married. Indeed, over 80% of Americans will get married at least once in their lifetime, and most people who get divorced will remarry (Cherlin 2013). Having a dream or simply an expectation of getting married is not altogether surprising. Long-term partnerships have some well-known benefits: trust, companionship, sexual intimacy, shared finances, and a joint project of raising children.

But what about the dream of having a *wedding*—a ceremony, a tuxedo or fancy suit, an elaborate white gown, a ring, and a big party to celebrate the union? Why is a wedding so culturally significant, especially a big wedding with all the trimmings?

Mai, an Asian-Canadian undergraduate student, told us that even though she is not currently in a relationship, she has all the details of her dream wedding mapped out, including the location (Disneyland), the ring (from Tiffany's, 2-carat), the centerpieces, and the wedding dress: "I always envisioned wearing an all-white lace gown with a sweetheart neckline, corset bodice, and flowing train stippled with Swarovski crystals." Mai's wedding fantasy may seem highly specific, but as the class discussion proceeded, it became clear that nearly every woman in the room had thought extensively about what her ideal wedding would look like, including what kind of rings and dresses would be involved. (Indeed, *Brides* magazine reports that a quarter of its readers are not yet planning a wedding; Ellin 2014.) The discussion became especially animated when it came to gender expectations. Ismael, a Somali-Canadian student, described the long hours he had to work to pay for his own recent wedding, an elaborate event with 500 guests that he felt allowed his Somali-Canadian wife to be a "princess for a day". (To pay for the event, Ismael worked the night shift as a security guard while attending university full-time.) After hearing this story in class, Ismael's fellow student, Mike (a White-Canadian) half-jokingly quipped that if he provides a big diamond and an elaborate wedding for his bride-to-be, then he wants to retain the right to tell her to stay at home and look after the kids.

In an age of high income inequality with a lot of people working long hours to make ends meet, it is somewhat surprising that the idea of a big wedding with an expensive dress and a large diamond is so powerfully entrenched in the collective conscience. As this particular classroom discussion unfolded, it became clear that the wedding dream was not limited to White upper-

The Big White Wedding

Kate Middleton and Prince William's wedding on April 29, 2011 was a highly anticipated affair, and a very large white wedding watched by millions on television. Speculation as to what Kate would wear carried on for months. The elaborate dress (designed by Sarah Burton for Alexander McQueen) was carefully studied by fashion commentators and quickly replicated for brides to purchase.

Source: Gettyimages.com # 157652124

middle-class heterosexual men and women. It is a dream shared by people from multiple race and class backgrounds and with different sexual orientations. In this chapter, we use our sociological imagination to shed light on wedding consumption. In particular, we look at how the cultural ideal of the heteronormative family is reproduced (and resisted) through the act of publically celebrating a wedding.

The next section provides a brief overview of sociological approaches to marriage and the family. After that, we unpack the phenomenon of the "white wedding". We can think of the white wedding as "a spectacle featuring a bride in a formal white wedding gown" mashed up with some combination of formally attired bridesmaids and groomsmen, flowers, table arrangements, special foods, drink, gifts, and a honeymoon (Ingraham 2008: 5). Of course, not everyone chooses to get married with this kind of lavish ceremony—or to get married at all—but the white wedding is sociologically significant as a hegemonic cultural ideal. Throughout the chapter, we also explore how the institution of marriage has become increasingly available to gay and lesbian couples, and consider the ways in which gay marriage both challenges and reproduces traditional notions of family.

2. MARRIED WITH CHILDREN? A BRIEF PORTRAIT OF OUR SHIFTING INTIMATE RELATIONSHIPS

When you think of the "family", what images come to mind? For many, the word family evokes the picture of a mother, father, and their children, and maybe a pet dog or cat. Perhaps you envision the ideal family pictured on TV sitcoms, featuring a hard-working father, a sexy stay-at-home mother, and two or three rascally kids. Our ideas about what counts as family can have powerful

A 1950s TV Family

A 1956 still from television series Father Knows Best, *in which insurance agent Jim Anderson, his wife Margaret, and their children Betty, Kathy, and Bud navigate the ins and outs of middle-class family life.*

Source: Gettyimages.com # 51887400

Modern Family

The cast of Modern Family *at the 64th annual Primetime Emmy Awards in 2012.*

Source: Gettyimages.com # 152710287

DIVERSE FORMS OF MODERN FAMILIES

While families vary significantly across cultures and over time, the institution of the family continues to be widely regarded as the foundation of society. During the 2012 American election, the *New York Times* reported that both Barack Obama and Mitt Romney had named *Modern Family* as one of their favorite television shows—a rare point of agreement between candidates with vastly different viewpoints on most issues (Leibovich 2012). What makes this television family "modern"? There are many ways in which this sitcom's family differs from traditional images of the family, including gay and lesbian families, internationally adopted children, remarriage and blended families, as well as inter-racial/inter-ethnic relationships. The show reflects just a few of the diverse family forms that we see throughout North America today. (Although one kind of family that is glaringly absent from the show—and from virtually all television sitcoms—is the working-class, financially struggling family.) *Modern Family*'s depiction of shifting family structure reflects historical processes like global migration, as well as changing social norms, such as attitudes toward gay and lesbian relationships.

social implications, not only for feelings of acceptance and belonging, but also for social policies and access to state entitlements. Many of you—like us—have lived in families that don't fit this image. You may have familial relationships that differ from the hegemonic ideal (e.g. a gay parent, a single mother, a childhood spent in foster care) and you may have experienced social stigma as a result. The reality of contemporary life is complex; today more than ever, the social meaning of "marriage" and "family" are up for debate.

We can think of the family as a cultural ideal, a set of intimate social relationships, as well as a longstanding institution. It might seem strange to use the term "institution" to describe what we often think as a private, intimate sphere. However, through a sociological lens, we can see how the family operates as an important social institution that organizes social behavior and also contributes to forms of social inequality. Scholars conceptualize the family as a set of intimate relationships where people share resources to sustain the lives of adults and children. Relatedly, academics use the term social reproduction to describe the financial, physical, and emotional care work that goes into reproducing people on a daily and generational basis.

Speaking of reproduction, that is something we are doing less of when it comes to children. In economically advanced countries around the globe, birth rates have been falling for decades. On average, women in a society need to bear 2.1 children over their lifetime in order for the population to remain stable (without immigration). The calculation of how many children the average woman would bear over her lifetime is called the total fertility rate. In Canada, the most recent data show that the fertility rate is 1.61 and has been below 2.1 for over 40 years (Statistics Canada 2016). In the United States, the rate in 2014 was 1.86, also below replacement level (Hamilton et al. 2015). At the level of individual families, this means that the stereotype of a family typically having parents with multiple children is becoming out of date. While such families are still quite numerous, there are more families that differ from this pattern than conform to it. At a societal level, the change is momentous. Countries in North America, Europe, and some in Asia are facing population declines that can only be offset through immigration. These populations are also, on average, getting older, as the proportion of young people falls with fertility rates.

As we see changes in cultural ideals and demography, it is clear that there is no universal family. The structure of the family has shifted throughout history and across cultural contexts, and includes a variety of intimate relationships, sexual pairings, and strategies for social reproduction. To understand the extent of this historical variation, we begin by reviewing shifting motivations for marriage that occurred with the advent of modern industrial economies. Then, we look at how the institution of marriage maps onto Western ideas of "modern love"—both in its idealized romantic version, and its grittier, everyday realities.

2.1. Love: From Working Partnerships to Love Matches

In pre-modern, pre-industrial times, marriage was more about practical considerations than steamy romance or finding your soul-mate (Coontz 2005). Physical survival was a fairly pressing issue: food supplies were often scarce, and many children did not live to see adulthood. The family was the unit of production, and couples across different class backgrounds primarily got married to address economic concerns—such as the need to produce children to carry on bloodlines (for more elite folks), and the need to produce children who could work in the fields (for the common peasant). Marriage was also a way to organize inheritance, produce a male heir, and regulate women's sexuality. Marriage typically had a norm of monogamy, but the rules of monogamy were typically applied more strictly to women than men (Ingraham 2008: 146–7). Forging and strengthening family connections, as well as making alliances with other families, were key motivations for pre-modern marriage. Cousin marriages were very common historically, and remain common in certain parts of the world today. In pre-industrial times, marriage matches were not focused on nurturing interpersonal relationships or sexual compatibility. These bonds may have involved affection and care in day-to-day life, but as an institution, pre-modern marriage was not primarily a love-based arrangement. As marriage scholar Stephanie Coontz writes, "only rarely in history has love been seen as the main reason for getting married" (2005: 15).

With the emergence of capitalism and industrial economies, the locus of labor moved from the family unit to the factory. This shift was particularly pronounced in capitalist England and the United States at the turn of the 19th century. With this shift, several significant changes in marriage emerged which have stayed with us to the present day: the valorization of the nuclear family, the emergence of separate public and private gender spheres, and a belief in "love" matches. We discuss these shifts below, since each plays a part in contemporary wedding dreams.

In pre-industrial societies, it was common to live in an extended family with aunts, uncles, cousins, and grandparents, all living and working together. When people left the farm to work in factories, this shift in work life was accompanied by a shift to smaller family units in the city. This gave rise to the nuclear family: a familial unit comprised of a heterosexual couple and their dependent children. Even today, this is what many people consider the "ideal family": dad + mom + kids. The traditional nuclear family is based on a model of patriarchy (discussed in chapter 7), a set of social relationships where masculine roles and ideals are organized hierarchically in relation to femininity. This masculine/feminine hierarchy emerged alongside a division of social spheres that occurred with industrialization. This resulted in two spheres: 1) the *public* realm of work dominated by men and 2) the *private* realm of the home dominated by women. (Many working-class women and women of color did work outside the home, but often within the private sphere of wealthier White women.) In this context, women aimed to "marry well", which meant partnering with someone successful in the public world of work. An ideal husband was not just a hard worker, but also a good *earner*—a man with a good income who could protect women and children from poverty and economic exploitation. To be a good wife meant being a good companion (and worker) in the private realm, creating a warm, domestic respite from the harsh world of work.

With this separation of public and private realms, industrialization also gave rise to the "cult of domesticity". This was not a literal cult, but a cultural belief that romanticized women's domestic responsibilities—cooking, cleaning, child rearing, and general homemaking. The cult of domesticity first emerged in the 1800s and experienced a resurgence in the 1950s, but has stayed with us in some form to the present day. (Think here of the popular idealization of culinary "goddesses" like Martha Stewart, Nigella Lawson, and Giada de Laurentiis.) Like many modern ideals, the cult of domesticity emerged out of early capitalist structures and dynamics. High-status women in industrializing England and the United States stayed at home, and homemaking became a kind of "art" and status symbol. Privileged (White, affluent) women spent countless hours on tasks related to food, entertainment, decorating, hosting guests, and needlepoint. The home was seen as a place of refuge from the harsh world of the industrializing economy and the smoky, crowded city. Consider the following tips given to women in an 1888 advice book: "Whatever have been the cares of the day, greet your husband with a smile when he returns. Make your personal appearance just as beautiful as possible . . . Let him enter rooms so attractive and sunny that all the recollections of his home, when away from the same, shall attract him back" (Hill 1887: 167). Idealized feminine gender roles came to center on being a good "wife"—a helper, nurturer, permanent sexual companion, and stable base of domestic support. This history helps explain why traditional wedding vows for women usually involve some element of domestic service: "Will you obey him and serve him, love, honor and keep him, in sickness and in health?"

Alongside the ideal of the perfect, domestic, feminine wife, the ideal of romantic love also entered the marital picture during industrialization. It's difficult to say exactly *why* this ideal emerged. Perhaps it was a way of making women feel better about being enshrined in (and confined to) the private realm of domesticity. Also, the emergence of romantic love may have reflected the transition from an agricultural to an industrial economy. In an agricultural economy, parents controlled access to land and inheritance, and played a large role in determining who could marry whom (Coontz 2005). With the transition to a capitalist market economy, young adults' marriage decisions weren't as closely tied to parents' permission and the associated promise of inheriting land. With a move away from agricultural ways of life and towards urban living, it became increasingly possible for people to independently decide whom they wanted to marry. By the late 1700s, the notion of "love

"Domestic Goddess" as Personal Brand: Nigella

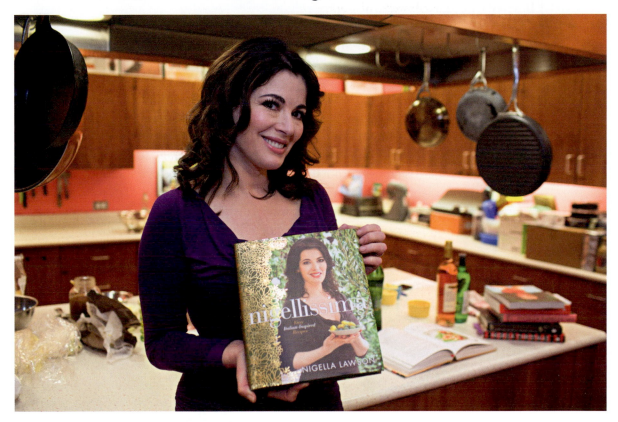

The author of popular culinary books like How to Be a Domestic Goddess, Nigella Bites, *and* Nigellissima, *Nigella Lawson has transformed her penchant for traditionally gendered domestic work into a personal brand (see chapter 10).*

Source: Gettyimages.com # 170797540

matches" gained traction, meaning that people started to expect, or at least dream about, a marriage that was based on love and possibly sexual desire. Since sex before marriage was looked down upon, marriage represented a socially acceptable form of sexual release. However, it's important to understand that *mutual* attraction in marriage wasn't a requirement of romantic love until about a century ago. In fact, in Victorian England, many people believed that women were asexual beings; these matches were seen as a way of satisfying men's distinct sexual needs (Coontz 2005).

ARRANGED MARRIAGE

Until the 18th century, many (if not most) people around the world had arranged marriages where an elder, matchmaker, or family member would bring the bride and groom together (Das Dasgupta 2009). Today, versions of arranged marriage are practiced in various countries in Asia, the Middle East, and sub-Saharan Africa, as well as in various diasporic communities (e.g. South Asian families that have migrated to the West). With globalization, arranged marriages have increasingly incorporated ideas of autonomous love matches, and partners often have a say over the suitability of the match. Interestingly, studies of marital satisfaction indicate that love matches do not necessarily lead to happier, more successful outcomes (Das Dasgupta 2009). As young people in the West struggle to find a suitable partner in large urban centers, "matchmaking services" for couples of various ethnic backgrounds have made a revival, offering a more personalized approach than online dating websites.

2.2. Modern Love: Ideals and Reality

Let's jump forward to the present day, which we will refer to as the era of "modern love". Although arranged marriages still exist, autonomous unions or "love matches" are a contemporary norm, and many people expect to find their future spouse through their own efforts. Romantic love is a key motivation for modern marriage, and also a key theme in mass media depictions of marriage and weddings. The dream of romantic love is also key to feminine **socialization** processes. (The concept of socialization was discussed in chapter 7. Think here of gendered products ranging from Bridal Barbie, to teen romance books, to "chick-flicks", to sitcom plotlines.) In this section, we explore contemporary Western ideals of love and marriage, and consider how they compare to empirical data on modern love and marriage trends.

While the ideal of marriage based on romantic love dates back to the 19th century, what is relatively new is the belief that this union involves gender equality. Historically, marriage wasn't firmly rooted in principles of equality, even when love ideals entered the picture. For example, in the United States, marital rape was legal in many states until the 1970s (meaning that a woman had no legal recourse if her husband forced her to have sex without her consent) and women often could not get credit cards or open bank accounts in their own names. Husbands commonly maintained control over family income, debts, and assets. In the US, these norms began to change around 50 years ago, with the rise of the feminist movement. In many contemporary heterosexual relationships, partners have an expectation of gender equality— that is, the belief that they will be equal partners in a marriage. Many wedding ceremonies have changed to reflect these shifting ideals. For example, many couples leave out talk of "obeying" in their marriage vows, and many brides work to avoid the impression that they are being "given" from father to husband (e.g. keeping one's own last name after marriage, or having their father *and* their mother walk them down the aisle).

While a cultural belief in marital equality has become more common, the roles available to couples on their wedding day remain highly gendered. Being a "bride" is a valorized feminine gender role that is not equivalent to the role of "groom". Brides are often expected to be the center of attention on their wedding day—a tendency that explains why many of our female students have thought in detail about their future wedding day, while few male students have given it serious thought. Indeed, the wedding day is sometimes described as the "most important day" of a woman's life—a phrase not often uttered to men. The role of the bride is socially valued as a performance of femininity, but it is generally not as powerful or flexible as the masculine role of groom. If a woman's "most important" day is her wedding day, then we can assume that she won't have future days in the public realm that are more significant (e.g. being sworn into office, saving somebody's life as a doctor, or breaking a world record for a sports accomplishment). Thus, even though many couples enter marriage with a belief in gender equality, the modern wedding's focus on brides (over grooms) reflects the continued emphasis on domestic femininity as a key source of women's value and identity. In contrast, men can remain a bachelor into their later years, perhaps never taking on the "groom" role, and not be seen as a failure. In part, this is because men are more defined—and judged—by their success fulfilling roles in the public sphere— as a worker, leader, breadwinner.

How do modern love ideals compare with marital realities? For one, the connections between marriage, sex, and childbirth have changed quite dramatically from earlier eras. For example, over 95% of Americans have at least one sexual relationship prior to getting married, suggesting a relatively flexible link between sex and marriage (Cahn and Carbone 2010: 175). Both sex and childrearing increasingly happen outside of a formal marital union. In 1960, 5% of American children were born outside of marriage, but by 2014, 41% of American children were born outside of marriage (over half of those children were born to cohabitating couples) (Livingston 2014; Curtin et al. 2014: 4). The link between women and homemaking has also shifted in recent decades. Most American and Canadian women do not expect to reside exclusively in the domestic realm of unpaid work, and the majority now work outside the home (US Department of Labor 2015; Status of Women Canada 2015). This has unsettled the binary of male/breadwinner/public realm versus female/bread-maker/private realm. Gender economic equality has not been reached (women still earn much less than men, on average), but women today are less financially dependent on men than they were in the past (Carbone and Cahn 2014). This has made it increasingly possible for women to have children and sex outside of marriage, since they are not as reliant on men for economic support.

While the *ideal* of everlasting romantic love is a powerful cultural factor motivating modern marriage, this ideal is not always manifest in marital

Changes in the American Family

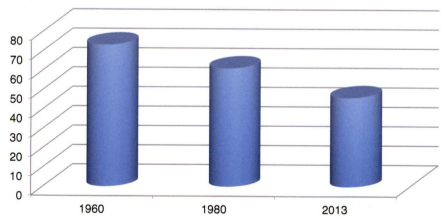

Percent of US children living with 2 married parents in their first marriage

Note: *In this data, the category of married parents only includes heterosexual couples. Notice how dominant definitions of "marriage" and "family" may lead researchers to neglect the existence of certain family forms, and thus to omit these families from official statistics.*

Data Source: Livingston 2014

realities. Most marriages begin with romance, but many marriages (almost half) end in divorce (Kennedy and Ruggles 2014). Getting a divorce is more socially acceptable than it was in the past, and also legally accessible. For many decades, couples had to provide proof of fault (e.g. adultery, cruelty) in order to attain a divorce. Women's increasing independence (through greater access to contraception, higher education, and employment opportunities) helped spur the implementation of no-fault divorce in every US state between 1969 and 1985 (Carbone and Cahn 2014: 111–13).

These marriage and divorce trends do not impact everyone equally. Americans with a college education tend to marry later, marry in greater numbers, and divorce less; Americans without college degrees tend to marry earlier, have lower rates of marriage, and divorce more frequently (Cherlin 2014a; Coontz 2014; Thompson 2013). Marriage rates also differ by race; in the US, Whites are more likely to be married than Blacks, and this difference has increased over time (Pew Research Center 2010: 2). What sociologists sometimes call the "marriage gap" or the "divorce divide" reflects the link between social inequality and marriage rates. Having a stable, long-lasting marriage is closely connected to stable employment and a regular income, something that is increasingly elusive for working-class families with low education levels (Coontz 2014; Cherlin 2014a). Sociologist Andrew Cherlin (2014a) argues that class-differentiated rates of marriage are not a reflection of value differences (i.e. that elites value marriage more than the poor), but a result of increasing inequality. He explains:

> College-educated men and women are the privileged players in our transformed economy: They can pool two incomes and provide a solid financial foundation for a marriage. In contrast, we have seen declines in marriage among high school graduates who are stuck in the middle of the labor market, where they can no longer find the kind of steady, decently paying employment that supported their grandparents' marriages.
>
> (Cherlin 2014b)

Relatedly, Coontz (2014) argues that broader patterns of social inequality may also help middle- and upper-middle-class marriages survive because those couples can afford to pay for low-wage labor to do tasks that couples often bicker about: "in some ways *inequality actually makes life easier for such couples,* since more Americans are available to work as nannies and house-cleaners for relatively low wages".

While marriage and divorce statistics vary across social groups, what is much more consistent is the *dream* of marriage. A survey conducted by the Pew Research Center found that "those with a high school diploma or less are just as likely as those with a college degree to say they want to marry" (2010: i). So the *ideal* of marriage continues to hold wide cultural resonance, but not everyone has the resources required to access this ideal, or even make a wedding plan in the first place. At the same time, we see growing acceptance of diverse family forms, including cohabitation, raising children without marriage, and single-parent households (Pew Research Center 2010). As sociologists, we want to recognize the links between social inequality and the marriage gap, but avoid valorizing or denigrating married life as though it were

INTIMATE PARTNER VIOLENCE

Intimate partner violence is another way that the lived experience of marriage differs from love ideals. Marital and partner violence is shockingly common. Women are statistically much more likely to be harmed by somebody in their family than by a stranger (Catalano et al. 2009: 3). For many women, marriage and romantic relationships are the major way they experience brutality, bullying, and violence. Data from the National Intimate Partner and Sexual Violence Survey indicate that nearly 1 in 10 women in the United States has been raped by an intimate partner, while 1 in 4 women has experienced severe physical violence inflicted by a current or former partner (Breiding et al. 2014: 1, 13). Women are more likely than men to experience individual and multiple, minor and severe forms of intimate partner violence, and to experience negative impacts associated with such violence, including anxiety, substance abuse, physical injuries, and missing school or work (Breiding et al. 2014: 65). Based upon this seeming gender asymmetry in the experience of intimate partner violence (bolstered by experiences of hospital, court, and law enforcement officials), feminist scholars argue that violence against women in intimate relationships is a specific manifestation of the patriarchal domination of women by men, differentiated from other kinds of family violence by its gendered nature (Lawson 2012: 588).

superior or inferior to other family forms. In this way, sociological work on the family has produced new understandings of family dynamics and patterns that have sometimes contradicted traditional assumptions that were driven by values rather than by evidence.

Certainly, our contemporary Western culture of **individualism** makes marriage and long-term partnerships more difficult to maintain, as people may be less willing to subordinate their own needs to the family unit. An ethos of individualism in intimate relationships means less rigid rule-following and a greater expectation of equality (Morgan 2007). These trends can be both empowering and destabilizing for the institution of marriage. An expectation of full partnership can lead to marital discontent when ideals of equality are

Same-Sex Wedding

A newlywed couple at the Grand Pride Wedding, a mass LGBT wedding held in Toronto on June 26, 2014 as part of the World Pride Festival. Over 100 couples tied the knot.

Source: Gettyimages.com # 500956167

A Timeline of the Fight for Marriage Equality

- **A Timeline of the Fight for Marriage Equality**

1972
- The US Supreme Court dismisses Baker v. Nelson, a case brought by a gay Minnesota couple challenging the fact that they were denied a marriage license.

1973
- Maryland becomes the first state to pass a statute explicitly banning same-sex marriage.

1975
- A Colorado couple launches the first federal lawsuit pursuing the freedom to marry for same-sex couples. The federal court later rules that Colorado law only recognizes different-sex marriages.

1989
- Denmark allows same-sex couples to register as domestic partners, becoming the first country to do so.

1996
- On September 21, President Clinton signs the Defense of Marriage Act (DOMA), which upholds states' rights to ban gay marriage and prohibits the federal government from recognizing same-sex marriages

1997
- Hawaii becomes the first US state to offer same-sex couples domestic partnership benefits

2000
- The Netherlands becomes the first country to legalize same-sex marriage

2004
- After the Massachusetts Supreme Court ruled in favor of same-sex marriage in 2003, on May 17, 2004, Massachusetts becomes the first US state to allow same-sex couples to marry.

2005
- California's legislature is the first to pass a bill allowing same-sex marriage; the governor later vetoes it.
- Spain and Canada legalize same-sex marriage

2006
- South Africa becomes the first African country to legalize same-sex marriage.

2008
- Connecticut becomes the second US state to legalize same sex marriage, while California voters approve Proposition 8 – a constitutional amendment restricting marriage to different-sex couples.

2009
- Sweden and Norway legalize same-sex marriage, as do Iowa, Vermont, and the District of Columbia.

2010
- CNN releases the first poll to show a majority of Americans supporting same-sex marriage.
- Argentina becomes the first country in South America to legalize same-sex marriage

2011
- The Respect for Marriage Act, aimed at overturning DOMA, is introduced to the US federal legislature.

2012
- President Barack Obama becomes the first sitting president to publicly support same-sex marriage.
- The Democratic Party endorses same-sex marriage in its party platform.
- Citizens in Maine, Maryland, and Washington vote to allow same-sex marriage.

2013
- The US Supreme Court overturns Section 3 of DOMA, requiring the federal government to recognize same-sex marriages conducted where they are legal.
- An appeals court restores the right to marry in California.
- England and Wales, Brazil, France, New Zealand, and Uruguay legalize same-sex marriage, as do Delaware, Hawaii, Illionois, Minnesota and Rhode Island.

2014
- Federal court rulings legalize same-sex marriage in 13 states, and Supreme Court actions effectively require 5 more states to allow same-sex marriage.

2015
- On May 22, 62% of Irish voters vote to amend the constitution to allow same-sex marriage, making Ireland the first country to legalize same-sex marriage through popular referendum.
- On June 26, a 5 to 4 US Supreme Court decision enables same-sex couples to marry in all 50 states.

Timeline sources: Freedom to Marry (2015); Masci et al. 2015; Pew 2015.

not reflected in the home. For example, while women now have high rates of participation in the labor market, this has "not translated directly into an egalitarian allocation of household labor" (Lachance-Grzela and Bouchard 2010: 767). Women continue to do most of the unpaid work involved in family life, such as cooking, cleaning, and childcare (Lachance-Grzela and Bouchard 2010: 767). Sociologist Arlie Hochschild (2003) coined the term the **second shift** to refer to the fact that many women perform a "first" shift at their paid jobs, as well as a "second" shift of domestic responsibilities when they get home. The inequities of domestic life—especially when both partners work full-time—can lead to marital dissatisfaction as people realize that the romantic expectations of wedded bliss aren't always fulfilled in reality.

Finally, the nuclear family expectations of husband, wife, and children have been challenged in many national contexts by the legalization of gay marriage. Until recently, marriage laws throughout the Western world reflected what sociologists call **heteronormativity**—that is, the belief that hetero-sexuality is the only "natural" or "normal" sexual orientation. As an institution that was only available to heterosexual couples, marriage has historically been an example of **heterosexual privilege**. In 2001, the Netherlands became the first country to legalize same-sex marriage. In Canada, same-sex marriage was legal nationwide by 2005. In the United States, same-sex marriage was first legalized in Massachusetts in 2004, and in the following decade extended to many states, but was banned in others (e.g. Kansas, Kentucky). In June 2015, a landmark US Supreme Court ruling legalized gay marriage nationwide. This meant that no matter what state policies had been held up to this point, gay and lesbian couples could marry anywhere in the country and have their marriage legally recognized. As many celebrated this historic ruling, Facebook offered users the option to overlay their profile picture with rainbow colors, as a show of support for marriage equality.

While cultural understandings of marriage, love, and family have under-gone significant shifts over the past two centuries, the idea of a big traditional "white wedding" is enjoying a moment of tremendous popularity. In the next section, we look more closely at the way many people enter into marriage: with an elaborate (and often expensive) wedding ritual.

3. THE WHITE WEDDING: A PRICEY (AND IDEOLOGICAL) RITUAL

3.1. Wedding Expenses and the "Wedding Industrial Complex"

At this point, you might be wondering why we included a chapter on weddings in a book on consumption. To answer that question, let's begin by addressing an issue on the minds of many brides- and grooms-to-be: what is the average price of an American wedding? The short answer is this: weddings cost a lot, and they aren't getting any cheaper. The average cost of an American wedding

A DIAMOND = ETERNAL LOVE?

The connection between diamonds and marriage today is commonplace, but this link has been crafted by powerful corporate actors in the diamond industry. For 83% of US weddings, the first wedding purchase is an engagement ring, which usually has a diamond (Ingraham 2008: 78). However, the idea that a diamond ring is a mandatory component of the wedding ritual is a relatively recent association. Historically, diamonds were thought of as jewels for the ultra-rich. For example, Tiffany's began as a store for America's wealthiest families, like the Vanderbilts and the Huttons (Wexler 2010: 83). Diamonds become more widespread in the late 19th century United States, with the expansion of diamond mining in Africa (Wexler 2010: 85). By 1938, the diamond company De Beers introduced the idea that two months' salary was a good price for a ring. Today, wedding guidelines in magazines and jewelry stores suggest men should spend three months' earnings on a ring (Wexler 2010: 84). In the late 1940s, De Beers launched its "a diamond is forever" campaign (Wexler 2010: 87;

Love = Diamond: Tiffany Ad

Advertising by jewelry companies reinforces the connection between diamonds and marriage. Seen here is advertising material by the luxury jewelry retailer Tiffany and Co., which makes the connection between love and a diamond ring explicit.

Source: Website screen capture: www.tiffany.ca (8/2/2016)

Ingraham 2008: 79), which encouraged people to see diamonds as tributes of lifelong romantic love—an idea that now has tremendous cultural resonance. In 2006, the film *Blood Diamond* (starring Leonardo DiCaprio) brought a brief period of attention to issues of violence and exploitation in the diamond industry, especially in the diamond mines of Sierra Leone and Angola. Some consumers now seek out "conflict-free" diamonds and there is now an international certification process in place to reduce the number of conflict diamonds in the supply chain. Still, the problem is far from solved. Corrupt companies and criminal networks use free trade zones like Dubai to disguise unethically mined diamonds, evade taxes owed to diamond-producing countries, and devalue legitimately sourced African diamond exports (Partnership Africa Canada 2014: 16). Ultimately, "consumers remain unable to purchase a diamond with certainty that it was not illicitly mined" (Winetroub 2013: 1426). (See https://www.globalwitness.org/campaigns/conflict-diamonds/)

quadrupled from the mid-1980s to the 1990s (Otnes and Pleck 2003: 2). Today, the average wedding costs about $30,000 (Khazan 2014), which is considerable given that 53% of Americans earn less than $30,000 a year (Social Security Administration 2015). The average wedding has 136 guests and involves considerable spending on each component: the reception venue ($14,006), invitations ($439), flowers and décor ($2,141), and photos ($2,556) (Jacobson 2015). In keeping with the gendered understanding of weddings as especially important for women, many wedding expenses center on the bride. On average, brides spend $1,357 on a wedding dress and $617 on wedding day accessories, including jewelry, a headpiece, and/or veil (Jacobson 2015; Market Wired 2014). Spending on engagement and wedding rings has also grown. Whereas a half-carat diamond ring was the norm for brides in the 1980s, the one-carat ring has become a "new standard," and more and more brides wear diamond rings in the two- and three-carat range (Wexler 2010: 80–1, 86).

How do we describe this kind of lavish (and expensive) wedding event? As we mentioned earlier, scholars use the term "white wedding" to describe a marriage celebration featuring some combination of the following elements: a bride in an elaborate white gown, numerous attendants and witnesses wearing formal outfits, a special ceremony (religious or secular), bouquets of flowers, a sumptuous meal and/or a party, and a honeymoon (Ingraham 2008: 5; Arend 2014; Otnes and Pleck 2003: 3). This kind of expensive wedding ritual became popular in North America in the 1950s—an era that emphasized rigid gender roles, along with a renewed cult of domesticity. White weddings declined in popularity in the 1970s, but regained their status in the 1980s, and have been "dominant to the present" (Arend 2014).

The wide range of white wedding expenses (from flowers, to gowns, to centerpieces) has generated a multi-billion-dollar wedding industry. This industry services all different kinds of weddings, and interestingly, lavish weddings are found in all walks of life. Indeed, wedding scholars Otnes and Pleck write: ". . . except on the lowest rungs of the socioeconomic ladder, the decision to plan and execute elaborate weddings is rarely questioned, and seems now to be considered not only a rite but also a right in North American culture" (2003: 3). The wedding industry has become so expansive that Ingraham describes it as the "wedding industrial complex", an industry worth about $58 billion in the US (Ingraham 2008: 41; The Wedding Report 2014). Wedding costs have grown around North America, and are even higher in more expensive locations, like New York City or San Francisco. As people are getting married later in life (28 is the average age in the US), more couples are paying for their own weddings. Parents may still foot some (or all) of the bill, but over half of couples contribute to their weddings, and about 30% pay for their entire wedding (Rivers 2010: 3). Of the couples who completely self-finance their weddings, 10% take out loans and 49% put at least some expenses on credit cards to do so (Rivers 2010: 3).

In an age of massive income inequality, frequent divorce, and widespread pre-marital cohabitation, the rise of bigger and more expensive white weddings is a bit puzzling. Scholars have put forward multiple theories to explain the continuity of this ritual. For one, the popularity of elaborate weddings likely reflects both a continued belief in the value of marriage, as well as social anxieties about its tenuous status (i.e. concern about the possibility of divorce can renew interest in having an elaborate wedding that shows one's commitment to the union) (Otnes and Pleck 2003: 5, 7).

Another way to understand the popularity of the white wedding is to recognize its status as a **ritual**. As discussed in chapter 6, sociologists understand rituals as a set of cultural practices that people perform for symbolic reasons. A ritual is less about achieving a practical goal, and more about the collective meaning it carries. Rituals display and cement a cultural idea—like the idea that marriage is a sacred bond between two people. More generally, rituals provide order in society, foster social solidarity, and inspire a sense of transformation for participants (Otnes and Pleck 2003: 4). For example, think back to your high school graduation. Was it really necessary to gather all those people together in funny gowns in order to hand you your diploma? Of course not. This ritual was a way of collectively celebrating your achievement and symbolically marking your transition to life after high school. Otnes and Pleck argue that the big wedding has become popular as a ritual escape from the world of the mundane, and an opportunity to experience a kind of magic. In that way, white weddings "embody our sacred beliefs in marriage and religion and feature luxury goods that make the couple feel like celebrities for a day" (2003: 13). While our everyday purchases are often bound by the limits of our pocketbook, we are told that this is a day to spare no expense—to dream big, and make that dream a reality. Otnes and Pleck summarize why the wedding ritual retains its popularity, and its inextricable connection to consumer culture:

> The rite of the lavish wedding is increasingly popular because it glorifies both romantic love and the love of "romantic" consumer goods, promises transformation to its participants, provides a repository of memories of this magic and romance, and offers the promise of perfect (e.g. boundless and guilt-free) consumption.
>
> (2003: 19)

For many, the ritual of the white wedding revolves around the bride's dress. The tradition of wearing a white gown is relatively recent, dating back to Queen Victoria's wedding in 1840 (Ingraham 2008: 59). Throughout history, white was not a practical color for working people, as it is hard to keep clean. In European culture, white was the color elite young women wore at the court when they socialized with royal families; as such, this color came to connote a higher social standing (Ingraham 2008: 60). Royal wedding fever kicked in with Queen Elizabeth's 1947 wedding to Prince Philip, leading to an upsurge in popularity of the white wedding dress in the years following World War II (Ingraham 2008: 60). Today, most women plan to get married in some variation of a white gown. Of course, you could actually wear *anything* to get married—jeans and a t-shirt, your pajamas, a Halloween costume, a basic black dress. However, the *white* dress is an important part of the wedding ritual because it embodies a host of symbolic associations—purity, virginity, tradition, and so forth. Having a dress that is white—and that is so special that it is reserved for a single occasion—helps elevate the wedding dress to the ritual level of the sacred, and transcend the everyday level of the profane.

Wedding Dresses: Historic and Modest

Wallis Simpson wears a simple wedding dress when marrying The Duke of Windsor, formerly Edward VIII King of Great Britain, in France on December 10, 1936.

Source: Gettyimages.com # 2639222

Wedding Dresses: Big and Bold

Britain's Lady Diana Spencer's wedding dress (1981) was the source of much admiration and many attempts to copy its grand design. It exemplified the turn in the 1980s towards bigger, more elaborate white wedding dresses; it featured hand embroidery, pearls, antique hand-made lace, as well as a 25-foot long train.

Source: Gettyimages.com # 77494468

When we look at various aspects of the wedding ritual and how they have evolved over time, we see that the desire for a white wedding is not "natural" or inevitable, but a socially constructed ideal. As sociologist Chrys Ingraham writes, "one is not born a bride or with the desire to become a bride", even though the meaning behind weddings is often seen as natural, or "normal" (2008: 4). Indeed, we become accustomed to the idea of a white wedding through processes of socialization that teach us about appropriate gender roles for men and women that are related to cultural ideals of the "good life". In other words, weddings can be seen as a socializing ritual that ushers men and women into state (and sometimes religious) sanctioned marriage. Heterosexuality has a sexual element to it, but it is not simply about sex or romantic attraction. Scholars like Ingraham suggest that heterosexuality is

SOCIOLOGISTS IN ACTION: HISTORICAL COMPARATIVE RESEARCH

History is an academic discipline all its own, but sociologists often find cause to borrow the techniques that historians have developed to provide historical evidence. This borrowing speaks to the overlap that commonly exists between academic disciplines in the social sciences. Between sociology and history, this overlap occurs when researchers use historical methods of data collection and analysis in order to investigate questions about social relationships and social theory. One analytical tool for addressing such questions is the use of comparisons of different sorts. For example, we can understand better why people get married if we compare marriage rates between groups of people with different education levels or different political beliefs or who live in contexts of differing economic constraints. In historical comparative research, the analytical tool of comparison is applied across different historical contexts. This can mean that two or more different societies are compared at a single time in history regarding a specific topic of interest, or that an issue is compared across different historical periods in a single society. Or it might involve a combination of both forms of comparison. Data drawn from historical periods can take on a wide variety of forms. We might have documents from government offices, personal artifacts, mass media productions, corporate files, or evidence from other organizations like churches or voluntary associations.

Did you know that before World War II it was very unusual for a man to wear a wedding band in North America? This finding is explored in a historical comparative article entitled "A 'Real Man's Ring': Gender and the Invention of Tradition". In this research, Vicki Howard (2003) examines etiquette books, bridal magazines, religious publications, and jewelry advertisements over the 20th century in the United States to demonstrate the historical timing of a move to wedding bands for men. (Women's wedding bands have a much longer history.) Howard shows that the establishment of the "double ring ceremony" as a wedding standard can be traced to the 1940s and 1950s. To investigate the question of why this change occurred, she compares the social circumstances under which the double ring ceremony became widely accepted with an earlier period when a proposed change for men's rings was socially rejected. In the 1920s, when the jewelry industry was busy promoting the importance of diamonds for women's engagement rings, they also developed an advertising campaign for an "invented tradition" of men's engagement rings. As we know, the campaign never caught on; today, we find no real tradition of men receiving a diamond engagement ring. However, the jewelry industry's efforts at inventing a tradition of men's wedding bands had more success; it now seems so normal that it is like it has always been true. Why the difference? Howard points to the gender symbolism of each type of ring, and to the changing beliefs and attitudes about the nature of marriage between the 1920s and the 1940s. With the mass separation and loss of World War II, the wedding band for men served as "a token of love and commitment". She writes that "jewelers' efforts to popularize the double ring ceremony succeeded in part because wedding consumption became a patriotic act . . . a wedding band could be presented as a manly object" (Howard 2003: 847).

an institutional force framed around sharply differentiated masculine and feminine gender roles. While there are multiple cultural events that reinforce heterosexuality—such as the high school prom—the wedding is the heterosexual ritual par excellence. In Ingraham's words, "weddings have served as one of the major events that signal readiness and prepare heterosexuals for membership in marriage as an organizing structure for the institution of heterosexuality" (2008: 7). As we discuss below, weddings organize, ritualize, and reflect social issues relating to gender, heterosexuality, race, and class.

3.2. The Wedding "Ideological" Complex

The white wedding is not just a declaration of love or a display of wealth, but can also operate ideologically to promote certain ideals and obscure various forms of inequality. Sociologist Chrys Ingraham (2008) speaks about a wedding *industrial* complex, but she also suggests the presence of a wedding *ideological* complex. To be clear, speaking about the ideological dimensions of a white wedding does *not* mean that brides and grooms are "brainwashed", or that people should feel ashamed of their wedding dreams (a sentiment expressed by some of our students when discussing this topic in class). In chapter 3, we discussed how the term **ideology** refers to an idea, or a collection of ideas, that works to mask relations of domination or exploitation—or to make these things seem natural. We also emphasized that ideology is a *process*, rather than a concrete, unchanging *thing*. Our goal here is to think critically about various dimensions of the white wedding ritual in order to investigate how this ritual can operate ideologically. Next, we discuss how the white wedding relates to various kinds of inequalities.

3.2.1. Gender, Weddings, and Ideology

First, let's look at the relationship between white weddings, gender, and sexuality, and the ways this ritual reinforces patriarchy and heteronormativity. Sociologist Patricia Arend, writes:

> White weddings ritualize and dramatize patriarchal and heteronormative gender relations through such actions as bridal showers that equip women for taking care of a home, the "giving away" of the bride, usually by her father or other male relative, a hyper-emphasis on her appearance relative to the groom's, and the announcement of her name change as part of the couple at the ceremony and/or reception.
>
> (Arend 2014)

We can unpack this idea further by looking at how weddings allow us to perform and police gender (e.g. Kimport 2012: 875; Ingraham 2008; Arend 2014). The white wedding involves two realms that are typically associated with femininity: 1) consumption (especially consumption of decorative items like flowers, fashion, and centerpieces), and 2) love (especially romance and relationship building) (Otnes and Pleck 2003: 11). The white wedding doesn't just reinforce cultural ideals of femininity, but works ideologically to normalize and reproduce gendered *inequalities*. The bride's **femininity** is valorized in the wedding, as seen in the emphasis on her beauty, purity (the white dress), demureness (the wedding veil), and need for protection (she is "given" from father to groom). These feminine ideals naturalize the idea of a weaker, fairer gender, and position the bride in contrast with the groom's **masculinity**, which is associated with greater power. In various wedding rituals we see evidence of the groom's ability to provide financially (he bought her an expensive ring), his strength (he can carry her across the threshold), and his relative dominance in the relationship ("you may now kiss the bride" or "I now pronounce you man and wife"). Some scholars have argued that white weddings are an assertion of traditional gender norms in an age where gender norms are shifting towards more equitable ideals (Coontz 2014). At the same time that women are demanding more power in the public sphere and in their relationships, white weddings reassert the value of traditional femininity. In this way, our cultural interest in the wedding as a sphere of gender segregation and differentiation can be seen as a kind of backlash against women's progress towards equality.

Another way the white wedding sustains gender inequality is in the planning of this ritual. While "wedding planner" is now a paid job title within the wedding industrial complex, most wedding preparations come about as a result of *unpaid* labor. Tamarra Sniezek (2005) interviewed 20 heterosexual couples in California to see who performed the wedding planning labor, and how men and women understood the division of this work. She found that even when couples said they shared this work equally, much more of it was performed by women. Not a single man in her study had purchased or read a wedding magazine or book, or used a wedding organizer to keep track of tasks. Women made strategic efforts to involve men in the planning work, so as not to overwhelm the groom with consumer choices. For example, a bride would do the groundwork researching a wedding item like invitations or centerpieces, and then present her fiancé with two options to choose from at the end of the process.

How did couples make sense of the inequitable burden of wedding planning? Sniezek found that wedding planning was a "tool participants use to understand and construct their relationship" (2005: 222). This meant that even if the woman was doing more of the work, she would assert that the work was equitably divided. When couples did acknowledge inequalities in their wedding planning work, they attributed them to personality (e.g. I *like* these tasks, and my partner doesn't) (2005: 228). Sniezek concludes that the wedding planning process helps construct a "myth of equality" about the relationship that will be used in years to come (2005: 231). This "myth" allows men to do less wedding work, but avoid any scrutiny or blame. Instead, the wedding planning process reinforces the stereotypical idea of women being better suited to certain kinds of tasks (e.g. researching consumer purchases, thinking about the aesthetics of product choices), and men being naturally uninterested and unskilled in these tasks. At the same time, by engaging in this ritualized display of femininity—by being beautiful, the center of attention, and putting on a successful event that everybody enjoys—the bride "gains control over the wedding and a degree of status and attention" (2005: 231). Yet, the social rewards of this day come at a significant cost, as the work of wedding planning is "time-consuming, under-appreciated and stereotypically women's work" (2005: 231). Thus, brides-to-be are faced with an ongoing tension between the benefits and burden involved with the gendered work of planning a white wedding.

3.2.2. Heteronormativity and the Same-Sex Wedding

In addition to gender roles, the wedding ritual involves an ideological process related to **heteronormativity**. As noted above, heteronormativity posits heterosexual relationships as "normal"; the flipside of this norm is that same-sex relationships are seen as **deviant**. Heteronormativity relates to binary gender roles, as it promotes the idea that there are two different types of people—masculine men and feminine women—who are naturally opposite and sexually attracted to each other (Ingraham 2005). Thus, the white wedding perpetuates heteronormativity through the idealized image of a masculine groom and a feminine bride who are engaged in a heterosexual relationship.

The heteronormative legal foundation of white weddings has been challenged with the legalization of gay marriage in multiple national contexts. This is certainly a win for gay people who have been fighting for the right to marry, and who have been historically excluded from the wedding ritual. More and more gay and lesbian couples are taking advantage of the legal opportunity to get married. Between 2013 and 2014, the number of married same-sex couples in the United States tripled to 390,000 (Jow 2015). An estimated 70,000 of the 150,000 same-sex couples living in states where marriage is newly allowed will marry in the next three years (Jow 2015). As a result, some expect that spending on gay weddings could reach $2.62 billion within the first three years of nationwide legality (Williams Institute 2015). But does gay marriage really represent a radical challenge to heteronormativity?

Some activists and scholars argue that the institution of marriage can never be fully reformed from its patriarchal, heteronormative roots (Duggan 2002; Valverde 2006). For example, Suzanna Danuta Walters writes that "marriage is a seriously problematic institution historically rooted in ownership and gender inequality. Put *that* on your wedding cake" (2013: 84). Instead of welcoming the state sanctioning of gay relationships, she argues that "love is no more legitimate or good or valuable if the state makes it official, and garnering a basic victory is not the same as making the world a more genuinely amenable place for sexual difference" (2013: 84).

The legalization of same-sex marriage also raises the question of what other issues may be overshadowed by the focus on marriage rights. For example, the legal status of adoption for gay and lesbian couples remains murky in many states (Carroll 2015), and there are fears that some states may add clauses that allow adoption agencies to discriminate against gay and lesbian couples in response to the legalization of gay marriage (Gates 2015). These inequities persist despite the fact that the American Sociological Association submitted a court briefing stating that "The clear and consistent social science consensus is that children raised by same-sex parents fare just as well as children of different-sex parents" (Manning et al. 2014). Thus, while we see gains in the fight for marriage equality, scholars must remain attentive to the continued oppression faced by LGBTQ families.

While the legalization of gay marriage is understood by many as a victory for gay rights, a key question remains: does the legal possibility of having two grooms or two brides challenge the heteronormative ideas and imagery at the root of traditional white weddings? To address this question, Patricia Arend (2014) surveyed and interviewed women—gay and straight—to investigate why they wanted a white wedding, and asked them to keep a diary detailing their ideal weddings. Arend found that the white wedding was taken for granted as the right way to get married for all of her participants, regardless of sexual orientation. For example, consider this passage about one participant's ideal wedding:

> I think of a large wedding, in a beautiful building or possibly outside, with a guest list of about 300–400 people. A formal event, me in a tux (but with a special style) her in a beautiful wedding dress . . . about five people on each side of the wedding party. Good food, open bar, and a night of dancing, laughing and happiness. Although the number one thing that makes it ideal would be my lover and I being utterly completely in love and glowing as we see each other for the first time on that day.
>
> (Arend 2014: 9)

This vision of an ideal wedding is fairly conventional, but what is exceptional is that this description was elaborated by a lesbian named Janice. For Janice, a 26-year-old White, middle-class ex-Catholic, white weddings are important because they are "beautiful, emotional and romantic" (11). While Janice's access to marriage is an important step towards inclusivity, Arend argues that "heteronormativity is also part of Janice's vision of a wedding, even though she is a lesbian" (11). For example, Janice rejects the idea of two lesbian brides both wearing white wedding gowns, and makes clear that she wants a vision of masculinity and femininity to make it a "real" wedding. Of course, the fact that Janice herself will be wearing a tux challenges conventional ideas of masculinity, since she is performing this role as a woman. Nevertheless, it is striking that this vision of gender differentiation in a white wedding is common in both straight and gay couples. To put this in the terms of the "wedding ideological complex", the white wedding fantasy can work ideologically to normalize the idea of a feminine bride and a masculine groom as foundational to marriage itself, even when white wedding practices are adopted by lesbian couples. Notably, a study of wedding photographs did not find this kind of gender differentiation among gay men (Kimport 2012). In these weddings, both men were shown wearing suits or tuxedos—a display that upholds masculine expectations, but disrupts heteronormativity in that there is not a bride figure in these wedding photos (2012: 875). Thus, we can see how aspects of gay and lesbian weddings can both reinforce and challenge the gender roles and heteronormativity traditionally associated with the white wedding.

3.2.3. Class Inequality, Racial Representation, and the White Wedding Fantasy

The white wedding can also operate ideologically through its relationship to social class, wealth, and inequality. North American popular culture fetishizes glamorous weddings with bejewelled white gowns, large diamond rings, and stretch limos. At the same time, we live in an era of unprecedented inequality. Ingraham writes that the romance of the white wedding works ideologically by "providing images or representations of reality that mask the historical and material conditions of life" (2008: 23), especially the growing gap between the rich and poor. At one level, the romance of a white wedding masks (or at least minimizes) the challenge of *staying* married, especially when you are struggling to make ends meet. As mentioned above, marriage rates are lower and divorce is more common for Americans with less education and lower incomes (e.g. Cherlin 2014a; Coontz 2014; Thompson 2013; Francis and Mialon 2014). This trend reflects the heightened challenge of sustaining a marriage over the long term with chronic financial stressors, and explains why divorce is more likely among those with fewer resources. In short, the material realities of financial family struggles in the United States (and elsewhere) are ideologically obscured by the white wedding's focus on the drama, romance, and luxuries of the day itself (Khazan 2014; Francis and Mialon 2014).

The white wedding also has clear links to the **new consumerism** and **upscale emulation**. Weddings are not just a personal event, but are deeply social and relational, inspired by those around us—including popular celebrity weddings and those portrayed on television shows. Many sitcoms feature a wedding plot, and there are countless wedding-themed reality television shows, like *Say Yes to the Dress, Bridezillas, Four Weddings*, and *I Found the Gown*, just to name a few. Magazines like *People* and *US Weekly* devote numerous pages to celebrity weddings and multiple magazines focus exclusively on wedding preparation. Television shows give visuals to idealized weddings, and give brides-to-be ideas about what their perfect nuptials will look like. For example, many fans of *Sex and the City* coveted the black diamond ring received by the main female protagonist—a ring soon identified as a 3.27-carat, square-shaped, emerald-cut ring worth about $60,000 (Wexler 2010: 88). A black diamond wedding ring trend soon followed, and interested viewers could actually buy the exact ring on designer Itay Makin's website (http://www. itaymalkin.com/collections/sex-and-the-city/products/sex-and-the-city-ring). In short, in a consumer culture, many of us compare our own weddings to the idealized weddings we see in celebrity lifestyles and popular culture— a trend that can lead to overspending, as well as an ideological disconnect between wedding fantasies and classed material realities of marriage.

In addition to obscuring class inequality, the white wedding operates ideologically in the perpetuation of racial inequality. If you scan through the channels of reality television shows or flip through the pages of a bridal

Wedding Ideology for Kids: Bride Barbie

Children can learn to fantasize about a white wedding and its gendered roles through toys like this Princess Bride Barbie (see chapter 7).

Source: Gettyimages.com # 1309888

magazine, it becomes clear that Whites are disproportionately depicted as brides-to-be. For instance, a study of 6,000 advertisements in 57 issues of bridal magazines over 5 years found that only 70 ads (less than 2%) depicted an African American woman as a bride. Moreover, none of the issues featured an African American bride on the cover (Frisby and Engstrom 2006: 12).

Much of the popular literature and marketing in the white wedding industry assumes that its participants are White (Ingraham 2008). When we discussed wedding magazines in class with our students, several women of color pointed out that they did not see themselves reflected in the idealized images on display. In addition to the lack of racial diversity in wedding marketing and popular culture, the reality of the white wedding can be quite different for people from different ethnic and racial backgrounds. For example, some American and Canadian couples have a "two wedding" model where they celebrate with a marriage ritual that is linked to their ethnic heritage (e.g. a traditional Indian or Chinese wedding) as well as having a Western-style white wedding (Otnes and Pleck 2003: 14). Also, not every couple is set on spending as much as possible on the wedding ritual, and rates of wedding expenses vary across racial groups. For example, the average Black couple in the US spends $12,152 on a wedding—less than half of the national average (Ingraham 2008: 49). This evidence suggests that the cultural ideal of the white wedding is not universal, and its links to whiteness go well beyond the bride's white gown. At least some African Americans are less invested in the white wedding fantasy than their White counterparts.

While we don't want to overgeneralize the appeal of the white wedding, there is also sociological data on the growing popularity of this event on a global scale, beyond simply an American phenomenon. Of course, the American white wedding itself is highly globalized, since most of the products are made around the world—the wedding gown sewn in Bangladesh, the diamonds mined in the Congo, and the honeymoon in Fiji. Destination weddings are the fastest-growing segment in the wedding industry (Ingraham 2008: 48), and almost all wedding gowns are made overseas, mostly in China (Ingraham 2008: 70). The Union of Needletrades, Industrial and Textile Employees (UNITE) revealed in 1997 that the seemingly "ethical" gowns for Alfred Angelo, a Philadelphia-based company, were actually produced in Guatemalan factories that employed children for illegally low wages and in unsafe conditions (Ingraham 2008: 74). Brides hoping to break out of the white wedding mold by ethically sourcing their wedding elements, particularly their dress, face a dilemma—ethically sourced dresses can be very expensive, and those you can afford might not be the ones you want to wear (Lipkin 2012:

The White Wedding in Japan

While only a small percentage (1–2%) of Japanese are Christians, 75% of Japanese weddings have a Western-style white wedding ceremony (Ingraham 2008: 74). The white wedding tradition can be employed in a way that is not religious. In this photograph, a Japanese couple is married in a non-religious ceremony in front of 500 shoppers in Mitsukoshi, a luxury Tokyo department store that offers its own wedding services.

Source: Gettyimages.com # 483378942

185). Some high-end retailers are now trying to capitalize on bridal desires for more ethical options. For example, Alfred Angelo released a "Purely Alfred Angelo" line of eco-friendly bridesmaid dresses that are made of natural fabrics like silk and cotton and marketed as waste-reducing because you'll definitely be able to wear them again.

The globalization of the white wedding is not limited to global commodity chains; the ritual itself is now found in multiple national contexts. In Japan, the market for white weddings is on the rise, whereas the number of traditional

Shinto weddings has fallen dramatically (Ingraham 2008: 57). The advent of online image sharing and increasing presence of American-made advertising campaigns in international markets have made wedding photography a potent site of transnational exchange (Lieu 2014: 138). In her study of Taiwanese bridal salons and photography, Bonnie Adrian found that photographers and young couples incorporated elements of Western-style bridal photography into their images (e.g. specific poses, the centrality of the bride, focus on romance, Victorian-style wedding dresses) (2003: 10–12). While these practices sometimes conflicted with local customs and beliefs, these innovations allowed young couples to express generational differences and forge a new vision of marriage as a rite of passage (ibid.).

We have also learned about the globalization of the white wedding from our students, including a Nigerian student named Esther. Esther described how her imagined future wedding combined her own Nigerian wedding ideals with white wedding consumption standards—even though she was not currently in a relationship:

> Coming from a culture [Nigerian] that insists on two weddings, a traditional ceremony and a "white" wedding, I see weddings as a monumental celebratory event in one's life. As a result, I follow various wedding blogs, social media accounts, and designers to keep track of the latest wedding trends. Thus, without a fiancé, I have everything from my wedding venue (country club), reception chairs (chivari), to my dress (Vera Wang), floral arrangement, and makeup planned.

Esther's words demonstrate how the dream of a white wedding holds tremendous cultural appeal. The white wedding has clear links to inequalities of class, race, gender, and sexuality, yet it remains a potent cultural symbol inspiring people—especially young women—in the United States and around the world. This romantic and expensive ritual stimulates billions of dollars in consumer spending. It also creates serious problems of consumer debt, and may work to stigmatize people who can't, or don't want to, fully participate in the white wedding ritual. By enshrining the wedded couple as the normative ideal, unmarried and divorced people may feel like their lives are incomplete, or less socially valued. Even if a person does achieve the cultural "holy grail" of white wedding bliss, the realities of married life often contrast with romantic love ideals. After the honeymoon, the "happy couple" may find themselves with some beautiful photos, a slew of credit card debt, and the challenging work of staying happily married.

THINKING FRAMES

How can each thinking frame help us ponder the sociology of weddings?

Material / Cultural	The white wedding is a powerful cultural ritual that symbolizes ideals of romantic love and promotes heteronormativity. On a material level, this ritual is part of a multi-billion-dollar "wedding industrial complex"; one wedding commodity that has drawn criticism is the diamond ring, and yet ring sales continue.
Think about . . .	Why do you think a diamond ring is such a potent cultural symbol in a wedding? Do you think greater knowledge of the material elements of the diamond industry would challenge its cultural prominence?

Structure / Agency	Ideals of marriage and family have been, and continue to be shaped by structural forces. Capitalist industrialization created a dual sphere model of public sphere roles for men and a feminine cult of domesticity. Now that many women work outside the home, marital roles and expectations have shifted, although equality remains elusive.
Think about . . .	How do working conditions impact our romantic relationships? Do you think the structural conditions of your work life (e.g. pay level, work schedule, status) might impact your sense of agency in your private, romantic life?

Micro / Macro	Microsociological research helps us understand how individuals make sense of the white wedding ideal, and how this ideal is negotiated between couples (e.g. during wedding planning). Macrosociological research has shown how rates of marriage and divorce differ across class, race, and level of education—patterns that have been dubbed the "marriage gap" and the "divorce divide", and which show how marriage is linked to social inequality.
Think about . . .	If you got married, how would you (ideally) divide up the labor of planning a wedding? How do you think the division of labor for wedding planning might reflect larger gender structures? Do you think this might differ for heterosexual and gay/lesbian couples?

ACTIVE LEARNING

Online

"The Bride in Her Head":
Read writer and actor Lena Dunham's (2015) reflections on her own complex relationship with the white wedding dream. How have her feelings about this ritual shifted over time? Source: Dunham, Lena. 2015. The Bride in Her Head. *The New Yorker*, 10 July 2015. http://www.newyorker.com/culture/cultural-comment/the-bride-in-her-head

Going solo:
Read this NYT article by sociologist Eric Klineberg on living alone. After reading it, would you say that living alone is a bad outcome? What are the pros and cons of living alone? How are single people stigmatized in our society? http://www.nytimes.com/2012/02/05/opinion/sunday/living-alone-means-being-social.html?_r=2&pagewanted=all

Discussion/Reflection

Wedding dreams:
Have you ever fantasized about your future wedding? (Or if you are already married, did you fantasize in the past?) If so, when did this fantasy begin, and what does it entail? If not, why do you think the "white wedding" dream doesn't appeal to you? (Hint: consider the role of class, gender, sexual orientation, race/ethnicity, socialization).

Beyond the white wedding:
Have you ever attended a marriage ritual that differed from the traditional white wedding? What were the key features of this ritual? What values were emphasized? (E.g. did these differ from the white wedding's focus on romantic love and consumption?) In what ways did this ritual reproduce or challenge gender roles and heteronormativity?

Sociology Outside the Classroom

Here comes *which* bride?
Look at a popular wedding magazine (e.g. *Brides* or *Martha Stewart Weddings*), or online wedding website (e.g. www.theknot.com). Conduct a mini-coding

exercise where you count the race/ethnicity of the brides depicted across a group of images. Code at least 50 different images, and keep a tally sheet to record their race. Are Whites over-represented in your sample of popular media sources on weddings? How is the "ideal" bride predominantly depicted in these sources?

Regulating same-sex marriage:

Research same-sex marriage policies in different settings around the world. What nation-states have the most and least supportive policies for same-sex marriage and same-sex families? Can you come up with an explanation of why some states are more supportive than others?

Chapter 9

I <3 MY PHONE: TECHNOLOGY AND SOCIAL NETWORKS

INTRODUCING KEY CONCEPTS

In this chapter, we shed light on the tension between group connection and separation by examining a ubiquitous technological device: the phone. Understanding this tension—between group solidarity and social isolation—is central to the modern sociological project. A case study of the phone allows us to examine how sociologists study feelings of togetherness, drawing upon concepts of social capital, social networks *and* homophily. *Phones can be used to create* virtual communities, *allowing consumers to become* prosumers *that create their own culture and sometimes mobilize to demand* social change. *On the other hand, more critical voices suggest that the constant connectivity made possible through our phones can paradoxically produce social isolation, while distracting us from engaging with important social and personal issues. A sociological perspective leads us to question whether alarm about smartphone usage can be classified as a* moral panic *that exaggerates the threat they pose to society. While technological devices like cell phones are clearly an important part of our everyday lives, sociologists caution against* technological determinist *arguments that overemphasize the power of technology driving social change, and tend to produce overly optimistic or pessimistic conclusions.*

1. INTRODUCTION: CHARGING UP OR SHUTTING DOWN?

In 2013, Filipina-American actress and film-maker Charlene deGuzman posted a video to YouTube called "I forgot my phone" (https://www.youtube.com/watch?v=OINa46HeWg8). In this two-minute video, Charlene is shown going through her day phoneless (e.g. hiking, eating at a restaurant, celebrating a birthday). In each of these settings, she finds a world absorbed in their cell phones, paying more attention to their small screens than the people and events going on around them. The video went viral: after a few days, it had been viewed more than 10 million times. At the time of this writing (in 2016), the video had been viewed almost 50 million times.

What was it about this video that struck such a chord? Certainly cell phones have become a ubiquitous part of our consumer landscape and our daily life. They are commonly framed more as a "need" than a "want". Seventy-eight percent of American teenagers have a cell phone (Madden et al. 2013), and the average teen sends about 60 text messages a day (Lenhart 2012). One study suggested that the average American looks at their smartphone for roughly two hours and 57 minutes daily, which is more time than we spend watching television (Brustein 2014). Should we be frightened of a world of spaced-out zombies staring blankly at their tiny screens while important life events unfold around them? A world of smartphone addicts who can't stop themselves from obsessively checking for new messages, or playing countless rounds of Flappy Bird? New technological developments are often simultaneously celebrated and regarded with suspicion, especially new technologies that are used by youth (Payne 2008). As Thurlow states: "On the one hand, young people are talked about as being somehow naturally technology inspired and literate, on the other hand, an image is promoted of young people as being . . . tragic victims of technology" (2007: 219).

As you reflect upon the debates surrounding the smartphone in this chapter, we encourage you to consider whether concerns about this new technology might be considered a **moral panic**. The concept of moral panic was developed by sociologist Stanley Cohen in his 1972 book *Folk Devils and Moral Panics: The Creation of the Mods and Rockers*. In the opening passage of the book, Cohen (1972: 1) defines the concept as follows:

> Societies appear to be subject, every now and then, to periods of moral panic. A condition, episode, person or group of persons emerges to become defined as a threat to societal values and interests; its nature is

presented in a stylized and stereotypical fashion by the mass media . . . socially accredited experts pronounce their diagnoses and solutions . . . Sometimes the panic passes over and is forgotten, except in folklore and collective memory; at other times it has more serious and long-lasting repercussions.

Drawing upon Cohen, we can define a moral panic as widespread anxiety about a particular phenomenon (like a new technology) or group (like youth) that is seen to threaten the fabric of society. Often perpetuated by mass media, moral panics give an exaggerated impression of an issue, representing it as a profound **social problem**.

Given that both technology and youth are seen to represent the future, it is no surprise that young people's relationship to new technologies is the source of particular concern (Livingstone and Haddon 2009). Have you ever heard someone lament the fact that "kids these days" are so technologically connected that they are missing out on the joys of childhood? These kinds of concerns often revolve around ideas of vulnerability. Children are understood to be threatened by the danger of online predators, the deleterious effects of screens on brain development, and the replacement of outdoor play with hours spent in front of a screen. Beyond ideas about the vulnerable child, young people's technology use is also seen as a threat *to others,* whether in the form of cyberbullying, or concerns about a generation of "media-obsessed", self-absorbed youth who don't know how to spell. Scholars of youth and media studies have suggested that part of this anxiety lies in a perceived threat to adult authority (Mazzarella 2007). That is, as young people gain technological skills, they begin to access information directly without the mediation of parents, and are mastering tools that may appear foreign or incomprehensible to older generations (Spigel 2001). Concerns

American Moral Panics: Reefer Madness

Other moral panics in the United States have been concerned with issues like sexuality, terrorism, and drug use. Pictured here is a poster for the 1936 film Reefer Madness, *which attempted to demonstrate the dangers of marijuana use by portraying its users as becoming violent and deranged as a result. While viewers today may find the depictions amusingly exaggerated, the film is emblematic of the moral panic over marijuana in the 1930s.*

Source: http://www.loc.gov/pictures/item/yan1996 000470/PP/OR Gettyimages.com # 153084787

about the risks of new technologies are often used to justify parental surveillance and regulation of young people's social media activities (Shade 2011). Are these practices warranted, or are they the product of a moral panic?

In this chapter, we examine the fears and the possibilities associated with the technology of the smartphone. We begin with a brief story of how the phone entered our homes and eventually became a kind of virtual appendage that we can't leave the house without. Then, we explore paradoxes embodied in the smartphone. Paradox is a common theme when sociologists study technological innovation. Rather than seeing technology as an exciting panacea for the world's problems (a utopian view) or a dangerous threat to society as we know it (a dystopian view), a sociological approach works to appreciate the complexities and contradictions of technological developments. More specifically in this chapter, we want to explore how the technology of the phone sheds light on the paradoxical modern phenomena of connectivity combined with social isolation.

2. A BRIEF HISTORY OF THE PHONE

Try to place yourself back in time. Imagine a world where communication was conducted primarily in person, or perhaps through a handwritten letter or the pages of a printed text. For most of human history, this was how humans communicated—between real people, or by written correspondence at a slow pace. The telephone was invented by Alexander Graham Bell in 1876, and emerged alongside other miraculous new technologies of the industrial age, like steam-based transportation systems. At the time, this incredible new technology was seen as both a wonder and a cause for alarm (Green 2007; Fischer 1992). The idea of people speaking in real time across great distances was truly amazing, but it was also frightening. The invention of the telephone—as well as the invention of steam-powered trains and ships—made it possible to move ideas (and capital) more quickly than was previously possible (Fischer 1992). It also blurred the boundaries between the public realm of work and the private realm of the home, as intrusions of the outside world could now enter into domestic life (Marvin 1988: 6; Katz and Aakhus 2002). Originally, it was thought that the telephone was a technology that men would use to do business from the comfort of their own home. However, it soon became apparent that telephone usage was not restricted to men, but also allowed women to communicate with each other in their private roles. At this time, some worried that speaking on the phone would compromise, or even replace face-to-face communication (Fischer 1992: 1). This concern about isolation and compromised social relationships is a worry that we hear echoed today in relation to more recent technological innovations.

Today, the idea of basic telephone technology is a mundane feature of everyday life for most of us in the Global North. In fact, Alexander Graham Bell's version of the wired telephone might seem archaic to you, since many people no longer even own a landline. Cell phone technology expanded dramatically in the 1980s and 1990s in Europe and North America. Instead of relying on "old-fashioned" telephone wires, cell phones are a highly sophisticated form of radio, sending signals out over hundreds of radio frequencies. A key change that this technology brought to phone communication is mobility. Your phone not only allows you to communicate with faraway people in real time, but also allows you to do this as you yourself are moving (provided you have a cell phone signal). The mobility of cell phones has allowed people to plan events more spontaneously—a phenomenon that scholars call "microcoordination" (Gardner and Davis 2014: 94). (Indeed, one of us—Kate—was the last person to get a cell phone in her social circle, and she remembers friends expressing frustration that they had to plan ahead in order to meet up.)

With the release of the iPhone in 2007, the world of cell phones became a world of *smart*phones. In its new form, your phone was not only a mobile communication device, but a place to check email, listen to music, take and store photos, get directions, watch TV, and play videogames. With the rise of social media sites like Facebook, Twitter, Instagram, and Tumblr, your phone is a device for viewing as well as contributing to Internet culture—for instance, by updating your status on Facebook, sharing a photo on Instagram, retweeting a link on Twitter, or posting a video to YouTube. Media scholar Henry Jenkins describes the new roles fostered through digital technology in terms of "participatory culture". He suggests that "[r]ather than talking about media producers and consumers as occupying separate roles, we might now see them as participants who interact with each other according to a new set of roles that none of us fully understands" (2006: 3). Other scholars have used the term **prosumer** (an amalgamation of *producer and consumer*) to describe the emergence of a new hybrid role within Internet culture: culture that we don't simply consume, but also actively produce (Ritzer and Jurgenson 2010). Smartphones are one of many new technologies that allow us to become prosumers, producing and consuming content simultaneously. Yet Jenkins warns that although we may be engaging in participatory culture, power relations persist, since "corporations—and even individuals within corporate media—still exert greater power than any individual consumer"

The Facebook Wall

Social media users become prosumers by creating content and sharing it in online venues like their Facebook friends' "walls". At Facebook headquarters in San Francisco, this kind of "participatory culture" is fostered through a physical "Facebook Wall."

Source: Gettyimages.com # 463388657

(Jenkins 2006: 3). This makes participatory culture a great case for exploring dynamics of structure and agency. You may decide what content to share on Facebook, but this platform is the creation of a massive corporation. Facebook not only controls the layout and features that structure the site, it also profits from your participation through targeted advertising. No matter how many "friends" you have, this is not an even playing field.

While smartphones facilitate our connections to others, they are a highly individualized technology. Telephones were once a shared household item, but smartphones are now typically linked to a particular person, with each member of the household possessing their own device. With its own collection

WHO MADE YOUR PHONE?

Many of you probably own an Apple product. In 2015, Apple CEO Tim Cook announced that the company had sold over 700 million iPhones (Gallagher 2015). One survey found that half of American households owned at least one Apple product, with the average household owning 1.6 devices (Gralnick 2012). Have you ever thought about where these millions of iPhones, iPads and MacBooks come from—that is, beyond the Apple Store? If the answer is "no", you're not alone. When Nicki Lisa Cole and Tara Krishna (2013) compared how Apple was covered in American and Chinese news media, they found that American coverage tended to focus on the brand image—the cultural ideas that we associate with Apple products and consumers. Often overlooked in these stories are the structural and material conditions in which Apple products are made, such that many North American consumers are unaware of the "systemic and extensive labor and environmental abuses coursing throughout Apple's Chinese supply chain" (Cole and Krishna 2013: 331). A particularly glaring absence in American media coverage is the voice of Chinese factory workers, who are often poor migrants from rural peasant communities. These workers describe horrendous labor conditions involving long hours in unsafe environments with no legal recourse—a situation that leads to a range of physical and mental health issues, as well as high rates of worker suicide (Cole and Krishna 2013: 336). In addition to labor exploitation, the ongoing expansion of new factories into the countryside has led to the razing of agricultural land and the forced relocation of rural communities, as well as air, water, and soil pollution. Poor air quality from the factories has caused some nearby residents to keep their windows closed at night to avoid dizziness and nosebleeds (Cole and Krishna 2013: 344). A follow-up report in 2015 found that despite Apple's claims to have addressed these issues, serious labor and environmental violations persist (Cole and Chan 2015). So while phones help some people forge virtual connections nearby and even around the world, a sociological perspective reminds us these are material goods produced within a global supply chain—one that has deeply troubling connections to labor exploitation and environmental degradation.

of photos, music, apps, and perhaps a distinctive protective case, each smartphone is a unique reflection of its owner. As Gardner and Davis (2014: 60) write,

> The apps arrayed on a person's smartphone or tablet represent a fingerprint of sorts—only instead of a unique pattern of ridges, it's the combination of interests, habits and social connections that identify that person.

Because of its connection to various social media tools, like Facebook and Twitter, your smartphone is also an electronic embodiment of your **social**

iPhone Factory Conditions

This image depicts workers on the assembly line at a Foxconn electronics manufacturing plant in Jiangxi Province, China. Foxconn is the world's largest electronics maker and its employees assemble and make parts for many well-known products, including the iPhone.

Source: APimages.com # 120518174954

networks—a concept we will explore below. Your phone is not simply a device for making calls, but also a tool for facilitating social connections to your close friends, faraway family, and distant acquaintances.

The story of the smartphone will continue to unfold. New versions are regularly released, with new features and new capabilities. Apps are continually being developed. Consumers are usually not content to simply own a phone; about half of smartphone users get rid of a working phone to replace it with the newest model available (Swift 2015). While many consumers assume that newer is better, our sociological imaginations encourage us to dig deeper. How do sociologists evaluate the ways that technologies like smartphones impact our social lives?

3. TECHNOLOGY AND SOCIAL CHANGE

There is no single theory to understand technological innovation, but a few key concepts are helpful to get started. First, what do we mean by "technology"? The term technology is relatively recent; it rose to prominence in the 1900s with new forms of machinery and industrialized mass-production processes (e.g. railroads, steam-powered engines). A basic, but still useful, definition of technology was coined by sociologist Read Bain in 1937. According to Bain, technology refers to "all tools, machines, utensils, weapons, instruments, housing, clothing, communicating and transporting devices and the skills by which we produce and use them" (860). Bain insisted that technology was not limited to *material* objects (i.e. the *stuff* of technology), but also included non-material *cultural* factors, like the knowledge and skill required to make those objects (1937: 862). Bain's writing makes clear that 1930s sociologists were already studying how technology allowed people to forge connections across time and place. He observed how "new types of social integration are dependent upon the printed word, the radio, the cinema, science, new machines, rapid movement from place to place and the still more rapid diffusion of knowledge of what is happening thousands of miles away" (1937: 863).

New technologies create possibilities for social connections between people who are not physically close, but they also generate new challenges and concerns. A useful way of understanding technology's mixed impact is the concept of the "integral accident" developed by the French theorist, Paul Virilio (2007). An integral accident describes how technological innovation brings with it the possibility that each invention will create its own set of problems. Therefore, to invent a new technology is simultaneously to invent

Imagined Communities

According to social thinker Benedict Anderson, one specific technological innovation—the printing press and mass distribution of newspapers—led unprecedented numbers of people to consider themselves members of the same national community, despite never meeting. Anderson described this as an imagined community (a concept introduced in chapter 6). The headline in this image shows how even basic technologies like a newspaper can work to generate social connections. In this case, the newspaper creates a sense of a unified Japanese nation facing the threat of a missile attack.

Source: Gettyimages.com # 508807316

an "accident". As Virilio describes, "to invent the sailing ship or the steamer is to invent the shipwreck. To invent the train is to invent the rail accident of derailment. To invent the family automobile is to produce the pile-up on the highway" (2007: 10). In each of these cases, the accident is *integral*, or inherent, to the technology itself. We could add to this list: to invent the cell phone is to invent texting while driving, or less catastrophically, lonely meals where everybody glances at their screen instead of talking to each other. The concept of the integral accident draws attention to a key technological paradox: technological innovation facilitates the possibility of positive social transformation as well as the potential to contribute to social problems.

As sociologists, we can approach technology as a lens focusing on the dynamics of a changing society. The idea of **technological determinism** positions technology as the key driver of **social change**: the widespread alteration of norms, values, practices, and/or institutional arrangements within or across contexts. Sociologists typically reject this idea, and see technology as one of many factors that shape social transformation. Even so, the concept of technological determinism is useful because we often see this idea at work within popular debates—whether the power of technology is presented through a utopian or a dystopian view.

A utopian view of technological determinism is evident in statements suggesting that the Internet will overcome all social barriers, or that cell phones can create a radical new sharing economy that eliminates loneliness and benefits all. A dystopian view of technological determinism comes through in claims that cell phones are corrupting today's youth, or that Facebook is making us image-obsessed and socially isolated. These extreme positions have a long history—as noted above, people have feared and praised new technologies throughout the ages. But the deterministic perspective undermines a key facet of sociological thinking, which is to see technology as just one of many complex forces shaping human life. As we will see below, technologies like the cell phone do not have universal impacts—either positive or negative.

DO "EASY" TECHNOLOGIES NECESSARILY MAKE OUR LIVES EASIER?

Technology theorist Timothy Wu argues that contemporary American culture promotes the **hegemonic** ideal that technology should always be as easy as possible. "Easy" or "convenience" technologies require "little concentrated effort and yield predictable results" (Wu 2014), like heating up a frozen pizza. Indeed, it's hard to argue with the pleasures or the appeal of easy technology. Simplicity is a big part of the genius of Apple products like the iPhone (Edson and Beck 2012; Thomke and Feinberg 2009). You pull your phone out of the clean, modern box and encounter a set-up that is very simple and straightforward; within minutes, usually without reading any kind of instruction booklet, you are ready to operate your new device. Can you imagine if operating this handheld computer required a detailed understanding of its workings? Without easy technologies like our phones, we wouldn't be able to quickly order a pizza, let alone post a review of the pizza place on Yelp, or Instagram an artful photo showcasing its delicious toppings.

While easy technologies create the pleasure of convenience, Wu suggests that there is a dark side to this ease. First of all, easy technologies haven't delivered on the promise of giving us more time for thought, reflection, and leisure (Schor 1998). Today many people feel hopelessly overworked. Their cell phones don't free them from work, but electronically tether them to the job so that they are always on-call (even in non-emergency professions like "college professor"). Many workplaces now use messaging apps like Slack, which facilitates constant connection among employees and was described in the *New York Times* as "one of the fastest growing business apps in history" (Manjoo 2015). The upside of this technology is "freedom from the job site" (Agger 2011: 120), allowing employees to work remotely, or to travel while on the job. But with that mobility comes the issue of "no downtime" so that many workers feel like there is virtually no time when they are off work (Agger 2011: 120–1). Wu argues that as each individual task may have become "easier" (e.g. it's easier to send a quick text or email than write, stamp, and send a handwritten letter), we are now left with a larger volume of small jobs (e.g. addressing an inbox with hundreds of new messages). In Wu's words, "we have become plagued by a tyranny of tiny tasks, individually simple but collectively oppressive" (2014). So we might be left with the question: is convenience technology really all that convenient?

To be clear, it's not that "easy" technology always or only creates social problems. Many of us appreciate the fact that cell phones are now so simple to use that even self-described technophobes can get the hang of texting or consulting a map on their phone. As Wu writes, "it isn't somehow wrong to use a microwave rather than a wood fire to reheat leftovers". We don't want to romanticize labor-intensive ways of life any more than we want to overstate the emancipatory impact of new technologies. At the same time, it seems that "easy" technology may not always free up time, and may conveniently facilitate the expansion of capitalist work cultures into more and more aspects of our lives.

In sociology, and in the social sciences more generally, we try to avoid technological determinist perspectives because they are too simplistic. Technology is important, but it is not the only factor shaping social change—nor does it shape all of our lives in the same way. We also need to consider factors like culture, class, gender, and age in the uses and implications of technology. One of the many factors overlooked by technological determinist approaches is the significance of individual agency within our technology-saturated lives. As we discuss below, attention to agency has been particularly important for youth studies scholars who have challenged the image of a technology-controlled teenager to instead emphasize the diverse ways young people use digital technologies to forge identities, meaning, and community in their everyday lives (e.g. boyd 2014; Buckingham 2006; Jenkins 2006).

4. PROMISE OR PERIL? THE PARADOX OF NEW TECHNOLOGY

Technological innovations like smartphones often have paradoxical implications within society. Taking a sociological approach to smartphones, we can see how they simultaneously bring us together (e.g. allowing us to share jokes with friends by texting throughout the day), and drive us apart (e.g. causing feelings of isolation, as shown in the video "I forgot my phone"). One of our students, a White Canadian student named Caroline, reflected upon her own ambivalent relationship to her phone:

> I didn't get a cell phone until I was in grade 10. I felt like I was the last one to get one and once I did I felt like I finally fit in with the crowd and was considered "cool". But over the years my cell phone has, in many ways, become a distraction. Unfortunately, it is still something I would not be able to live without because I rely on it too much and because it has been a part of my life for so long.

For Caroline, getting a phone was a key part of "fitting in" and connecting with others. Nevertheless, she worries about the central place that this technology now holds in her life. Our smartphones offer new possibilities, but also create new problems. In this section, we discuss these contradictions in relation to two central sociological paradoxes of the smartphone and its ability to forge social connections while simultaneously creating social isolation. The first paradox concerns the loneliness and isolation that may coexist with instant connection in our wired worlds. The second paradox concerns the potential of smartphones to distract us, while also providing opportunities to facilitate projects demanding social change.

Paradox #1. The Loneliness of Instant Connection

The first sociological paradox surrounding the smartphone involves the potential and pitfalls of instant connection. Mobile devices clearly have much to offer our social lives, allowing us to connect, communicate, and cooperate. However, there are those who question the social value of this connection. Some research suggests that mobile communication tools may, paradoxically, be linked to loneliness and social alienation. In this section, we use the concepts of social capital and alienation to investigate the positive and negative aspects of cell phone connections.

The concept of **social capital** (discussed in chapters 4 and 6) refers to the form of social currency that comes from your relationships with others—how many people you know, who they are, and the degree to which these relationships can help you access opportunities. To some extent, the idea of social capital can be traced back to the classical sociological idea that being connected to others can have positive consequences, and serve as an antidote

Alone with Our Phones

Together but alone at a Connecticut Starbucks.
Source: Gettyimages.com # 469934006

to **anomie** (Portes 1998: 2) (see chapter 5 for a discussion of anomie). Today, the term social capital is often used to describe the connections, information, and social relationships that help people expand and capitalize on their social networks. Have you ever got to skip the line at a bar because of your connections? Or accessed free childcare from a neighbor? That's social capital at work. Within sociology, these kinds of social ties are referred to as **social networks**—the links we have to others through social interactions (Chriss 2007). Social networks can consist of strong ties (i.e. people you know very well, like close friends and family) as well as weak ties (i.e. acquaintances you might not confide in, but can help connect you to opportunities) (Granovetter 1973). While our close relationships often feel the most important to us, sociologist Mark Granovetter (1973) found that *weak* ties are also a powerful source of social status. This is especially true in the working world, where the question of "who you know" can often be the ticket to a new position or promotion. Weak ties provide access to different networks, since our distant acquaintances tend to know people we don't. What's more, sociological research has found that our access to networks is clearly shaped by our social location (e.g. gender, race, class). In part, this is because social networks tend to reflect the pattern of **homophily**: the tendency to form bonds with those who are similar to us. In the words of McPherson, Smith-Lovin, and Cook (2001), "similarity breeds connection".

While having a lot of social capital has a positive dimension (e.g. helping people out), it is not without its pitfalls: strongly linked communities can create a culture of conformity, promote nepotism, and marginalize people on the basis of age, race, gender, or other characteristics that mark them as a social outsider (Portes 1998: 15–17). Even if you are someone who values diversity, there is a good chance that many people in your social network will share aspects of your social location, such as your social class, ethnicity, or level of education. The sociological significance of these patterns is not only about understanding similarity and difference, but also about inequality and discrimination. In a world structured by racism, sexism, and other inequalities, some people have access to more connections to others, and those connections have different social power. For example, a White, upper-middle-class kid who takes tennis lessons at a country club will have access to powerful social networks from a young age, and these connections can open up a range of future opportunities. Recall from our earlier discussion in chapter 4 that Bourdieu theorized three types of capital: 1) economic, 2) cultural, and 3) social. In this case, the child's social capital can be converted into future economic capital, such as when he uses his tennis club connections to get a job. It can also be converted into cultural capital, such as when his parents use their friendship network to gain insider knowledge on the best school for their kids (Ball 2003).

Many sociologists believe that social capital has been declining since the 1950s. One of the most well-known versions of this story was put forward in Robert Putnam's (2000) famous book, *Bowling Alone*. Putnam emphasizes the positive dimensions of social capital. In his words, "Working together is easier in a community blessed with a substantial stock of social capital" (1993: 35–6). He argues that civic association has been steadily declining across cohorts born after World War II, and that a decline in social capital has emerged alongside a growth in **individualism**. For example, since the 1980s, the number of very close friends that people regularly confide in has declined by one third (McPherson et al. 2006), and the level of trust people have in strangers has also diminished (Gardner and Davis 2014: 99). The title of Putnam's book presents the case of bowling as an example of these larger trends: although many people still go bowling, significantly fewer people bowl in *leagues* than in previous decades. Putnam argues that the decline of social capital has problematic implications for a thriving democracy, which requires networks of citizens who are actively engaged in social life.

What does the decline of social capital and the rise of individualism have to do with technology? Some sociologists argue that new Internet technologies (like smartphones) facilitate the formation of **virtual communities** that can compensate for the loss of social capital in our offline lives. Even if we go "bowling alone", as Putnam claims, we may form online communities that are socially and emotionally supportive (Shirky 2008). Online networks extend beyond our physical proximity, allowing us to connect with like-minded individuals outside of our immediate surroundings. This can be particularly important for marginalized groups, such as LGBTQ youth who lack access to supportive relationships offline. In their research with American youth, Gardner and Davis point to a "broadening of acceptable identities" linked to the expansion of online technology, meaning that it is now "OK to be a geek; it's OK to be gay" (2014: 61). The girl bloggers in their research emphasized the value of having the opportunity "to express their more marginalized identities online" (Gardner and Davis 2014: 90). At a time when "confidant networks have closed in on a smaller core group" (McPherson et al. 2006: 372), technology can also facilitate the formation of ties that bridge social boundaries; people who frequently use the Internet and share photos online tend to have larger and more racially and politically diverse discussion networks (Hampton et al. 2009: 27–8).

While virtual communities clearly provide opportunities for connection, some scholarship cautions that social media can promote broad social networks that are relatively shallow. Even if we're "friends" with a lot of people on Facebook, these relationships may be relatively superficial, and unhelpful in times of need. In these conditions, people may feel isolated despite their membership in online communities, and networks may lack norms of reciprocity. (Consider your own network of Facebook friends. How many of these people would you feel comfortable asking for help on moving day?) Bourdieu's concept of social capital was not only about the *number* of connections we have, but also the *strength* of these bonds. In a context of deeply connected virtual lives, we may nevertheless experience a sense of **alienation**. In chapter 3 we discussed how Marx used the concept of alienation to describe the way workers are alienated from the goods they produce in a capitalist system. Beyond this specific Marxist usage, scholars use the term alienation in a more general sense to refer to estrangement from oneself and others. When we feel socially isolated, out of touch with ourselves, and lacking a strong sense of purpose, we can describe ourselves as alienated. These sorts of feelings may

Virtual Communities, Offline Connections

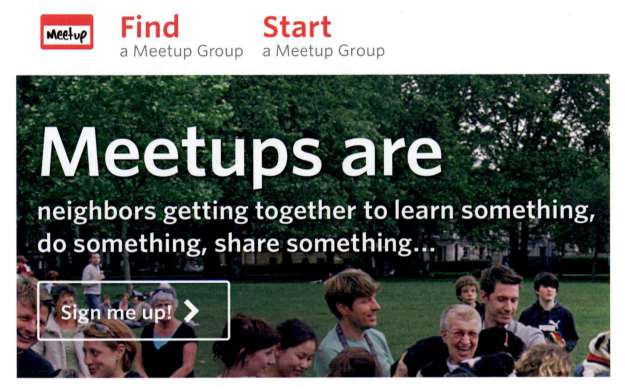

Virtual communities can also promote the development of offline connections. Online services like Meetup, one of the largest of its kind, allow users to form groups around a particular interest or concern and to organize local face-to-face gatherings with like-minded people.

Source: Website screen capture: meetup.com

arise from shifting a significant proportion of our social networks online (Turkle 2011).

While some studies have raised concerns that virtual communities leave us alienated and lacking social capital, others have pointed to evidence that we use cell phones and social media to facilitate social connections. Williams and Merten (2011: 165–6) found that parents "perceived family connectedness to improve with technology [use] that increased family members' exposure to one another"; more Internet connections can mean more communication and connectivity within the family. In addition, there is now a considerable body of research documenting the diverse ways young people use digital technologies to forge and strengthen social bonds outside of the family, rather than

The ME ME ME Generation

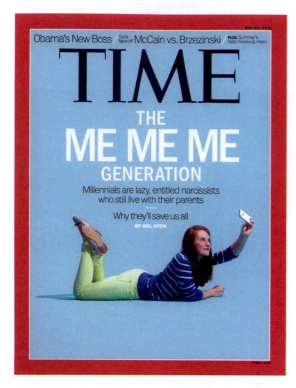

This cover for a 2013 issue of TIME *Magazine features a young woman taking a "selfie" and offers a common adult depiction of young people and Millennials as a cohesive group obsessively preoccupied with technology. The large font text "ME ME ME" and the young woman's positioning on her stomach with her feet in the air portray youth as particularly self-absorbed and ineffectual. Recent critical research on youth and technology takes issue with dominant portrayals like this one and suggests that they overstate technology's influence on young people's lives.*

Source: *TIME Magazine* cover: http://content.time.com/time/covers/0,16641,20130520,00.html

eroding them (boyd 2010; Buckingham 2006; Jenkins 2006; Ito et al. 2010; Kahne, Lee and Feezell 2013). Mimi Ito and colleagues (2010) at the University of California conducted extensive research exploring youth's engagement with new technologies, involving over 5000 hours of online observation and over 800 interviews. They found that most young people used social media to extend and develop the networks they were a part of offline through school, sports, local organizations, etc. Their use of technology was primarily a virtual means of "hanging out". Many of the teens in this study reported that "engaging with social media is important for maintaining and developing friendships with peers" (boyd 2010: 79). A smaller group of young people in the Ito et al. (2010) study used new technologies to participate in communities that they didn't have access to offline, forging connections with distant others who shared interests in things like creative writing, hip-hop, or video editing. In addition to expanding their social networks, these youth also valued the knowledge and sense of expertise they gained through connecting with a broader community of young people who shared a specific set of interests. While emphasizing these kinds of positive tech experiences, many youth studies scholars warn against romanticizing the relationship between youth and technology—a utopian vision of technologically savvy young people who are liberated by their smartphones. Herring (2008) critiques common assumptions about the "Internet generation" (largely perpetuated by adults), which ignore the diversity of young people's lives and exaggerate the extent to which youth are determined by technology.

Cell phone, Internet, and social media usage generate new challenges for youth and their families, such as cyberbullying (Williams and Merten 2011: 166). Those who are concerned about the negative impact of smartphones also suggest that the pressure to present the best version of yourself via real-time social media

SOCIOLOGISTS IN ACTION: SOCIAL NETWORK ANALYSIS

Social network analysis is an area of sociology that explores patterns in the formation, composition, and strength of social bonds. While qualitative methods like ethnography and focus groups allow us to observe interpersonal interactions, quantitative methods are useful for understanding the broader constellation of relationships in which these interactions emerge. Social networks can be depicted using sociograms, which are models representing networks of social ties. Social ties are conceptualized as personal relationships, from loose acquaintances (which are called weak ties), to close friends and family (called strong ties). Networks can vary in their size (the number of ties to other people) and in how densely they are organized. In some networks, everyone knows everyone else in that network, making it high density. In other networks, people are connected through only knowing one or a few other people in the network, making it low density. The people who connect many others in a network who would otherwise be unconnected are central nodes. Through understanding people's ties, the size and density of their network, and their centrality within a network, sociologists can better understand a large number of important outcomes, such as people's employment opportunities and successes, their health status, and their consumption choices. Sociologists have been graphing and analyzing social networks since the 1930s (Wasserman et al. 2005), but interest in this area of research has intensified with the emergence of the Internet and new communication technologies.

In 2009, the Pew Research Center released a report on "Social Isolation and New Technology" (Hampton et al. 2009), which compared the social networks of people who use various forms of technology (including cell phones) with those who don't. Among people with similar demographic characteristics (such as education and age), the study found that "ownership of a mobile phone and participation in a variety of Internet activities were associated with larger and more diverse core discussion networks" (Hampton et al. 2009). In addition, they found that those who were active online were also engaged within public spaces, such as libraries and community centers. This research challenges the claim that our technology-filled lives are making us socially isolated. The authors were careful to point out that their analysis couldn't identify cause and effect (e.g. they couldn't claim that cell phones are the cause of expanded social networks); however, they could confidently state that "technology use is often strongly associated with larger and more diverse social networks" (Hampton et al. 2009). (Refer back to chapter 7 for the distinction between correlation and causation.) Thus, while historical data shows a decline in the size and diversity of our social networks since the 1980s, this research suggests that our cell phones are not a clear culprit.

updates can contribute to anxiety and alienation. One study found that college students who logged more time on Facebook thought of their own lives as less happy than other people's lives; people who had a lot of "friends" that they didn't know directly also believed that other people were happier (Hui-Tzu, Chou, and Edge 2012). Gardner and Davis also found that "youth take care to present a socially desirable, *polished* self online", and that at least for some youth, managing this "externally oriented" self is exhausting and stressful (2014: 63, 67) (In chapter 10, we'll look more closely at sociological theories of how the "self" is constructed through interactions with others). Though our phones allow us to do many amazing things, some believe that they aren't "well suited to support the kind of deep connection that sustains and nourishes relationships" (Gardner and Davis 2014: 102).

The question of whether our connections are enriched or impoverished through cell phones and social media is not at all straightforward. In fact, sociological research challenges us to move beyond "either/or" debates to explore the diverse and sometimes contradictory implications of new technologies within our lives. A sociological perspective critiques a technological determinist approach that adopts a singular focus on technology as the sole agent driving change. Sociologists examine how our social lives are shaped—and compromised—by technologically mediated relationships, but also how people use technologies to deepen and extend social networks.

Paradox #2. Virtual Distractions and "Real"-World Problems

Anyone who has a smartphone knows that this technology can provide us with seemingly endless entertainment, creative outlets and positive distractions. In addition to mindless games that keep us occupied while riding the bus or waiting in line, such entertainment can also be a source of connection to others. For example, dana boyd shows how young people use Snapchat—an app for sharing photos or videos that disappear after 10 seconds—to share "inside jokes, silly pictures and images that were funny only in the moment" (2014: 64). As we discussed earlier, within participatory culture we are not simply consuming media produced by others; instead, we take up a new hybrid role as prosumers. We may be entertained by our phones, but we are also entertaining others—whether by writing imaginative fan fiction, or simply commenting on a friend's Instagram photo.

While smartphones keep us connected and entertained, some have suggested that this technology can distract us from learning about and mobilizing to address real-world problems and social issues. For example, we may be really, really good at Candy Crush, but know very little about the workings of government. Of course, cell phones aren't the first thing in history to be criticized as a mind-numbing distraction. Critics of the Roman empire (circa A.D. 100) noted the power of "bread and circuses" to keep the poor distracted from their plight. Karl Marx once said that religion is the "opiate of the masses", meaning that religion was like a drug that made people passive about the oppressive society they were living in. Building on Marx, Herbert Marcuse wrote about the "distractions" of the culture industry in the 1960s. He was part of a group of theorists called the **Frankfurt School,** who brought a Marxist perspective to culture. The term "culture industry" was developed by two other Frankfurt theorists, Theodor Adorno and Max Horkhiemer, who drew attention to the link between popular culture and capitalism. They argued that just like other goods, pop culture is churned out in a system of mass production that is ultimately designed to generate profit. Building on Adorno and Horkhiemer, Marcuse argued that through this process capitalism creates "false needs" once people's basic needs are satisfied. In the context of consumerism, these false needs drive a cycle of endless desire, shopping and purchasing. From this perspective, new consumer technologies can help resolve the crisis of meaninglessness and alienation people experience in capitalism, and thus keep the system going. They give us something to get excited about and to save money for (e.g. the new iPhone is out!), and distract us from the forms of inequality and exploitation that surround us. Drawing from these critiques, Ben Agger (2011) argues that we are now living in a kind of "iTime" characterized by a lack of clear boundaries between private time and professional time; work expands out of the 9–5 office into the home, evenings, and weekends. Agger suggests that because our smartphones blur the line between work and play, they may make us less likely to identify exploitation—like Apple's troubling labor and environmental practices, discussed above. In Agger's words, "The Internet is a massive culture-industry machine" in which we are "diverted from our own alienated everyday lives and from the larger questions" (2011: 126). From this perspective, as we become enmeshed in the world of our smartphones, we become detached from our own lives, as well as the broader social and political issues shaping our lives and generating social exploitation.

Does this mean that new technologies always have the effect of dulling our political consciousness? Not necessarily. In fact, our smartphones—and the social media that they connect us to—can also alert us to injustices going on around the world, encourage a more expansive **framing** of social problems, and even allow us to become involved in **social movements** (see chapter 3). At a moment when mainstream news outlets are owned by a small number of powerful corporations, we can use new technologies to seek out a range of alternative perspectives through independent media, and add our own voices to a more inclusive public conversation about what are the key social problems of the day. Citizens can use the connectivity of a smartphone to find out about social injustice, to sign online petitions, and to get more involved politically. For example, new technologies were credited with at least some of the activism that took place during the Arab Spring, a series of political uprisings through-out Tunisia, Egypt, and several other countries in 2011 (Duffy 2011). Of course, many activists and scholars have been quick to point out that it was the *people*, not the *technology* itself that created this social movement. (There's that pesky technological determinism again.) But there is no denying the important role that technology played in facilitating the formation of activist networks and communications, at both local and transnational scales. It is also worth noting that cell phone users are more likely to belong to voluntary associations (e.g. a youth group, church, or community organization) in their communities than are non-users (Hampton et al. 2009).

Returning to the topic of youth and technology, scholars have challenged the commonly held perception that young people today are "apathetic" by pointing to the diverse ways in which many youth become politically engaged online (Kahne, Lee, and Feezell 2013). For example, young people have made

Facebook and the Arab Spring

Activists used social networking platforms like Facebook to organize protests during the Arab Spring. Pictured here is an Egyptian man holding a sign praising Facebook during a demonstration in Cairo's Tahir Square in 2011.

Source: Gettyimages.com # 108877129

important contributions to the "Black Lives Matter" social movement through various social media campaigns. After the 2014 police shooting of 18-year-old Michael Brown in Ferguson, Missouri, youth of color drew attention to the contrasting images of Brown that circulated in the media—images that gave very different impressions of the young man who had been killed. Using the hashtag #IfTheyGunnedMeDown, African American youth posted contrasting photos of themselves—one fitting stereotypes of a "respectable" student, the other fitting stereotypes of a "troublemaker"—and asked, "What photo would the media use?" Using their phones, these young people inserted their voices into the public conversation about issues of systemic racism, media

Hashtags in the Real World

Source: Gettyimages.com # 459689190

A sign with a hashtag during a protest against police violence in a Missouri shopping mall on Black Friday, one of the busiest shopping days of the year. Hashtags often take on a symbolic role in protest movements, going beyond their practical use as a means of organizing online content.

representation, and police violence. This tactic was effective, and worked to frame police brutality against African Americans as a serious social problem. This example brings us back to the complex relationship between technology and social change. While a social media campaign cannot be seen as a panacea for the problem of police violence, smartphone technologies have enabled new forms of social connection, allowing youth to publicly critique racialized

Smartphones and Police Violence

Demonstrators use a cell phone to document a 2015 demonstration at New York's Union Square held in solidarity with Baltimore protests after the death of Freddie Gray. Gray died of a spinal cord injury sustained when police failed to properly secure him in the back of a van and ignored his requests for medical help. Six officers were indicted by a grand jury and faced charges of murder, manslaughter, and assault. The officers were eventually found not guilty.

Source: Gettyimages.com # 471890088

police violence. Such a profound, and complex social problem won't be solved easily, but this organized effort to build solidarity and highlight racism speaks to the power of this technology. It also suggests that a moral panic surrounding youth and cell phones is not only simplistic, but could thwart the political potential opened up through this new technology.

THINKING FRAMES

How can each thinking frame help us ponder the sociology of the smartphone?

Material / Cultural	New technologies like the smartphone have facilitated the rise of a "participatory culture" where we perform hybrid roles as "prosumers". Alongside the cultural dimension of new technology, smartphones are also material goods produced within a global supply chain characterized by labor exploitation and environmental degradation.
Think about . . .	How do corporations like Apple maintain a positive brand image while being charged with exploiting workers and the environment? Why do you think there is a gap between the glossy promise of new technology and the unglamorous world of technological manufacturing?

Structure / Agency	Sociologists continue to debate the extent to which new technologies like cell phones build social capital and expand social networks. Scholars also draw attention to the diverse ways people exercise agency through their use of new technologies, challenging a technological determinist approach.
Think about . . .	How do the uses and meanings of smartphones vary among different social groups (e.g. across age, gender, social class)? What features of smartphones seem enabling and empowering? What smartphone features feel like a constraint, or a form of social control?

Micro / Macro	Smartphone technology has altered social relations, changing the way we make plans, express our dissent, and behave at work. Our phones provide opportunities for self-expression, but also enable new forms of social control and heightened work expectations. Drawing on the Frankfurt School, some theorize these micro shifts in behavior within the macro context of capitalism: as a way to extract more labor (e.g. unpaid email overtime), while providing distractions that inspire an endless desire to consume.
Think about . . .	What new strategies have workers developed to manage the demands of "iTime"? How do cell phones facilitate or encourage consumption?

ACTIVE LEARNING

Active Learning

Online

Apple: Let the revolution begin (or at least, "think different"):
Apple has a long history of presenting itself as a kind of "revolutionary" company. Watch these 3 short Apple advertisements. How do they present themselves as a countercultural company? How believable is this message today, given that Apple is the largest technology company in the world?

"Think Different—Crazy Ones" (1997): https://www.youtube.com/watch?v=nmwXdGm89Tk

"Get a Mac—Better" (2006): https://www.youtube.com/watch?v=48jlm6QSU4k

"MacBook Air—Stickers" (2014): https://www.youtube.com/watch?v=OzQh6wDb2oE

Apple: Who makes your smartphone?
Watch this 45-minute video on Apple's broken promises. http://www.cbc.ca/player/News/Technology+and+Science/ID/2648627032/

Take notes about key issues in the smartphone commodity chain. Also, ask yourself, "how much do consumers really know about how their phones are made?"

Discussion/Reflection

The "integral accident" of cell phones:
How does Virilio's concept of the "integral accident" apply to smartphones? How many "accidents" or social/environmental problems can be traced to cell phones?

Cell phone capabilities:
Do you think a cell phone today is a "want" or a "need"? Why? Make a list of all the things your smartphone can do. How long is your list? Which of those functions have come to feel like necessities in your everyday life? Compare your list with your classmates. What are the downsides of the smartphone's "easy" technological capabilities?

Cell phone coordination:
How have cell phones changed the way we make plans and connect with people?

Sociology Outside the Classroom

Technology and social change:
Visit Change.org and Avaaz.org. Sign a petition, and forward a petition to a friend. Do you think signing an online petition is an effective way to create social change?

Survey research on teens and social media:
Visit the Pew Research Center website and explore their 2015 survey research on Teens, Social Media and Technology (http://www.pewinternet.org/2015/04/09/teens-social-media-technology-2015/).

What key trends do they find in teens' digital technology usage? How do these patterns differ by gender, race, and class? Do any of these findings surprise you? If you could conduct a follow-up study related to these issues, what would you want to know?

PART III

Standing Out: Individuals Negotiating the Social World

BRANDING YOUR UNIQUE IDENTITY™: CONSUMER CULTURE AND THE SOCIAL SELF

INTRODUCING KEY CONCEPTS

This chapter examines how we develop our sense of self and manage our multiple identities in a consumer society. While acknowledging our individuality, sociologists view the self as a fundamentally social creation. Our multiple identities are shaped by our social location (e.g. gender, race), enmeshed in our relationships with others, and managed through everyday interactions. This chapter introduces the sociological tradition of symbolic interactionism and explores key concepts relating to a social sense of self: Cooley's looking-glass self, Mead's generalized other, and Goffman's dramaturgical theory. Then, we examine how the self is configured in consumer culture, where we are encouraged to "brand" ourselves and purchase items that create a coherent lifestyle. While brands can provide a source of collective identity, they also profit from consumers' free labor in the creation of brand culture. This chapter lays the foundation for future chapters where we look at how specific consumer goods and brands are used to shape our social identities.

1. INTRODUCTION: INDIVIDUALISM IN A MASS-CONSUMPTION CULTURE

To a certain extent, everybody wants to feel unique. Just as no two snowflakes are the same, we may believe that each person possesses a special combination of qualities and strengths. Our feelings of individuality often relate to inner qualities like personality, interests, or sense of humor, but a key way that we express that uniqueness is through the things we purchase and display to the outside world—the decorations we hang on our walls, the clothing we wear, the car we drive (or the bicycle we ride). We may refer to ourselves in branded terms—"I'm a Chevy kind of guy", or "I'm a Mac person", or "I'm a Coke drinker—not a Pepsi person". Today, we may even feel compelled to brand our personal identities, especially as we see the fame and fortune that can come with self-promotion on reality television (Hearn 2008). For example,

Ourselves in Branded Terms: "Get a Mac" Ad Campaign

Apple's "Get a Mac" TV advertising campaign, which ran from 2006 to 2009, depicted the Windows operating system as a dull older man in a suit and tie who was interested in office work. The Mac was shown as a laidback younger man in casual clothing, interested in music, photography, and movies. Advertising critics argue that these kinds of advertisements encourage consumers to think of themselves in branded terms, for example, as either a Mac or a PC.

Source: https://en.wikipedia.org/wiki/File:Getamac.png

the Kardashian clan's long list of companies and products includes the "Kardashian Kard" credit card, Kim Kardashian Fragrance perfume, and the Kardashian Kollection clothing line for Sears. In addition, various Kardashian family members have served as the public face of Skechers "shape-up" toning shoes, Carl's Junior, Estée Lauder, Babies 'R Us, Opi nail polish, Quick Trim diet products, Gillette razors, Hype energy drinks, and a line of "waist trainers". While not everybody aspires to self-brand at a Kardashian scale, the pressure to market oneself is also felt by average folks looking to land a good job or attract a romantic partner. While the act of promoting oneself is nothing new, scholars suggest that what *is* new are the "cultural forces and discourses that have given rise to the overt practices of self-branding" (Hearn 2008: 201). In her book on branding, Sarah Banet-Weiser describes her realization that "my own students, eager for career advice, were now asking me about how to build a 'self-brand'" (2012a: 3).

Consumption can certainly afford us a sense of individuality. A collection of consumer items, shopping habits, and style decisions can come to feel like they express something about who we are. However, there is a paradox at work here: in contemporary consumer culture, the things we buy and covet are purchased and coveted by many other people— and that's often why we want them! Thus, the very things that express our uniqueness also align us with a larger group. We often employ brand names to convey our sense of self to others. Think here of a Coach bag (signaling your sophistication and wealth), a pair of Air Jordan sneakers (demonstrating your connection to basketball and hip-hop culture), a Chevy truck (suggesting that you're the rugged, off-roading type), or a pair of Lululemon yoga pants (showing off your body and/or interest in fitness). Even a lifestyle group known for their aversion to mainstream brand labels—hipsters—can seem to be following a kind of eccentric dress code— e.g. knitted hat, thick-rimmed glasses, ironic t-shirt, colorful cardigan, and messenger bag. In this chapter, we explore this paradox: the search for individuality and uniqueness in a broader consumer culture where most items we purchase are mass-manufactured, mass-marketed, and branded by transnational corporations.

Hipster Olympics

Contestants sign up for the second Hipster Olympics in Berlin, Germany, in 2012. With black t-shirts, body art, and horn-rimmed glasses in tow, they can compete in the Vinyl Record Spinning Contest, Skinny Jeans Tug-O-War, Cloth Tote Sack Race, and Make Your Own Ironic Hipster Moustache Competition.

Source: Gettyimages.com # 148985280

People with Seemingly Eccentric Yet Similar Outfits

Standing out or fitting in? People dress to express themselves as individuals, but our efforts to express our personalities take place within a shared cultural environment that influences how we express ourselves. In this picture we can see how individual fashion choices can paradoxically produce some conformist outcomes.

Source: http://bit.ly/2cNmgLl

Understanding the paradox of individualism in a mass-consumption culture requires an appreciation for how identities emerge in a social context. Put simply, we develop our sense of self *in relation to others*. Our desire for individuality may feel like it comes from deep within, but we also live in a social world that shapes who we are. In this chapter, we look at key sociological theories that help us understand the self as a social creation. Then, we connect these theories to consumer culture, looking in more detail at the way we craft lifestyles and meaning in brand culture.

2. THE SOCIAL SELF: KEY THINKERS AND CONCEPTS

Most people don't think about their "self" as a sociological concept—it's just who you are! Our sense of self enables us to see our own lives and perspectives as distinct from those of others. Although it may feel entirely personal, sociologists see the self as a *social* creation. In this section, we discuss three major sociological thinkers who developed the idea of a social sense of self: Cooley, Mead, and Goffman. These scholars were key thinkers within the sociological tradition known as **symbolic interactionism**—a theoretical perspective that emphasizes how our social world is created through our everyday relationships and interactions. While symbolic interactionists are a diverse bunch, they share a common focus on **microsociological** dynamics of everyday life. Sociologists working from this perspective examine how we construct meaning—and selves—through our interactions with others.

The idea of a social self can be traced back to the work of Charles Cooley (1864–1929), a key member of the first generation of American sociologists. At the time of his writing, many thinkers endorsed the idea of an innate, unified self, known as the "Cartesian ego", taken from the philosopher Descartes. According to this perspective, the self emerged from within; the isolated, introspective individual could come to full self-understanding on one's own. Challenging this notion, Cooley put forward the concept of the **looking-glass self** (1964 [1902]). According to Cooley, our self develops through an *imagined* sense of how others see us and judge us, as well as the feelings we get from imagining these perceptions (Cooley 1964 [1902]: 184). The idea of the looking-glass self suggests that the expressions and actions of others provide a kind of mirror onto our self. For example, if a young girl is frequently told she is pretty, she might come to understand her physical appearance as central to her sense of self—rather than, say, her intelligence or sense of humor. Cooley taught us that our sense of self is always relational, based on our emotional responses to the perceived evaluations of others (e.g. Do we feel ashamed because we believe we are disrespected or ridiculed? Do we feel proud because we believe that others admire us?). With the looking-glass self, Cooley introduced the idea that how we think about ourselves is shaped by how we think others perceive, react to, and evaluate us. Put simply, without the mirror of the social world, we can't fully understand ourselves.

George Herbert Mead (1863–1931) engaged with Cooley's ideas to further theorize the social foundations of the self. Mead began his career as a philosopher, but became a major figure in early American sociology. He believed that our self emerges through a kind of internal dialogue between what we like, what we want, and how we think we will be seen by others. He referred to this as the dialogue between the "I" (the impulsive part of your self), and the "me" (the socialized self). According to Mead, young children are driven solely by the "I"—e.g. "I want a cookie!"—but gradually develop a sense of the "me" through socialization—e.g. "May I have a cookie, please?" The dialogue between the "I" and the "me" shapes how we act in various social situations. For example, you may think of yourself as a generally ravenous, food-loving person and take pride in your ability to polish off a pound of chicken wings. Despite this food-loving streak, you may restrict how much you eat on a first date because you want to convey a sense of self that is respectable and in control, a dilemma that is especially profound for women who feel pressure to restrict their eating in public (Young et al. 2009). Mead argued that participation in social life required people to not just think about themselves, but to assume the perspective of others. He believed that this ability developed through early socialization, as the "me" begins to take shape. Initially, the "me" develops in relation to "significant others"—people who are important to us and whose approval we desire, such as parents. Eventually, the socialization process results in a sense of the **generalized other** (1962 [1934]), which refers to an overall, internalized sense of societal expectations that allow us to act appropriately in a variety of situations. For Mead, a core aspect of socialization is learning to understand the context-specific nature of the generalized other. For example, children are expected to (eventually) learn that you behave differently at the dinner table from how you do on a playground. In our early years, this lesson comes from specific people around us, such as parents and siblings (whom Mead would call "significant others"). Eventually, we no longer need this guidance, as we come to internalize social norms, and thus develop a sense of the generalized other.

A third major figure developing a sociological notion of the self was the eminent 20th century sociologist, Erving Goffman (1922–1982). Goffman saw face-to-face interactions as crucial to understanding social life. His perspective on the self is known as **dramaturgical** because he used metaphors of the theatre to emphasize how our sense of self is performed for others on a kind of social stage. How we present our self depends on the particular "stage" we are on, and also the kind of impression we seek to convey to our "audience". This is not to say that people are faking it, but rather that we are concerned about what others think of us, and so we adjust our actions accordingly. Goffman developed the concept of "impression management" to describe the work that goes into managing the self we display for others. For example, you likely present yourself differently when speaking with your professor (playing the role of student) than when you are at work (playing the role of employee). Our presentation of self also differs according to the "region" of the per-formance: whether in a more public "front" region, or occurring "backstage". Think of the kind of interactions that take place between the staff in the back of a restaurant, as opposed to the more formal behavior that occurs at the front of house with customers. What Goffman's dramaturgical theory emphasizes is that your presentation of self will differ depending on the people you are engaging with, as well as the context of the performance.

Pulling all these threads together, it becomes clear that sociologists have discredited the idea of a single, static, asocial self. Instead, they suggest that we have multiple selves that are shaped by the particular situation and relationships we are engaging in. This idea might seem strange at first, since people are always saying to "be true to yourself", as though there is only one core self. We hope that the examples above make clear that people are continually managing their self through social interactions. This doesn't make any particular version of your self any less "true" than others; it just means that our sense of self is necessarily social, and always constructed in relation to others.

Early theorizing on the self by sociologists like Cooley and Mead shaped later sociological thinking about identity (Vryan 2007). The concept of **identity** helps connect our multiple selves to larger social structures (Stets and Burke 2003). Identities reflect the different aspects of the self as they relate to a role (e.g. student), a situation (e.g. restaurant diner), or a social group (e.g. Canadian). Sociologists study a range of identities, including "sex/gender, family, race and ethnicity, nationality, religion, occupation, sexuality, age, and voluntary subcultural memberships" (Vryan 2007). Consider the many different ways that you could complete the following statement: "I am a . . ." For instance, you might say, "I am a man, a son, an African American, a student, a coffee barista, and an athlete." Each of these statements expresses something about who you are as an individual, but these identity statements also connect you to others, highlighting the multiple social groups that you are a part of. We often manage multiple identities with little thought, but sometimes that process creates conflict (e.g. if you are both a devout Christian and an erotic dancer, or you work for an oil company but also consider yourself a committed environmentalist). Identities are experienced and processed cognitively and emotionally—we think about them, and we feel them. But it is often external cues that signal our identities to others (Stone 1981). Think of the identity conveyed by a teenager with multiple facial piercings dressed all in black, versus a middle-aged man driving a BMW convertible. In these instances, a sense of self is communicated before words need to be exchanged—by the piercings and clothing in one instance, and the pricey automobile in the other.

Goffman was one of the first sociologists to examine the work of identity management. He noted that your identity is not simply "given" to you at birth,

Communicating Identity on Campus: Greek Life

North American students may be accustomed to seeing the Greek letters of fraternities and sororities on clothing worn at their universities. What kinds of identities do these external cues signal?

Source: APimages.com # 340170572234

but is an ongoing social process—a kind of social accomplishment and for some, a social struggle. Goffman (1963) emphasized the especially difficult work of managing stigmatized identities. The concept of **stigma** describes a "deeply discrediting attribute" (Goffman 1963: 3) that is socially devalued or looked down upon (Kusow 2007). It is important to emphasize that the attribute itself is not the source of stigma; rather, stigma results from the social process in which this attribute is devalued. For example, an individual might experience stigma because of a disability, religious belief, sexual orientation, or mental illness. When an attribute is stigmatized, the group or individual is positioned in a distinct, and less valued identity category, leading to **stereotyping, discrimination** and a loss of **status** (Link and Phelan 2001).

One of Goffman's key insights is that a stigmatized attribute is socially constructed and maintained—it is not inherent or "natural", and thus will vary across time and place.

Consider the example of gays and lesbians. In the United States, homosexuality was classified as a mental illness until 1973 and criminalized in some states until 2003. In this context, being gay was heavily stigmatized, and those who openly claimed this identity were seen as deviant. In the contemporary US and Canada, gays and lesbians are viewed very differently; while we have certainly not overcome the problem of homophobia, shifts in social attitudes and institutions (like marriage) have led to the de-stigmatizing of gay and lesbian identities. We have also developed more inclusive language, shifting from the singular category of "homosexual" to the multifaceted acronym LGBTQIA: Lesbian, Gay, Bisexual, Transgender (see chapter 7), Queer (an umbrella term for non-heterosexual identities), Intersex (see chapter 7), and Asexual (a term for people who do not experience sexual attraction). The use of this acronym acknowledges a diverse range of sexualities that exist beyond heterosexuality, and suggests that they should not be stigmatized. However, it's important to recognize that these shifts in norms, laws, and terminology are both historically and culturally specific. In Russia, for example, although homosexuality was decriminalized in 1993, the federal government passed a law banning the spread of information regarding "non-traditional sexual relations" to minors in 2013. The law effectively makes speaking positively about LGBTQIA sexualities, identities, and families in public an offense punishable by fine, detention, and/or deportation (Human Rights Watch 2014).

Goffman (1963) emphasized that stigma is a relational process involving judgment and identity management in interactions. When you have a stigmatized attribute, you must manage your "spoiled identity" or discredited social status. This might involve hiding the stigma (e.g. covering up a gang tattoo), distancing yourself from the stigma (e.g. denying a mental health issue), compartmentalizing the stigma (e.g. avoiding discussion of your gay partner in a homophobic workplace), or embracing the stigma (e.g. reclaiming a stigmatized label like "fat" or "queer" to describe yourself) (Snow and Anderson 1987). Strategies for managing stigma also depend on the visibility of a stigmatized identity. Some stigmatized identities are highly visible (e.g. using a wheelchair or belonging to a marginalized racial group), whereas others are only revealed through social interactions and can be selectively concealed (e.g. membership in a persecuted religious group or having a criminal record) (Kusow 2007). For example, being raised in poverty can be

IDENTITIES ON DISPLAY: PERFORMING MOTHERHOOD

The stuff we purchase and display to others provides a key resource for managing our identities. This process is clearly illustrated in an article by Deborah Freedman Lustig exploring the significance of baby photos for Latina and African American teenage mothers. During her research with a teen parent program in a California high school, Lustig noticed that many young mothers displayed photos of their children on lockets or in plastic frames on their purses and jackets. The photos were often taken by a commercial photographer (like Sears), and depicted well-groomed children wearing special outfits, sometimes surrounded by toys—evidence that they were well cared for. For these young mothers, who were stigmatized within the school, the display of studio portraits signaled pride in their maternal identities and a sense of responsibility toward their children. In Lustig's words: "Both the photos themselves and the consumerism depicted in the photos demonstrate the teen mothers' status as good providers/good consumers" (2004: 184). The display of commercial baby photos allowed these young women to proudly claim their maternal identities, and thus to challenge the stigma associated with teen motherhood.

Baby Pictures on Display

covered up, to some extent, by wearing the right clothing, or acquiring knowledge of high-end consumer items. A key sociological point here is that stigma positions particular identities outside of "normal" society, so that particular people come to be viewed as deviant. This "outsider" status will, in turn, impact individual and group identities. Nevertheless, it's important to note that stigma, self,

Commercial photographs—of babies, families, or happy couples—represent one way that a sense of self is constructed and displayed through a commodity form.
Source: Alamy E8FWTP

and identities are not fixed and stable, but constantly in process. Over time, as certain traits become socially stigmatized (e.g. smoking) or de-stigmatized (e.g. depression), possibilities for individual and group identity also shift.

Sociologists have shown how our sense of self and identity are socially constructed. But this social construction does not occur out of thin air—it requires the stuff of material culture. Consumer culture, with its focus on brands, labels, and self-promotion, provides a key resource for constructing identities.

3. SHOPPING FOR A SELF-CONCEPT IN CONSUMER CULTURE

To understand the relevance of consumer stuff to identity, we need to appreciate the relatively fluid nature of self-concepts in contemporary times. In pre-modern, traditional societies, identity was more fixed, being closely linked to the realms of family, work, and religion. In this context, a child's future was thought to be laid out for them, as key aspects of their identity were inherited and seen as a given—that is, determined by tradition. In contrast, in many contemporary settings around the world, people encounter more choice in their lives. We may choose not to adopt the religion of our parents, or pursue studies in a field that means not taking over the family business. While such expanded choices bring new possibilities, they also generate new challenges when it comes to establishing our sense of self. British sociologist Anthony Giddens (1991) argues that this lack of a prescribed future means we must actively work to construct our identities. In his words, "What to do? How to act? Who to be? These are focal questions for everyone living in circumstances of late modernity—and ones which, on some level or another, all of us answer, either discursively or through day-to-day social behavior" (1991: 70). Giddens's concept of the "reflexive project of the self" describes how we continually reflect on who we want to be, and actively work to construct our sense of self—through our everyday actions (including our consumption choices), and the stories we tell about ourselves. Giddens believes that this reflexive project of the self is a hallmark of modern life. Of course religion, work, and family still matter to our identity—as do other aspects of our social location, like race and gender—but in a post-traditional world our identities are more ambiguous and open-ended. In this context, consumer culture provides a key resource for contemporary reflexive projects of the self. What we buy (and don't buy) communicates a great deal about how we understand ourselves and how we hope to be perceived by others.

Closely related to the reflexive project of the self, the concept of **lifestyle** provides a useful way to describe how our consumer choices contribute to our sense of self (Giddens 1991; Featherstone 1987). In the context of our modern lives, Giddens suggests that "the question, 'How shall I live?' has to be answered in day-to-day decisions about how to behave, what to wear and what to eat— and many other things" (1991: 14). A lifestyle is not captured in a single commodity choice; rather a constellation of multiple choices come together to express a coherent sense of self. For example, a person who is concerned about environmental sustainability may make a range of consumer choices that fit within a "green lifestyle". This person might buy locally and organically grown vegetables to ensure they weren't shipped long distances or grown with pesticides, choose an "eco" brand of laundry detergent to avoid polluting the water with harmful chemicals, and take the bus or subway instead of driving. While these consumer choices reflect a personal commitment to environ-mental sustainability, they come together to form a "green" lifestyle that positions this consumer as a particular type of person. Even if they aren't consciously working to craft a green identity, these lifestyle choices both reflect and reinforce this person's sense of self, as well as how they are perceived by others. While some of these "green" choices can be pricey, the process of crafting a lifestyle is not reserved for affluent elites; Giddens argues that in a post-traditional society, we all engage in this practice through the many choices we make each day about how to live.

While the shift to a post-traditional order opened up new possibilities for crafting identities, scholars debate the implications of this array of lifestyle choices. Some argue that a fluid and flexible sense of self reflects a broader context of postmodernity, where our lives are characterized by fragmentation and flux, and where universal truths are called into question (Featherstone 1987). Consumer choices are integral to the postmodern self, as "people use consumption to cobble together a coherent identity within the context of fragmented society" (Ahuvia 2005: 172). Some scholars theorize this process as a liberation from the confines of national, class, or racial identities, and emphasize the creativity consumer culture affords for crafting our sense of self (Firat and Venkatesh 1995). Other scholars question the claim that we have been freed from the shackles of social structure, and point to the ways gender, race, and class continue to shape the identity and consumption options available to us (Catterall et al. 2005; Skeggs 2004). Shopping for identity may feel simultaneously freeing and oppressive, excitingly open-ended but also costly and overwhelming. While we may enjoy crafting a sense of self through our consumer choices, we may find it difficult to gain a sense of self that is

Buying Green

A participant in the 2015 Annual World Bicycle Forum in Colombia shows off a statement bike bell. This gathering views urban cycling as part of a lifestyle conducive to environmental sustainability.

Source: Gettyimages.com # 464539610

satisfying and meaningful—especially given the abundance of choice in a highly corporatized, profit-driven environment where there is always something newer, more fashionable, and more exciting on offer (Hearn 2008). As a result, we may consume in an effort to solidify our identity, but never really feel satisfied with our selves, leading to a relentless (and expensive) treadmill of consumption.

Whether you are more hopeful or more pessimistic about the idea of "shopping" for identity, there is no denying the significance of possessions, commodities, and consumer culture in crafting our sense of self. Writing at the end of the 19th century, philosopher William James mused, "It is clear that between what a man [sic] calls *me* and what he simply calls *mine*, the line is difficult to draw" (cited in Belk 1988: 140). Today, the connection between our possessions and our self takes on a particularly significant role given the rapid expansion of stuff in consumer culture, combined with our more tenuous relationship to traditional sources of identity. In this context, Belk (1988) describes a process whereby people develop an "extended" sense of self based on their possessions. He conceptualizes this extended self in terms of concentric layers (like a target); some possessions are more important to your sense of self and are positioned closer to the center, whereas other items are more peripheral. Think here of the difference between a teenager's frequently used and much loved skateboard versus their toothbrush. The location of items on these concentric layers will differ between individuals and across cultures, but will also shift for the same person over time, as they experience new roles and life transitions. For example, as a university student, you probably value different items than you did in elementary school, although some of these (like a treasured family photo) may persist over time. Belk argues that the connection between your self and your belongings is not simply a two-way relationship between a person and a possession; he theorizes a three-way relationship between a person, a thing, and the social relationships that surround them (Belk 1988: 147). For example, a child may request a set of Pokémon cards not only because this is a fun toy to play with, but also because they want to be seen as cool. The desire for this toy is not just about the child and the cards; it also involves other children who create a cultural context where these cards are valued, and where not having this consumer item may lead to social stigma.

Even within Belk's model of the extended self, there are multiple ways that our possessions connect to our sense of self. For one, material items can be powerful symbols of the past (Belk 1988: 148–9). The things in our life become infused with memory and emotion, carrying traces of our personal history and family tradition. For example, the frayed armchair in your parents' living room might seem like an eyesore to an outsider, but remain important to your sense of self because it evokes memories of time spent watching soap-operas with your grandmother. We can also see the connection between possessions and identity in the things we collect (Belk 1988: 154). Whether we're amassing shoes or spoons, comic books or tattoos, the act of collecting can legitimate our desire to acquire things—we're not greedy, we're just building our collection! In addition, collecting a particular type of consumer item can bolster the self with a sense of control. As Belk explains "[w]e may not be able to control much of the world about us, but the collection, whether of dolls, depression glass, or automobiles, allows us total control of a 'little world'" (1988: 154).

Further illuminating the link between our possessions and our sense of self, Ahuvia (2005) found that people tend to have a few consumer items that they "love", which "play a special role in consumers' understandings of who they are as people" (2005: 182). For many of us, our loved items provide a way

A DAY IN YOUR SHOES: SNEAKERS AND THE SELF

Has anyone ever told you to spend a day "in someone else's shoes"? While they were likely using "shoes" as a metaphor for taking another person's perspective, footwear can provide a powerful resource for expressing our sense of self. Take the case of sneakers. Historically associated with basketball and hip-hop culture, sneakers have been an important source of status and self-expression for African American youth. In the 1980s, marketing campaigns featuring basketball star Michael Jordan (Nike) and rappers Run-DMC (Adidas) elevated sneakers as icons of Black youth culture (Chertoff 2012). Scholars have debated whether sneaker culture empowers or exploits the youth who purchase multiple pairs of shoes to express different aspects of their identities (Keyser 2015). Today, some young people have developed identities as sneaker collectors, sometimes called "sneakerheads" (Hines 2013). These youth exercise agency as experts within this cultural milieu, trading limited edition sneakers online and at collectors' shows—often for a hefty profit. But in contemporary fashion culture, sneakers are not limited to youth. In 2014, the Style section of the *New York Times* ran a story on the growing popularity of sneakers among "fashion-forward" businessmen—or even paired with tuxedos by prominent celebrities on the red carpet. The symbolic ties to teens and hip-hop culture persist; by wearing sneakers, these men signal their awareness of the latest trends, as well as a youthful identity that is valued in many modern American workplaces (Williams 2014).

of "synthesizing" competing aspects of our identities (Ahuvia 2005: 181). For example, one of Ahuvia's research subjects felt a desire to be feminine and girly, but also strong and independent. Her collection of vintage purses allowed her to balance these two sides of herself, as objects that were "pretty" and girly, but that also demonstrated her ability to find a good deal and appreciate something unusual and unique. Besides our love for certain objects, we also express our sense of self through the things we dislike, hate, or reject (Wilk 1997). For example, Johnston and Baumann's (2015) research with "foodies" revealed that a foodie identity was solidified not just by the foods interviewees enjoyed, but also by the things they hated and ardently avoided. Many foodies expressed their aversion to chain restaurants like the Olive Garden, distinguishing their tastes from the average, middle-brow eater. This is an example of what Ahuvia calls a "demarcating" strategy for managing possessions in relation to our sense of self (2005: 181). By rejecting certain things, we draw **symbolic boundaries**; we signal who we are by creating distance from consumer items we dislike.

The connection between our stuff and our sense of self is also exemplified through the *loss* of material possessions (Belk 1988: 142). Goffman (1961) showed this in his study of "total institutions" like prisons, mental hospitals, and military training camps, where people are cut off from the rest of society for a prolonged period of time. A key ritual when entering such institutions is the removal of personal belongings, part of a larger process that Goffman called the "mortification of the self" (1961: 23). By stripping away the inmate's stuff, the prison strips away their sense of self; the institution subsumes one's individuality. In the case of the military, this process is designed to instill a group identity that is cemented through shared or similar possessions, such as a uniform, a gun, and shared living quarters. While Goffman focused on the ritualized removal of personal belongings within total institutions, Belk notes that people who have been robbed may also experience a loss of self. Having something stolen from you can feel like your very sense of self has been violated (Belk 1988: 142). The forced removal of personal belongings is particularly traumatic, but a loss of self can also result from voluntarily giving things away. Belk describes how people who give away their old clothes can feel sad, nostalgic, and regretful (1988: 143). Even if you will never again wear that pair of ripped jeans, or you feel too old for your beloved stuffed animals, it can be hard to part with objects that are powerfully associated with your sense of self. Collins and Janning have shown the significance of household items within children's experience of divorce. They note that "if an object is lost or taken away, part of one's identity that is attached to that object may be changed, if not eliminated" (2014: 165).

The significance of possessions to our sense of self is not universal, but will differ depending on historical and cultural context. One study in Hong Kong found that Chinese consumers crafted a sense of self through gift-giving, with particular focus on luxury gifts (Wong et al. 2012). Wong and colleagues found that expensive gifts conveyed powerful messages about the importance of the recipient, as well as the honor and status of the giver (2012: 938). For example, parents who receive an expensive gift from their children can "gain face by displaying their conspicuous goods to their friends as evidence that their children care about them" (Wong et al. 2012: 943).

Interestingly, when asked about items that were important to them, the Chinese participants in this study consistently mentioned items no longer in their possession, specifically referencing things they had given away as gifts (Wong et al. 2012: 943). This exemplifies a different relationship between consumption and the self from what has been documented in American and Canadian contexts. Mention of these gifted possessions suggests the importance of giving in this cultural context, where gifts represent a bond with loved ones, as well as the development of oneself as generous and honorable. In this context, consumption is still integral to the development and expression of self, but this relationship is defined more through *giving* than *acquiring* possessions—a striking example of how our sense of self is constructed in relation to others in a specific cultural setting.

4. BRANDING GOODS, BRANDING THE SELF

For many people today, our stuff is not simply categorized by its general function. You don't just wear *shoes*, you wear Nikes or Doc Martens or Keds. You don't just drink *soda*, you drink Coke or Pepsi or 7 Up, or maybe your favorite brand of carbonated water. Similarly, your phone isn't just a *phone*, it's an iPhone, or a Samsung, or a Blackberry. In this chapter, we've been discussing the link between our possessions and our sense of self. In contemporary consumer culture, a key part of this link involves our attachment to brands.

At a basic level, brands are a way to differentiate similar stuff; a brand sets apart one product line from its competitors. From a sociological perspective, a brand is much more than a corporate logo. Instead, a brand is "the total constellation of meanings, feelings, perceptions, beliefs, and goodwill attributed to any market offering displaying a particular sign" (Muñiz 2010). Peel below the obvious surface layer, and brands are symbolically rich and deeply relational performative tools (Lury 2004). More than just labels, brands are communicative objects that convey symbolic messages to others, and for that reason, they provide a significant resource for identity construction (Arvidsson 2005; Schroeder 2013). In the words of consumption scholar Alison Hearn, we live in a moment when brands increasingly "comprise the tools for the creation of self" (Hearn 2008: 200; also Holt 2002: 94). Today, Cooley's "looking-glass self" operates, in part, through branding. For example, when a classmate glances at your luxury handbag, you might imagine that she associates you with the brand's upscale associations.

SOCIOLOGISTS IN ACTION: PHOTO ELICITATION

The use of visual data can help sociologists further investigate the link between consumption and identity. **Photo elicitation** is a relatively new but increasingly popular research method that combines visuals and narratives by "inserting a photograph into a research interview" (Harper 2002: 13). In this method, images may be provided by the researcher or by participants themselves—either pre-existing images (like family photos) or photos they have taken for the study. Discussing these images can help researchers gain insights into participants' perspective, both in the photos they select, and in the way they interpret these photos for the researcher. Scholars have advocated photo elicitation as a technique to evoke rich narratives, given the link between images and memory and emotion. This technique can also help to establish rapport with interview subjects, as it provides a shared focal point and positions the interviewee as expert on the images they are describing (Clark-Ibáñez 2004).

Rosaleen Croghan and colleagues (2008) used the photo elicitation technique to explore the relationship between consumption and youth identity in the UK. They gave disposable cameras to 28 young people (ages 12–17) and asked them to take pictures of "consumer goods that were of significance to them" (346). Given that our sense of self is always constructed in relation to others, Croghan et al. interpreted their participants' photos as "exercises in self-presentation in which participants emphasized particular positively sanctioned aspects of self" (349). Within this presentation of self, brands emerged as an important symbolic resource. These young people were "acutely aware of the consequences of brand association, and would position themselves carefully in relation to brands" (351). If the photo depicted a brand with positive associations, then they talked about why it mattered to them; if the photo depicted a brand with negative associations, then they distanced themselves from it in order to preserve their sense of self. This study reveals how visual data can generate new insights into the relationship between branding and identity. While a traditional interview might elicit narratives on participants' likes and dislikes, Croghan and colleagues note that the "uncompromising nature of the visual image occasioned a marked degree of explanatory or repair work in relation to issues of branding" (351). Put in more simple language, the visual presence of the brand in the interview worked to focus and sharpen discussions, and provided additional insights when compared to an abstract discussion of consumer ideals.

While people have long crafted a sense of self through their possessions, the cultural significance of branding is relatively new. Prior to the 1900s, the goods available for purchase were not linked to a brand (Muñiz 2010). If you ran out of soap, you went to the store and bought just that, *soap*, without having to choose between different logos, packaging, and scents. Branding became significant with the shift to mass-manufacturing and distributing goods on a national scale (Muñiz 2010). Early branding was designed to communicate quality; a trusted brand was thought to separate the leading choice from a generic, or low-quality knock-off. A brand that is associated with quality and status allows a business to charge a premium: seemingly identical products can be sold for different prices because one is emblazoned with a respected logo. However, brands are not just about maximizing profit and guiding consumers' decision-making. The names and symbols associated with our purchases are fundamentally about *meaning*; some theorists have gone so far as to suggest that brands are one of the main sources of meaning in contemporary consumer culture (Holt 2002). Today, brands are applied not only to the goods we encounter on store shelves, but to things that people have long considered separate from the marketplace, like universities, religions, politicians, and charities (Muñiz 2010; Banet-Weiser 2012a). In a competitive economic climate, many people feel pressured to self-brand—build a meaningful, impressive, and recognizable snapshot of the self that will catch the attention of potential employers, customers, or social media followers. Brands facilitate "a process of positioning, or 'negotiation' of the self in relation to the shifting demands of everyday life" (Arvidsson 2005: 5).

How do brands come to carry such powerful meanings? Scholarly accounts of this process have shifted over the years. In the early period of advertising following World War II, it was thought that a brand's meaning was developed by marketing executives and propelled down to the lowly consumer (Banet-Weiser 2012a: 7). From this perspective, a brand had a clear creator (marketers)

Favorite Teen Brands

A group of teenagers in Rio de Janeiro, Brazil, looks at a Nike store window display featuring Brazilian soccer star Neymar. Considered to be one of the best players in the world, Neymar has achieved extreme financial success and international renown at a young age. When he scored the goal that clinched his team's prestigious Champions League win in 2015, Neymar did so wearing Nike Hypervenom shoes and a uniform featuring a Nike logo. Nike remains the most popular clothing brand with teens in the US, and controls over half of the American athletic footwear market (Piper Jaffray 2015; Powell 2014).

Source: Gettyimages.com # 149242954

who established a fixed meaning that was internalized by consumers—a kind of "hypodermic needle" approach to brand meaning. Today, scholars see the meaning of brands as the result of a more complex process in which consumers play an active role. From this perspective, brand meaning emerges through an "exchange" between markets and consumers, rather than a one-way "injection" of meaning into consumers' mindsets (Lury 2004). Scholars use the term "brand culture" to describe the interplay between the *production* of the brand and the cultural reception and *usage* of the brand (Schroeder 2013). To build a successful brand requires brand management from marketing experts, as well as consumer meaning making. A major element of this participation now occurs through social media, allowing consumers to inject their voice into brand culture. For example, when you "like" a brand on Facebook, you are contributing to the meaning of that brand, and also presenting yourself as a particular kind of person with particular tastes. While such consumer-generated content often reinforces a brand's image, our contributions as **prosumers** can also work to *resist* or alter a brand's meaning (see chapter 9 for more on "prosumers" and the blurring of boundaries between production and consumption in digital culture). For example, when you share a spoof ad—like those mocking Matthew McConaughey's Lincoln commercials—you similarly contribute to the cultural meaning of the brand. Once again, your sense of self is also at play in this process.

Endorsing a Company Through Humor?

In this widely watched mock ad, comedian Jim Carrey mocks Matthew McConaughey's advertising campaign with the car company, Lincoln. While the spoof undoubtedly draws critical attention to the actor's motivations in this endorsement, it also brings more media attention to the Lincoln brand.

Source: https://www.youtube.com/watch?v=dI6tvCbPePg

While we are active agents in creating brand meaning, this does not mean that the individual consumer has the same power as a brand owner. Brands are still managed by corporations, and millions (if not billions) are spent to maintain their image. Brand management is now less about telling people what a brand means, and more about "defining the contours of what the brand *can* mean" as it is used within people's lives (Arvidsson 2005: 245). For example, Starbucks can construct a brand image that is about quality coffee, taking time to re-charge, and a comfortable **third place** environment (see chapter 4), but this message may not appeal to all consumers. Nevertheless, the market dominance and geographic range of Starbucks today suggest that this brand message has been wildly successful. What's more, the recognition of consumer agency doesn't mean that consumers and marketers benefit equally from the exchange of meaning in brand culture. Drawing upon a Marxist approach, Arvidsson argues that brand meaning relies upon the exploitation of consumers' free labor, since the "value" of a brand is built, in part, from "people's ability to create trust, affect and shared meanings" (2005: 236). Our emotional investments in a brand translate into economic value for the company; as consumers participate in this process of creating brand meaning, the brand becomes valuable as an entity in its own right (Hearn 2008: 200). So while your favorite brands may provide tools for self-expression, you are simultaneously contributing to the value of this company—a contribution that some scholars see as free labor and a form of exploitation.

As we have learned from classic sociologists like Cooley and Mead, our sense of self as an individual is always constructed in relation to others. Similarly, the objects that express our individual sense of self can also contribute to our sense of *collective* identity (Belk 1988: 152). Collective identity refers to "an individual's cognitive, moral, and emotional connection with a broader community, category, practice, or institution" (Polletta and Jasper 2001: 285). Collective identities are based on the perception of a shared status, whether that is a favorite sports team, geographic region, ethnicity, or music subculture. While collective identities have long been expressed through symbolic goods—like a team logo, cuisine, or national flag—today some people unite around a shared love of certain brands to form a kind of brand community. A brand community is "a specialized, non-geographically bound community, based on a structured set of social relationships among admirers of a brand" (Muñiz and O'Guinn 2001: 412). For example, Muñiz and O'Guinn have studied the formation of brand communities around Macintosh computers and the Swedish car brand, Saab. Members of these communities "share a social bond around a branded, mass-produced commodity" (2001:

418), and may also derive a sense of status over opposing brands, like PCs and Volvo's. These brand communities provide consumers with a source of "connection"—not only to the brand, but also to each other—creating a sense of "we-ness" (418). For example, Saab owners describe waving to each other when they pass on the road, or stopping to help another Saab owner fix a flat tire. In an Internet age, brand communities are not limited by geographic boundaries, and also exist as **virtual communities** (see chapter 9)—as with fans of Mac lipsticks, Sony Playstations, or Marvel comic book superheroes.

While brands are a powerful resource for identity construction at the individual and the collective level, we don't want to overstate their influence. Yes, brand culture contributes to our sense of self, but other forces remain

American Apparel Hoodie

While it displays no visible logo, many would recognize this hoodie as an American Apparel product. If a logo-free item carries the meaning of a brand, is it really unbranded?

Source: Gettyimages.com # 462864058

A Logo-less Brand Strategy: Oliver Peoples

The American luxury eyewear brand Oliver Peoples offers products that it claims embody a distinctive Los Angeles lifestyle. Notably, its website explains that the brand avoids placing obvious logos on its glasses, opting instead for "subtle details [that] are distinctive to the brand and recognizable to the discerning consumer". The brand claims that it "has never relied on a logo but instead on fostering relationships with like-minded consumers who appreciate and respect our approach", suggesting a marketing strategy that creates brand identity by purposely avoiding logos. Seen here is a similarly subtle window display at their New York City store.

Source: Gettyimages.com # 169724364

important—such as our work, family, or race and ethnicity. Some of the possessions that are most central to our sense of self may not be attached to a specific brand, like a family heirloom, photo album, or scarf that was knit by a friend. What's more, we are always much more than any one brand we consume. Belk writes that no single brand can be equated with a person's complex and fluid sense of self; instead, we need to recognize how a "complete ensemble of consumption objects" represent the "diverse and possibly incongruous aspects of the total self" (1988: 140). We also live in a time of growing backlash against branding. A critique of multinational corporations is not limited to radical activists, but is now shared by many consumers who are concerned about human rights violations and environmental degradation perpetuated by corporate giants—or those who simply resist being defined by a logo. Writer and activist Naomi Klein's (1999) book *No Logo* was an international bestseller, charting the rise of the anti-globalization movement and the growing resistance to an increasingly corporatized and commercialized world. Over the past decade, the market for "artisanal", handcrafted goods has exploded—a trend that may signify consumers' search for meaning beyond the branded world of mass-produced goods. Nevertheless, it is important to recognize that even when we resist brands, we are still constructing our sense of self in relation to brand culture. By refusing to wear logo-emblazoned clothing, or ordering handmade goods on Etsy, we cultivate different kinds of identities—whether as hipsters, activists, or bargain hunters.

As sociologists have emphasized since the turn of the 20th century, our sense of self does not simply emerge from within. We are social beings with a fundamentally social sense of self. Even if we wish to declare our identities a "no logo" zone, we live in a heavily branded world, and can't simply step outside of it. What's more, the pervasiveness of brand culture means it may no longer be seen as "selling out" to fashion an identity through brands. When the brand is everywhere, our understanding of what is "authentic"—that is, "real", non-commercial, genuine, sincere—can become a kind of brand in itself (Banet-Weiser 2012a). In this context, an American Apparel unbranded hoodie may feel "authentic" and non-commercial, as opposed to a Nike hoodie with a large swoosh, even though American Apparel is a for-profit corporation. Whether we embrace our favorite brands as a site for expression and community, or build a sense of self that resists and critiques big brands, consumer culture continues to provide us with tools to construct and manage our identities. In the remaining chapters, we explore three key sites for constructing a sense of self through consumption: the crafting of our physical appearance, the music we listen to, and the cars we drive (or don't drive).

THINKING FRAMES

How can each thinking frame help us ponder the sociological relationship between our stuff and our sense of self?

Material / Cultural	The material objects in our lives are deeply linked to our sense of self. Our possessions become invested with meaning and provide a key symbolic resource for communicating our identities to others. This relationship differs across cultural contexts.
Think about . . .	What material objects are most significant to your sense of self, and how do you think they reflect the cultural values you are immersed in?

Structure / Agency	Consumers don't passively receive the brands that are marketed to them, but actively participate in their creation. While consumers exercise agency in this exchange, some scholars argue that consumers' contributions to brand culture are a form of labor that is exploited by corporations.
Think about . . .	Have you ever been caught up in a brand's positive image and "liked" them online? How do you think you have contributed to the brand's value?

Micro / Macro	Symbolic interactionism is a theoretical perspective that focuses on microsociological dynamics of face-to-face communication and impression management. While brands provide communicative tools within specific social interactions, these individual exchanges occur within a broader, macrosociological context. When we look at these broader structures, we see that transnational corporations exert considerable power over the tools available for constructing and expressing our sense of self.
Think about . . .	How might somebody resist the political-economic power of big-name brands in their personal lives? Could reshaping the micro-meanings of the brand eventually impact the structural position of the brand in the broader economy?

ACTIVE LEARNING

Online

A few of my favorite things:
Visit the website for "Making Modern Motherhood," a study conducted by UK scholars Rachel Thomson, Mary Jane Kehily, Lucy Hadfield and Sue Sharpe. As part of this study, researchers asked children to describe their "favorite things". Click on the "favorite things" links to tour children's bedrooms and hear them talk about the stuff they love. What insights can you gain into the children's sense of self? http://modernmothers.org/index.html

Sneakerheads:
Check out Jian DeLeon's "Fieldguide to the Modern Day Sneakerhead" (http://www.complex.com/sneakers/sneakerhead-guide/). How does this "guide" relate to the link between consumption and identity? As you read through the various "types" of sneaker collectors, take note of the connections made to other aspects of social location—such as gender, race, and class—whether stated explicitly or implied in the description and/or illustration.

Discussion/Reflection

Mapping the self through stuff:
What objects are important to your sense of self? Draw a map of your self with concentric circles; put your possessions on that map, and then describe why some items are closer or further away from the center, symbolizing their relative significance to your sense of self. What items do you *love*, and why? Do any of these loved items synthesize competing aspects of your identity?

Brands and the self:
What brands are most closely connected to your sense of self? What brands do you dislike or "demarcate" yourself from (using Ahuvia's terminology)? Why?

The story of your stuff:
Dump out the contents of your backpack or purse. What do these items say about your sense of self? Can you see multiple identities reflected in your stuff (e.g. a student ID, a ticket stub, a bike helmet, a work uniform)? Compare the contents of your bag with a classmate. How might the similarities and differences in your stuff reflect identities that you share (e.g. student), and identities where you differ (e.g. gender, employment, hobbies)?

Sociology Outside the Classroom

Image analysis:

This chapter introduced the method of photo elicitation, which incorporates images into a qualitative interview. Another potential source of visual data can be found in our social media profiles, where we assemble images (as well as posts and links) in order to craft an online identity. For this exercise, analyze the images that a celebrity has shared over the past year on a highly visual social media platform, such as Instagram or Facebook. Looking across time, how do these images convey a sense of self to others? Keep a tally of the consumer practices displayed, including not only personal belongings like clothing and food, but also activities like attending concerts or traveling. Does this visual display of consumption choices work to craft a particular lifestyle?

Chapter 11

LOOKING GOOD: IDEOLOGY, INTERSECTIONALITY, AND THE BEAUTY INDUSTRY

INTRODUCING KEY CONCEPTS

What do you think of as "beautiful" or "attractive" in a person? Our ideas of physical attraction feel deeply personal and have powerful implications for our self-worth and relationship to our bodies. While people often say that beauty is in the "eye of the beholder", sociology can show us how beauty ideals are socially constructed. In this chapter, we look critically at beauty ideals through the lens of intersectionality—a sociological perspective that examines how various systems of inequality work together. We examine how beauty is both an ideology and an industry. As an ideology, physical appearance ideals can obscure inequalities relating to gender, race, and body size. As an industry, beauty is implicated in the drive to sell more products, as well as a sense of body dissatisfaction—a culture of "lack"—that motivates us to keep shopping.

1. INTRODUCTION: CAN ANYONE BE BEAUTIFUL?

Our physical appearance is loaded with sociological meaning. Many of us scrutinize our personal "look" on a regular basis, hoping to determine which outfits, products and workout routines will help us look our best. When we ask our students who is attractive, beautiful or simply "hot", many of the same names pop up—Channing Tatum, Angelina Jolie, Beyoncé, Kim Kardashian. These celebrities are admired for their famous faces and figures around the world. Not everybody can look like a celebrity, but even non-famous people aim to maximize their physical attractiveness. We often feel like our appearance is evaluated on a daily basis. Sometimes those evaluations involve a casual glance on the street; other times they are made explicit in virtual space. The "Hot or Not" website was launched in 2000 as a way for average people to evaluate the hotness of other average people in submitted photos. Many websites that followed—the dating/hook-up website Tinder, Rate your Professor, even the earliest version of Facebook ("Facemash")—allowed users to evaluate the physical attractiveness of others.

Thinking about who is "hot" seems like an obvious, though personal, question. Our aim in this chapter is to show how ideals of physical appearance are sociologically complex and revealing; they tell us a great deal about the kinds of traits that are socially valued. To observe this point, try typing "beauty" into a Google image search. When we do this from our American and Canadian computers, our screens are flooded with a sea of similar images featuring thin, young White women, many of them wearing or applying makeup. There are no men on the screen and very few women of color. These images suggest a few things to an observant sociologist. First, they suggest that beauty is strongly associated with femininity; as a result, women experience a lot of pressure in relation to physical appearance. The frequent depiction of makeup suggests an understanding of beauty as something that women must work toward, purchasing appropriate consumer products to maintain an attractive appearance. Indeed, the search for beauty takes place within a consumer culture where multi-billion-dollar industries profit from the promise of flawless skin, perfect hair, a firm physique, and a fashionable look. These images also suggest that in contemporary American and Canadian culture, idealized beauty is predominantly associated with youth, thinness, and pale skin. While children are often told that "beauty comes from within", the dominant messages that surround us in popular culture suggest that only a very narrow range of bodies are attractive.

Googling "Beauty"

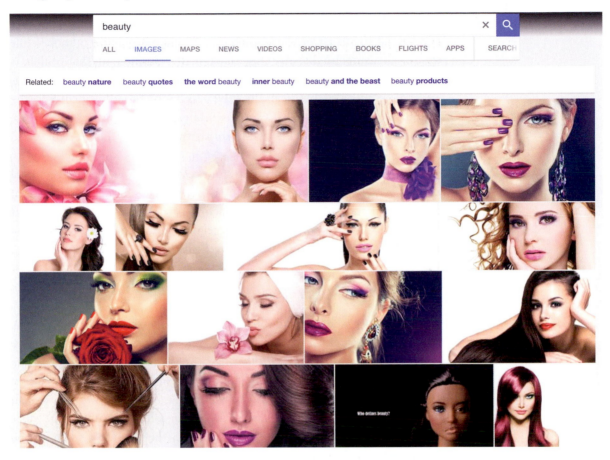

This is what came up for us when we searched for "beauty" on Google Images. According to these images, what does it mean to be beautiful?

Source: Google image search for "beauty". Screen shot.

The array of pale, thin, feminine faces revealed through our Google image search highlights the way that beauty is **socially constructed**—a concept introduced in chapter 6, and that we explore further below. Briefly, to say that beauty is socially constructed means that appearance ideals are not simply natural, but are created in specific historical and cultural contexts. In part, we know this because fashion and beauty ideals are far from universal. In North American and European cultures there is a significant fear of fat, and fashion models typically have very thin, tall bodies. In other parts of the world—like the South Pacific islands of Samoa and Fiji, or the West African nation of

Mauritania—female fatness is socially prized and not considered a social **stigma** (see chapter 10 for more on stigma). In this chapter, we show how ideals of physical attractiveness are socially constructed, and examine how these social standards privilege some groups and marginalize others. While we are focusing on beauty, this chapter isn't limited to that which is "beautiful"—an ideal that is dominantly associated with femininity. Rather, we explore ideas of physical attractiveness more broadly, including the appearance norms associated with masculinity. Throughout the chapter, we pay particular attention to the relationship between beauty ideals, gender, and race.

The first part of the chapter introduces a sociological, intersectional approach to beauty—not as a natural, universal quality, but as a social construction and an ideology. In the second part of the chapter, we look at the fashion and beauty industries, and consider their impact on social ideals— as well as the products we consume to feel worthy and avoid social stigma.

2. BEAUTY: A POWERFUL CULTURAL IDEAL

We are constantly bombarded with advice on how to improve our appearance. *Buy these razors for the smoothest shave! Lose body fat with this great new cleanse! Brighten your smile with the latest teeth-whitening technology!* While these messages proliferate in contemporary consumer culture, our focus on the body as an important marker of personhood is historically unique. British sociologist Mike Featherstone writes that "within consumer culture, the inner body and the outer body become conjoined: the prime purpose of the maintenance of the inner body becomes the enhancement of the appearance of the outer body" (1991: 171). Previous eras valued a person's appearance, to be sure, but physical appearance was not as clearly linked to individual value, character, and personhood. Scholars use the concept of **body work** to refer to the labor that people perform (or hire others to perform) in order to manage and manipulate their bodies to fulfill a variety of cultural expectations (Gimlin 2007). Today, popular body work practices include makeup, exercise, tattoos, hairstyling, hair-removal, teeth cleaning and whitening, clothing selection, dieting, and, increasingly, cosmetic surgery (Carr 2007).

Recall from chapter 1 that a central goal of sociology is to *make the familiar strange*—that is, to question taken-for-granted aspects of everyday life. One way to see the strangeness of our contemporary focus on external appearance is to compare the personal dreams of young women at the end of the 19th and the 20th centuries. That is precisely what historian Joan Jacobs

Brumber (1997) did in her book, *The Body Project*, through the analysis of girls' diaries. A girl writing in her diary over 100 years ago (in 1892) described self-improvement in purely "inner" terms, noting that she was "[r]esolved, not to talk about myself or feelings. To think before speaking. To work seriously. To be self restrained in conversation and actions. Not to let my thoughts wander. To be dignified. Interest myself more in others" (quoted in Brumber 1997: xxi). These goals differ substantially from a diary entry from 1982: "I will try to make myself better in any way I possibly can with the help of my budget and baby-sitting money. I will lose weight, get new lenses, already got new haircut, good makeup, new clothes and accessories." In this second diary entry, we see the influence of consumer culture, as the girl aspires to buy new things to improve herself. We also see an emphasis on appearance—losing weight, getting contact lenses, and improving her face, hair, and style. This historical comparison reveals a striking shift in ideals of self-improvement, from the internal betterment of one's thoughts and feelings, to the external betterment of one's physical appearance. As Brumber's research illustrates, our emphasis on beauty is not "natural", but has been created within a specific cultural and historical context—what sociologists call a social construction.

2.1. Beauty as a Social Construction

Ideals of beauty and attractiveness are experienced at an individual level; we may feel insecure about our bodies, nervous about a new haircut, or admiration for a friend who always seems to look good. While these feelings are deeply personal, sociologists draw our attention to the social processes that underpin collective ideas about looking good. The concept of **social construction** refers to the fact that many of the categories we use to make sense of the world are *socially* created, rather than naturally occurring or biologically inevitable. In part, this is because humans don't experience the world directly through our senses; as complex, intelligent, social creatures, we create conceptual models, or categories to make sense of the world around us. These socially constructed categories allow us to organize our experiences and interpret our surroundings, using labels like "beautiful", "handsome", "hot", and "sexy". These words come to feel obvious and are experienced as individual thoughts, but their underlying meanings are socially derived.

To say that beauty is socially constructed means that ideas about physical appearance emerge within a particular historical and cultural context. For example, sociologist Lisa Wade (2013) has drawn attention to the shifting significance of high heels. Now seen as a sexy feminine accessory, in the

1600s, high-heeled shoes were a status symbol among men in the European aristocracy. As Wade writes, "The logic was: only someone who didn't have to work could possibly go around in such impractical footwear." Our understandings of beauty are fashioned by specific group norms, values, and social processes. These socially constructed ideals come to take on a life of their own, influencing our thoughts and actions. Thus, social constructions may be a kind of social *idea*, but their effect is very real. This dynamic was summed up by the sociologist W. I. Thomas, who stated, "If men [sic] define situations as real, they are real in their consequences" (Thomas and Thomas 1928: 572). So while our understanding of beauty has been created by society—and perpetuated by media and advertising—this idea will powerfully influence our self-perceptions and efforts to shape our own appearance. Even if they are not "natural" or universal, social constructions have powerful effects in our lives, shaping collective understandings, social actions, and material realities.

To appreciate the power of social construction, consider how dominant appearance ideals impact our lived experiences. We compare ourselves to the images that surround us—on billboards, magazines, movie screens, and online—and assess our own appearance accordingly. Our experience of this process will vary depending on our **social location** (e.g. gender, race, age). As we noted earlier, beauty is closely associated with femininity, placing particularly intense pressure on women. But not all women experience these pressures in the same way. Dominant perceptions of beauty also privilege whiteness, so women's experiences of these images are shaped by the intersection of gender and race. Social construction is not only about creating categories to interpret the world: these categories are deeply shaped by social inequalities, and work to advance the interests of dominant groups. Thus, the social construction of beauty perpetuates both **sexism** (see chapter 7) and **racism** (see chapter 6). In a 2014 speech, Academy Award winning actress Lupita Nyong'o reflected on how the racist beauty ideals perpetuated in the media compromised her sense of self-worth as a child growing up in Kenya—even as someone who was eventually named one of *People* magazine's "Most Beautiful People in the World".

I want to take this opportunity to talk about beauty. Black beauty. Dark beauty . . . I remember a time when I too felt unbeautiful. I put on the TV and only saw pale skin, I got teased and taunted about my night-shaded skin. And my one prayer to God, the miracle worker, was that I would wake up lighter skinned. The morning would come, and I would be so excited about seeing my new skin that I would refuse to look down at myself until I was in front of a mirror because I wanted to see my fair face first. And every day, I experienced the same disappointment of being just as dark as I was the day before. I tried to negotiate with God, I told him I would stop stealing sugar cubes at night if he gave me what I wanted, I would listen to my mother's every word and never lose my school sweater again if he just made me a little lighter. But I guess God was unimpressed with my bargaining chips because He never listened.

(http://www.essence.com/2014/02/27/lupita-nyongo-delivers-moving-black-women-hollywood-acceptance-speech)

Because socially constructed beauty ideals emphasize whiteness, the market for skin lightening products is a growing, multi-billion-dollar industry. These products equate beauty with white skin and promote the idea that lightening dark skin is both achievable and desirable. The popularity of skin lightening products demonstrates how socially constructed ideals have a powerful impact on material realities. However, cultural ideals are not static, and material practices can be shifted as beauty ideals change. In that same speech quoted above, Nyong'o reads from a letter written by a young fan: "I think you're really lucky to be this Black but yet this successful in Hollywood overnight. I was just about to buy Dencia's Whitenicious cream to lighten my skin when you appeared on the world map and saved me." Of course, it is not only celebrities like Lupita Nyong'o who have challenged the socially constructed association between light skin and beauty. In a 2016 Twitter campaign, women of color took to the Internet to critique the skin lightening product "Fair and Lovely"—and the Eurocentric beauty ideals it represents—by posting photos of themselves with the hashtag #Unfairandlovely. The idea for the campaign originated in a photography project by Pax Jones, a Black student at the University of Texas (Blay 2016). Jones's original photos featured South Asian sisters Mirusha and Yanusha Yogarajah. The hashtag soon went viral, and hundreds of women of color shared

Black Skin and Beauty Images

In 2014, Lupita Nyong'o won an Academy Award for her performance in Twelve Years a Slave. She used her acceptance speech as an opportunity to draw attention to racist beauty ideals.

Source: Gettyimages.com # 476327917

#Unfairandlovely images of themselves as a public statement against racist beauty ideals.

2.2. Beauty as an Ideology

In addition to a social construction, we can also think of beauty as an **ideology** (see chapter 3). While some sociologists see ideologies as neutral forces, others—like ourselves—argue that ideologies work to reinforce and naturalize power hierarchies (Johnston and Taylor 2008: 944). Ideologies are organized around a set of ideas, normative claims, and value structures, and have an emotional component that enhances their popular appeal (Johnston and Taylor 2008: 944). To put this in everyday language, ideologies work to convince us that inequality is natural, and therefore not a problem.

When ideological beliefs become part of our everyday common sense, we describe them as **hegemonic** (see chapter 3 for an introduction to Gramsci's concept of hegemony). For example, the assumption that an ideal feminine body is thinner and more delicate than an ideal masculine body—often presented as larger and more muscular—is a hegemonic beauty ideology (Dworkin and Wachs 2009). Nevertheless, it is useful to remember that hegemony is not a synonym for "brainwashing". Beauty ideologies are frequently challenged, resisted, and reshaped. What's more, not all people absorb beauty ideologies in the same way. For example, a classic American study by sociologist Melissa Milkie (1999) examined how White and Black girls interpreted the images in fashion magazines. While both White and Black girls found the magazines' depictions of beauty unrealistic, the White girls more strongly identified with these idealized images, and felt worse about themselves after viewing them (Milkie 1999: 201–2). In contrast, the Black girls in the study were critical of the magazines' overwhelming whiteness, and the images appeared to have less of an impact on their sense of self (1999: 200–2; See also, Lovejoy 2001). Lisa Duke found a similar pattern in her research. She writes that "Black girls generally viewed magazines as biased and largely irrelevant to their ideas about beauty" (2000: 384). In short, not everybody engages with beauty ideologies in the same way; our interpretation of these ideals is shaped by our social location.

While hegemonic body norms are contested, sociological research can help us understand how beauty ideals relate to gender inequality, racism, and fat-phobia. In order to understand how these systems of inequality work together, we draw upon the feminist sociological perspective of **intersectionality**. This term was originally coined by legal scholar Kimberlé Crenshaw (1989), and

EVALUATING BEAUTY AND BODY WORK PRACTICES: A CHECKLIST

To evaluate if a specific beauty or body work practice has an ideological element, we need to ask critical questions. These questions aren't designed to make normative judgments (e.g. "high heels are bad"), but to identify ideological processes at play. Consider a specific body work practice, like bikini-waxing, body-building, or skin-lightening. Then ask yourself the following questions:

- Does it reflect a hegemonic ideal (e.g. that women should be smaller than men, or that light skin is preferable to dark skin)?
- Does it naturalize power hierarchies between social groups (e.g. men over women; Whites over people of color)?
- Does it reinforce consumerism and capitalist exploitation? Does it justify profitable but exploitative industries (e.g. skin-lightening, sweatshops)?
- Is it internalized and rationalized? When a person violates the norm does it create stigma (e.g. for a woman to wear a sleeveless shirt without shaving her underarms; for a man to be smaller and less muscular than his girlfriend)?

If you have checked yes to one or more of the above questions, you may be dealing with an ideological beauty or body work practice!

has been further developed by myriad feminist and anti-racist scholars to understand the complexity of inequality and oppression. In the last chapter, we discussed how our identities are never singular, but are shaped by multiple social factors, such as race, gender, class, age, sexual orientation, migration status, disability/ability and religion. Intersectionality draws attention to this multiplicity; in this approach, sociologists examine how these different aspects of our social location *intersect* to shape social advantages and disadvantages. For example, early feminist scholarship highlighted issues of sexism, but tended to focus on the lives of middle-class White women—experiences of womanhood that are by no means universal. Black feminist scholars like Patricia Hill Collins (1998) have drawn attention to the significance of race and class in shaping women's experiences. For example, while the 1960s feminist movement is often framed as facilitating women's entry into the labor market, many working-class and African American women worked outside the home long before this—sometimes in the homes of affluent White families, as nannies, cleaners, and cooks. Intersectionality draws our attention to the way that race, gender, and class intertwined to shape women's experiences, rather than viewing a single social factor in isolation.

An intersectional perspective is also crucial for understanding masculinity. In previous chapters we discussed how men have access to certain privileges within patriarchal societies—for instance, they tend to have higher incomes, and have greater access to positions of power in business and politics. Therefore, we can say that men are privileged as a group. But are all men privileged in the same way? Absolutely not. Thinking intersectionally, we see how race *intersects* with gender in the construction of masculinity. For example, because of racist **stereotypes** that associate Black men with crime, the very traits that are seen as desirable in White men—like physical strength—can be seen as threatening in Black men (Ferguson 2001). Conversely, some traits that are stigmatized for White men are valued in the performance of Black masculinity. For example, C. J. Pascoe's (2007) research in a California high school showed how a keen sense of fashion was valorized for African American male students. For these boys, it was important to have nice clothes in order to avoid being seen as "ghetto" (a label that emerges at the intersection of race and class). By contrast, if White male students showed an interest in clothing, they risked being called a "fag"—a label that emerges at the intersection of race, gender, and sexuality (Pascoe 2007). These examples highlight the importance of intersectionality in the study of beauty and appearance regimes; the question of what it means to "look good" and how we are expected to strive toward this ideal is shaped by multiple, intersecting social factors.

When examining the intersecting nature of appearance ideals, it's helpful to unpack three key dimensions: gender, race, and body shape. Femininity has historically involved a focus on appearance as an indicator of self-worth and social value. Traditional feminine beauty has been associated with inactivity, passivity, and submissive body language. You can see some of these features in images of classic cover-girl pin-ups from the 1940s.

In many depictions of feminine beauty—from classic pin-up images to today's magazine covers—women are seen as objects that are desired by men, not as subjects with agency who desire on their own terms. This imagery reinforces stereotypical notions of feminine passivity and **heteronormative** desire (see chapter 10). While women have long been expected to work on their appearance, men are increasingly encouraged to focus on how they look as well. Studying men's and women's fitness magazines, Dworkin and Wachs identify

Classic Pin-up

Betty Grable, an American model and actress, poses for a photoshoot in 1943.

Source: Gettyimages.com #56022068

Spoof Image of Male Pin-Up

One way we can investigate if gender differentiated ideals still exist is when we switch the roles and find them ridiculous—as can be seen here with this spoof image of a male pin-up

Source: http://petapixel.com/2011/10/04/men-photographed-in-stereotypically-female-poses/

several key areas of gender convergence. Specifically, men and women now face similar pressures on three points: 1) a fear of fat; 2) bodily objectification; 3) the marketing of body products, like fragrance and skin-care (2009: 34). While these three trends are now apparent in both women's and men's fitness magazines, this convergence does not mean that sexual objectification and body pressures operate in identical ways for men and women. Ideal masculine bodies are depicted as large, muscled, dominant, athletic, and sexually powerful, whereas ideal feminine bodies are presented as small and "toned", with less emphasis on athletic ability (Dworkin and Wachs 2009: 49). What's more, a fear of fat has different implications for men and women. Because reducing body fat has had feminine connotations

Getting Toned or Getting Ripped?

Both men and women's magazines encourage a fat-free body, but the emphasis on building muscle is socially constructed in gendered terms. Put simply, men are expected to get "ripped", whereas women should be "toned". This gender contrast can be seen in this image, which shows participants in the 4th of July Muscle Beach competition in Venice Beach, California. The event features body building as well as a bikini contest for women.

Sources: (*left*) Gettyimages.com # 487246128; (*right*) Gettyimages.com # 487245616

historically, men's fat reduction is presented in masculine terms through a focus on building muscle. Men get "ripped" or "jacked", and work to get a six-pack (or even an eight-pack!). By contrast, women get "toned" and "firm", and are discouraged from becoming too muscular (2009: 37). In sum, while there is definitely more emphasis on masculine appearance today than there was in the past, objectified images of masculine bodies work to reinforce hegemonic ideas of masculine strength and aggression.

Besides gender inequalities, beauty images also work ideologically to naturalize racism, and to present whiteness as the ideal beauty type (Collins 1991; Kwan and Trautner 2009: 61–2). People of color are "symbolically annihilated" (Tuchman 1978) in advertising and fashion imagery, meaning that their presence is typically marginal, or absent altogether. Dworkin and Wachs found that 80% of images in women's fitness magazines were of White women, and 97% of images in men's fitness magazines were of White men (2009: 52). In the world of high fashion, Ashley Mears's research on the fashion industry found that people of color comprised less than 4% of models on the high-fashion catwalk; many top fashion shows had no Black or Asian models, and listings of top models featured only a handful of people of color (2010: 23–4).

The ideological process at work here reinforces a Eurocentric conception of beauty that builds on and naturalizes colonial and racist attitudes. When women of color *are* featured in advertising campaigns, as Beyoncé is in L'Oréal advertisements, their skin and hair color are often significantly lightened.

In a study of over 2000 people appearing in advertisements in popular magazines, Baumann (2008) studied the lightness and darkness of models' complexions, as rated according to a color pallet from 1 (lightest) to 10 (darkest), with a focus on comparing White and Black models of both genders. This research documented how a fair complexion beauty standard operates in a particularly gendered way. More specifically, the fair beauty standard applied to Black women more intensively than Black men insofar as Black

Getting Ripped, or Ripped Apart?

Despite being one of the most successful tennis players of all time, and having appeared on the cover of Vogue, Serena Williams has faced critiques for her muscular physique throughout her career. Some tennis players feel self-conscious about their bodies, and seek to balance the potential "on-the-court" rewards of bulking up with pressure to conform to perceptions of ideal femininity.

Source: http://bit.ly/2cDQrpR

Fairness and Beauty Ideals

Internet commentators noted that Indian actress, Freida Pinto, looked uncharacteristically fair in this 2009 Vanity Fair photo shoot. In 2011, L'Oréal advertisements featuring the actress generated similar speculation. Pinto has spoken out about the uncomfortable experience of auditioning for skin lightening commercials as a young model in India, and has encouraged others to embrace their natural complexion.

Source: Gettyimages.com # 88585750

women were systematically portrayed with lighter complexions than Black men. Moreover, White women were portrayed with lighter complexions than White men. These findings were replicated in an analysis of advertisements from the 1970s, showing that the gendered nature of the fairness ideal is not just a product of the period when the research was conducted. An in-depth analysis of a subset of White women models showed that the darker the woman's complexion, the more likely she was to be depicted as sexualized and less sophisticated, demure, or refined. The advertisement analysis suggested that the meaning of fairness corresponded to dominant schemas for ideal femininity, and that these ideals were less achievable for Black women—and not relevant for men of either race.

Besides gender and race, a third significant beauty ideology involves body size. Scholars use the term fat-phobia to describe this pervasive fear of—and prejudice against—fat bodies. (Note: these scholars follow the lead of fat activists and deliberately use the word "fat" in an effort to reclaim the word from its negative connotations.) Our social fear of fat (and cultural valorization of thinness) has a powerful ideological dimension. The average American woman's body (who weighs about 166 pounds) is virtually never depicted within the beauty industry, and most media images feature women with extremely low levels of body fat. Thin bodies are not only idealized as physically attractive, but are also commonly associated with health, responsibility, and discipline. This equation positions fat-free bodies as the social ideal, and reinforces stereotypes of fat people as lazy, unhealthy, and irresponsible. The hegemonic idea that "thin" = "healthy" is nearly universal in mass-media imagery. Even when fitness magazine articles promote self-acceptance, they are often accompanied by visuals portraying a body that is nearly fat-free. While the equation between "thin" and "healthy" is ubiquitous in popular culture, this is not a straightforward epidemiological fact. Thin bodies can be unhealthy bodies, diminished by smoking, cancer, or anorexia. At the same time, bodies that are categorized as "overweight" can be healthy. People with a body mass index (BMI) of 25–30—which is technically "overweight"—may still exercise regularly and consume a healthy diet (Saguy 2013: 52).

If thin bodies aren't necessarily healthy bodies, why are we constantly bombarded with messages about how to reduce body fat? Drawing from the work of British sociologist Mike Featherstone (1991), Dworkin and Wachs describe a "culture of 'bodily lack' that requires constant maintenance" (2009: 36). The idea of "lack" works ideologically to focus attention on how we fall short of appearance ideals, and the resulting need to do more, and *buy more*, to approximate those ideals. Instead of focusing on what your body *can* do, in a culture of "lack" we often focus on what we do not possess—a six-pack, a big bust, fat-free thighs, or "perfect" skin. Because having close-to-zero body fat is the cultural ideal, we are encouraged to always be on the lookout for products that move us towards this elusive standard. We can see a similar dynamic in relation to youthful body ideals. Because looking young is the cultural ideal, the adult consumer must continually invest in products that counter the inevitable appearance of aging, such as wrinkle creams and hair plugs. In short, a culture of "lack" is a culture that encourages a treadmill of consumption to meet elusive body standards.

Given that so many appearance ideals are unattainable for most of us, why do we invest heavily in the pursuit of socially constructed ways of "looking good"? For one, body work can yield emotional rewards. We may enjoy wearing makeup, or derive satisfaction from working out to achieve a muscular body. As feminist research has shown, women can find pleasure in the consumption of beauty products at the same time that they are critical of the beauty industry (Taylor et al. 2014). Hegemonic beauty ideals—like the svelte feminine body and muscular masculine body—carry considerable social power in shaping our beauty norms and practices, even when we reflect critically upon these standards.

3. LOOKING GOOD: A GROWTH INDUSTRY

While the concepts of social construction and ideology draw our attention to the *cultural* dimensions of looking good, sociologists also examine the links between physical appearance and political-economic structures (the *material* dimension of our material/cultural thinking frame). Consider the case of the manicure. Getting a manicure/pedicure has come to feel like a habit for many Western middle-class women, symbolizing self-care and professionalism.

While the manicured hand carries cultural resonance, it has a deep material connection: the availability of other groups of women who do the work of making manicures cheap and accessible. In this case, the body work involved in a manicure is not just about work on the self, but the work performed by marginalized others within a broader labor market. Sociologist Miliann Kang researched the world of manicures in Korean-owned nail salons in New York City, and notes that "while some women's bodies are manicured into objects of beauty, other women's bodies serve as tools for enacting these beauty regimes" (2010: 2). Thus, inequalities are perpetuated not only through the images that are idealized in billboards and magazines, but also in the labor relations that underpin the beauty industry. Whose bodies are managed to align with socially constructed beauty ideals, and whose bodies perform the actual labor of body work?

A sociological perspective can help us investigate how capitalism and advertising shape ideals of physical attractiveness, body practices, and fashion cycles. How do structural forces shape our personal sense of "looking good"?

3.1. The Dove Campaign for Real Beauty: Feeling Empowered to Buy Stuff

To explore the business side of beauty, it's helpful to look at a marketing campaign that has received widespread popular support: the Dove "Campaign for Real Beauty".

Dove describes the campaign as promoting a "wider definition of beauty" by "featuring real women whose appearances are outside the stereotypical norms of beauty" (http://www.dove.us/Social-Mission/campaign-for-real-beauty.aspx). From billboards to more recent viral videos, the Dove "Campaign for Real Beauty" has been widely successful and long-lasting (Banet-Weiser 2012b; Aaker 2013; Nack 2014). The goal of the campaign was not simply to help women feel better about themselves, but to revitalize a faltering brand, establish customer loyalty, and boost Dove's sales. Did it work? The answer is a resounding yes. The campaign has garnered numerous advertising awards and remarkable success in economic terms, leading to an estimated 700% increase in Dove sales (Anker and Kappel 2011: 294). This was an impressive development for a brand that many thought was hopelessly old-fashioned and no longer relevant for young women.

Central to the Dove campaign's success was its ability to capitalize on consumers' frustration with narrow beauty standards. Commodifying dissent —that is, turning resistance into a product that can be sold—has become a

Dove: A Champion of "Real" Women?

Dove's 2012 "Show Us Your Skin" campaign asked women to have their picture taken at the Real Beauty Photo Studio in New York or upload pictures online to feature in Times Square billboards, digital ads, or an online gallery. This "living ad" campaign was Dove's largest campaign to date featuring "real women".

Source: Gettyimages.com # 143134501

key feature of contemporary capitalist culture (Frank 1997). One of the earliest, most infamous examples of this strategy was the 1968 Virginia Slims campaign that crafted the idea of a feminist cigarette using the slogan, "You've come a long way baby".

Dove's Campaign for Real Beauty provides a recent example of selling products through women's empowerment: it presents a feminist message in the critique of narrow beauty ideals, but it also promotes consumerism by encouraging women to buy Dove products (Johnston and Taylor 2008). In this highly successful campaign, we see how individual discontent with beauty ideology can be channeled back into a brand preference. Notably, the campaign does not question the assumption that beauty is an important feminine ideal.

You've Come a Long Way Baby . . . (1) ("Women's Bank Accounts in 1957")

This 1991 advertisement plays on Virginia Slims' 1960s highly successful campaign slogan, "You've come a long way, baby". This slogan uses the idea of women's empowerment to sell a product—cigarettes. This advertisement also reminds women "what most women's bank accounts looked like in 1957", as many women could not freely open bank accounts in the United States until the 1960s. While promoting women's financial independence is undeniably positive, this advertisement has a paradoxical twist: it promotes consumption of a carcinogenic product that is the world's leading cause of preventable death, killing 6 million people a year.

Source: Virginia Slims Ad 1 http://goo.gl/WPnNjj

You've Come a Long Way, Baby . . . (2) ("Rosemary for President")

This 1970 Virginia Slims advertisement captures the aspirations of feminists seeking to break through the glass ceiling in all spheres of life . . . someday. Like other Virginia Slims advertisements, it employs a feminist message of empowerment to encourage women to buy a cancer-causing product.

Source: Virginia Slims Ad 2 http://goo.gl/WPnNjj

Instead it seeks to democratize beauty—to make it available to everyone. Thus, the campaign for Real Beauty perpetuates a broader ideology of compulsory beauty, which suggests that all women should *strive* to be beautiful (Taylor, Johnston, and Whitehead 2014; Kwan and Trautner 2009: 59). This ideology of compulsory beauty is also promoted by make-over television shows. In these shows, women who have made bad fashion and beauty choices—often women from working-class backgrounds—are taught how to style themselves more skillfully, develop better taste, and achieve a more "respectable" appearance (Rafferty 2011). While these style interventions may have an impact on women's self-esteem, feminist activists and scholars argue that gender inequality is upheld when women are defined by their appearance (Kwan and Trautner 2009: 59–60; Bordo 2003). From a political economic perspective, critics have also raised questions about Dove's connection to other troubling beauty products. Dove's parent company, Unilever, also sells Fair & Lovely, a "fairness cream" that is marketed through the promise that it is "proven to lighten the skin". Unilever also sells Axe Body Spray, which is marketed as a way of making men irresistible to women. So while Dove adopts a seemingly feminist message, it has economic ties to companies that profit from racist and sexist ideals.

The Dove campaign illustrates a key dynamic at play in consumer capitalism. On the one hand, consumer products offer an opportunity for feelings of empowerment and self-expression. On the other hand, consumer culture must promote a feeling of "lack" and a need to buy things. Consider the Dove campaign: for this campaign to be successful, women must feel empowered by Dove's positive messaging, yet remain motivated to purchase Dove firming cream. Ads strategically present you, the viewer, with something you are lacking, and then offer a solution to this problem. If you don't feel beautiful, you can buy some makeup for a quick pick-me-up. If you don't feel muscular enough, you can buy a fitness magazine to help you work on your body. This dynamic of self-expression and consumption/conformity is particularly evident in the fashion industry.

3.2. Fashion: Expressing Yourself While Conforming to Trends

German sociologist Georg Simmel (1858–1918) was one of the first sociologists to theorize the **fashion cycle**. He described the "trickle-down" process of trends, whereby elites initiate a fashion trend but must find something new to distinguish themselves when the trend is copied by the masses (1957 [1904]:

545). Simmel believed that fashion was especially appealing to women and other disadvantaged groups who lacked control of their own lives and craved some kind of change (1957 [1904]: 556). In his view, fashion allowed an avenue for individualism, differentiation, and visibility in a larger context of social inequality, making it especially attractive to society's most marginalized (1957 [1904]: 557). Simmel also insightfully noted that fashion synthesizes a desire for individuality and conformity—standing out and fitting in. You can be uniquely "you", but also be "in fashion" (part of a larger social trend). In his words, fashion combines the "tendency towards social equalization [and fitting in] with the desire for individual differentiation and change" (543).

Today, scholars acknowledge the wisdom of Simmel's insights on the fashion cycle, and the "trickle-down" of trends. However, compared to Simmel's world of the late 19th century, fashion is much faster and more complex today. There is not *one* fashion market, but multiple types and tiers of markets (Crane 1997; Thompson and Haytko 1997: 16). While the "trickle-down" dynamic of the fashion cycle persists, lower-status groups and subcultures also initiate trends that "trickle-up" into the consumption patterns of elites (a phenomenon explored more in chapter 12) (Crane 2000: 14). Scholars also recognize the importance of **lifestyle** as a driver and organizer of fashion (Crane 2000: 10, 134–6) (the concept of lifestyle was discussed in chapter 10). While our class position undoubtedly shapes what fashions we have access to, people have some degree of agency to craft their own lifestyle, rather than simply imitating elites (Giddens 1991). Fashion provides an avenue to express one's identification with, and ambivalence towards a range of identities, such as youthfulness and sophistication, masculinity and femininity, or conservatism and rebellion (Crane 2000: 13).

Research on fashion has revealed a wide range of emotions that motivate our clothing purchases—both positive and negative. Besides the feeling of confidence that comes with looking good, researchers also document "concerns, anxieties and fears experienced over one's personal appearance and the reactions of others to it" (Rafferty 2011: 241). Fashion involves a competitive, relational element, as consumers strive for the latest and greatest trends (Rafferty 2011: 243). As sociologists following Bourdieu (1984) have emphasized, displaying one's "good taste" is a way for people of higher social classes to feel superior to others (see chapter 4 for more on Bourdieu). Possessing the "good taste" of fashion is no exception. In one study of young women fashion-consumers in Ireland, "good taste" for upper-class consumers was symbolized in the ability to purchase "classic" pieces from high-end luxury brands, rather than buying cheap, ephemeral fads (Rafferty 2011: 253).

In contrast, women from lower economic classes felt more pressure to keep up with the fashion cycle and bought large numbers of cheaper fashionable pieces. For some participants, this process led to contradictory feelings of pride at being stylish, but shame, distress, and even depression at the expense devoted to clothing purchases (Rafferty 2011: 246).

Fashion culture is dynamic, constantly changing and involving multiple voices. Research done by Jeff Murray (2002) demonstrates how people can use fashion to mediate between tradition and modernity. This mediation was made clear in Murray's interview with a Sikh man named Surendra, who had immigrated to the United States. While Surendra viewed the Sikh turban as a positive symbol of his traditional culture, he felt that its compulsory nature represented the perceived conservatism of older Sikhs who rejected Western fashions. Surendra proudly displayed the turban in his home and also wore a Sikh Kara (a steel bangle on the right wrist). At the same time, he perceived Western fashion as a form of "liberation", allowing him to express an identity that was less constrained by traditional culture. Surendra said that when he eventually stopped wearing the turban and cut his hair, he felt "really good because now I could have the kind of hairstyle I wanted, and look like I wanted to" (Murray 2002: 430). Surendra's feelings toward the turban are not representative of all Sikhs; nevertheless, his experiences highlight how our clothing and appearance can both reflect and mediate experiences of migration across cultural contexts.

Today's fashion world is more complex than it was at the time of Simmel's classic writings, but the dualism between individual expression and social conformity persists (Thompson and Haytko 1997: 15–16). Fashion allows consumers to express identities and distinguish themselves from others. It also embeds them in a fashion cycle that involves dissatisfaction with the "old", the shift from conformity to "cool", and built-in obsolescence as new products become fashionable.

American sociologist Ashley Mears's research provides insight into the conformist culture of high fashion. As a graduate student, Mears was approached by a modeling agent in a Manhattan Starbucks and told she had a "great look". She took him up on his offer and worked as a professional model in New York and London for two years, all the while carrying out sociological research on the modeling industry. While working as a model, Mears took field notes, reflected on her work experiences, and interviewed other models and industry actors, including stylists and the bookers who connect models with clients. Immersed in the fashion world, Mears gained insight into the behind-the-scenes production process that makes modeling such a

THE MATERIALITY OF FAST-FASHION AND THE GLOBAL GARMENT INDUSTRY

Today's fashion cycles change so quickly that they are often described as "fast fashion". In this context, runway trends are transformed into products that appear on store shelves just six weeks later—a transformation that is made possible by a globalized, flexible and fast-moving production chain. Fast-fashion global giants like H&M and Zara promise consumers a constantly shifting range of low-priced products, allowing shoppers to continually update their wardrobes with the latest trends. Some consumers experience the fast-fashion cycle as a source of freedom, as trendy items are available for an affordable price, even if they are more frivolous than durable. As one young consumer observed, "A Zara sweater pills up the fourth time you wear it, so maybe you throw it away; but you knew it was going to be like that" (Gabrielli 2013: 214). But in production terms, the rise of relatively low-cost, trendy clothing raises questions about environmental and human costs. As clothing consumption increases and quality decreases, more clothing items end up in landfill (Lee 2007). In labor terms, it is workers in China, Vietnam, and Bangladesh who produce much of the US and Europe's fast-fashion finds (only 2–2.5% of American garments are made in the US) (IGLHR 2014). The low wages and poor working conditions in these countries gained widespread concern with the 2013 Rana Plaza tragedy in Bangladesh—a country whose garment industry is second in size only to China's. In what labor scholars believe is the worst disaster in global garment industry history, an eight-story factory collapsed, killing over 1100 people and injuring 2500 (Siddiqi 2015: 167). The factory employed mainly girls and young women who made clothing for global chains like Benetton, Walmart, and Children's Place, earning between 12 and 25 cents an hour and working 14-hour days (IGLHR 2014). The tragedy raised questions of accountability in global garment supply chains—questions without easy answers in a complex global system of subcontracting where major brands distance themselves from exploitative labor practices.

high-status, but brutally competitive and low-paid form of employment. For example, it may surprise you to learn that the average model in 2009 made about $27 thousand a year (2011: 11). Mears's research documented the humiliation, rejection, and waiting that characterized work as a fashion model, as well as the widespread under-reporting of ages and body measurements (describing a model as younger/thinner than she actually was), and relentless

SOCIOLOGISTS IN ACTION: CONTENT ANALYSIS

To research the portrayal of social groups in mass media, sociologists often use the method of **content analysis**. With content analysis, scholars literally count how many times a phenomenon of interest—like someone's gender or race, or the word "beautiful"—is depicted across a large grouping of textual materials, like print advertisements or television shows. By systematically counting the frequency of a particular word or trait, scholars are able to empirically document depictions of social groups that reflect (and can reproduce) dominant cultural perceptions of those groups. For example, one group of researchers looked at fashion magazine covers, which they argued reflected predominant beauty ideals (Sypeck, Gray, and Ahrens 2004). They examined the covers of the four most popular American fashion magazines between 1959 and 1999 in order to see whether the covers changed in systematic ways over time. The particular phenomena they counted were the body size of the models depicted using a standardized scale, as well as the proportion of the body shown (depiction of faces alone, vs. faces and upper torsos, vs. full body). The pictures were rated independently by multiple raters to ensure reliability. The researchers found there was a statistically significant trend towards depicting thinner bodies over time, as well as a trend over time to increasingly show full-body depictions on magazine covers. The authors argue that these objectively measurable trends represent changes in more abstract cultural ideals about the focus society places on thinness and women's bodies. By carefully documenting the prevalence or appearance of a particular phenomenon across a wide range of texts or images, content analysis can provide insight into cultural patterns that are difficult or impossible to perceive through casual observation.

pressure to be thin amongst a group of already very thin women. Even though Mears was 5′9″ and 125 pounds, she describes how she was subtly—and not so subtly—encouraged to lose weight. In one fitting where she struggled to pull on a pair of pants, the designer slapped her thigh and made a joke about "child-bearing hips" (2011: 105).

Mears endured the low points of model work in order to investigate a sociological research question: why is the definition of "beauty" in the fashion world so narrow? In particular, Mears was interested in understanding the industry's focus on models who are not only ultra-thin, but also White. Of the 200 models in one agency she studied, only 20 were women of color (2010: 37). The online pop-culture magazine *Jezebel* has documented the lack of racial diversity among high-fashion models in New York's fashion week since 2008; they found that White models made up around 80% of modeling spots in the 2014 shows (Dries 2014; Sauers 2013).

To research the narrowness of beauty norms, Mears studied how culture—in this case, fashion culture—is made and manufactured. This is an approach that sociologists refer to as "the production of culture" since it focuses on the people and institutions that produce the cultural items we consume. Many fashion scholars believe that we can't fully understand the culture of fashion without looking at the fashion industry (e.g. McRobbie 1997; Aspers and Godart 2013: 181). Indeed, this approach led Mears to some important insights. One of the key findings of her study was the existence of a high degree of uncertainty in the modeling industry. Taste in models is highly subjective and there is a flood of new models to fill a limited number of high-status jobs. Because of this uncertainty, the industry works to minimize risk by bowing to conventions and stereotypes—a practice that ends up reinforcing the whiteness of the industry and perpetuating distorted representations of women (2010: 25). Mears writes that the "implicit frame of beauty is so narrowly molded around whiteness that any deviation from a White, bourgeois body is viewed as problematic" (2010: 37).

This vision of beauty leads people in the fashion industry to reject most models of color, except the few who possess facial features associated with whiteness. As one NYC booker put it, "people want a White Black girl" (Mears 2010: 40). A New York stylist explained that a high-fashion "ethnic" model means the following: "the only thing that is not White about you is that you are Black. Everything else, you are totally White. You have the same body as a White girl. You have the same aura, you have the same the old, aristocratic atmosphere about you, but your skin is dark" (2010: 39). Thus, studying industry actors allowed Mears to shed light on the connection between uncertainty in the industry and racist beauty ideologies. She shows how the narrow beauty standards in high fashion modeling produce an "ironic result": in this seemingly "edgy" field, decision-makers are not "rule-breakers", but are instead guided by "imitation, routine and rules of thumb" (2010: 36). The end result is to produce a high-fashion vision where few women of color gain acceptance, and oppressively narrow depictions of beauty persist.

In short, the worlds of beauty and fashion appeal to many, but do not empower all equally. Dove's "Real Beauty" campaign calls for all women to feel beautiful, and its sister company, Axe, suggests that all men become irresistibly sexy with just one spritz. Dreams of beauty, hard bodies, fashionable clothing, and all-round sexiness may be widely appealing, but they are often elusive goals—especially for those who are marginalized by socially constructed ideals.

THINKING FRAMES

How can each thinking frame help us ponder the sociology of beauty and fashion?

Material / Cultural	The worlds of fashion and beauty embody cultural ideals; at the same time, they are supported by industries that are growth-oriented and profit maximizing. These industries must sell a vision of physical attractiveness that is inclusive enough to encourage mass participation, but restrictive enough to create a culture of "lack" motivating further consumption.
Think about . . .	What are the specific cultural ideals of attractiveness that encourage *you* to buy products (e.g. clearer skin, fashionable clothes, a muscular physique)? Could those cultural ideals be achieved without consuming?

Structure / Agency	One person alone can't change beauty standards, and many people feel restricted by narrow cultural ideals of beauty (e.g. light skin, thin bodies). At the same, time, the realm of fashion encourages self-expression and creative manipulation of styles, leading many to associate "looking good" with feeling free and authentic, like themselves.
Think about . . .	How empowered do you feel to *resist* dominant appearance ideals?

Micro / Macro	To a certain extent, beauty is in the eye of the beholder. At the same time, sociology teaches us that the individual's "eye" will vary tremendously depending on social location: cultural upbringing, geographic location, social class, sexual orientation, gender, age, race, and ethnicity. Local cultures of fashion and beauty exist, but they interact with macro forces of global industries that have a transnational, mass-media presence.
Think about . . .	Can you think of a specific setting or micro interaction where broader beauty norms are resisted, rejected, or irrelevant?

Active Learning

ACTIVE LEARNING

Online

An Oscar-winning beauty:
Watch Oscar award winner Lupita Nyong'o speak on the subject of black skin and beauty. https://www.youtube.com/watch?v=ZPCkfARH2eE

What are the key points she makes about beauty and blackness?

Teens, race, and beauty:
Watch the short documentary *A Girl Like Me*, made by teen film-maker Kiri Davis. What insights does this documentary reveal about the intersections of race and gender within hegemonic beauty standards? www.youtube.com/watch?v=YWyI77Yh1Gg

Critiquing White beauty standards:
Watch this short MTV video, in which women of color discuss White beauty standards. According to the video, what are White beauty standards? What specific examples are provided? What are some of the effects of these beauty standards in women's lives? http://www.colorlines.com/articles/watch-video-breaks-down-real-problem-white-beauty-standards

Girl, you don't need makeup:
Watch Amy Schumer's short spoof video, "Girl, You Don't Need Makeup". https://www.youtube.com/watch?v=fyeTJVU4wVo

What socially constructed norms of beauty are evident in this video? How does the video reveal the fine line feminine beauty walks between being "natural", and being "an effort" requiring an investment of time and products?

Simply irresistible:
Robert Palmer's 1988 video, "Simply irresistible", was one of the most distinctive and memorable music videos of the 1980s. Check out the original, and then watch indie-singer Ingrid Michaelson's spoof of this video. Girls Chase Boys: https://www.youtube.com/watch?v=5GBT37_yyzY

Why does this video seem so silly? What is the video challenging?

Fashion's narrow reach:
Read this critique of the extreme lack of racial diversity in *Elle* magazine's 30th anniversary fashion spread. http://www.huffingtonpost.com/entry/elle-look-diversity-in-fashion_55d48ae5e4b055a6dab22658

Why do you think the fashion world continues to be so narrowly drawn to images of White beauty?

Discussion/Reflection

Democratizing beauty for all women: A worthy goal?
Drawing from what you have learned, discuss the idea that all women should be encouraged to feel beautiful. What role does the ideal of beauty hold for women? How do you think young girls come to adopt this as an important pursuit, worthy of extensive time, energy, money, and thought? Should girls and women reject the invitation to strive for beauty?

Body pressure: An equal opportunity endeavor?
Research suggests that girls and women experience body pressures in uniquely potent ways, but that boys and men are also subjected to appearance ideals that prioritize body work and discriminate against fat. How do body pressures for men and women differ? How are they similar?

Sociology Outside the Classroom

Who's hot?
Find a list of "attractive celebrities". Many such listings exist in magazines (e.g. *People Magazine*'s annual listing of the "most beautiful people in the world"),

and in the online world of celebrity gossip. Look carefully through the list to see the range of bodies presented, and the prevalence of certain types of bodies. If you were an alien species judging beauty from this list, what would you think of as beautiful? How does beauty reflect gendered, racialized, and fat-phobic ideals?

Counting beauty:
Conduct a mini-content analysis to develop a systematic account of "beauty" as it relates to gender, race, ethnicity, and skin tone. To do this, identify a source of images, like a health magazine/website, or a fashion magazine/website. Identify at least 50 discrete images of people, since a bigger data pool will allow you to draw stronger conclusions. Count how many men are depicted versus women. Count the racial depiction of the people depicted (e.g. White, Black, Latino, South Asian, East Asian—to the best of your ability, knowing that we can't always determine someone's race based on appearance). Count how many people are depicted with visible body fat. What conclusions can you draw from your mini-content analysis?

A trip to the drugstore:
Put your sociological imagination to work with a trip to your local pharmacy. Look closely at the range of products sold and consider how they may emphasize sexist or racist beauty ideals (e.g. consider the amount of space devoted to women's and men's products, or the skin tones reflected in products like Bandaids and makeup). Given this array of products, who appears to be the target consumer? How are different groups of consumers targeted differently?

Chapter 12

WHAT'S ON YOUR PLAYLIST? SUBCULTURES, RACISM, AND CULTURAL APPROPRIATION

INTRODUCING KEY CONCEPTS

Music is an important source of cultural symbolism, and a way to articulate dissent. Sociologically, music can teach us about tastes, subcultures, and the power of subcultural capital. Our ideas of "cool" music are not simply dictated by the music industry. Coolness often emerges from subaltern social classes— those who are economically disadvantaged and/or racially oppressed. Through music, African Americans have played a large role in shaping cultural concepts of cool. The case of hip-hop is used to reflect on dynamics of racism (including prejudice, discrimination, and institutional racism) as well as White privilege, cultural appropriation and color-blind ideology. Musical icons that are edgy and critical can be commercialized and turned into a mass-market commodity. At the same time, music is considered a form of art, and continues to offer a powerful medium for collective protest to oppression and injustice. In terms of economic sociology, music can teach us about the impact of digital technologies on our consumption practices, and the immense (but challenged) power of the music industry.

1. INTRODUCTION: HOW MUSIC MATTERS

Many things we have discussed in this book involve necessities. We need food and clothing in our daily lives. Many of us need coffee. We may feel like we need smartphones to be functioning members of society. Many of us need a car to get around, especially when public transit is underdeveloped. But do we *need* music? Technically speaking, music is not something we need to survive, although our favorite musicians may help us get through difficult times. Music is not a biological necessity but it *is* culturally ubiquitous: it exists all around us, it is played in multiple global cultures, and it has been developed and enjoyed throughout history. Music's omnipresence provides a clue about its tremendous sociological importance. Throughout this chapter, we examine the sociological significance of music for cultural survival and resistance to oppression, especially **racism**. In addition, we look at how musical resistance can be transformed into a **commodity** that is consumed by many different kinds of people in a capitalist economy.

To set the stage for our discussion of musical resistance (and commodification), we begin by outlining music's sociological relevance and complexity. Sociologically, we can think about music in three key ways: 1) as an art form, 2) as a commodity, and 3) as a tool of cultural resistance. Let's start with its artistic dimensions. Sociologists usually approach music as part of the world of **art**. Something that is "art" (as opposed to a craft) doesn't have a function, like a teapot or a phone. Instead, music is fundamentally aesthetic. The French sociologist Pierre Bourdieu declared that "music is the 'pure' art par excellence" (1984: 19).

While some kinds of art can feel intimidating (e.g. going to an expensive art gallery or attending the opera), many people enjoy listening to music. Not everybody can name drop their favorite painter, but we would guess that most people reading this book can easily list musical artists that suit their tastes, or think of a song that sets a mood for having fun. However, music is not *just* entertainment. As an art form, music is incredibly rich with symbolism, and this allows people to find many different meanings that are experienced at a personal level. Music's symbolic richness helps explain why identities are so powerfully expressed through musical preferences. When we decide what is good music and bad music, we are simultaneously saying something about who we are, and who we are not. In sociological terms, we use music to satisfy and express our **tastes**, as well as to draw **symbolic boundaries** (see chapter 4). As Bourdieu famously wrote in *Distinction*: "nothing more clearly affirms one's [social group membership], nothing more infallibly classifies, than tastes in

Feeling the Music

As an art form, music can generate a powerful sense of belonging and social solidarity (see chapter 5). The positive feelings you experience at a live show come not only from the musical performance, but also from the social experience of appreciating this art form with others who share your musical tastes.

Source: Shutterstock 233870467

music" (1984: 18). Many social groups in high school are defined by their distinctive tastes in music—electronica listeners don't embrace country music, and country music fans usually don't listen to hip-hop. On social media, we often perform identities through our music affiliations, whether by "liking" certain bands, sharing a favorite music video, or posting photos of a recent show we've attended. By saying "I like this music", we are also saying, "this is who I am". Historically, music tastes have been associated with class differences as well. Up until about the 1960s, social elites were almost exclusively the only groups in society who tended to like classical music and opera, and they rarely appreciated other genres. At least part of this taste preference can be attributed to the formal musical training that elites were more likely to have had, which can enhance appreciation for classical music (this connects to the concept of **cultural capital**, discussed in chapter 4). Elites were also socialized into a taste for musical forms through their families, who may have had a habit of listening to classical music or a tradition of regularly attending the symphony or opera. Today, although class differences in tastes still exist, they are much less likely to be strongly patterned around classical music and opera, as people with high economic and cultural capital have widely varying tastes and appreciate a wide range of musical genres.

Besides being a symbolically rich art form, there is a *second*, more contemporary reason why music is sociologically interesting: music is a significant commodity in consumer culture. Of course, we can certainly sing in the park with friends or pick up a guitar and make music at home. But in the current moment, that's not what many of us do. As a commodity, music supports a billion-dollar global industry of songwriters, musicians, technicians, producers, and business executives, among others. However, that industry has faced a significant crisis with recent technological change, facilitating the rise of digital downloading and streaming. While digital purchases have grown, they have not been large enough to compensate for the loss of revenue from traditional physical musical sales. The graph below (taken from *The Atlantic*) shows diminishing physical music sales over time. It's important to note the stabilization trend here. Music sales actually *rose* 0.3% in 2012, a trend which can be attributed to increased subscriptions to streaming services, as well as a global crackdown on music piracy (Weissman 2013). There are other significant forms of revenue within the music industry that are not reflected in this graph, such as attending live shows. While the music industry has faced a crisis of revenue (which we discuss more below), musicians are certainly not disappearing from our social world. They are major celebrities and style icons who provide a soundtrack for our daily lives.

There is a *third* reason why music is an important sociological case study; beyond its status as art and commodity, music is a tool of cultural resistance. The significance of music as a form of political expression is perhaps most clearly illustrated in the phenomenon of the "protest song". Protest songs have existed for hundreds, if not thousands of years, and can be found throughout the world. At its core, the protest song marries music with a message of resistance and a vision for social change. In North America, common targets have included slavery, women's rights, environmentalism, poverty, war, and police violence. Hip-hop scholar Tricia Rose describes how music provides a crucial source of political expression in the context of oppression:

> Under social conditions in which sustained frontal attacks on powerful groups are strategically unwise or successfully contained, oppressed people use language, dance and music to mock those in power, express rage, and produce fantasies of subversion.
>
> (1994: 99)

Many examples of protest songs can be found within American folk music, which has a long history of telling stories drawn from the poor and the working class. A classic example is the music of Woodie Guthrie, whose trademark guitar displayed a sticker stating, "this machine kills fascists". Guthrie traveled through migrant labor camps during the Great Depression of the 1930s US, and lived amongst the people who were suffering. One of Guthrie's most famous songs, "This Land is Your Land", celebrates the natural

Music Sales

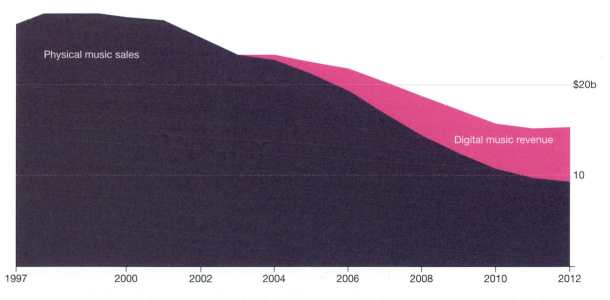

Note: Digital music revenue includes downloads, subscription services, and advertising revenue from free media-hosting sites such as YouTube. Revenue from concerts not included. All values in 2012 dollars.

While music remains a significant global commodity, the music industry has suffered a decline in revenue with the shift from physical to digital music sales.

Source: http://www.theatlantic.com/business/archive/2013/02/think-artists-dont-make-anything-off-music-sales-these-graphs-prove-you-wrong/273571/

beauty of the American landscape, but also protests the injustices faced by poor and working-class Americans. In one of the verses Guthrie sings: "By the relief office, I'd seen my people. As they stood there hungry, I stood there asking, Is this land made for you and me?" Guthrie was a major influence on later folk singers, like Bob Dylan, Joan Baez, and Pete Seeger.

Besides folk music, African American music has a long history of social protest, from the early days of slavery through the civil rights era, and continuing today. In the early 1900s, jazz emerged as a uniquely American musical form that was rooted in the African American experience. In musical terms, jazz grew out of ragtime, and combined syncopated beats with songs from slave plantation folk music. Jazz music thrived in the prohibition era of the 1920s, as speakeasies offered Whites spaces to drink while being entertained by African American musicians. Early jazz singers like Billy Holiday sang about classic themes of heartbreak and good times, but they also sang about the racism they experienced in the US. For example, the classic jazz song "Strange Fruit" combines a beautiful but haunting melody with a critique of lynching—a horrific practice where Blacks were hanged by White mobs after the end of slavery. First performed by Billie Holliday in 1939, the song paints a disturbing picture of racial violence: "Southern trees bear strange fruit / Blood on the leaves and blood at the root / Black bodies swinging in the southern breeze".

More recently, music has played an important role in the Black Lives Matter movement. This struggle for racial justice has emerged in response to police killings of unarmed Black people in the United States, such as Trayvon Martin, Michael Brown, Eric Garner, and Freddie Gray. In 2014, a video of Eric Garner's death (captured on a civilian's cell phone) showed him struggling for breath as police pinned him to the ground, and he could be heard pleading, "I can't breathe". Garner's words became a key chant for the movement, in addition to the statement, "Hands Up, Don't Shoot". Amidst ongoing political demonstrations, poet Luke Nephew wrote a song as a tribute to Garner—and to the many Black people who face violence at the hands of police—which became a core protest song for the Black Lives Matter movement:

> I still hear my brother crying "I can't breathe"
> Now I'm in the struggle saying "I can't leave"
> Calling out the violence of these racist police
> We ain't gonna stop till our people are free
> We ain't gonna stop till our people are free

Hands Up, Don't Shoot

The Black Lives Matter movement has generated a number of protest songs, following a long history of using music as a tool of cultural resistance. Here, protesters are shown chanting "Hands Up, Don't Shoot" at the Reclaim MLK march in St. Paul, Minnesota, January 19, 2015.

Source: APimages.com # 828209983315

This song could be heard at protests in the streets throughout the United States, from New York to Oakland. The role of music within the Black Lives Matter movement has not been limited to singing in the street; prominent artists like Alicia Keys and D'Angelo have also released tributes to victims of police violence. On the night a grand jury declined to indict Darren Wilson (the police officer who killed Michael Brown, an unarmed 18-year-old, in Ferguson, Missouri), Grammy-winning rapper Killer Mike delivered a passionate speech at a live show. As millions of Americans took to the streets to protest the verdict, Killer Mike addressed his audience. "I would like to say Rest in

Peace to Michael Brown. I would like to give all thoughts and prayers to the people out there peacefully protesting," he said. After speaking about racial and economic injustices, and the need to stay strong in the face of fear, he ended his comments by saying, "the one thing I want you to know is that it's us against the motherfucking machine!" (quoted in Young 2014).

In Canada, the First Nations hip-hop group A Tribe Called Red has risen to cultural prominence making music that discusses colonization and the oppression of indigenous people. Their songs have tackled issues such as the colonial underpinnings of Thanksgiving, the appropriation of indigenous culture, and the racist iconography promoted by professional sports teams (an issue we discussed in chapter 6). In media interviews, A Tribe Called Red members often highlight the significance of music as a tool of political protest. As DJ NDN (Ian Campeau) told fans during a 2015 Q&A in Sault Ste Marie, Ontario: "There's this tradition through history of people who are oppressed, people who have no voice, that's where they find it, they find it in the arts" (Petz 2015).

The protest song is a rich site of sociological meaning, with clear connections to the thinking frames featured in this book: material/cultural, structure/agency and micro/macro. Protest songs are a form of cultural expression that responds to material conditions of marginalization and oppression, such as a racist system of policing. They are also a way that members of oppressed groups have historically exercised agency through a collective critique of structural inequalities. Thus, protest songs—like many complex sociological phenomena—are shaped by material and cultural dynamics, highlight the interrelation of structure and agency, and can be explored through macro and micro lenses.

Later in the chapter, we discuss how hip-hop has carried on the tradition of the protest song. But first, we begin with a concept that is crucial for understanding music's sociological significance: subcultures.

2. THE STATUS OF SUBCULTURES

Up until this point in the book, we have spent a lot of time looking at trends of aspirational consumption, especially as represented by things associated with the upper-crust of society. Indeed, upscale emulation is a dominant theme in consumer culture. Many of us would like a yacht, or a set of Louis Vuitton luggage, or a Ferrari. But this is not the only game in town when it comes to consumer culture. Sometimes the rich simply don't provide much in the way of style iconography. Politicians and business executives are not generally known for kick-starting fashion trends. In fact, people in positions of power are often symbolically connected to tradition and convention, and also to mainstream, rather than alternative or avant-garde, cultural practices. So it is not too surprising that politicians and business executives tend to exemplify traditional cultural cues. As a result, they do not typically come to mind as trendsetters for style. In fact, trendsetters are quite often not situated within the dominant, mainstream culture, but instead are associated with a distinct subculture.

Indeed, a subculture—like hip-hop—can have incredible influence over mainstream conceptions of "cool". Within sociology, the concept of **subculture**

Politicians and Business Executives: Representing the Dominant Culture

US Secretary of State John Kerry and advisors meet with business executives in this January, 2015 photo. Many of these people are rich and/or powerful, and so they intentionally dress in ways that are boring as part of their social roles.

Source: https://commons.wikimedia.org/wiki/File:Secretary_Kerry_Meets_With_Business_Executives_to_Discuss_the_USA_Pavilion_at_the_Milan_Expo_2015_(16214573026).jpg

Pharrell Williams and his Stylish Hat

Hip-hop artist and song-writer, Pharrell Williams, is known for not only his catchy music, but also his iconic hat, which first made a splash at the Grammy's in 2014. The "Buffalo" hat—originally designed by Vivienne Westwood in the early 1980s and inspired by a hat worn by indigenous Peruvian women—has become a signature style piece popularized by Williams, and even spawned its own Twitter account. When Pharrell's Grammy hat was put up for auction (to benefit a children's charity), it was purchased for $44,100 by the fast-food chain, Arby's, which has a similar shaped hat in its logo.

Source: Gettyimages.com # 465271741

refers to a "group with certain cultural features that enable it to be distinguished from other groups and the wider society from which it has emerged" (Muggleton 2007). Subcultures unite around their own sets of norms, values, and symbols, which are often defined in opposition to those of mainstream society. Indeed, sociological research has shown how subcultures can "point out the inconsistencies in the larger culture, the gaps between a society's values and its reality" (Haenfler 2010: 46). For example, hip-hop regularly highlights inconsistencies between the ideals of the American dream and the reality for young inner-city Blacks. Black people's lives are significantly shaped by **racism**. (As we explored in chapter 10 on beauty ideals, racism combines racial prejudice with institutional power and authority.) Inner-city Blacks experience racism on an individual level, but also experience racism in the ways they are portrayed in mass media, and in their inter-actions with institutions like schooling and policing. Alongside racist oppression, African American youth have an incredible musical and stylistic influence through hip-hop culture (Patterson and Fosse 2015), and a small number have achieved material wealth as musical artists. From the very beginning, the subculture of hip-hop developed followers not only for its music, but also for its fashion sensibility. Hip-hop artists have become style icons in themselves, and many have developed their own clothing lines, like OVO (Drake), Ivy Park (Beyoncé), and Phat Farm (Russell Simmons, co-founder of hip-hop label Def Jam). Sociologist Ross Haenfler writes that "hip-hop has arguably had a greater influence on all youth style than any other subculture, as White, Latino, and Asian, upper, middle, and lower class kids alike adopt hip-hop imagery, speech patterns, and fashions" (2010: 44).

Hip-hop has now been embraced as a style worth emulating by youth around the world. This is a relatively common dynamic within consumer culture. The music and style of specific musical subcultures—

whether it be punk, grunge, or hip-hop—is often taken up by the broader culture and by the mass market. This happens, in part, because the music and the culture of a disadvantaged group provide mainstream culture with a source of excitement, rebelliousness, and a kind of edginess. Sociologist Patricia Hill Collins writes of the long history of White interest in Black culture, noting that White consumers are attracted to what Greg Tate has called "everything but the burden" of African Americans' lived experience (2009: 141).

The appeal of Black music to White consumers is certainly not new. Here, it's helpful to return to the history of Jazz. Jazz is a distinctly American musical genre that originated in the early decades of the 20th century and was pioneered by African American musicians. As Paul Lopes (2002) has documented, jazz did not originally command a lot of respect among broad audiences or within the music industry. However, over time the genre became more popular, especially among highly educated White audiences. The evolution of jazz as a cool music scene paralleled changing attitudes about race relations in the US. For culturally progressive Whites, appreciating jazz music and the cultural symbols attached to jazz earned them a kind of **status**. One of the cultural symbols related to the jazz world was the zoot suit, which was a kind of anti-suit that was popular with African American jazz musicians in the 1940s. It later became a fashionable way of dressing for Whites who listened to jazz, as well as other cultural groups, like Latinos and Italian Americans who participated in the jazz subculture.

The idea of something being "cool" emerged alongside jazz, and the notion of "coolness" was heavily associated with African American culture. As Alphonso McClendon (2015) has written, the jazz subculture spawned a wave of fashion trends that became more broadly popular but were still symbolically connected to the subculture, notably with a focus on ornamentation and twists on formal dress. Importantly, a defining element of coolness was a sense of defiance. Black jazz musicians like John Coltrane and Miles Davis made clear that their music was not designed to please Whites, and sometimes literally turned their back towards their predominantly White audiences as an expression of this defiance (Cashmore 2007). Nevertheless, the cool image associated with jazz was embraced by Blacks and Whites alike, as "cool" ways of dressing, acting, and walking were taken up in social settings far from their original creation. A similar dynamic of appropriating "cool" would later occur with hip-hop. Below, in our discussion of cultural appropriation, we'll consider some of the thorny questions that arise when a socially powerful group adopts the cultural practices of disadvantaged groups as though they were their own.

Jazz, Style, and the Birth of "Cool"

Ella Fitzgerald was a major figure in the jazz music scene beginning in the 1930s and she achieved success in related genres as well over the following decades. She was widely recognized as one of the most influential and successful jazz artists, and her popularity afforded her many television and film appearances. Her fashion style originated in the jazz aesthetic and was the epitome of glamour in the 1940s and 1950s; she is still known today for having been a fashion trendsetter.

Source: Alamy BPTXPF

We can think of subcultures, like jazz and hip-hop, as possessing a kind of "capital", or social currency. Sociologists use the term **subcultural capital** to refer to the status gained by insiders in a "cool" scene (Thornton 1996). By displaying specialized knowledge of a particular subculture, individuals demonstrate their authentic membership, accruing subcultural capital that distinguishes their own specialized tastes from those of mainstream culture. In his research on hip-hop, sociologist Jason Rodriquez explains that the status of subcultural capital is rooted in "alternative taste hierarchies embedded in youth cultures that stands apart from the dominant [hierarchy]" (2006: 664). In this way, a connection to hip-hop culture can provide a kind of subcultural capital. Yet, the status of hip-hop is complicated, given its connection to the past and continued oppression of African Americans. Stylistic cues associated with hip-hop can be interpreted differently depending on one's **social location**. We explore the complexities surrounding hip-hop, racism, and cultural appropriation in the next section.

3. PRODUCING AND CONSUMING HIP-HOP: RACISM, WHITE PRIVILEGE, AND CULTURAL APPROPRIATION

In order to understand how hip-hop evolved to become a mass-market commodity, we need to look at the history of this subculture. In a contemporary context, hip-hop is sometimes criticized for its apparent materialism, sexism, and glorification of violence, but this subculture is rooted in a historical context of racism and social struggle. Sociologist Michael Eric Dyson argues that hip-hop offers insight into race, history, and politics and suggests that "at its best, hip-hop gives voice to marginal Black youth we are not used to hearing from on such topics" (Dyson 2010: xvi). Indeed, sociologist Andreana Clay notes how often "academic and popular constructions of youth of color portray them as gang affiliated, 'troubled,' and potentially dangerous" (2012: 3). Countering this portrayal of hip-hop as the music of "troubled" youth, Clay highlights hip-hop's political potential. She describes how "some youth embrace hip-hop culture, music, and performance to articulate their ideologies and create political identities, as this genre most accurately reflects the lives, language, and rhythms of youth of color, particularly in urban areas" (2012: 8).

Originating in the 1970s, hip-hop was created by African American and Latino youth living in the impoverished South Bronx. As the most economically devastated neighborhood of New York City, the Bronx had been hit especially hard by state cuts in funding for low-income housing and social services. In this context, hip-hop emerged as a local expression of young people's everyday struggles with poverty, crime, drugs, and police brutality. While it is best known for its music, the subculture of hip-hop included other key elements of cultural expression, such as graffiti and breakdancing. Young people came together to share music and dancing at block parties, nightclubs, and in city parks, reclaiming these urban spaces. While the atmosphere was often celebratory, hip-hop carried an element of social critique. Grandmaster Flash and the Furious Five's "The Message", released in 1982, is widely regarded as the first example of what came to be known as "conscious rap".

The political messages conveyed through conscious rap critiqued the racism embedded within the structure of society, including inequalities in housing, education, wealth, and the criminal justice system. Taking a cue from these early musical influences, hip-hop offers an illuminating case study for key concepts in the sociological study of racism.

Sociologists who study racism often distinguish between prejudice, discrimination, and institutional racism. You are probably familiar with the first two terms. **Prejudice** refers to biased *beliefs* about a particular social group, while **discrimination** (discussed in chapter 6) refers to unequal *treatment* of members of a social group. We often think about racial prejudice and discrimination on an individual level, such as when a White store clerk holds negative views of Black youth (prejudice), and thus follows a young Black shopper around the store (discrimination). While individual beliefs and actions are certainly an important component of racism, our sociological imagination pushes us beyond the individual to examine how racism operates on a structural level. The concept of **institutional racism** refers to systems of racial advantage and disadvantage that are maintained through social institutions like education and the criminal justice system. While these institutions maintain the appearance of fairness, a close look at the numbers reveals vast inequalities. For example, the "Black Girls Matter" report released in 2015 shows striking racial disparities in school discipline (Crenshaw 2015). Data from Boston and New York City public schools indicate that "Black boys are disciplined more than any other group", with Black boys being suspended three times more often than White boys. For girls, the racial disparity is even higher: Black girls are suspended six times more often than White girls (Crenshaw 2015: 18). The authors of the report link these statistics to zero tolerance policies, which mandate severe disciplinary action for minor infractions. While such policies have the appearance of fairness, they often disproportionately target students of color, particularly Black youth. Sociologist Ann Arnett Ferguson writes of how Black boys are "adultified", such that "their transgressions are made to take on a sinister, intentional, fully conscious tone that is stripped of any element of childish naivety" (2001: 83). The same rule violation may be seen as more or less severe, as teachers' perceptions are filtered through racial stereotypes. In her ethnographic research in a West Coast elementary school, Ferguson found that "in the case of African American boys, misbehavior is likely to be interpreted as symptomatic of ominous criminal proclivities" (2001: 89). Thus, the racial disparities in school discipline are a product of both the racial prejudice among individual actors, and the institutional racism of school policies.

We can also see racial inequalities in the education system by comparing the resources available to students in different schools. The American Civil Liberties Union notes that in poor communities, "overcrowded classrooms, a lack of qualified teachers, and insufficient funding for 'extras' such as counsellors, special education services, and even textbooks, lock students into second-rate educational environments" (American Civil Liberties Union 2015). Given the intersection of race and class in the United States, students of color are much more likely to attend such impoverished schools. In 2014, the US Department of Education released data revealing striking racial inequalities in American schooling, not only in suspension rates, but also in the breadth of courses offered. For example, high schools with the highest percentage of Black and Latino students were much less likely to offer upper level math and science courses compared to predominantly White schools (Rich 2014). Thus, public education—at a *systemic* level—can reinforce broader patterns of racial inequality.

The institutional racism that youth of color experience in the education system does not end when they finish school. Scholars and activists draw attention to a "school-to-prison pipeline", where punitive school policies work to funnel students into the criminal justice system—a pattern that disproportionately affects students of color. Students who are regularly suspended as a result of zero tolerance policies may fall behind in classes, disengage with schooling, and eventually find themselves "pushed out". Critical education scholars and activists refer to school "push out" rather than "drop out" in order to highlight the institutional factors that drive many marginalized youth out of school. Students who are pushed out of school are much more likely to enter the criminal justice system. Sociologist Victor Rios writes of the **youth control complex** to highlight the multiple institutions that work to penalize, stigmatize, and eventually criminalize youth of color. He conducted ethnographic research with Black and Latino boys in Oakland, California, and found that school disciplinary practices—such as labeling a student "at risk"—can subject boys of color to heightened surveillance, restricting the opportunities available to them as they are placed under scrutiny within schools, the community, and the criminal justice system. The link between schools and the criminal justice system has become even more apparent as police gain a greater presence within schools themselves. It is now common for police to patrol school hallways as a "school resource officer", increasing the likelihood of school-based arrests (American Civil Liberties Union 2015). The role of police within schools entered the media spotlight in 2015 after a video went viral depicting a White police officer's violent arrest of a Black female student, who had apparently been reprimanded for using her cell phone in class. Understanding the school-to-prison pipeline is a pressing sociological concern in an era of mass incarceration. The United States imprisons a greater proportion of the population than any other country in the world—716 per 100,000 people (Walmsley 2013: 1)—and more than 60% of those incarcerated are people of color (The Sentencing Project 2014). Black men in America face a 32% chance of imprisonment over the course of their lifetime (The Sentencing Project 2014).

What do schooling and the criminal justice system have to do with hip-hop? Throughout the book, we have emphasized the interplay between material and cultural dimensions of social life. In order to understand the *cultural* phenomenon of hip-hop, we need to understand the *material* conditions in which this subculture emerged—and this requires an understanding of the racism that is embedded within American society. Not all hip-hop has an explicitly anti-racist message, but a lot of it does, especially early work from "conscious rappers" like Public Enemy, founded in 1982. Consider this lyric from the song "Fight the Power": "Elvis was a hero to most / But he never meant shit to me / Straight up racist, the sucker was / Simple and plain". Public Enemy's Chuck D later clarified that the lyric was not meant to suggest Elvis was personally racist; instead, he sought to draw attention to the racism within White culture, where Elvis was labeled "The King" without acknowledging that his music borrowed heavily from Black music of the time (Haenfler 2010: 47). In keeping with the sociological claim that subcultures often highlight inconsistencies within the dominant culture, hip-hop has powerfully critiqued the notion that we live in an equal society where racism is a thing of the past.

The sociological study of racism is not limited to the oppression of people of color. Like any form of inequality, the disadvantaging of some groups is accompanied by the privileging of others. The concept of **White privilege** refers to the advantages that White people experience as a result of their race. Privilege often comes in the form of access to opportunities, and the removal of barriers experienced by oppressed groups. For example, White youth who wear baggy pants and hoodies with their hoods up are much less likely to be viewed suspiciously by store clerks or law enforcement than Black and Latino youth wearing the same outfit. This is an example of White privilege, which opens up particular opportunities for Whites that are not available to people of color. Another example of White privilege is being able to turn on the television or look through the newspaper and easily find people who look like you represented in positions of economic and political leadership. Whites are also more likely to live in affluent neighborhoods and attend well-resourced schools. Because it involves the absence of barriers, and access to rights and opportunities that are often taken for granted, privilege may be invisible to those who have it. Thus, many White people are unaware of the advantages they receive as a result of their whiteness. Given the problem of White privilege, and the history of hip-hop as a response to racism and inequality, how can we understand the sociological significance of White people producing and consuming hip-hop?

As the influence of hip-hop music and style has achieved massive popularity within mainstream culture, the practice of producing and consuming hip-hop has expanded well beyond the Black urban communities who are credited for its origins. Major White hip-hop artists have risen to the top of the charts, claiming the industry's highest honors. For example, in 2014, White rapper Macklemore won four Grammy Awards, including best hip-hop album of the year. The expanded audience for hip-hop is even more striking. White youth now make up the largest segment of the American hip-hop market (Radio + Television Business Report 2012), notwithstanding the fact that African Americans and Hispanics are more likely to be fans than the general population (Nielson 2015). Of course, White fans do not all relate to hip-hop in the same way. Some White youth may be attracted to the anti-racist themes of hip-hop, and may identify with this subculture as a form of political expression. Others may identify with the violence and sexism of gangsta rap. What's more, hip-hop is now a global phenomenon, taken up in different ways by youth around the world.

While hip-hop's mainstream popularity might be celebrated as a success story for a subculture with humble beginnings, the cultural dissemination of hip-hop raises questions about who has legitimate access to this music. Broadly speaking, **cultural appropriation** refers to the use of cultural elements (such as modes of

Hip-Hop Goes Global

Hip-hop has traveled a long way from the South Bronx, and is now popular with diverse audiences around the world. Sri-Lankan British hip-hop artist M.I.A. brings hip-hop's legacy of political critique to an international context, addressing issues of war, colonization, and global inequality. In this image, she is shown performing for Paris Fashion Week, further showcasing the powerful connection between hip-hop, style, and fashion.

Source: APimages.com # 560186425226

speech, dress, or forms of music) by an outsider—someone who is not a member of the cultural group historically associated with this tradition. While we may want to applaud the sharing of cultural traditions in a diverse society, this dynamic can become problematic when members of a privileged group (like Whites) appropriate cultural elements from an oppressed group (like Blacks). Given that hip-hop has emerged from a history of struggle in the face of racism, do Whites have the same right to produce and consume this music without having endured these struggles themselves?

Debates about who has a legitimate right to produce hip-hop are ongoing. In 2014, many of these conversations centered on the rise of Iggy Azalea, a middle-class White Australian who raps with a Southern US accent. Azalea's music includes controversial lyrics that allude to histories of oppression that appear disconnected from her own social location. Consider the following lines, from the song "d.r.u.g.": "When the relay starts, I'm a runaway slave . . . Master, hitting on the past gotta spit it like a pastor". Iggy Azalea has achieved massive commercial success and a Grammy nomination, but she has also been the target of substantial criticism from Black artists like Azaelia Banks and Chuck D of Public Enemy. Gender and race scholar Britney Cooper writes of how she cringes when she hears Azalea sing "tell me how you love dat". From Cooper's perspective as an African American woman who grew up in the South, "the line is offensive because this Australian born-and-raised White girl almost convincingly mimics the sonic register of a downhome Atlanta girl" (Cooper 2014).

In 2014, rapper Q-tip publically lectured Iggy Azalea on the complexity of these issues. Using Twitter as an educational platform, he emphasized the historical significance of hip-hop, and the problem with borrowing from this subculture without acknowledging this important context (http://ca.complex.com/music/2014/12/qtip-iggy-azalea-history-lesson).

"*HipHop is a artistic and socio-political movement/culture that sprang from the disparate ghettos of NY in the early 70's*", Q-tip tweeted. "*Coming off the heels of the CIVIL RIGHTS MOVEMENT and approaching the end of the Vietnam war it was a crossroads 4 America*" . . . "*specially for Blacks in the US our neighborhoods were PROLIFERATED w/a rush of HEROINE*" . . . "*our school systems here in NY dungeon traps with light for learning*"

Yet, Q-tip notes that out of this context of hardship and struggle emerged cultural expression: "*it was a neighborhood thing really. Black and Latino Kids were carving out their space and it became infectious*" . . . "*the music was undeniable! It moved from NY N became national and even GLOBAL*"

Addressing Iggy Azalea directly, Q-tip emphasizes the significance of hip-hop's origins: *"you have to take into account the HISTORY as you move underneath the banner of hiphop. As I said before"* . . . *"hiphop is fun it's vile it's dance it's traditional it's light hearted but 1 thing it can never detach itself from . . . is being a SOCIO-Political movement."*

Central to the debate surrounding Iggy Azalea's music is her own failed understanding of racism, White privilege and the history of rap. Many artists have criticized the ignorance she has displayed on Twitter, something that Q-tip's tweets sought to rectify. For scholar Britney Cooper, a key problem with Azalea's music is her lack of recognition for the struggles that she is profiting from. Cooper (2014) writes that "while she may love hip-hop, [Iggy Azalea] has very little appreciation of Black culture or the problematic ways that White privilege can colonize that culture to the tune of millions of dollars." Taking an **intersectional** approach, Cooper draws attention to the intersection of race and gender in Azalea's problematic mode of performance. She writes "Iggy profits from the cultural performativity and forms of survival that Black women have perfected, without having to encounter and deal with the social problem that is the Black female body".

Thinking sociologically, we can see how dynamics of cultural appropriation reveal the deep interconnections between material struggle and cultural expression. When White artists produce hip-hop without paying credit to its history, they benefit from the culture of an oppressed group without enduring the hardships African Americans (or other members of the Black diaspora) continue to face. In 2015, then 16-year-old actor Amandla Stenberg produced a video called "Don't Cash Crop My Cornrows," which presented an eloquent take-down of cultural appropriation that quickly went viral. In Stenberg's words, "appropriation occurs when a style leads to racist generalizations or stereotypes where it originated but is deemed as high-fashion, cool or funny when the privileged take it for themselves" (quoted in Workneh 2015). Providing examples from hip-hop as well as Black hairstyles, Stenberg illustrates how the mainstream popularity of a subcultural style does not necessarily inspire respect for those who produced it. Indeed, as one journalist notes, "sagging pants, gold grills and cornrows—things that lead to stigmatization and marginalization when worn on Black people—are 'edgy' and fashionable when featured on high-profile White folks" (Williams 2015). Brilliantly illustrating this hypocrisy, Stenberg leaves viewers with a provocative question: "What would America be like if we loved Black people as much as we love Black culture?"

Musical Innovation vs. Appropriation

Stromae is a Belgian hip-hop artist whose music has been popular in Europe for several years and is now gaining fans in the US and elsewhere. His music exemplifies how genres can be adapted and merged from around the globe; it is recognizably hip-hop, but combines influences from African and European traditions. Stromae is a Black European musical artist, with an African father who died in the Rwandan genocide of the 1990s. Why is Stromae not accused of cultural appropriation? In part, it is because Stromae's social location and personal biography demonstrate experiences of oppression and outsider status akin to the African American experience, even though he is not African American.

Source: https://en.wikipedia.org/wiki/Stromae#/media/File:Stromae_@_BSF_2011_ (6070934641).jpg

How are we to make sense of this disjuncture between the apparent love of Black culture and the continued oppression of Black people? Sociologist Jason Rodriquez (2006) sheds some light on this issue in his research with White rap fans. He suggests many Whites who consume hip-hop downplay the significance of racial inequality, embracing what sociologists call **color-blind ideology**. In Rodriquez's words, color-blind ideology espouses "the assertion of essential sameness between racial and ethnic groups despite unequal social locations and distinctive histories" (Rodriquez 2006: 645).

Color-blind ideology is not limited to hip-hop fans; it is a dominant ideology within contemporary America, and one that works to justify and obscure the vastly unequal racial status quo. Rodriquez argues that the mass-marketing of hip-hop promotes a color-blind ideology that allows White fans to experience a sense of social similarity to people of color that doesn't have much basis in reality.

To reach these conclusions on color-blind ideology, Rodriquez carried out ethnographic research with White youth who loved hip-hop. More specifically, Rodriquez hung out and interviewed people at conscious rap concerts in a college town in Massachusetts where most of the audience members were White. The town where he did the study was predominantly White, but it was surrounded by towns with larger populations of Blacks and Latinos. Through his observations and interviews, Rodriquez identified a common strategy used to justify the participation of Whites in hip-hop culture, and to avoid the awkward topic of cultural appropriation. Hip-hop fans said that many Whites like hip-hop more now because there are more White rappers—like Eminem— and that White people generally like a White MC. However, they usually distanced themselves from that general perspective—saying that *they* weren't like that. Instead, they claimed to not see race, drawing social boundaries to distinguish their own apparently color-blind approach to hip-hop. Unlike other people, Rodriquez's participants claimed that they didn't need their MC to match their skin color. Even after viewing a hip-hop concert with highly racialized messages—with references to activists like Marcus Garvey and Malcolm X—one teenage fan said the following:

> You have to make a bridge between the race differences, and you have to realize that it's all just people and no matter what the color of your skin, it just doesn't matter . . . it's all the same sort of message of freedom, independence.
>
> (Rodriquez 2006: 661)

Rodriquez suggests that the ideology of color-blindness allows White fans to replace the message of Black emancipation with one of universal emancipation. Universal messages of freedom are not themselves objectionable, but Rodriquez argues that color-blind ideology "provides the opportunity for Whites to use their racial power . . . to appropriate the culture of hip-hop, taking the racially coded meanings out of the music" (2006: 663). Put differently, these fans may genuinely love hip-hop, but they unwittingly wield their White privilege as they engage in cultural appropriation and downplay the enduring racism that animates hip-hop. At the same time, consuming hip-hop also allows White fans to benefit by positioning themselves as "cool". While White fans take on the subcultural capital associated with hip-hop, they often deny the relevance of racial inequality in their own lives. In other words, they deny their White privilege.

Hip-hop provides a rich sociological case study, illustrating how mass consumer culture works to culturally appropriate and commodify the coolness associated with a particular subculture. Indeed, we can see how advertisers take up hip-hop's themes of rebellion, style, and creativity in the midst of poverty, and use those themes to sell products. For a particularly glaring example of this commodification dynamic and color-blind ideology, consider the advertisement that sells Poweraid using the words of murdered rap artist, Tupac Shakur (https://www.youtube.com/watch?v=0GG-TsIu5Ik). Tupac, whose parents were members of the Black Panther party, wrote about racism and violence in the inner city. Featuring NBA star Derrick Rose, the ad promotes a message of perseverance in the face of adversity. Encouraging consumers to "Power through", the ad ends with words on the screen stating "we're all just a kid from somewhere". This universal message may have broad appeal, but it loses the specific history behind Tupac's lyrics. While we may all begin as "a kid from somewhere", the kind of struggles and opportunities we encounter are deeply shaped by our race, class, and other aspects of our social location. The uplifting message offered by an energy drink company may be pure marketing genius, but it also works to obscure racialized structural inequalities.

Within a capitalist society, music is not simply a form of cultural expression, but also a valuable commodity. In the next section, we shift to the *material* side of our material/cultural thinking frame, as we explore economic relations and technological shifts in the music industry.

4. THE MUSIC INDUSTRY

We tend to think of music as created by artists, but music is also shaped by the multinational corporations that promote and distribute most of the songs we listen to. In recent years, this industry has been the site of significant transformation. The corporate production and distribution of music relies on communication technologies to reach audiences, and the digital era has upended practices that music companies relied on for almost 100 years. Therefore, music provides an excellent sociological case study for exploring how industries respond to and manage technological change. While technology influences all industries, technological change has been exceptionally transformative in the case of music. Music is as popular as ever, but the ways that people get their music are changing, and the very meaning of accessing and listening to music is being redefined through changing understandings of the legality and social acceptability of file-sharing. Exploring these questions sociologically highlights the interrelation between production and consumption. Put simply, production shapes consumption, and consumption shapes production. Sound confusing? We explain these two sides of the music industry coin below.

First, the sociological study of music demonstrates how production shapes consumption by highlighting how people within the music industry make decisions about artistic creation and financial gain simultaneously. The case of radio playlists is an illuminating example. Throughout history, the music industry has had the power to shape what we end up hearing on the radio. The practice known as payola involves record companies paying bribes to radio DJ's (and later to radio company executives) to get playtime for their records. Getting exposure for their music through radio play translated into increased sales. Payola scandals were huge in the 1950s, and eventually the practice was outlawed in the early 1960s. Even though it is now illegal to use bribery to promote music, versions of the practice pop up intermittently in the present day. One way this occurs is through contests. For example, consumers may be invited to have breakfast in the Bahamas with Ke$ha because they called in after hearing two of her songs played consecutively. You might wonder why Ke$ha would want to have breakfast with random radio listeners. These kinds of contests are usually arranged by a musical artist's record label. While there is no formal quid pro quo, they result in more airtime for that artist, as well as more attention for the radio station. Although none of us likes to think of our musical preferences as so easily manipulated, the fact remains that these kinds of marketing tactics do influence sales figures and the popularity of musical artists.

Another way our consumption habits are shaped by production is due to the extreme concentration of ownership in the music industry. The music industry is what economic sociologists call an **oligopoly**: a market that is controlled by a small number of powerful sellers. Even though the digital age has made it possible for anyone to upload a clip of themselves on YouTube, big business continues to exert substantial control over the flow of music into our earbuds. Three major companies dominate the music industry: Universal, Sony, and Warner. The radio conglomerate I Heart Media dominates US airwaves, reaching 245 million listeners every month. In addition to owning

Why Are There So Many Boy Bands?

One Direction is the latest incarnation of a historically successful musical formulation known as the "boy band". Like earlier boy bands N'Sync and the Jonas Brothers, these musical acts feature a group of young men (and sometimes actually boys) who share the singing duties but are not known for playing instruments. Boy bands feature members who are maximally appealing to the average young, female fan. As an industry formula, boy bands have had tremendous success and record companies look to repeat past successes by finding new boy bands to sign and promote.

Source: Shutterstock 304270097

many, *many* radio stations, I Heart Media also controls the largest network of performance venues in the United States. These radio networks give top performers—like Beyoncé or Taylor Swift—enormous amounts of airtime. One perspective on the approach these companies take to musicians is that they are investments. As corporations, record companies and radio stations are necessarily motivated by profits. Making money through music requires a degree of innovation, as audiences are always looking for new songs. But too much innovation can be bad for business—new artistic directions are risky and may fail to resonate with audiences, and that means a loss of investment. As a result, the music industry generally sticks to familiar formulas that have been successful in the past.

Apple is another key player in music oligopoly. If you download music legally, you are most likely going through the Apple filter. In fact, 63% of digital downloads go through Apple, and critics complain that it is difficult to get your songs sold through this venue if you are not from a major record label. What we want to highlight here is how the *material* relations of production in the music industry shape the *cultural* output of music in our lives. Major record labels engage in a range of strategies to manage risk and maximize profits, which leads to a great deal of overlap in the kinds of artists and music that they develop and promote. As a result of all of this oligopoly power, our playlists have become very similar.

Another reason why we seem to listen to the same old songs has to do with how the music industry uses consumer data. Here, we see that production is not the only driving force in the music industry; consumption also shapes production.

The digitization of music has greatly diminished revenue, but it is not without a silver lining for the industry: the massive amount of consumer data generated through digital sales provides a rich source of information to industry actors, allowing them to predict what songs and artists will become hits. Through big data, the industry uses our consumer habits to make decisions about which musicians to give record contracts and which types of music to promote and target towards particular audiences. Not only does marketing happen at the level of social groups such as, for example, highly educated Latina women under 30, but it also happens at the level of the individual. When a person uses digital music services, she provides companies like Apple with an exact description of her musical preferences. Apple can then use its information database to market particular songs and artists directly to her—songs and artists that it knows, through analysis of its database, are most likely to appeal to her. More broadly, the music industry is using the information

The Strains of an Oligopolistic Industry

In 2015, as Apple introduced its music streaming service, Taylor Swift withheld her music from being accessible through the service. Apple had decided that it would not pay royalties to musicians and songwriters (the copyright holders) during the introductory period when it was allowing customers to try the service for free. Because of Apple's strong influence within the industry, it felt it could set its own terms, but Swift's protest got them to change their minds.

Source: https://commons.wikimedia.org/wiki/Category:The_1989_World_Tour#/media/File:Taylor_Swift_006_(18117144088).jpg

SOCIOLOGISTS IN ACTION: TEXTUAL ANALYSIS

Sociologists have employed a large number of different methods in studying music, including surveys of listeners, ethnographies of musical production and performance, and statistical analyses of industry output, among others. Some researchers have employed textual analysis to address questions about music's meaning. **Textual analysis** is a method for interpreting the sociological significance of a text, and can be used to investigate the meaning of music. When we say "text", we are not referring simply to the written word; any object produced for the purpose of audience reception can be analyzed as a text. For example, a text can take the form of written or spoken language (e.g. song lyrics), visual representations (e.g. album covers), or other artistic media (e.g. music videos). Textual analysis aims to bring a theoretical perspective to bear on texts in order to provide an understanding of them that would not be immediately or casually available to an audience. With textual analysis, the sociologist seeks to explain the meaning of texts through interpretation (rather than developing an argument about **causation**).

As the music industry grew over the 20th century and became a mass medium, it also developed sociological significance as a popular art form that both influenced and reflected youth culture. It is in this context that Donald Horton (1957) carried out a textual analysis of popular songs in the 1950s. Horton analyzed a body of song lyrics published in music magazines in 1955. His method of textual analysis involved carefully reading lyrics and developing a set of preliminary insights about the nature of the lyrics holistically, and then returning to the lyrics to refine those insights in an iterative fashion. Horton found that the songs tended to deal with romantic relationships and to fall within a series of acts that roughly mirrored the trajectory of a relationship—wishing and dreaming, courtship, the honeymoon period, the dissolution of the relationship, and being alone. His interpretive insight about popular songs was that, as a whole, they functioned as a "vicarious discourse" where the lyrics provided a set of normative prescriptions for how to behave and how to feel within modern romantic relationships. By focusing on romance, pop songs outline a contemporary cultural schema for youth who are looking for tools to navigate the tricky world of dating, especially as norms and values around relationships are in flux. Horton also argued that popular songs provide a language for identity formation, as song lyrics described ways of understanding the self in relation to others. Although this study took place in the 1950s, a textual analysis of today's popular music would likely reveal a different yet equally revealing set of prescriptions about contemporary romantic relationships. (See the "Sociology outside the classroom" exercise at the end of this chapter.)

generated from digital sales and streaming at the aggregate level to make decisions about future musical production.

Some critics have argued that the use of big data within the music industry has led to a shallower and less creative pool of pop songs, as consumer tastes drive the industry toward repetition (Thompson 2014). But are consumers wholly responsible for the current state of pop music? Insights from economic sociology paint a more complex picture. Part of what appears to be driving contemporary pop music trends is a wave of industry conservatism in the face of declining revenue streams. As we mentioned earlier, recorded music revenues have dropped significantly over recent decades. Downloads and digital subscriptions are projected to increase, but the overall revenue stream has diminished substantially. Today, the average person spends about $25 a year on music, compared to $71 in the late 1990s (DeGusta 2011). Ten years ago the average American spent almost three times as much on recorded music products as they do today. Twenty-six years ago they spent almost twice as much as they do today. Research in economic sociology has shown how financial crises can encourage cultural industries to either radically innovate (as Hollywood did in the 1960s after audiences shrank because of increased TV watching) or to become more conservative in order to minimize losses. When they behave conservatively, industries produce more of the same and take fewer chances, which means that we—as consumers—may be left with few innovative or exciting acts. Consumers are an important force shaping the industry, but an understanding of production processes and decision-making is also crucial for understanding industry trends.

As a discipline, sociology has analyzed almost every corner of society. Through better understanding the nature of particular social objects and practices, we develop concepts and knowledge that in turn help us to understand the rest of society. Such is the case with music. As music sociologists William G. Roy and Timothy J. Dowd note: "Music is a mode of interaction that expresses and constitutes social relations (whether they are sub-cultures, organizations, classes, or nations) and that embodies cultural assumptions regarding these relations" (2010: 184). This statement crystallizes an important sociological insight—that symbolic creations like music are the outcome or expression of how groups relate to one another. The trick for the sociologist is to ask the right questions about what music can tell us about social groups and their interrelationships, and then to find the right method to gather evidence to answer those questions. In this chapter we have shown how musical tastes can generate insights into race relations, as well as how musical production and distribution practices can shed light on the ways organizations manage risk and negotiate complex technological issues. The content of music itself—its lyrics and other sonic qualities—can illuminate significant sociological phenomena ranging from romantic relationships and boy bands to the economic challenges facing the music industry. Through analyzing the social contexts of music's production and reception, we can see how a consumer product that generates strong feelings of personal identity and group belonging is also powerfully connected to broader structural features of society.

THINKING FRAMES

How can each thinking frame help us ponder the sociology of music?

Material / Cultural	Protest songs are a form of cultural expression that respond to material conditions of marginalization and oppression, such as poverty or a racist system of policing.
Think about . . .	Do any of your favorite songs carry a message of social protest? What material conditions are these artists critiquing in their music?

Structure / Agency	People choose to listen to music that they like. At the same time, the music that we like is highly influenced by the ways that particular artists and genres are distributed and promoted by the music industry.
Think about . . .	What radio stations or websites do you listen to? How does the music that is made available to you on these stations or websites constrain or expand your musical preferences?

Micro / Macro	Research on music subcultures often takes a microsociological approach in order to investigate how individuals construct meaning and draw social boundaries through interactions with others. Macrosociological research can shed light on how music industry trends are shaped by changes in technology and economic relations.
Think about . . .	How do you feel about music companies collecting and using information about your personal listening habits in order to a) target marketing efforts toward you, and b) build databases for understanding consumer preferences?

ACTIVE LEARNING

Active Learning

Online

Coopting "cool":
Watch the Poweraid ad discussed in the chapter which features Tupac's music in the background. Can you find other examples of corporations using hip-hop's "cool" status to sell products? https://www.youtube.com/watch?v=0GG-TsIu5Ik.

"On Fleek":
Music is not the only form of expression that can be subject to cultural appropriation. Check out this article describing how corporations benefit from the viral content generated by Black teens—a contemporary example of how powerful actors appropriate Black culture for profit. Do you think these teens should be financially compensated for the digital culture they create? http://www.thefader.com/2015/12/03/on-fleek-peaches-monroee-meechie-viral-vines

The Shazam effect:
Watch this short *Atlantic Monthly* video on shifts in the music industry. According to this video, who is to blame for increased uniformity on the radio? Do you think this is a fair explanation? Using your sociological imagination, can you think of factors that might be missing from this account of changes in the music industry? http://www.theatlantic.com/magazine/archive/2014/12/the-shazam-effect/382237/?single_page=true

Discussion/Reflection

High school subcultures:
Music is an important way to form identities and mark social boundaries. Can you think of social groups in your high school that were defined by their taste in music? Did these music subcultures overlap with elements of social location, such as race, class, or gender?

Appropriation or appreciation?
In this chapter, we have focused primarily on White appropriation of Black culture. Can you think of other examples where forms of cultural expression historically associated with an oppressed group have been appropriated by Whites? Are there ways for White fans to enjoy hip-hop music without engaging in cultural appropriation?

Sociology Outside the Classroom

The evolution of hip-hop lyrics: textual analysis:
What are the major themes that are addressed by hip-hop lyrics and how have these changed over time? Textual analysis can help you find out. Go to billboard.com/charts/year-end and make a list of the top 50 hip-hop songs from the most recent year and also from 10 years earlier. You can find song lyrics from many sites online, such as songlyrics.com or azlyrics.com. Review the lyrics from the earlier year multiple times, making note of the main concerns of the songs, such as love, desire, happiness, protest, conflict, etc. Refine your list of themes and how the themes relate to each other through multiple readings of the lyrics. Be open to finding other themes and to the different ways these themes can be presented, such as happiness through consumption or happiness through relationships. Then repeat this process for the lyrics from the later year. Compare and contrast how the themes have evolved.

Chapter 13

OUR LOVE–HATE RELATIONSHIP WITH THE CAR: MASCULINITY, INDUSTRY, AND ENVIRONMENTAL SUSTAINABILITY

INTRODUCING KEY CONCEPTS

Cars are an ideal example for understanding how our stuff has profound cultural and material dimensions. Cars are not only a means of transportation but a powerful marker of identity. How you get around—whether by car or truck, bike or bus—depends on your financial means, but it can also say something about the image you want to project. Certain cars are strongly associated with masculinity, *and can also be a way to signal racial or ethnic identities. Cars are symbolically dense cultural commodities, but they are also material goods that can help us understand shifting economic structures, especially the transition from a* Fordist *economy of industrial manufacturing to a* post-Fordist *economy. Car culture also offers a clear example of how* social structures *work to shape our decisions by providing specific opportunities and constraints regarding our transportation. Outlining these social structures promotes a systemic understanding of social outcomes, an understanding that greatly improves on explanations that focus on individuals' decisions. North Americans' love affair with the car is longstanding but has its share of challengers. Choosing different modes of transportation (e.g. bikes, buses, hybrid cars) has become an important way to signal environmental concern about climate change and greenhouse gas emissions, and may also offer an exit strategy from the stresses of mainstream car culture (e.g. car payments, traffic, road rage). As such, thinking sociologically about cars demonstrates how people do not uncritically accept consumer culture; the car industry is powerful, but it does not erase human* agency. *Car culture inspires desire amongst consumers for the latest products, but knowledge of the material implications of car culture works to animate* environmentalism *and* social movement *engagement.*

1. INTRODUCTION: CAR DREAMS AND CAR REALITIES

What kind of car do you imagine driving in the future? Is it a relatively modest and attainable model like a Honda Civic or Chevy Volt, or do you image something more distinctive—like a high-priced Land Rover, a flashy yellow Lamborghini, or a high-tech (and electric-powered) Tesla?

Teaching sociology to undergraduate students, we have noticed a distinctive trend when discussing the topic of the car: many male students tend to give a lot of thought to car purchases. While women often have specific ideas about their future wedding dresses (see chapter 8), men in our classes frequently have elaborate ideas about the kind of car they might one day own —both in their fantasy future life where money is no object, and in a more realistic future where they have to make their own car payments. In one of our classes, a student named Gvinder stated that his dream car would be a Ferrari. When asked why, he explained how his father immigrated from India with virtually no money, but with big dreams for his son's economic future. When his son was born, he gave him the name Gvinder—deliberately dropping a vowel in the spelling (i.e. Govinder) so that his name would fit on the personalized license plate of his future Ferrari. While Gvinder shares his father's dream of owning a Ferrari, he is also realistic; he tells the class that he will probably buy a Honda when he saves up enough money. The other male students nod approvingly. Gvinder's female classmates have very different ideas about cars. One woman imagines a car that would fly like the car in Harry Potter. Another says she focuses mainly on the color of the car, one says she would let her brother pick her car, while another says she would like to have a car to match each of her outfits. (The men in the class laugh uproariously at this last comment.) While the women take the car discussion less seriously than the men, they realize the high stakes of car ownership—especially since most of them live in a suburban setting with minimal public transit options. Car decisions matter—both practically and financially, even if one isn't deeply invested in car aesthetics. For example, one student, Mindy, whose parents don't speak much English, described how she became very involved in the family's recent purchase of a Toyota because her parents needed help negotiating with the car dealer and the insurance broker to get the best deal possible.

In this chapter we shed sociological light on car fantasies and car ownership. What shapes the desire for a car—say, versus riding a bike or taking public transit? Why are cars and trucks so closely linked to our cultural ideas of masculinity? While taking stock of the car's symbolic significance, we also examine car manufacturing and emerging challenges to car culture. How does car culture relate to economic growth? With the shift of manufacturing jobs out of the United States and Canada and into lower-wage locations, the dream of regularly buying a new car or truck becomes more elusive for many working-class and middle-class consumers. Put simply, without a well-paying job (or two well-paying jobs), car fantasies cannot be turned into automotive realities.

The **material** significance of the automobile is staggering. The automotive industry is the largest manufacturing sector in the world. By 2011, there were an estimated billion cars on the road—a number that doubled from 25 years prior (Newman 2011). While environmentalists worry about the impact of cars on the atmosphere, car ownership is on the rise. In the United States alone, drivers will travel an estimated trillion miles annually by the year 2050 (Silberg et al. 2015). The car is an enormously important material object whose manufacturing generates billions of dollars and supports millions of workers, while its practical functions structure many North Americans' everyday lifestyle. About 86% of Americans commute by car to work (while 2.8% walk and 5% take public transportation) (Werback 2013). In the United States, 87% of the driving-age population has a driver's license (US Department of Transportation 2014).

As we have been emphasizing throughout this book, consumer objects have both a material *and* a cultural dimension. Put differently, the car is a manufactured material object and it is also a potent cultural symbol. Cars (and trucks) are often imbued with ideals of masculinity—as shown in testosterone-driven films like *The Fast and the Furious*. In our classrooms, students are often vehement about the association between certain cars and gender. For example, if you are a guy, they tell us, you should drive a masculine car (*not* a Yaris), whereas "cute" cars (e.g. a MINI Cooper) are often associated with female drivers. Cars are also closely linked to race and ethnicity. For example, in one classroom moment our students told us that the Buick brand is associated with "old White people". Sociologist Amy Best's study of car culture (2006) demonstrates the importance of low-riders (a customized car that rides low to the ground) for Chicano youth's identity and pride in San Jose, California. The car you drive also speaks to your social class. Consider the contrasting impression given by showing up on a first date in a Mercedes SUV versus a rusted-out Hyundai. Cars are what Best calls "status conferring objects" (2006: 4). Cars also represent nostalgia for simpler times. This nostalgic appeal was vividly demonstrated in the Disney movie *Cars,* where anthropomorphized cars tried to re-create the glory days of cruising along Route 66 (a historic US interstate highway). Even today, many people enjoy going for a drive, plan vacations around a scenic road trip, or relish time spent detailing, tinkering with, or modifying their car.

Our key point here is that the car is not only a commonplace and materially significant feature of modern life, but also a commodity with both positive and negative symbolic resonance. Perhaps most significantly, driving has become strongly associated in our collective psyche with *freedom*. Think of the freedom many teenagers feel when they first get their license, and are able to go out driving with their friends (and not their parents!). Imagine the freedom of barreling down the highway on a road trip, sun shining, windows down, tunes blaring. Yet the freedom to drive is a paradoxical kind of freedom. Most obviously, driving a car is far from free; having a car requires money, and a considerable amount of it. For financial and practical reasons, the poor, the young, and the elderly frequently lack access to a private automobile. Even when we can afford a car, it is unclear how much freedom we have to drive. Often, alternatives like public transit, cycling, and walking are near impossible choices to make, and so people reluctantly end up driving to their destination. As Amy Best writes, "we are a car-dependent people, even if we hate to admit it" (2006: 6). Another sociologist, Dennis Soron, describes driving as a form of "compulsory consumption", given that many urban environments are "heavily biased towards automobile use" (2009: 182). Cars have become safer over the years with the innovation of new safety features, but the automobile is still a significant source of injury and death, killing about 34,000 people a year in the United States (LaFrance 2015). While cars are a source of pain, death, and expense, many of us still want a car because they seem to make life easier, and convey a sense of status and success. For at least some of us, car ownership delivers a feeling of pride and pleasure. For all of these reasons, we can say we have a "love–hate" relationship with the car—a theme that we will revisit throughout this chapter. In Amy Best's words, "the car is both a symbol of freedom, progress, and prosperity *and* a harbinger of the perils of rapid industrialization and the wreckage foisted on humanity by corporate capitalism" (2006: 4).

Our goal in this chapter is to shed light on our love–hate relationship with the car. In the next section, we examine the rise of car culture, what sociologist John Urry refers to as a system of "automobility" (Sheller and Urry 2000; 2004). When we use terms like "car culture" or automobility, we are referring to the multiple symbolic *meanings* associated with automobiles, as well as the social, economic, and political factors that allowed automobiles to emerge as a dominant mode of transportation. Throughout the chapter we reveal the

Car Accidents and Inequality

The inequality of who dies in car crashes

Motor vehicle crash deaths per 100 million vehicle miles traveled among people aged 25 or older.
Shading indicates 95% confidence intervals.

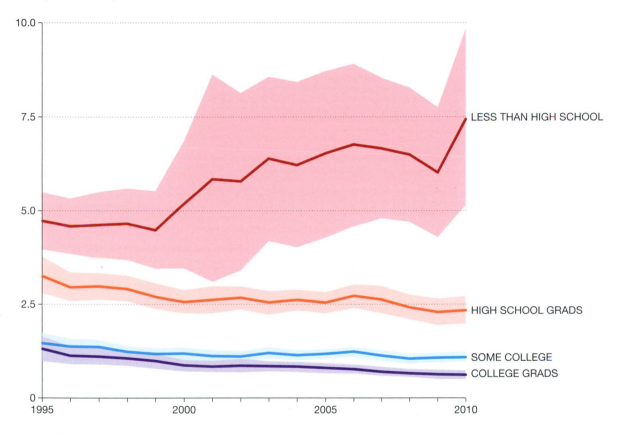

Sociologists are interested in understanding social inequalities, and car accidents are a worthy study in inequality. This graph relates levels of education to the number of motor vehicle crash deaths per 100 million vehicle miles traveled (for adults over 25 years of age). Doing so demonstrates the inequality of automobile fatalities: the least-educated Americans are 4.3 times more likely to die than the most educated Americans—and the gap appears to be widening. The higher death rate can be connected to the fact that poor Americans drive cheaper cars with fewer safety features (e.g. side air-bags, automatic warning systems), and receive poorer health care when they are involved in a traffic collision. Poor Americans also are more likely to be killed as pedestrians (Badger and Ingraham 2015).

Source: https://www.washingtonpost.com/news/wonk/wp/2015/10/01/the-hidden-inequality-of-who-dies-in-car-crashes/

insights of a sociological approach to the car, with a special focus on connecting this commodity with masculinity, economic growth, environmental change, and social movement mobilization.

When thinking sociologically about cars, it's helpful to examine key features of car culture, or *automobility*. When Sheller and Urry (2000) coined the term automobility, he was not referring to individual vehicles, but to an entire *system* of values, norms, practices, and infrastructure that supports the dominance of automobile travel in our society. As Urry notes, the system of automobility "spreads world-wide, and includes cars, car-drivers, roads, petroleum supplies and many novel objects, technologies and signs" (2004: 27). Automobility includes many elements—like vehicles, licensing systems, and dealerships—and these elements work together to create a system with considerable inertia. Car culture—like capitalism—tends to expand globally, absorbing and suppressing other modes of transport (like biking) in its path. In this chapter, we examine several critical features of automobility, including its systemic qualities, mobility, symbolic power, linkages to mass production and consumption, and contested nature. These features demonstrate the powerful cultural and material dimensions of this important global commodity. Below, we discuss each of these features, demonstrating how they help us think sociologically about car culture.

2. CAR CULTURE IS SYSTEMIC

Car culture involves much more than how we *feel* about cars (thumbs up or thumbs down). Rather, automobility is a *system* that has emerged to promote and perpetuate routinized car ownership and car driving. Analyzing car culture as a system has much in common with **functionalism**, a sociological approach that sees society as operating through a set of interlocking, complementary parts that work together to support the greater whole (see chapter 5). By seeing car culture as a system, we are encouraged to look beyond individual car ownership and appreciate the "technical and social interlinkages with other industries, car parts and accessories; petrol refining and distribution; road-building and maintenance . . . car sales and repair workshops; suburban house building; retailing and leisure complex; advertising and marketing; urban design and planning; and various oil-rich nations" (Urry 2004: 26). Just as the multiple parts of a car engine work together to allow the car to run, multiple **social structures** (see chapter 1) work together to create a system that promotes driving over other mobilities (e.g. walking, cycling, traveling by rail), and shapes how we organize our housing, leisure, and work schedules (ibid.).

We have developed powerful and ubiquitous social structures to facilitate car ownership and usage—structures that are legal, economic, physical, technological, and cultural. The systemic elements of car culture give automobility a kind of inertia, or what some sociologists refer to as path dependence (Urry 2004: 27, 31–32). **Path dependence** means that once society adopts a certain course of action, early decisions—like building highways and gas stations—can be self-reinforcing and can have a great deal of influence on later decisions. Once we created infrastructure and cities that relied on cars, later transit decisions were shaped by those earlier choices. Moving away from our primary reliance on cars isn't impossible, but it is certainly more difficult because of earlier commitments to a car-based way of life.

The systemic features of automobility are not always transparent to the casual observer. While today it can feel very natural to jump in a car to run an errand, the development of a systemic car culture was not inevitable—it was socially and economically produced through a complex historical interplay of corporate decisions, consumer choices, and state strategies. Scholars of urban planning and car culture document how the infrastructure for car manufacturing, consumption, and travel was laid down throughout the 20th century. The United States was the first country to experience the shift towards a system of mass motorization. When cars first appeared on the transportation scene in the 1890s United States, they were an elite mode of transportation only available to a privileged few. This situation gradually changed, as cars shifted from being a relatively exclusive mode of transportation to a mainstream, "normal" way of getting around. Henry Ford's Model T was hugely important in this story, as it was the first affordable car in the marketplace (something that we discuss more later in the chapter). The Model T was the car that incorporated the average worker into a system of automobility. By the late 1920s, there was one car for every five Americans—a sizeable difference from countries like France and England where there was only one car for every 44 people (Volti 2004: 56). Between 1969 and 1997 the number of two-car households doubled from 30% to 60% (Best 2006: 5). In 1995 car ownership reached a critical peak when the population of licensed drivers was equal to the number of cars and light trucks in the US (Volti 2004: 155). Today, the US has the largest number of private automobiles of any country on earth (Sousanis 2011). In the US, the average household owns approximately two cars (TEDB 2015), and a significant number of households own three cars.

The expansion of a system of automobility is not just about having more cars on the road, but has also involved a reshaping of the American landscape

Household Vehicle Ownership, 1960–2010

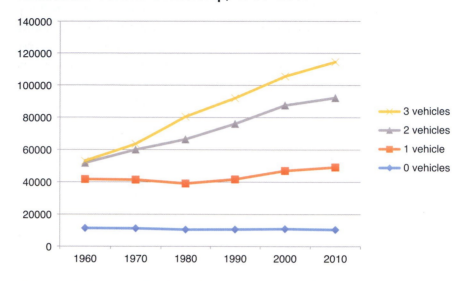

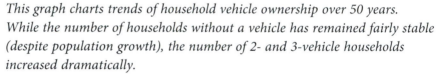

This graph charts trends of household vehicle ownership over 50 years. While the number of households without a vehicle has remained fairly stable (despite population growth), the number of 2- and 3-vehicle households increased dramatically.

Source: AASHTO 2013: 8

to privilege car travel. Social historians have documented the deliberate tactics used by General Motors in the 1930s to promote private car transport (e.g. Kunstler 1993). One key strategy was to put electric streetcars out of business throughout the United States and replace them with gasoline-powered buses (Kunstler 1993: 91–91). GM also worked with Standard Oil and Firestone to close down electric railroad companies and move traffic onto newly built highways (Kunstler 1993: 211–2). These car campaigns were remarkably successful. Kunstler writes, "General Motors' ultimate goal was to replace public transportation with private transportation, meaning the car, and in this they triumphed" (1993: 92). Instead of relying on public transportation, over the course of the 20th century more and more of the population came to rely on car travel to move around, and cities were designed to facilitate a rapid flow of car traffic. A system of interstate highways helped fuel a key trend of the 1950s and 1960s: the expansion of suburban living, a trend that arose along-side a dramatic expansion in automobile ownership (Volti 2004: 109–10). As people owned more cars, they took more road trips, leading to a parallel expansion of roadside motels, franchised fast-food chains like McDonald's (conveniently located next to interstates), and the growth of drive-in movie theatres (Volti 2004: 111–13).

What this historic story of car culture makes clear is that a system of automobility is not entirely sustained by private car ownership, but also requires public spending. Cars are private property, but to travel in them, we rely on the infrastructure provided by the state—roads, signs, speed limits, speed traps, ambulances, laws against drunk driving and so forth. As sociologist Rudi Volti writes, "governments have played an indispensable role in providing the infrastructure essential to automobile operation. Cars are of little value if they do not have adequate roads to travel on" (2004: x). For this reason, we can conceptualize car travel as a "quasi-private" mode of transportation (Sheller and Urry 2000: 58). The historical record shows that the state—at least in the US and Canada—has tended to privilege a system of car transportation over the course of the 20th century (Holtz Kay 1997; Kunstler 1993). In 2014, 60% of government spending on transportation went to highways, while less than 25% went to mass transit (Musick and Petz 2015: 8). When the American Society for Civil Engineers issued a *Report Card for America's Infrastructure* in 2013, it gave America's transit system a "D", citing the fact that 45% of American households lack access to public transit options, millions are underserved, and many transit agencies struggle to stretch declining funding to meet increasing demand (2013: 7, 53). With budget crises of recent decades, the state has generally neglected to invest in alternatives to car transportation, like subways and other systems of public transportation, especially compared to the expansion of roadways for private vehicles (Best 2006; Holtz Kay 1997). Additionally, recent decades have featured politicians who promise to lower taxes. Voters may like to pay less tax, but public coffers need funds to invest in big ticket items like new subway and regional rail infrastructure, especially when existing systems are aging and pushed to capacity with population growth.

An integral component of car culture is the regulation of automobile ownership and operation. The case of the automobile highlights the important interaction between **law** and society. As cars grew in popularity, and as car technology evolved to produce more powerful machines, laws were required to organize how cars could be produced and operated. Some regulations address safety concerns. As cars became faster machines and as they became more common, a set of complex regulations for safety standards evolved to ensure that cars on the market had at least minimal safety features. Regulations about fuel efficiency and emissions standards are more recent additions to address concerns about pollution and climate change. Laws regarding how people use cars have evolved over time as well, with **crimes** related to cars being some of the most common and well-known kinds of illegal activities. Speeding is a prime example. In order for speeding to be a crime, speed limit laws must be enacted. Emerging in the early part of the 20th century as cars became increasingly popular, speed limit laws are part of a larger category of laws that manage how people can drive—laws that are frequently broken! Running stop signs and red lights, aggressive driving, and illegal turns are just a few of the many ways people violate the law when driving. Theft was long a crime before cars, but laws specific to car theft have been enacted in order to manage this particular **social problem**. As car culture has grown, the regulation of cars has

Car Ownership Globally (measured by number of cars per 1000 people)

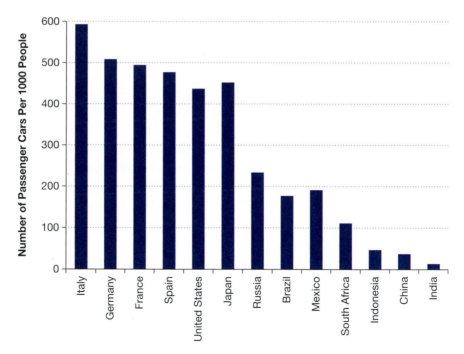

Scholars can chart the global growth of the middle class by looking at rates of car ownership per 1000 people, as shown in this figure (Uri Dadush 2012). In recent years, the US has dropped in this ranking, largely because rising inequality is squeezing the middle class. However, this graph shows that the US is still at the high end of the spectrum of car ownership, especially compared to a populous nation like China.

Source: http://carnegieendowment.org/2012/07/23/in-search-of-global-middle-class-new-index/cyo2#

Cars in China

Although China doesn't have a large number of cars for each 1000 citizens, it is the country that has added the largest overall number of cars to its national fleet in recent years. In 2010, China became the world's largest market for new cars, and is second only to the US in terms of overall number of cars.

Source: Shanghai Traffic Jam https://www.flickr.com/photos/carloszgz/15210144673/

become an essential and complex way that the system is sustained and managed. Laws cannot solve all of the social problems associated with cars—people still steal cars and drivers still have road rage. By using the law to formalize what kinds of **deviance** are socially unacceptable, most people find car culture manageable—or at least tolerable.

The system of automobility first emerged in North America, but it is now present in varying degrees in most countries (Urry 2004: 27). In the Global South, car transportation has lagged behind rates of usage in the Global North, but it is quickly catching up. Although rates of car ownership in the Global North are relatively stable, the number of cars in the world is projected to grow by 60% and reach 1.6 billion by 2025 (World Economic Forum 2013: 5). Countries with a developed middle class have higher numbers of cars for each citizen. Once a certain threshold of economic development is passed and the middle class expands, rates of car ownership go up dramatically (Dadush and Ali 2012).

3. CAR CULTURE IS CENTERED ON MOBILITY

The second key feature of car culture is an emphasis on rapid mobility. The mobility of the car impacts social expectations of how far and how fast we can travel in our daily lives. Research has shown that the flexibility of car travel encourages more trips than would be taken if one were reliant on other slower modes of transportation (Urry 2004: 28). The mobility offered by car travel has altered the way we organize our cities, social lives, and work lives. It allows us to separate our homes from our leisure spaces, and has created great distances between where people work and where they live. The car gives us elements of freedom and flexibility, but it also means that we live in "spatially stretched and time-compressed ways" (Urry 2004: 28). In many major US and Canadian cities, it is not uncommon to spend one hour driving each way from home to work. Americans in populous cities regularly contend with road networks congested for 6 hours a day on weekdays (Schrank et al. 2015: 5). Over 8% of American commuters spend 60 minutes or more traveling (including all modes of travel) to work, and nearly 3% commute 90 minutes or more (one way) to work (Jarosz and Cortes 2014).

Living in a culture organized around automobility, other modes of transit may come to feel inflexible, cumbersome, and fragmented, as expectations focus on moving around with maximum speed, privacy, and convenience. Because we have organized our social and physical environments in ways that are car-dependent, the mobility promised by the car can come to feel like a necessity, rather than a luxury.

Without denying the importance of status and identity concerns, an understanding of the attraction of cars for consumers must also emphasize the convenience of rapid mobility. One study of teen car drivers in Britain found that mobility is a key reason for driving and wanting a car (Carrabine and Longhurst 2002). One teenager was asked why she wanted to drive, and she replied:

Because I'll be more mobile. I'll be able to go and see my friends and go out for a quick drink and things, whereas at the moment I've got to get to a lift here, or, I've got to go and walk there and it's quite difficult to see each other.

(Carrabine and Longhurst 2002: 189)

The authors of this study conclude that there is an important cultural significance attached to the car because it helps youth "maintain and develop social networks, friendships and relationships" (190). For teens in the study, the desire for a car seemed less about acquiring a status object, and more about "facilitating sociability" (190). Not having a car put teenagers at risk of "social exclusion"; without this source of mobility, there is a danger of being "left out" (192). Lacking a car, young people often have to rely upon family members to get around, denying them the sense of freedom that can come with independent mobility.

The mobility of the car is both a blessing and a curse, bringing us back to the theme of our love–hate relationship with automobiles. The car is a kind of Frankenstein technology: it gives us power, but it can leave us vulnerable to its dark side—immobility! (Think back to chapter 9's discussion of technological change and Virilio's concept of the "integral accident".) The unprecedented number of people on contemporary roadways means that car trips often involve as much idling as driving. Sociologist Ben Fincham describes a paradox of mobility, wherein "[the] desire/need to be mobile is the major contributing factor to the motor-car being a source of immobility" (2006: 209). Today, the average American spends an entire workweek per year stuck in traffic—an amount of time that has grown rapidly in recent decades (Werback 2013). Traffic delays are estimated to cost the American economy $160 billion in lost time and wasted gas spent idling (Schrank et al. 2015: 1). And the problems don't end there; our expectations of automotive speed and mobility can lead to road rage, accidents, and a general sense of frustration. While today's traffic jams are unprecedented in size, the frustration of driving goes back to the early days of automobiles. Cultural theorist, Theodor Adorno wrote back in 1942, "[a]nd which driver is not tempted, merely by the power of the engine, to wipe out the vermin of the street, pedestrians, children and cyclists?"(cited in Urry 2004: 29). While this statement may seem extreme, those of you who must navigate heavy traffic on a regular basis may understand the sentiment. Our system of automobility seems to undermine the very ideals that it has promised us: freedom, convenience, and rapid mobility.

Besides the frustration of being stuck in traffic, it is worth noting that once you are strapped into the car, you are confined in a space where there is almost no kinesthetic movement expected from the driver (Urry 2004: 31). Your body

Traffic / Smog in China

In China, the rising rate of car ownership has presented serious problems for traffic congestion and air quality. On December 8, 2015, Beijing ordered its first ever "red alert" warning for smog. Half of all cars were ordered off the road, construction halted, and all schools were closed.

Source: Gettyimages.com # 502145646

becomes disciplined to the machine: you must keep your eyes on the road and you can't stretch out or stand up. Even a simple thing—like sneezing, adjusting the radio, or reading a text message—puts you at risk of an accident. Not surprisingly, public health experts point out that one of the main reasons we don't move enough as a society is because we spend so much time sitting still, moving in our cars. People who experience long automobile commutes are less likely to meet recommended levels of moderate-to-vigorous physical activity and are more likely to experience high blood pressure and problems with cardiorespiratory fitness (Hoehner et al. 2012).

Drive-Through Culture

Food writer Michael Pollan estimates that 19% of American meals are eaten in cars, and expresses concern about how our food system is reshaped by our love for the automobile: "As we move further away from eating food to eating highly processed, complicated food products—as we move from yogurt to Go-GURT—it takes more energy, and more energy in the packaging. We're putting a lot of time into redesigning our whole food supply so we can eat in the car" (quoted in Roberts 2006).

Source: Gettyimages.com # 462672444

4. CAR CULTURE IS SYMBOLICALLY POWERFUL

In addition to being systemic and focused on rapid mobility, car culture has powerful and enduring symbolic resonance. A car purchase is never symbolically neutral; it inevitably conveys meanings, identities, and values. Like other commodities discussed throughout this book, cars help us craft our identity and communicate messages about our gender, race, and social class. Just think of the many common **stereotypes** that link cars to particular types of people: soccer mom with a minivan, middle-aged businessman with an expensive sports car, and macho guy with a muscle car. These images reveal our tendency to connect specific types of vehicles with specific identities and symbolic values.

In addition to the particular associations of individual car brands, having access to a car—of any make or model—is an enormously important milestone for many young people. In the words of one of our students, "When I got my full driver's license, I felt free from childhood. The first time I drove in the car by myself I felt accomplished, independent, and a lot more mature." As this student notes, getting one's driver's license symbolizes a key transition on the path to independence. Indeed, all three of us grew up in rural areas and remember going for a driver's permit the day we reached the legal age. In many rural and suburban areas, the car offers an important means of mobility for a young person that literally has no substitute. While *driving* confers independence, North American car culture firmly associates car *ownership* with social success and status. Automobiles are perhaps the major item of individual consumption—after housing—that gives status to their owners. As Best writes, "[w]hether racing down the highway in a Mustang convertible, cruising down main Street in a Lexus, or observing a Hummer parked in the driveway of a palatial home, we see cars as a way to announce one's material successes (or lack thereof) to the world" (2006: 4).

Besides the status of actually owning and driving a car, cars are important symbols of our consumer desires—the stuff we want but don't have. Consumption scholar Colin Campbell (1987) argues that a key component of consumer culture involves fantasizing about commodities and the pleasures they will bring us. Even if we don't actually possess the coveted car—like Gvinder's Ferrari discussed at the outset of this chapter—it can embody our ideals, hopes, fantasies, and idealized pleasures. Perhaps for Gvinder and his father, the Ferrari came to embody the ideal of financial success and a luxurious way of life. In this way, cars function as a kind of **aspirational**, or **bridging good** that connects who we are with who we would like to be, the life we would ideally live (McCracken 1988; Nieuwenhuis 2008). Car culture's powerful symbolism rests, at least in part, on an escapist tendency coupled with dissatisfaction with one's current position in life. When we are unsatisfied with reality, we can displace our hopes and dreams onto symbolic objects—like cars—that connect us to a fantasy life.

You may not be entirely surprised to learn that many of the people who see cars as aspirational goods are men. Cars are a particularly salient symbol of masculinity (see chapter 7 for more on the social construction of gender). Car culture is frequently used to constitute masculine identities through symbols of power, speed, aggression, technological and mechanical sophistication, success, and dominance. Car culture also provides a space where men can form social bonds and communicate, often across generations (Best 2006: 4). At the same time, car culture "creates and deepens divisions among men", as men compare and evaluate who has access to the most prestigious sets of wheels (Best 2006: 4). To be clear, the longstanding connection between car culture and masculinity does not mean that women never enjoy cars, or don't participate in car culture. Some women are car enthusiasts, either on their own or in the context of heterosexual relationships (Best 2005: 58; D'Antonio 2015). In addition, there are certain kinds of cars (e.g. small cars, "cute" cars, minivans for moms) that are symbolically associated with femininity. Advertisers fully recognize the masculine and feminine symbolism imbued in car culture, as you can see with car advertisements.

While the symbolic connection between masculinity and cars might seem obvious, potentially less obvious are the *racialized* meanings associated with cars and car culture, and the use of cars to perform racial and ethnic identities. In sociology, the concept of ethnicity refers to a shared cultural or linguistic heritage. Best's ethnographic research in San Jose demonstrates how "many Chicano youth embrace the lowrider as an object to 'claim' an ethnic and national identity" (2006: 33). For many young people in Best's study, car cruising was a site of pride, visibility and respect, and an activity that connected them to a history of struggle to claim a place within a racially divided urban setting. As Best (2006: 33) writes:

Car Advertisements and Masculinity / Femininity

This 1967 Fiat 850 advertisement in Playboy plays on heteronormative masculine fantasies, showing that a man with a Fiat can have it all—a fully dressed woman to share a meal with, and a less-fully dressed woman to serve him.

Source: https://www.flickr.com/photos/91591049@N00/21294129226

SOCIOLOGISTS IN ACTION: ARCHIVAL RESEARCH

How can we understand the path that has led to the current place of the car in contemporary society? A historical approach is best suited to mapping and analyzing broad, long-term phenomena such as how industries and their place in society have evolved. Historical sociology most often relies on **archival research** to find evidence to address these kinds of questions. In archival research, the researcher identifies a collection of historical documents that are germane to a particular question. Such collections are often held by libraries, but archives are also maintained by a range of public and private institutions. The archival materials are then systematically reviewed in order to collect accurate information about important historical facts. Researchers can generate both qualitative narratives and quantitative databases from archival research, depending on the questions and data points they are interested in.

In a study of the history of automotive marketing, Margaret Walsh (2011) investigated how the American automotive industry understood the place of women within their consumer base. She was interested in the period of 1945–90, a time of great change for women in the American labor market and in society more broadly. The case of the automobile industry is ideal for investigating how industries respond to changes in their markets, especially since automobiles are a particularly gendered consumer product and have traditionally assumed a male buyer. Walsh's archival research accessed historical documents held by the John W. Hartman Center for Sales, Advertising and Marketing History at Duke University, including the business records of the J. Walter Thompson Company advertising agency (which held the Ford Motor Company's advertising account), as well as many images of car advertisements from the Roy Lightner Collection of Antique Advertisements. She also examined the photographs, car advertisements, automotive journals, and newspaper stories on the automobile industry contained in the National Automotive History Collection in the Skillman Branch of the Detroit Public Library. These different collections contained documents from all the decades she was

Ford Ad 1961

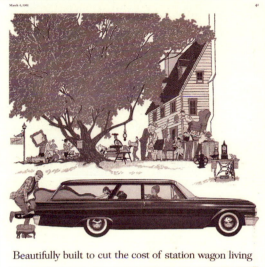

This 1961 Ford station wagon advertisement from The Saturday Evening Post depicts a woman in the driver's seat on an antiques shopping expedition. The ad's emphasis upon the beautiful and low-maintenance (it "takes care of itself") aspects of the vehicle appears to cater to the busy American housewife.

Source: Ford Ad 1961 https://www.flickr.com/photos/91591049@N00/15690138967

interested in studying, allowing Walsh to observe how changes in female consumers were incorporated into marketing practices. Walsh not only examined if women were included in car advertisements, but also investigated how advertisers and car manufacturers thought about women as car consumers. Walsh found that the automotive industry began to incorporate women into its advertising in the 1950s and 1960s, primarily focusing on the car as a helpful aid to housewives. These advertisements promoted the idea of a second family car so that wives and mothers could perform various domestic roles like driving to the grocery store and shuttling kids to their activities. With the social changes of the 1960s and 1970s, women were driving more, working outside the home, buying cars on their own, and actively involved in family car purchasing decisions. Interestingly, Walsh's archival research demonstrated that there was a significant lag in industry recognition of these changes; for decades, the industry continued to treat women as secondary car consumers who were most interested in a car's beauty and fashionability, rather than its functionality or reliability. By the 1990s, the automotive industry had caught up to changing realities for American women. Car advertisements became closely aligned with the diverse ways that women thought about cars, and spoke to the diverse factors they considered when making a car purchase like handling, dependability, safety features, and environmental impacts.

Today, cruising "slow and low" is a way some young Chicanos remain connected to this history of struggle. As they cruise, appropriating the distinctive style of their forebears, they create and maintain community, construct a coherent cultural identity, and symbolically struggle against the repeated assaults on the collective soul of their community.

The lowrider cruising scene was a source of cultural pride, but it was also a site of tension involving regular encounters with police who were there to enforce anti-cruising ordinances, usually designed to protect the interests of corporate development. Conflicts also emerged among Chicano youths themselves: some saw cruising as a negative symbol of Chicano culture, while others claimed it as a site of pride, authenticity, and a claim to space. For these young people, cruising served the "active reinvention of ethnicity, whereby they produce alternative understandings of being Chicano against the images, mostly negative, that they confront elsewhere" (2006: 33). While the car is often viewed as a highly individualizing commodity, for these Chicano youth the collective ritual of car cruising served as a form of community building, especially under the threat of being "whitewashed" (Best 2006: 36). The case of the lowrider demonstrates the symbolic potential of car culture, and the ways that cars go beyond an instrumental function of moving people around to acting as repositories of ethnic, racial, gender, and classed identities—as well as centerpieces for struggles of cultural belonging.

The case of the lowrider also demonstrates that it's difficult to talk about car culture in a *singular* sense. Even though we can talk about a **hegemonic** car culture, we also want to emphasize that car culture exists on multiple levels or scales (see chapter 3 for a discussion of hegemony). There is a global culture of luxury brands enjoyed by transnational elites (e.g. Ferrari, Rolls-Royce), but there are also brand associations with particular national identities (e.g. some US consumers' preference for half-ton trucks made in the US), as well as localized car **subcultures** (e.g. Corvette clubs, street racing groups, car modification enthusiasts). While hegemonic car culture puts a status premium on regularly buying a new car, there is also a significant subculture of classic car collectors, who value reclaiming and repairing old cars (Nieuwenhuis 2008). This classic car subculture is symbolically significant, because it demonstrates the emotional attachment that people develop to these commodities; these car aficionados may invest significant amounts of their time and energy fixing up an old car rather than purchasing a newer (perhaps more efficient) model. Nieuwenhuis's research on classic cars shows that people become emotionally attached to cars when they invest their labor into them; they enjoy a feeling of control that is "achieved through mechanical simplicity" which "allows the owner the ability to carry out his or her own maintenance and repair and personalize as appropriate" (Nieuwenhuis 2008: 653). By fixing and upgrading their car themselves, people come to form more of an emotional attachment to the car, and less of a willingness to casually get rid of it. Nieuwenhuis's research on classic car subcultures also shows how old cars can serve as a kind of **bridging commodity** that connects people to a historic, idealized past through a sense of nostalgia. This was also a key finding in D'Antonio's research on Corvette clubs, where she found that Corvette owners were highly patriotic, as well as nostalgic for an earlier, seemingly simpler era of American life (2015).

5. OBJECTS OF MASS PRODUCTION AND CONSUMPTION

Unlike other objects—like food or clothing—cars have primarily existed as a capitalist **commodity**. For this reason, Best writes, "car culture . . . should be understood as a culture inseparable from its market origins" (2006: 14). As mentioned above, when cars appeared in the 1890s, they were not a mass consumption item, since their high price made them affordable only by social elites. Working-class urbanites and rural people resented the rich cruising through the streets and speeding down peaceful country roads. Early cars involved a significant amount of artisanal labor, and often had elaborate carved wooden carriages that matched the tastes of the leisured elite. In 1906, future USA President Woodrow Wilson (then President of Princeton University) noted how the conspicuous wealth symbolized by the car could spark anti-elite resentment. He was quoted in the *New York Times* saying, "Nothing has spread Socialistic feeling in this country more than the use of automobiles. To the countryman [cars] are a picture of arrogance of wealth with all its independence and carelessness" (quoted in McCarthy 2009: 12).

Today, cars fill our streets, cities, and garages. Car ownership is often equated with adulthood, and as sociologist Bill Millard notes, in many North American cities, "the implicit equation of *motorist* with *citizen* remains the default setting" (2014: 33). At the same time that cars surround us, many people struggle to make car payments, especially when well-paying, stable jobs—like working on a car assembly line—are harder to find. Many people's access to a car depends on debt financing, cheap interest rates, attractive leases, and the second-hand car market. Others exit the car market altogether, and rely on cabs, public transportation, car-share programs, or walking and cycling.

How do we understand these dramatic shifts? How did cars transition from icons of arrogance and wealth, to a broadly accessible mass-market commodity that is ubiquitous—albeit far from universally affordable or desirable? To understand this story, we need to discuss the iconic auto-maker, Henry Ford, the development of a Fordist economic model (1910–70), and the eventual transition to a post-Fordist economy (1970 to the present day).

5.1. Fordism (1910–70): Mass-Produced Cars for Mass Consumption

Cars became mass-produced commodities in the early 20th century. Although the first cars were produced in Germany and France, mass-production techniques pioneered in the US made cars cheaper, more efficient, and widely available. Three major US car manufacturers—Ford, General Motors, and Chrysler—began to manufacture cars for the mass market in the first half of the 20th century, and were the dominant industry players until the 1970s. All of the "Big Three" US automotive companies were important in the history of the car, but the most dramatic changes began with Henry Ford.

Henry Ford (1863–1947) is credited with kick-starting a transition to mass industrial production—a transition that began with cars, but extended to other complex industrial items like television sets, radios, and computers. Ford built his first car in 1896 and established the Ford Motor Company in Detroit in 1903 (Volti 2004: xiv). He realized that car consumers were limited to elites, a feature that made the market fairly limited. In 1903, only 11,235 automobiles were sold in the US (Volti 2004: 23). Ford saw a bright future for a business that made cars accessible to the common person. Put differently, he had a vision of **mass production** that was complemented by **mass consumption**. Mass production involves large runs of standardized commodities produced with minimal modifications and efficient production methods. A key part of Ford's establishment of a system of mass production was introducing the assembly line, first used in 1913 (Volti 2004: xv). With an assembly line, workers stay in one place performing uniform tasks at high speeds on goods that move along a line. Assembly line production is a key part of what became known as **Fordism**. The wide-scale, efficient implementation of this technique revolutionized industrial manufacturing and allowed Ford to expand production and bring down the cost of cars. Ten years after introducing the assembly line, more than 1.8 million Model Ts had been produced and sold by the Ford Motor Company (Volti 2004: xv).

To create a system of mass consumption, Ford needed a mass of people who could buy his cars. He also needed to create incentives for workers to stay working on the assembly line. Assembly line production involved a new kind of labor arrangement that was noisy, repetitive, and involved very high worker turnover; in the early days of Ford's assembly line, 71% of new hires quit after only five days (Volti 2004: 26–7). Shortly after he introduced the assembly line, Ford implemented a $5 daily wage program. This program dramatically increased wages and created new car consumers (Gartman 2004: 177). Ford wanted to create consumers for his products, but he also wanted to quell worker discontent, and he understood this to be a smart financial decision— not simply a humanitarian act. To make cars more accessible to the common person (and his own workforce), Ford used company profits to lower the price of cars. When the Model T was first introduced in 1908 it retailed for $950. Remarkably, by 1924 one could buy the Model T for $290. Ford's strategy of using company profits to lower prices was contentious. At the time of these price reductions, John and Francis Dodge were shareholders in Ford. They went to court to sue Ford for channeling profits back into the company, rather than paying out large dividends to investors. The Dodge brothers won their case, and their victory reinforced the American business principle of "shareholder value". Ford was forced to pay out extra dividends of $19.3 million, some of which the Dodge brothers used to start up their own rival car company.

The first mass-produced car was the Model T, and it was basic, black, and had little concern for aesthetics. The Model T represents the consummate Fordist product: a mass-produced item offered to a mass of consumers in a uniform package. The Model T's production peaked in 1923; after this it faced serious competition from firms who offered consumers a bit more variety and luxury for their automotive dollars. The Model T "was welcomed in the 1910s as an instrument of democracy, bringing automobility to the masses . . . [however], by the 1920s it was commonly ridiculed as ugly" (Gartman 2004: 174). This is where General Motors entered the picture. As the Model T became accessible to working class people, social elites began to desire cars that set them apart as special and unique. Under the leadership of Alfred Sloan in the 1920s, GM began to mass-manufacture cars with stylish details that resembled luxury automobiles. From that point on, mass-manufactured cars in the US became stratified by stylistic details and price-point.

Ford's genius was making cars accessible to the average person, but GM recognized that consumers were interested in buying cars that set them apart and expressed their personal style preferences. In 1934, GM president

Henry Ford's Model T

Henry Ford believed that his business should turn a profit, but he was also famous for believing that business existed to generate jobs. In his own words, "My ambition is to employ still more men, to spread the benefits of this industrial system to the greatest possible number, to help them build up their lives and their homes. To do this we are putting the greatest share of our profits back in the business" (Dodge versus Ford 1919).

Source: Youth with Model T, Library of Congress: http://www.loc.gov/pictures/item/fsa1998007588/PP/

Alfred Sloan observed that "many people do not want to have exactly the same thing that the neighborhood has" (Gartman 2004: 178). At the top of the GM hierarchy stood the Cadillac; moving down the price hierarchy, consumers could choose from the Buick, Oldsmobile, Pontiac, and finally at the very bottom, the Chevrolet. In addition, GM developed another key car innovation that was also a brilliant marketing tactic: an annual change in each model (Volti 2004: 52). GM also introduced the idea of different colored cars, drawing from DuPont (a major GM shareholder) technology in fast-drying paint.

These innovations led GM to control 47% of the US car market by 1928. To be clear, GM cars were stylistically unique, but overall, cars in the Fordist era of mass manufacturing were actually quite similar, even though they had many superficial styling details that differentiated them into these different price brackets. From the 1920s to the 1950s, large automotive firms offered a variety of models that were qualitatively similar, but superficially differentiated by aesthetics and accessories. Cars began to change from season to season, like fashion trends, encouraging consumers to upgrade their model, even when their old car was still functional.

A key point to take away from the story of Fordism is that products—like cars—were mass-produced *and* mass-consumed. The 20th century revealed a symbiotic connection between automotive manufacturing, employment, and mass consumption. More broadly, the spread of Fordist production methods across a range of American manufacturing industries contributed to the spectacular ascendance of the American economy in the 20th century. Cars were not just popular; they were "one of the industrialized world's great growth industries during the first two decades of the post-World War II era" (Volti 2004: 89). As part of the post-WWII economic boom, the American working class enjoyed relatively high wages and historically high rates of unionization. Around 35% of American workers belonged to a union in 1954—a historic high point for the US (Mayer 2004). In the affluent period of post-WWII Fordism, high worker wages were used to establish a "separate realm of consumption in the home", a realm where workers "could find respite from and compensation for the realm of work" (Gartman 2004: 177). Of course, the boom times of Fordist mass consumption did not mean that everybody consumed in identical ways. Not everybody drove a Cadillac, even though many people admired them. However, the Fordist era was marked by an overarching belief that everyone would be able to access *some* version of mass market commodities, even if it was a lower priced Oldsmobile. In addition, the era of Fordism was an era of mass production and minimal product differentiation, even though there was growing acknowledgement that consumers sought to express a bit of creativity and personality through their purchases.

5.2. Post-Fordism (1970s–Today): Niche Markets

Car manufacturing is still a major global industry, employing about 5% of the world's workforce directly or indirectly (Graham 2010). However, production and consumption patterns shifted with the economic crises of the 1970s, and the world entered a period referred to as **post-Fordism**. The post-Fordist era roughly maps onto the era of **globalization** (see chapter 1)—from the late 1970s to the present day. There are many complex economic reasons for the transition to post-Fordism. Besides the economic turmoil that emerged in the 1970s (characterized by rising inflation, low growth rates, and high energy prices), the rise of globalized manufacturing processes made it difficult for nationally rooted automotive sectors to compete. To make the story relatively simple, we will concentrate on identifying post-Fordism's chief characteristics. This is especially important because it allows us to understand key elements of our current economic conditions, and how they shape possibilities for both employment and consumption.

In contrast to mass production and consumption, post-Fordism is characterized by flexible production and niche consumption. Instead of mass-produced cars with superficial styling differences, manufacturers have come to offer a greater number of cars that are fundamentally different in structure and engineering. Walking into a dealership reveals an extensive array of vehicles: "compacts, subcompacts, intermediate-sized cars, muscle cars . . . sports cars and personal luxury cars. Each type targeted . . . [to] a small, more specific market niche, based on non-class characteristics like age, gender, and family status" (Gartman 2004: 185). In consumer terms, a post-Fordist economy offers a massive amount of product differentiation, providing plenty of opportunities to distinguish oneself through consumption. Today's car consumer will find many different automobile choices available in their price range, and different options to show off their wealth and lifestyle. For example, if you are sporty you might want to buy a Subaru and attach a rack to carry your mountain bike. If you see yourself as a more intellectual type you might be more attracted to a Volvo. Both cars might be similarly priced, but they have different lifestyle messages and communicate different values.

To make all of these different types of cars, and to keep up with overseas competition, car manufacturing had to change. In short, production became more nimble, flexible, and global. In stark contrast to a Model T being rolled out on a single Detroit assembly line, cars are increasingly made at various sites around the world. When cars are assembled at a plant, the components being put together were themselves fabricated in factories around the globe. Moreover, consolidation within the industry has meant that technology is shared across brands. For example, some Audi and Volkswagen vehicles share their basic skeletons. However, even rival brands can "share" technology and manufacturing, a practice known as "badge engineering", where car companies "source models from competitors" to "round out their product lines without investing in the massive tooling needed to make each model in-house" (Fingleton 2013). The sourced model is then rebranded and sold as an entirely different car, often for an inflated price, as happened in the case of the Aston Martin Cygnet, which was actually a Toyota product (ibid.).

Within this context of the globalization of the industry, the three US car giants—Ford, GM, and Chrysler—were seriously shaken by foreign competition in the post-Fordist era. By 1971, Japan had risen to become the world's second largest auto producer (Volti 2004: xvii). In 1998, the German company Daimler-Benz acquired Chrysler—the largest industrial merger in history (Volti 2004: 146). This merger speaks to the increasing interpenetration and consolidation of automotive manufacturing. Even before the Daimler Chrysler merger, Chrysler owned 13% of Mitsubishi motors (ibid.). In 2008 the American car industry faced a serious financial crisis; although the reasons are diverse and complicated, the crisis arose in part due to the competition facilitated by post-Fordist production conditions and also due to miscalculations about consumer demand. GM and Chrysler filed for bankruptcy and were provided many billions of dollars in government loans in order to continue operating. All three companies needed to make major changes to their production processes, product lines, and relationships to their workers.

The decline of US automotive manufacturing reveals a great deal about employment prospects for US workers. Manufacturing still happens in the US, but it uses less labor, and that labor is much more specialized. In this context, it has become much more difficult, if not impossible, for somebody with minimal education to earn a middle-class income in an entry-level industrial automotive position. In a profile of the US company Standard Auto Parts, Davidson (2012) argues that this firm provides a metaphor for the new reality of US manufacturing. According to Davidson, this reality is a picture of "far fewer people, far more high-tech machines, and entirely different demands on the workers who remain" (2012). Most disturbingly for policy-makers who value full employment, the new automotive-parts manufacturing offers only minimal and tentative employment for unskilled workers. Today, automotive workers face the constant threat of being replaced by a machine or a lower wage worker abroad, and have virtually no opportunities for upward **social mobility** (see chapter 4). The Fordist system of employment and job training was relatively forgiving for people who came from disadvantaged backgrounds. Today in the post-Fordist era, the situation is quite different. Davidson writes, "I fear that those who are challenged now will only fall further behind." Indeed, the employment conditions of post-Fordism are characterized by

Michigan Building in Detroit

Formerly wealthy car-manufacturing cities, like Detroit, have been dramatically impacted by the post-Fordist era. Foreign automotive competition has led to the relative decline of the US automotive sector. Detroit used to be the global center of car manufacturing, but the city filed for bankruptcy in 2013. The picture above depicts the Michigan Building in Detroit. This historic theater is now used as a parking lot; it offers parking to office workers as a way to try to keep tenants from leaving the building altogether.

Source: Gettyimages.com #168251307

fewer opportunities for upward mobility, more persistent poverty, and a shrinking middle class. Though manufacturing employment in the United States remained relatively steady from the 1970s to the 1990s, the country lost an astonishing 5 million manufacturing jobs between 2000 and 2014. Moreover, of the 2.3 million manufacturing jobs lost during the 2008 recession, only 900,000 have been recovered (Scott 2015). Worker discontent has been quelled by low union membership (preventing collective mobilization), and the movement of industrial jobs overseas. It is much harder to organize a successful union campaign when you are competing with lower wage workers abroad, and when a much lower percentage of the population is employed in industrial manufacturing.

6. CAR CULTURE IS CONTESTED

Car culture is systemic, symbolically powerful, and embedded in enormous corporations, consumption desires, and global economic structures. However, the system of automobility is not static, and it has not gone unchallenged. In the 1960s and 1970s, public concerns about car safety, air quality, smog, and the uncertain future of gasoline supplies came to the fore of public debates (Volti 2004: 137). Interestingly, despite such critiques, the "automobile and the society it helped to create" showed "impressive staying power" (ibid.). This "staying power" of automobility speaks to the endurance of the systemic features we outlined earlier. However, we do not want to suggest that systems cannot and do not change or evolve. One of the dangers of systemic (or **functionalist**) ways of thinking in sociology is the tendency to reduce every social factor to its function. This tendency leads scholars to underestimate conflict, systemic disruptions, human **agency** and **social change**. As sociologist and car scholar David Gartman writes, "systems are abstractions—they do not act, only people do" (1994: 3). When we think about Gartman's comment in relation to the social system of automobility, we see that social *structures* are important, but people's *agency* works to shape and define social structures as they evolve. The system of automobility is not fixed; it has changed from a Fordist model to a post-Fordist model, as we have just discussed. Additionally, challengers to car culture have had a significant impact on how people view cars, and in some cases, have even altered transportation habits.

We can begin our discussion of car culture's critics by looking at the physical environment. Awareness of environmental problems has grown considerably in recent decades (Cotgrove and Duff 2009: 77–8), and some commentators see the car as "the single most important cause of environmental resource-use" (Urry 2004: 26). There are many environmental critiques of car culture, and these critiques only grow in magnitude as the planet's inhabitants face a worrisome future of global warming caused by fossil fuel dependency. Almost half of the oil used in the US is consumed as finished motor gasoline, and 90% of that is used in cars, SUVs and small trucks. Relatedly, 20% of all US carbon dioxide emissions come from gasoline combustion (US Energy Information Administration 2014). Expected increases in car ownership in China and India over the coming decades are worrying for the contribution they will make to smog and urban sprawl. Growing car usage evolves alongside the building of roadways, which leads to a loss of open space and traffic congestion. Car manufacturing is itself energy-intensive and incorporates materials such as plastics, paints, and batteries that have problematic environmental implications. The list of car culture's impacts on the environment is a long one.

Besides the car's association with fossil fuel and sprawl, automobility also creates a tremendous amount of waste when it comes to the cars we no longer drive. Life-cycle analysis, sometimes called cradle-to-grave analysis, documents all the energy that is lost when you factor in the resources required to make, use, and dispose of a car. This factor is not insignificant, especially considering that many people get rid of their cars when they are still functional. Why does automobility involve the premature disposal of so many cars? According to car scholar Paul Nieuwenhuis (2008), one key issue is product durability; many of our cars don't seem built to last, and are difficult to fix ourselves. However, Nieuwenhuis argues that the mainstream car industry has made more long-lasting cars, especially in response to consumer demands for increased quality that followed the entry of well-made Japanese cars into the American car market (2008: 648). Nieuwenhuis suggests that the issue of premature disposal is also cultural, and more specifically, occurs when consumers lose their emotional attachment to their cars. Of course, this pattern isn't limited to cars; when consumers lose a passion for a product, they are more likely throw it out and buy something new. This happens when goods—like cars—function as a "fashion product, rather than a true durable" (Nieuwenhuis 2008: 650). The presence of a **fashion cycle** in the car industry means that consumers come to desire the newest, most stylish vehicle, and distance themselves from older, "outdated" models. While it is sometimes possible to repair cars to extend their functionality, that is less likely to happen if consumers have lost their emotional attachment to their cars, which seem old and unfashionable. Nieuwenhuis's point is not that it is necessarily *easy* to hold on to your car for longer, but that it is possible to imagine a different kind of car culture where consumers are incentivized to repair and upgrade their cars, rather than simply replace them. We see this among classic car enthusiasts; in this subculture, a value is attributed to the skill of maintaining an old car, and the personal labor invested in the car works to reignite owners' emotional attachment to their vehicles (Nieuwenhuis 2008).

While some people upgrade their old cars for environmental reasons, a more common strategy for environmentally conscious car owners is to buy a more efficient, less polluting vehicle. Growing awareness of the connection

Rising Demand for Hybrid Cars and Electric Plug-In Vehicles

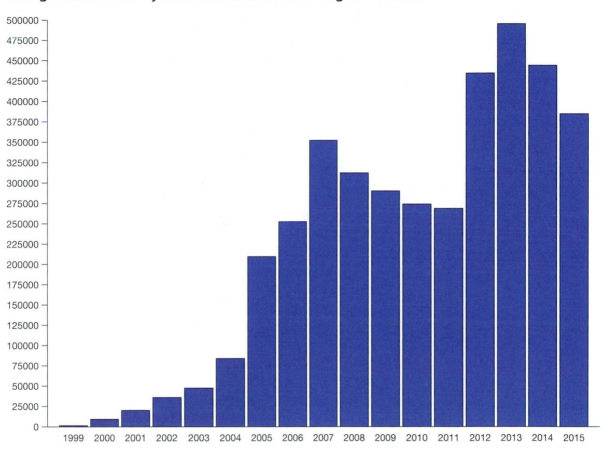

This chart shows the number of hybrid electric cars automobiles sold in the US between 1999 and 2015. Sales rose in 2005 as a cumulative response to government tax incentives and rebates, declined along with overall vehicle sales after the 2008 recession, and followed the upward trend of economic recovery in 2012.

Source: US Department of Energy. 2014. "Alternative Fuels Data Center: Maps and Data." http://www.afdc.energy.gov/data/.

between cars and environmental problems has fueled the remarkable growth of a consumer market for hybrid vehicles and plug-in electric vehicles.

Knowledge about the environmental issues linked to conventional vehicles motivates actions beyond just different automobile choices. Discontent with car culture also fuels **social movement** activism, a collective approach to making social change through organized, sustained activities that may target corporations, state regulations, and social habits (see chapter 3 for more on social movements). Environmental activists and sympathizers are cognizant of environmental problems (like many of us), but what distinguishes environmentalism as a social movement is the belief that our dominant way of life is flawed, and that industrial societies need to be reorganized to allow for a more humane and sustainable way of life (Cotgrove and Duff 2009: 77–8). These kinds of environmentalist values are sometimes referred to as **post-materialist**. Whereas materialist values prioritize economic growth, post-materialist values (which tend to emerge amongst those with a certain amount of economic security) prioritize social relationships, self-actualization, and living in harmony with nature (Cotgrove and Duff 2009: 80). Critiques of automobility often take on a post-materialist flavor: instead of just focusing on growing the economy and saving industrial jobs in automotive manufacturing plants, environmentalists argue that we must reorient our ways of life and transportation away from car culture to build community, expand human well-being, and live within the earth's limits.

Bicycle culture represents a post-materialist challenge to automobility. At a basic level, riding a bike is an alternate form of mobility. The convenience of the bicycle is particularly felt in urban contexts where roads are clogged with slow-moving vehicles and cyclists often find it easier to get around (and pay for) two wheels rather than four. But bicycle culture is not just a practical or strategic alternative to getting in a car; it often represents an expression of post-materialist values. This is most obviously demonstrated in the case of "Critical Mass", a bicycling protest movement that typically occurs on the last Friday of the month when cyclists gather *en masse* to celebrate the joy of biking, and to "reclaim" the streets from a hegemonic car culture. The event originated in San Francisco in the early 1990s (at an event called "Commute Clot"), and eventually spread to over 300 cities around the world. If you have ever witnessed (or participated in) this event, you may have heard the rallying cry, "We are not blocking traffic . . . We are traffic!". Some rides only involve a few dozen cyclists, while others have brought together tens of thousands of people. Critical Mass events are relatively decentralized; there is no chief authority, and various spin-off groups have formed. What unites these various bike activists is a collective social movement approach to social and environmental change. By regularly coming together in a public way, Critical Mass activities seek to politicize the issue of biking as an environmentally friendly, but publicly under-supported (and therefore risky from a safety perspective), form of mobility. More generally, we can think of Critical Mass as challenging the widespread assumption of "motorism", which takes for granted the idea that cars are, and should be, the kings of the road (Millard 2014: 34).

Critical Mass

A Critical Mass bike ride in Vancouver, British Columbia, held at the end of June, 2007, to celebrate the grassroots reclamation of public spaces and allow cyclists to move safely and freely around the city.

Source: https://www.flickr.com/photos/itzafineday/2615537456

An Organic Statement on Car Culture

The iconic "Garden Car" has been a feature of Toronto's Kensington Market neighborhood since 2007. Each spring "she" is moved back onto the street and replanted. The City allows the car to remain on the street as public art (without paying for parking), as long as it is insured and removed for the winter. Significantly, the caretaker of the car is an urban cycling consultant.

Source: https://commons.wikimedia.org/wiki/File:Art_at_Kensington_Market.jpg

Besides the environmental and social movement critiques of automobility, business commentators are raising questions about the extent to which young consumers can financially commit to car ownership. Cars are not easily affordable for many young workers. As we noted above, many workers in a post-Fordist economy struggle to make ends meet. This means that buying a house or a car is no longer a guaranteed rite of passage to adulthood, and middle-class status is more difficult to attain than in previous generations. While having a car is still an important source of identity and meaning for many youth, the overall trends suggest that young people are buying fewer cars and the proportion of teenagers with a license is also going down. In 1983, 46% of teens had a driver's license, but by 2014, only 25% of teens did (Beck 2016). The youth market for cars is sluggish, and carmakers are trying to create demand among young consumers. An article in the *Atlantic Monthly* titled "The Cheapest Generation" describes Ford's efforts to appeal to youth drivers with its Fiesta (Thompson and Weissmann 2012). Toyota has also made attempts to appeal to millennial drivers. The 1999 unveiling of the Echo was the first car "designed for strong youth appeal" (Best 2006: 11). Beyond this, Toyota launched an entire Youth Division, Scion, designed to sell low-cost sedans and SUVs to youth. Luxury cars, like Lexus and Mercedes, have also come out with smaller, cheaper "starter" models to try to generate brand loyalty at a younger age.

As carmakers attempt to appeal to young buyers, they also have to compete with the rise in the **sharing economy**. In the sharing economy, people use mobile devices and Internet connections to temporarily access consumer durables like cars or living spaces, rather than owning the good themselves. With our cell phones, we can book a Zip Car, catch a ride with Uber, or plan

THE UBER CHALLENGE TO CAR CULTURE

As we write this book, Uber faces major legal challenges in the various global cities where it has arisen, not to mention large-scale organized protests by conventional taxi drivers. The Uber case is sociologically interesting for several reasons. With respect to consumers, the case highlights how consumer expectations and desires can be a powerful force in creating change within industries. Consumers often pick Uber over conventional taxis given their lower prices and convenient hailing and payment system, which maximizes consumers' ability to meet their mobility needs and wants. The case also illustrates the precarious nature of work in a post-Fordist economy, and the need for the state's legal regulations to be rapidly and frequently overhauled in response to technological changes. Local taxi companies must comply with regulations around their operation and pricing, and they contribute to municipal tax bases. Uber is not a local business (except for its home base) and there is ongoing debate about how and whether Uber services can be regulated. Most taxi drivers are employees for legal and tax purposes. With Uber, drivers are independent contractors, which raises questions about insurance coverage and worker protections. As taxi drivers struggle to make a living in expensive urban locations, critics question whether Uber is truly a "sharing economy" model, or a private business that allows its actors to avoid paying taxes, insurance, and municipal fees.

a trip through Airbnb. These options make it less necessary for many consumers to buy their own car, or rent a car when visiting a city. Today, car-sharing options are relatively mainstream and low-budget. Car access (versus car ownership) is especially attractive for people living in urban settings where rents are high and parking is hard to find. In these settings, it can be more convenient to use mass transit and biking for some trips, and then access a car only when necessary.

So, what is the future of the car? Looking around us, it is clear that we are not yet in a post-driving, post-owning era. However, things are definitely changing. Our cultural standard of car ownership as a mandatory rite of citizenship is becoming unsettled, if not completely challenged. The

Taxi versus Uber

In December of 2015, taxi drivers in Toronto block traffic to protest what they see as unfair competition from UberX and to promote greater municipal regulation of the ride-sharing service.

Source: Gettyimages.com # 501718620

Fleet of Smart Cars

A fleet of Smart micro hybrid cars for Daimler's Car2Go rental service in Ulm, Germany. Car2Go allows users to rent low-emission Smart cars by the minute in thirty cities around the world.

Source: Gettyimages.com # 107979816

environmental problems of automobility don't motivate everybody to purchase an electric car (especially since many can't afford one), but they are present in the public consciousness. Perhaps in the future, as John Urry writes, "The cool way of travelling will not be to own but to access small, light mobile pods when required" (2004: 36).

THINKING FRAMES

How can each thinking frame help us ponder the sociology of the car?

Material / Cultural	The car is an industrial product with important economic and environmental effects, and also a culturally significant object that is implicated in individual and group identities.
Think about . . .	As more people choose alternatives to car ownership, how might the symbolism of cars change over time?

Structure / Agency	Cars are the primary form of transportation for most people because the infrastructure, market, and legal and cultural supports for driving are in place. But people are also increasingly looking to alternatives that are more environmentally friendly and budget conscious.
Think about . . .	Has your family always owned a car? How are your family's routines organized around having or not having a car? How are your family's transportation routines shaped by employment opportunities and your family members' position in the larger economic system?

Micro / Macro	At a personal level, driving a car can feel liberating and convenient and can fulfill practical transportation needs. At the same time, the broader picture of our societal reliance on cars is less positive because of the environmental drawbacks of smog and carbon dioxide emissions as well as the inefficiencies of traffic congestion.
Think about . . .	What do you think of efforts to push for alternative forms of transportation, such as public transit options and biking? Are such options good ideas for the community you live in, and are they realistic and attractive for you personally?

ACTIVE LEARNING

Online

Active Learning

Selling a dream:
Look online at car advertisements. Find examples that exemplify the idea of cars as a bridging commodity (aspirational good). Find examples that showcase how cars are advertised differently to men and women.

A decline in car culture?
How can we understand the decrease in the rates of car ownership among young people? Rates of both driving and ownership are down among younger age groups. Is this decline primarily economically based, or is it more cultural and related to different values and lifestyle priorities? http://business.time.com/2013/08/09/the-great-debate-do-millennials-really-want-cars-or-not/

Unequal transportation options:

Many people cannot afford to own a car. For some, public transportation is the only way to get to work or to school. Although there is a lot of diversity across cities, economically disadvantaged neighborhoods tend to have access to worse public transportation options. What are the social implications of this discrepancy? How can inequality in transportation access feed into broader inequalities? http://www.theatlantic.com/business/archive/2015/05/stranded-how-americas-failing-public-transportation-increases-inequality/393419/

Discussion/Reflection

Self-driving cars:

News stories about self-driving cars are appearing with predictions that we could have them on roads within the next ten years. Although these cars could be owned, they could also be hailed from a cell phone. What kinds of social changes might possibly result from the availability of self-driving cars? What advantages will they have over current cars? How well can they address current problems compared to mass transit options?

Automotive industry bail-out:

In the financial crisis of 2008, the US government spent billions of dollars in order to rescue the automotive industry from collapse. Given that American car companies employ many thousands of workers, the government justified the bail out as a way of protecting workers. Some people argued that this was "corporate welfare". How much government involvement in the market is appropriate?

Sociology Outside the Classroom

Cars and identity:

Interview people who own a car to understand how the car is related to their sense of self. Ask them not only what kind of car they own, but also what kinds of cars they like and do not like. Ask them what kinds of cars they hope to own in the future and what makes a car cool or not cool. How did they come to own their particular car—is it their ideal car or a car that is good enough for now?

60-mile traffic jam!

Read this news story, which describes an extreme version of an event that almost everyone has experienced—a traffic jam. http://www.dailymail.co.uk/news/article-1306058/China-traffic-jam-enters-11th-day-officials-admit-weeks.html. Thinking about this traffic jam, observe the state of traffic where you live. Does traffic flow well, or is it relatively clogged? Keep a log of the time you spend in transit for one week. How does that time break down by different modes of transit? Are your choices about how to travel relatively open, or are you strongly constrained to public transportation, car travel, or a non-motorized option?

ADVERTISING AND SOCIETY: AN OVERVIEW OF SOCIOLOGICAL METHODS

OVERVIEW

This appendix has two main goals. In the broadest sense, it describes the relationship between arguments and evidence in sociology. By analyzing the logic behind data collection and analysis, we will gain an understanding of how certain kinds of questions are best addressed through empirical social research, as well as how particular kinds of data allow us to make particular kinds of arguments. More specifically, this appendix also introduces the most common methods that sociologists employ. Through a close look at these methods of data collection and analysis, we will learn about their advantages and disadvantages, which will allow you to understand and critique social scientific findings and arguments of the kind that we encounter within academic publications and within the media more broadly. When you know which methods are available to sociologists and how they differ, you can understand the reasoning underlying researchers' methodological choices. This chapter features the case of advertising and will discuss how the production, content, and reception of advertising can be empirically investigated through sociological methods.

1. INTRODUCTION: ADVERTISING AND CONSUMER SOCIETY

People seem to have a conflicted relationship with advertising. Sometimes we find advertising entertaining and surprising and cool—Super Bowl ads on television and videos that go viral online are examples. But sometimes advertising is irritating—like when you are forced to watch an ad before you can access a webpage or when a movie's start time is delayed 15 minutes to show ads to the theatre audience. Like it or not, advertising is pervasive in society. It is especially prevalent in mass media, as advertising is central to media's business models. Media such as broadcast television, radio, and magazines get most or sometimes all of their revenue from advertising. Even if we feel like we avoid watching commercials on TV or online, advertising inevitably trickles into our daily routines in a variety of ways, including billboards, signs on buses and park benches, and through product packaging.

Advertising is pervasive because it is central to the functioning of capitalism and to consumer society. Through advertising, we learn about what we can spend our money on, and we are exposed to new options in the marketplace. We also learn pertinent information about products and services that can help us make consumption choices. More significantly, advertising is the mode through which brands are developed. It is the way that corporations communicate with consumers to develop their brands. Brands are identity markers for products and services, and they involve much more than an identifying name or logo. As we discussed in chapter 10, brands also include the image and associations that consumers attach to a corporate name, along with how they feel about that image. (For example, in our classes students often tell us that they have very different emotional associations with Coke and Pepsi, even when they believe that these two sodas taste relatively similar.) Through advertising, firms promote particular kinds of images with intended meanings for consumers. In this way, advertising is about not only relaying relevant information—about price and product performance—to consumers, but also about forging an emotional connection.

Given these layers of functions and uses, advertising is clearly a complex phenomenon. Complex social phenomena can be studied in many different ways, so advertising makes an ideal case for highlighting the range of sociological methods that researchers can employ. In this overview, we will describe in detail a set of common sociological methods and discuss examples that all relate in some way to advertising. Before reviewing these specific methods, we will illustrate a number of central methodological concepts that cut across multiple methods and that illuminate the common logic underlying empirical sociological inquiry.

2. THE NATURE OF EMPIRICAL EVIDENCE AND EXPLANATIONS

In most academic institutions, sociology belongs to the category of "social science". While the idea of "science" might bring to mind lab coats and test tubes, the term is not limited to lab research. More broadly, science refers to a system of acquiring knowledge based on a scientific method, as well as to the organized body of knowledge gained through such research. Social sciences are those academic disciplines that use some form of scientific inquiry to understand people (rather than, say, to understand galaxies or oceans or ant colonies).

There is a lot of debate over what actually counts as "science", and not all sociologists use the term to describe their work. Although we cannot explore these debates here, we can usefully characterize social science, like sociology, as centered on gathering and measuring empirical evidence and subjecting it to specific principles of reasoning. Academic traditions in the humanities provide a useful contrasting case of knowledge production. Take philosophy, for example. In that discipline, knowledge is generated from logical reasoning and from asserting values—labeling things as good or bad. Rather than collecting data, philosophers often use theoretical scenarios to illustrate their arguments. In contrast, sociologists primarily focus on using data to explain the world around them—how the world *is*. Although some sociologists do think deeply about how the world *should be*, they typically connect these thoughts to empirical observations of the world around them. (As we discussed in chapter 2, sociologists use the term **empirical** to describe approaches that use data collection about the world as it is, and use the term **normative** to designate ideas about how the world should be. Some scholars believe that sociologists should stick with the empirical, but normative approaches have a long history in sociology, especially for scholars concerned about class, gender, and racial inequality.)

2.1. Ways of Knowing

While sociologists may have ideas about how the world could be a better place, the search for sociological knowledge does not begin by labeling things good or bad. Instead, it is about reliably identifying social phenomena and explaining how social phenomena are related—what part they play in society more generally. Social science methods are good for finding out facts without relying on tradition or authority. By tradition we mean things that many people have thought for a long time. For example, the idea that smoking was not only harmless but could be good for you was something that people had thought for decades—because tobacco companies conveyed this message through advertising. After many years of this idea circulating in society, it was widely believed as a traditional truth. By authority we mean the power to persuade others that something is true because it comes from someone who has a certain position or status. In their advertisements, tobacco companies portrayed doctors as authority figures about tobacco's positive effects on health. Tradition and authority are ways of knowing that can be quite useful, but as can be seen in the example of the healthfulness of smoking, they can be wrong and cannot substitute for empirical methods to produce facts about the world.

As an alternative to authority or tradition, we can also rely on our own personal observations to learn about the social world. However, people often observe in ways where they make some common mistakes. For example, when observing an event, they might think they remember how things happen and all of the details, but human memory can be very unreliable, especially without setting out with a research plan in advance. Another common mistake is for people to take a few examples that they know about and overgeneralize from them, meaning they haven't done enough observing to really know the whole story; sometimes this is referred to as anecdotal evidence. For example, just because *your* little brother seemed to become more aggressive after watching an ad for the latest Marvel superheroes movie doesn't mean that *all* young boys would respond in this same way. In addition to overgeneralizing, another way that our own thinking can differ from scientific research is selective observation. This happens when we pay attention to some examples that we think are important, and ignore examples that contradict what we already think. For example, if you believe that ads for household cleaning products have begun to show more men than they did in the past, you might notice every time a man appears on screen doing laundry. Because your attention is focused in this way, you might miss the many other times when we see a woman depicted doing housework. Social science methods are designed to be systematic in order to avoid these common mistakes that people make in how they perceive and understand the world around them.

2.2. Theory, Cases, and Classes of Cases

Some research is carried out specifically to establish or describe new facts about social life. In other instances, sociologists make a more explicit plan to go beyond description and *explain* the social world. To offer an explanation, sociological research must build arguments, make claims based on sociological facts, and employ or develop theoretical concepts. A sociological theory is, at its core, an explanation about what things are or how they are related. In sociology, we aim to develop and support theories that are generally applicable. Theories, then, are explanations about classes of events or cases, rather than about specific, individual events or cases. This distinction is captured by the terms idiographic and nomothetic. **Idiographic explanations** provide a complete picture of what happened so that all the factors can be included in an explanation. Idiographic explanations often focus on a single case, or a small number of cases. An example would be a close reading of a single advertisement. In this case, the researcher would examine all the components of the advertisement's content and also examine the conditions under which that advertisement was produced. The goal would be to provide as comprehensive an understanding as possible of that specific ad. A **nomothetic explanation** looks less in-depth at a particular case and instead examines multiple cases to try to explain how variables are related. Put differently, nomothetic explanations involve generalization rather than close readings of a single case. In this way, nomothetic explanations tell us about a class of events or cases; this strategy usefully allows the sociologist to detect larger patterns, even if the explanation of a single event or case will not be as deep as it would be with a nomothetic approach.

How do ideographic and nomothetic approaches relate back to the goal of developing sociological theory? Idiographic explanations can serve as the building blocks for developing new theories by suggesting factors to consider and showing that they mattered in the one case at hand. However, idiographic explanations are not what we typically mean by the term "theory" in social science. Instead, ideographic studies are considered a resource that can be used to build theory. Nomothetic explanations, which try to explain classes of events or cases, are what we mean by theories in social science. However, without idiographic sociological research, it would be difficult to know where to start to create nomothetic explanations. That is why idiographic approaches are a good start for building theory, through in-depth examination of particular cases. Only then can we move on to think about explaining groups or classes of cases.

2.3. Types of Data

Data is a synonym for information that is treated as evidence. Sociological data exists in many forms. An important distinction to help understand the range of types of data in sociology is the difference between **quantitative** and **qualitative data**. Most basically, quantitative data is information that is represented numerically, and qualitative data is information that is represented through words. For example, quantitative data on advertising might take the form of statistics about the number of viewers, as evidenced in magazine circulation figures. Qualitative data about advertising viewers might take the form of a quote from an interview with an audience member about what they think of an advertisement. Some questions that sociologists pose are most effectively addressed through analysis of quantitative data, and other questions are best addressed through analysis of qualitative data. Below, we review a range of different methods, some quantitative and some qualitative.

To generate data, sociologists gather information about various attributes of a social phenomenon. **Attributes** are characteristics or qualities of a person or a thing. If our research involves people, then attributes include things like age and race. If we are studying things like an advertisement, then attributes include things like the product being advertised or the number of words used in the advertisement. Attributes describe people and things.

Variables are commonly accepted groupings of attributes, where a person or a thing can vary in the attributes that apply to them. For example, height is a variable made up of attributes like 5 feet 8 inches, 5 feet 9 inches, etc. People can vary in how this variable applies to them. Other common variables are age, gender, race, occupation, and education, but the list of potential variables is practically endless. In the study of advertising, some common variables include the advertising medium (e.g. television, magazine, etc.), length of a commercial in seconds, the size of a print advertisement in square inches, and the number of people appearing in an advertisement.

Sociological research often starts with a decision about what part of the social world we want to observe. **Operationalization** describes the process of making a decision about what to observe in order to get information about variables and attributes. Sometimes the way to operationalize a variable is obvious: if we want to know the length of a television commercial, we would probably measure the duration in seconds from the very beginning to the very end. However, many times there are many different potential ways to measure what we are interested in. For example, if you were interested in the concept of truth in advertising, how would you best measure whether a commercial is truthful? Our ideas of what counts as truth or falsehoods in advertising would influence our operationalization. One way you might operationalize truthfulness would be to record any written or spoken words, and then verify whether they are objectively true. If a commercial claims that a brand of toothpaste can whiten your teeth, you could research whether there is any scientific basis for the claim. Or if a commercial lists a price for a product, you could check to see whether the product can be purchased for that price. This is certainly one way to approach truthfulness in advertising. However, often when people discuss this concept, they are referring to a different kind of truthfulness: not what is explicitly said, but what is suggested or implied. When advertisements constantly portray young, successful, popular people using their products (think of beer commercials or clothing commercials), this association implicitly makes a claim for the lifestyle available to consumers when they purchase these products. This kind of truthfulness in advertising is much more difficult to operationalize, as there is no consensus about whether the portrayal of an available lifestyle is a claim that should be assessed as true or false.

The operationalization process is closely related to the task of **sampling**: selecting a subset of people or advertisements (or whatever it is that we are studying) that will be the focus of our research. On the one hand, we cannot observe everything we are interested in because of limitations on time and resources. On the other hand, we do not want to just randomly start making observations because we need to be able to justify that we are observing the right cases for our particular research question. For example, if we want to study whether advertising causes people to have materialistic values, whose values are we going to observe? We must decide which people will serve as the source of this information, and we need to create a sample of people whose values we will investigate further. At the heart of sampling is the idea that we need to set logical limits around the cases we will observe. We cannot observe everyone's values because no researcher has the resources to do that. We also want to avoid studying too few people, just in case these few people are unusual and not representative of the larger population of people that we are interested in. What is the right size of a sample, then? That question can only be answered with respect to the resources available and to the particular kind of study you want to do. After deciding on sample size and the characteristics of the sample, there are practical concerns around how to find these people so that the sample is random and not biased in any particular direction. For example, if you wanted to investigate the impacts of advertising on materialist values in American youth, you would want to create a sample of young Americans that reflected the general population in terms of gender, race, class, and engagement with advertising. If you *only* studied young women to answer this question, or only studied rural youth, then your data would be biased in a particular direction, and would not reflect the materialistic values of American youth in a general way.

Sometimes in sociology we are interested in determining how variables relate to one another. For example, does the type of product advertised influence the racial composition of people in that advertisement (e.g. do fast-food ads feature racial minorities more frequently than Whites?). Some sociological studies have examined the relationship between products advertised and racial groups to empirically assess whether advertisements reproduce racial stereotypes. Are certain kinds of products more likely to be associated with people of a particular racial group? To address this kind of question, we look at correlations between variables, and in this case we can approach these variables as having a **causal relationship**. In conceptualizing a causal relationship, we say that the **independent variable** influences the **dependent variable** (concepts that were introduced in chapter 7). In the case of advertising and race, the product being advertised is the independent variable, and the race of people depicted in the advertisement is the dependent variable. To take a more specific example, a sociologist could compare advertisements for fast food vs. table service restaurants to see if the restaurant genre (independent variable) shapes the decision of which actors to cast (dependent variable), namely the proportion of racial minority actors vs. White actors. In other words, when an advertising firm creates an advertisement, the kind of product in question influences the selection of whom to portray in the advertisement. This causal relationship is sociologically significant because it can inadvertently reproduce stereotypes about racial groups, healthy diets, and beauty ideals.

Of course, not all social science is interested in relationships between independent and dependent variables. Causal relationships are just one area of focus for sociology. Many studies are carried out in order to find out how things happen, rather than to find out causes of changes. Other studies are carried out in order to take a complicated and poorly understood phenomenon and make it more comprehensible. This kind of analysis breaks down big phenomena into more easily understood and identifiable smaller components.

2.4. Inductive and Deductive Reasoning

Inductive and **deductive** reasoning represent two different ways of producing knowledge. Which type of thinking is right for a particular study depends in part on how well developed knowledge is about a particular question. When more is known, then there are incentives built in to approaching a question with deductive reasoning. When less is known, then it is more natural to take an inductive approach.

Deductive logic involves reasoning from the general to the particular. In order to develop an explanation, you first start out with thinking about general principles, or explanations about whole classes of things. Where do you start to think about these things? You start by reading what other people have already studied and found and have claimed. Based on what is already known, you develop an idea about how to explain something you are interested in. You then take your idea and focus it into a proposition and then a **hypothesis**. The hypothesis, in order to engage with evidence, needs to be fairly narrow. To illustrate how to think of a hypothesis, we can start with the well-known proposition "sex sells". This is shorthand for saying that advertising relies on sexual imagery to be appealing to consumers. However, it is too vague to be a hypothesis; we need to develop a more specific idea about *how* sex sells. One idea might be that advertising portrays women in physical positions that subtly signify sexual receptivity. This is an idea that sociologist Erving Goffman developed through a textual analysis of print advertisements. A hypothesis based on this idea might be: Women will be depicted in advertising in reclined positions more often than men. Another hypothesis might be: Women will be depicted with more skin showing than men. The following steps will involve deciding how you will measure the attributes implicated in the hypotheses (gender, angle of body position, skin covered by clothing vs. exposed), constructing a sample of advertisements to collect observations on, and analyzing the findings to understand whether they support or contradict the hypotheses. Through deductive reasoning, we can refine our understanding of how sociological variables are related and we can test the theories that researchers in the field are working with.

Inductive reasoning involves thinking in the opposite direction. While deductive reasoning starts with a statement about how things are related and then involves observing cases, inductive reasoning starts with observing cases and then involves reasoning about them in order to formulate a statement about their general nature or how they are related. Many sociological studies start with the motivation that a topic is understudied or that a social problem is important to know more about. The first step is to specify an analytical focus and to begin making observations. The data are then analyzed by the researcher for patterns. These patterns can then be the foundation for proposing arguments or theories. To return to the example discussed above, in order to test a hypothesis about how sex sells in advertising, someone at some point needed to develop possible ideas about how this works. Erving Goffman's study of gender in advertisements was drawn on in order to develop a testable hypothesis. Goffman's study itself is a perfect example of inductive reasoning. His general interest in the ways that gender is signaled led him to study a large sample of advertisements, and based on his study he inductively developed a set of ideas about how women tend to be portrayed differently from men in the media and the meanings of those portrayals. Sociological research often involves a dialogue where inductive studies provide ideas that are tested and refined in deductive studies. Those findings and refinements can then spark new ways of understanding that lead researchers to undertake novel inductive studies.

3. SOCIOLOGICAL METHODS

So far we have been talking about the logic behind observing and measuring the social world. Now it is time to look at the specific methods that sociologists employ to collect data. In order to organize the overview of these methods in a way that facilitates comparisons between them, we can relate them back to studies of advertising. Advertising is a broad enough social phenomenon that it can be studied from different angles. This overview of methods will illustrate how different methods offer specific advantages and lend themselves to providing data that are well suited to some questions more than others. We'll examine methods in relation to the study of advertising production, methods that lend themselves well to the study of advertising content, and also methods that are well suited to studying how people receive and respond to advertising.

3.1. Being There: Ethnography and Participant Observation

A good way to learn about how people interact with other people is to enter into a social world and observe its dynamics firsthand. This type of data collection is broadly referred to as **ethnography** (discussed in chapter 3). This method involves the researcher entering into a social setting and observing social behavior as it naturally and normally occurs. A great advantage of this method is that it allows for observation of actual social behavior, rather than relying on reports or recollections of what happened. It also allows a researcher to observe the social context in which social interactions occur, so that their meaning and significance can be most accurately understood. Ethnographic methods are particularly well suited to facilitate inductive reasoning and generally produce qualitative data. Ethnography is often carried out over extended periods of time with multiple site visits. This allows the researcher to observe how social processes play out, and also provides an opportunity for the researcher to have a deep and nuanced understanding of the people involved, including their motivations, expectations, and social relationships. This method is also systematic as it involves extensive documentation and iterative review of observations, so as to minimize problems of observer bias or selective recall. The notes that the researcher makes are the data that are then analyzed, sometimes to address a question that the researcher had when beginning and sometimes to generate new understandings of social settings that had not been previously articulated.

Ethnography specializes at making social worlds easier to understand for those outside them. In this sense, ethnographic research can generate explanations of behaviors and attitudes. It generates understandings of "what is really going on". Often, social worlds look from the outside to make little sense. When doing ethnographic research, the researcher can see more details and can collect information about the perspectives and understandings of the participants in that setting. Only through this type of sustained study can the confusing surface be interpreted in a way that makes sense to the rest of us.

Ethnographic research can involve a researcher only observing a social setting, and this can work well if it is possible for the researcher to be relatively unobtrusive and not to disrupt the natural social dynamics (e.g. observing interactions at a fast-food restaurant). However, in some cases, it is awkward for the researcher to observe people, and so it is less disruptive if the researcher can more fully integrate into the social setting by becoming a participant. This kind of ethnographic work is called **participant observation**. A good example of participant observation research on advertising is Sharon Koppman's (2014) study, "Making art work: Creative assessment as boundary work". In this study, Koppman wanted to better understand how creative professionals defined creativity in their work and how they justified those definitions. She picked the advertising industry as a site for ethnographic work on how these workers made decisions and defended them. In total she spent 320 hours at her research sites. While all workers were made aware of her researcher status, she also functioned as an intern, which made her presence at the workplace less obtrusive and more natural. It also helped her see the workplace issues more readily through the eyes of the other workers. Through her observation of many social interactions at workplace meetings, Koppman was able to find patterns in the ways that creative workers determined some kinds of ideas to be creative while dismissing other ideas as illegitimate. Within advertising, creative workers used restrictive conceptions of what is creative in order to frame their own work as relevant and novel, while labeling other kinds of ideas that were outside their expertise or from other professional traditions as lacking in creativity. This study of how advertising work gets done helps us to understand the kinds of decisions that advertising workers make, which in turn helps us to understand the kind of advertising produced. We can see how participant observation was well-suited to collecting data on workers' thought processes and justifications for good and bad advertising. These are very subtle social interactions, and the workers themselves were likely unable to articulate how they thought about these issues because they are never raised as topics for discussion. They would require extensive reflection on the significance of what was said within the workplace, which most people tend not to engage in, but is the job of the researcher when doing participant observation.

3.2. Standardized Questions: Survey Research

A **survey** is a research method that involves administering a standardized questionnaire to a sample of respondents (survey research is discussed in chapter 4). Typically, surveys are administered to large samples for the purposes of description and explanation, though exploratory surveys also exist. The great advantage of surveys is that they ask the same questions to large numbers of people, which allows for comparisons across those people and across different groups of people within the sample. The prototypical survey is the census, in which the government attempts to gather basic demographic information from every household. Most surveys are much smaller scale, though, because most researchers face resource constraints. Surveys are typically sent to a sample of people that is large enough in order to reliably generalize from the survey results to the larger population that the sample is meant to represent. The administration of each individual survey requires relatively few resources (of time, money, and labor), which frees up resources to administer the survey to a large number of people. Compared to ethnography, which involves investing heavy resources into one or a few cases, surveys take the opposite strategy of investing lightly in a large number of cases (or respondents).

Surveys can be administered by a researcher, who poses questions to a research subject, either in a face-to-face setting or over the phone. Surveys can also be self-administered, where a research subject completes the survey on his or her own, either on paper which is then mailed in, or online. Survey questions have to be very carefully planned. Each individual question has to be designed to ensure that it is easily comprehensible to the research subjects and to ensure that it is eliciting exactly the information that the researcher is looking for. This is relatively easy in terms of asking people about their age or their gender identity, but it can be much more difficult when asking people about their opinions, values, knowledge, and beliefs. For this reason, the technique of pre-testing surveys to verify that different research subjects will understand what the questions are asking for is an important step in survey construction.

Survey research can be a useful way to collect data about how advertising is related to values and beliefs. Critics of advertising have argued that advertising promotes materialistic values, and because advertising is so pervasive, it has the potential to influence values in society. Survey research can provide evidence that helps us to determine whether this claim about the effect of advertising has empirical support. A study by Buijzen and Valkenburg (2003) reports on the use of a survey to observe whether advertising viewing frequency was associated with holding materialistic values. The survey was administered to students between 8 and 12 years of age in a sample of classrooms in public schools. The researchers received 360 surveys. One of their main independent variables was advertising viewing frequency. It is impossible to precisely measure the actual amount of advertising any person views without constantly monitoring all that person sees or hears. Like many survey questions, then, the measurement of advertising viewing frequency was designed to be a reliable *indicator* of the frequency, which would allow comparisons between research subjects. In the case of this study, the survey presented the titles of 10 commercials that had been broadcast on television during the data collection period and asked the children to indicate whether they had seen each of the commercials often, sometimes, or not at all. They then created an overall measure of advertising viewing frequency, using these example commercials as indicators. One of the key dependent variables they were interested in was materialism, or the extent to which people believe that possessions are important and necessary for happiness. Because this belief is somewhat abstract, they chose indicator questions to measure it: (a) Do you think it is important to have a lot of money? (b) Do you think it is important to own a lot of things? And (c) Would you like to be able to buy things that cost a lot of money? Children were given the choice of responding on a four-point scale ranging from (1) no, not at all to (4) yes, very much. Through statistical analysis, the researchers were able to determine that children who had higher advertising viewing frequency were more likely to hold materialistic values. Keep in mind that one survey can never definitively "prove" the existence of a relationship between variables, especially when they are as difficult to reliably and validly measure as the ones in this study. Also keep in mind that this main relationship was subject to moderation in certain circumstances; the researchers found that "the effect of advertising on materialism was significantly weaker for children in families that often discuss consumer and advertising matters" (Buijzen and Valkenburg 2003: 498).

Survey research is a highly sophisticated method, and there are many technical aspects to survey design that cannot be covered here. Survey analysis, likewise, is a highly advanced field of data analysis in the social sciences. Researchers have developed entire traditions of data analysis that employ surveys. One such tradition is **social network analysis** (discussed in chapter 9). In this field, researchers survey respondents about who they know and the nature of their connections to other people, in addition to other topics of interest. Through cataloguing people's social networks, researchers can see how people's network size and density is related to a range of social outcomes, like health and employment status, among many others. Social network analysis is more than just a survey method: it is also a theoretical approach to understanding network ties as important causes of social outcomes. As a field, the theoretical stance of social network analysis has led to the creation of specialized survey questions that are designed to best measure people's social networks. There are other specialized forms of survey analysis, such as panel-data analysis, where researchers survey the same group of people over multiple periods to understand changes over time. Another specialized form of survey analysis is multi-level modeling, where researchers survey people who are clustered into levels. For example, people can be surveyed as individuals, but also be conceptualized as a member of a group, such as within a family, school, neighborhood, or city. Such modeling can help researchers understand, for example, how advertising has an effect on children's values, but also how that effect can be dependent on the characteristics of their family's interactions, school, or where they live.

3.3. Exploring In Depth: Qualitative Interviews and Focus Groups

Interviewing people in order to pose questions to them is a basic sociological research tool. Interviews can take different forms, though. In the example of survey research above, technically the administration of a survey can be done through interviewing a person. However, that kind of interview is constrained to standardized questions to maximize comparability across subjects. The label of **qualitative interviews** signifies a very different kind of interview (discussed in chapter 2). In this method, the goal is to facilitate an interaction between the interviewer and the research subject so that the subject can talk as much as possible and participate in guiding the course of the interview. The interviewer has a general plan for what he or she wants to find out about, but there is room to focus on what the respondent finds important or interesting or relevant. The flexibility of qualitative interviewing is one of its strengths. Unlike in a survey, the depth of the interview allows for some variation in the questions, so that more can be learned about what is different about respondents, or how they think differently about the same questions. It also allows for the researcher to explore new thoughts and ideas that emerge through the interview. This makes qualitative interviews well-suited to developing new theory, because they can uncover ideas about topics that the researchers would never have thought of.

Qualitative interviews are generally done with much smaller sample sizes than a survcy, while the questions are generally "deeper". They ask people to elaborate on what they think and know and feel, to justify their positions, to illustrate their answers with concrete examples from their lives, and to be as detailed as possible. Each interview can generate a lot of data. An advantage of this way of posing questions is that the researcher has a high degree of clarity about what the respondent means in their responses. There is ample opportunity to explore nuances. This strength is carried over into the mode of analysis of interview data. Researchers generally transcribe interviews and then review the transcriptions to begin to identify important themes that are related to the initial research questions. There is usually an iterative process where researchers develop a coding of the interview transcripts that characterizes their main themes and how they are related to one another. These themes are then analyzed in order to make an argument about how they relate to existing sociological theories and perspectives.

How can qualitative interviews be used to study how advertising impacts consumers? We know that advertising is designed to increase the likelihood that consumers will direct their spending towards a specific brand. While there are many theories of how and why advertising influences behavior, it is difficult to generalize about how advertising actually influences consumer choices. People make decisions differently for different kinds of products. With this in mind, Frosch et al. (2011) carried out a study of how people responded to advertisements for drugs that treat cardiovascular disease. Pharmaceuticals advertisements promote a medical product that can address a condition that is also linked to changes in exercise and diet. The researchers wanted to know how people interpreted these advertisements. More specifically, they wanted to know whether these ads influenced consumers' understanding of the nature of cardiovascular disease—as something that was the result of lifestyle changes, or as primarily a question of bodily tendencies and responses to the environment beyond individuals' choices. The study involved qualitative interviews with 45 people. Interviewees were shown commercials and asked to talk about their reactions to the ads—as well as their understandings of the sources of cardiovascular disease and how it should be addressed. The researchers found that watching these pharmaceutical advertisements can shift people's understanding of the nature of cardiovascular disease and whether it can be effectively addressed by lifestyle choices alone. This study pointed to the need for further research to examine how advertising influences consumers' understanding of the causes of medical problems, as well as consumers' perceptions of the boundaries of medical expertise and responsibility.

Sometimes researchers believe that they can get more valuable perspectives and information from interviewees in a group setting. When qualitative interviewing is done with a small group of interviewees, researchers are employing the research method of **focus groups** (discussed in chapter 5). The logic of focus groups is that the kinds of things that people say in a discussion in a small group setting can be different from what they would say to a researcher one-on-one. The small group setting can feel more natural to some interviewees, and some people will feel more free to say things as part of a group discussion. Focus groups generate a kind of dialogue that is different from a one-on-one interview, which is likely to elicit longer personal narratives rather than social interaction. There will, of course, be some topics and some settings where focus groups can be counterproductive. Some questions are too intimate, and some people do not want to discuss certain topics with particular other people. For example, a focus group about workplace satisfaction would be difficult if the focus group included supervisors as well as the employees they supervise. These obstacles aside, focus groups can provide insight into people's motivations, opinions, and understandings. Just as with interviews, focus groups produce qualitative data, where the discussion is transcribed and the transcriptions are inductively analyzed to identify common themes. There is no rule about the size of a focus group, but it must be large enough to facilitate a group discussion and small enough so that all the interviewees can participate. Typically, a study will run multiple focus groups to look for commonalities across the discussions. Focus groups are, in fact, a key research tool for marketers. Both marketers and sociologists use focus groups to study people's perceptions of advertising; the difference is that marketers then use these insights to generate more persuasive advertisements.

3.4. Document Analysis: Content Analysis, Textual Analysis, Comparative Historical Research

In the methods reviewed above, the observations come from people directly. However, many times it is not possible or not preferable to get the information a researcher needs directly from people. At those times, researchers can turn to the study of documents that are produced by people, groups, and organizations. The different forms of documents used for analysis have the virtue of being stable data points: the documents are produced not for the researcher, but for some other original purpose. They exist before the research is carried out. We know that their production and content have not been influenced by the presence of the researcher. The production of documents is central to many realms of society. Businesses produce sales records, earnings reports, employment records, supply orders, and many other kinds of records of business activities. Governments produce records of virtually all important decisions made for the sake of transparency and accountability, not to mention all the documents that governments produce specifically for the purpose of providing information to researchers and policy-makers. The media produce books, magazines, newspapers, and many other kinds of printed materials, but we can expand our understanding of "documents" to include radio, television, cinematic, and other electronic forms of communication like websites, blogs, podcasts, Instagram posts, and tweets. All these different kinds of documents can tell us important information about the actions, knowledge, and understandings of people, from individuals all the way up to the level of the nation.

The category of document analysis is broad and can accommodate many different approaches to the collection and analysis of data. Document analysis can be qualitative or quantitative in method, depending on the nature of the documents and on the nature of the questions that are being addressed.

Content analysis (discussed in chapter 11) is a category of document analysis that most commonly involves the following steps. First, the researcher selects a sample of documents. In many cases, the sample is designed to be as large as resources allow for, so as to make the sample representative. Second, the researcher develops codes to apply to the documents. Each code will become a variable in the analysis. For example, in coding advertisements, the variable of "gender" is created and can take a value for each person appearing in the advertisement. Codes can be situated on a spectrum from manifest to latent. Manifest codes are those that are most objective and require the least amount of interpretation; they have high reliability as most people would readily agree on the value of the code for a particular advertisement. For example, one group of researchers carried out a content analysis of 345 of the most viewed US television shows to see how depictions of ethnic minorities changed over two decades (Tukachinsky et al. 2015). This study relied centrally on manifest coding of the racial identity of people portrayed in commercials (the vast majority of people in commercials are portrayed with distinct racial identity cues). This study revealed a gross under-representation of Asian Americans and Latinos and a virtual absence of Native Americans. For example, Latinos make up roughly 16% of the US population, but their prevalence on US television shows increased from less than 1% in the 1980s to only 3% in the 2000s (Tukachinsky et al. 2015: 24–5). In contrast, latent codes are those that require more interpretation and are not obvious "on the surface", and so must be very clearly and narrowly defined to be reliable. An example of a latent code is whether a model in an advertisement is sexualized. The presentation of sexiness is something that most people think they can recognize, but not everyone agrees on what is sexy. What degree of sexiness is required before a model is coded as sexualized? Given this ambiguity, it is always preferable, when possible, to develop manifest codes that can be used as indicators of the latent concept of interest. For example, sexualization can be broken down into a combination of narrower components such as proportion of skin covered by clothing, tightness of clothing, bodily position, and the prominence of sexualized body parts like cleavage or abdominal muscles. Each of these codes is more reliably coded. At the same time, not every latent concept can be broken down into smaller parts, and so many content analyses involve a mixture of both manifest and latent coding.

In some ways, **textual analysis** is to content analysis as qualitative interviews are to surveys. Rather than a focus on representative samples and comparability of variables' values across documents, textual analysis (discussed in chapter 12) is much more focused on providing a deep, qualitative analysis of a smaller number of documents. Sometimes called "discourse analysis", textual analysis specializes in uncovering layers of meaning within documents. This method uses theoretical tools to guide investigation, often drawing from traditions such as feminist social theory, Foucauldian analysis, or semiotics, which specify particular phenomena of concern and particular kinds of relationships to examine. These tools encourage an interpretive approach to analyzing evidence, and textual analysis provides qualitative rather than quantitative data. Textual analysis was employed by a researcher who was interested in understanding the changing nature of a well-known, long-running advertising campaign (Wang 2016). The campaign was "Singapore Girl" for Singapore Airlines and featured beautiful airline stewards carrying out their service roles. The researcher closely examined 10 television commercials which were part of the campaign between the 1970s and 2013. While the campaign had previously been criticized for playing on harmful stereotypes of Asian women as subservient, the more recent commercials moved away from stereotypical depictions. Through qualitative analysis of more recent commercials, the researcher analyzed fine details such as editing choices, scene sequencing and transitions, and narrative elements. With feminist analytical tools, the researcher showed how, despite the move in more recent commercials away from a focus on the women attendants' faces and bodies, the commercials convey a subtler kind of stereotype through visual references to an "authentically" feminine interpersonal brand of service offered by the airline. This is a meaning that is not on the surface, but one that requires deep interpretation, guided by a close interpretive reading of the text and feminist theory.

The method of **historical comparative research** (profiled in chapter 8) is similarly based on the analysis of documents. While the tools and aims are different from either content analysis or textual analysis, the boundaries of these methods are quite fuzzy and can certainly overlap with one another. Even so, comparative historical research is characterized by its explicitly historical focus, by the use of comparisons across cases and/or across time periods, and by a research goal of relating large-scale outcomes affecting many people to societal level social factors. Comparative historical research can rely on quantitative (e.g. a corporation's advertising expenditures) or qualitative (the text of a company's annual report) historical data sources. For the most part, comparative historical research produces data, even when using quantitative historical sources, that are themselves qualitative in nature.

3.5. Controlled Comparisons: Experiments

Methods that use experimental design are based on the premise that we need to make controlled comparisons between cases. By controlled we mean that we ensure that we know that two cases are the same in every significant way except for a variable that we are interested in examining, and that we control which group is subjected to the influence of that variable and which group is not. This degree of control allows us to isolate and observe an independent variable's influence on a dependent variable. Experiments are fundamentally about understanding causal influences between variables, based on deductively derived hypotheses, and are a quantitative data method. The basic idea of comparing outcomes between cases is one that motivates a lot of social research. Using survey data, for example, we might compare the incomes of people who graduated from college with those who have lower levels of education. While we can learn a lot about the relationship between education and income from this kind of survey data, it is not a good way to confidently establish a causal relationship. The reason is that the people who graduate from college might be on average different in various ways from those with lower levels of education before they even go to college—deciding to go to college and having the ability to be admitted imply that people have certain personal characteristics and resources that could affect their incomes as well. This means that, using survey data, the size of the causal relationship between education and income is hard to tease out from the other influences on income. In this way, survey analysis employs a "quasi-experimental" design, where only some of the important variables are controlled, but not all of them.

Experimental research is a core scientific method that is common in the natural sciences as well as in the social science of psychology. In sociology, experiments have traditionally been most common in the area of social psychology, an area in which sociology overlaps with some psychological research. In the past, experiments were carried out in laboratory or similar settings, where participants are recruited to participate and are aware they are in an experiment, even if they do not know the specific nature of the experiment or the researchers' hypotheses. In recent years, researchers have developed tools for running experiments online, using web-based applications for providing information and stimuli, and recording subjects' responses.

Given their focus on causal effects, experiments are well suited to understanding how advertising influences consumer behavior. In an interesting study of influences on young people's college choice (Oakes and North 2013), researchers used television and radio advertisements for a university; these advertisements had not yet been broadcast (and so had not yet been seen or heard by anyone). In one set of advertisements, they added classical music in the background, and in another set they used the same advertisements except the background music genre was dance music. As a control, they used no music at all in a third set of advertisements. They then randomly assigned groups of volunteers to hear or watch one set of advertisements, and then they posed a set of questions about what the young people would expect these universities to be like and how likely they would be to apply. For the experiment to be valid, it is important that the research subjects not be aware that the focus is on the effects of the music, because that awareness might influence their responses. The findings revealed that the young people in the experiment extended the stereotypes associated with each music genre to the university depicted in the advertisements. Compared to the control group and the classical music genre group, the group that watched or heard the advertisements with dance music reported being more likely to apply to that university. The group that watched the classical music genre advertisements perceived the university to be more sophisticated and to likely have higher tuition fees. The design of the experiment allowed the researchers to be confident that the different perceptions across groups of research subjects was caused by the differences in music genres, as they had controlled for all other potential influences.

While experimental design has obvious strengths, sometimes researchers are interested in questions that cannot be studied in a typical experimental setting. For example, if they are studying something that plays out over weeks or months, research subjects typically are not available to put their lives on hold for the sake of an experiment. Just as importantly, often researchers are interested in outcomes that cannot be replicated in an artificial setting, but must be studied in a natural setting. A common critique of experiments is that because subjects know they are being observed and because the experimental conditions are hypothetical, the experimental results cannot be generalized to the real world. In the example above, asking people where they will apply for college does not provide exactly the same findings as actually observing their application process. To address some of these problems, researchers may carry out a **field experiment** (discussed in chapter 6). A field experiment attempts to apply the principles of experimental design as rigorously as possible to a real-world setting (out "in the field"). The great advantage of field studies is that they allow researchers to observe the actual behavior they are interested in rather than an indicator of that behavior. In the case of advertising, researchers would almost always prefer to observe how consumers' choices are actually influenced by advertising through measuring how consumers spend their money, rather than relying on what consumers say they would do in a situation that resembles a consumption choice. A field experiment would involve using real advertising for an actual business, where the study design interacts with the design of the advertising campaign. For example, an advertising campaign might vary the race of the models it shows in website banner advertisements randomly across visitors to a site, and then track which visitors were more likely to click through depending on which advertisements they were shown. Field studies are, however, expensive and difficult to carry out, and not every research question can be examined with this method.

4. CONCLUSION: A DIVERSE METHODOLOGICAL TOOLKIT

In this overview of some of the most common methods employed in sociological research, we have seen that the need to meet a diverse range of empirical challenges has inspired the development of a diverse set of methodological tools. When assessing the value of sociological research, it is necessary to evaluate the match between the method employed in the research and the nature of the research questions posed. In the end, we want to use the method that produces the kind of data and analysis that are most closely tailored to the specific research question. For this reason, it is important to understand the advantages and disadvantages of each method. To help you see how these methods share some similarities and differences, the graphic shows

Research Methods: Key Traits

This graphic provides a bird's-eye view of research methods. As you can see from the top row of the graphic, coming up with a clear, defined research question is an important first step for many (if not most) sociological projects. Knowing your question helps you decide what sort of data (qualitative or quantitative) is most helpful to meaningfully answer the question. On the third row of the graphic, you will find a summary of key traits associated with qualitative and quantitative research. The bottom row lists the common methods discussed in this chapter. Note that methods listed in the middle of the bottom row can be seen as more likely to generate both qualitative and quantitative data. However, all methods

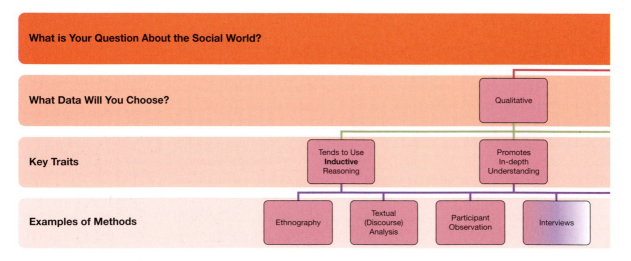

how these methods tend to be used. The graphic is not meant to suggest that these methods are starkly different in the traits they necessarily exemplify, but rather that researchers have a tendency to use them in these ways.

One implication of the trade-offs across methods is that there can be distinct advantages to combining methods. Multi-method studies have become increasingly common in sociological research because the weaknesses of one method can be bolstered by the strengths of another. It is fairly common, for example, for a researcher to study associations between variables through survey analysis, and then to employ qualitative interviewing to better understand why and how those variables are related. While a survey can tell us that women are more likely than men to respond positively to celebrity endorsements in advertisements, we would need interviews to help us uncover the reasons why this relationship exists. A study that employs both methods will be much more revealing into the broader trends, as well as the nuanced meanings that women associate with celebrity endorsements.

Sociological methods are dynamic: the set of empirical tools available to sociologists has developed over time as the discipline has evolved, and this

have some flexibility in how they are used—even surveys can generate qualitative data, and sometime even ethnographic work can produce some quantitative data. It's also worth noting that some sociologists have at times had a tendency to view the pros and cons of qualitative vs. quantitative research as a struggle for the legitimacy of one over the other. While it is natural to develop expertise in certain methods, it is now broadly recognized that it is a great strength of the discipline of sociology to be able to integrate multiple methods and both qualitative and quantitative modes of analysis.

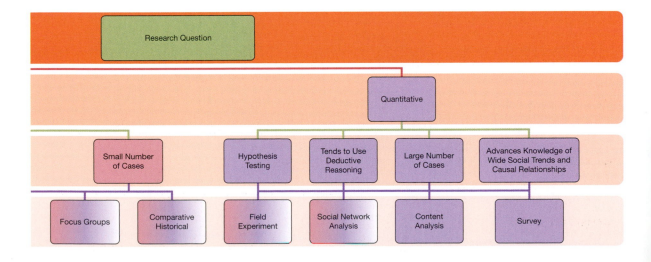

evolution has occurred through dialog with other disciplines. Ethnographic methods, for example, are frequently employed by anthropologists, and there has been extensive borrowing between the fields to refine the method. The same can be said about experimental methods in psychology and statistical analysis of survey data in economics. While neighboring disciplines have been influential in shaping these methods, so has technology. Statistical analysis has been transformed by increases in computing power, while computers have also provided techniques for the transcription and coding of interview data that make it more efficient to do and to carry out the research within a team setting. The Internet has provided new channels for surveying respondents or for collecting experimental data, or for collecting large amounts of textual data like thousands of Twitter posts. In short, the tools we have now are subject to change as researchers in the social sciences make methodological innovations and as technology makes new ways of collecting and analyzing data possible. As we have mentioned, this overview has focused on the most common methods that sociologists employ. Variants of these methods abound (e.g. photo elicitation, oral history, participatory action research, feminist methodology), and these variants can be seen as growing out of theoretical or technological changes that point researchers towards new empirical tools or towards new ways of using existing tools.

REFERENCES

Aaker, David. 2013. "A Beauty of a Brand Builder." *Marketing News* 47(8): 12–13.

AASHTO, American Association of State Highway and Transportation Officials. 2013. *Commuting in America 2013. The National Report on Commuting Patterns and Trends.*

Adrian, Bonnie. 2003. *Framing the Bride: Globalizing Beauty and Romance in Taiwan's Bridal Industry.* Berkeley: University of California Press.

Agger, Ben. 2011. "iTime: Labor and Life in a Smartphone Era." *Time and Society* 20(1): 119–36.

Ahuvia, Aaron C. 2005. "Beyond the Extended Self: Loved Objects and Consumers' Identity Narratives." *Journal of Consumer Research* 32(1): 171–84.

Allegretto, Sylvia, Marc Doussard, Dave Graham-Squire, Ken Jacobs, Dan Thompson and Jeremy Thompson. 2013. "Fast Food, Poverty Wages: The Public Cost of Low-Wage Jobs in the Fast-Food Industry." Report released October 15, 2013. UC Berkeley Labor Center / University of Illinois at Urbana-Champaign.

American Civil Liberties Union. "What is the School-to-Prison-Pipeline?" Retrieved December 17, 2015 (https://www.aclu.org/fact-sheet/what-school-prison-pipeline).

American Society of Civil Engineers. 2013. *2013 Report Card for America's Infrastructure.*

Anderson, Benedict. 1983. *Imagined Communities.* New York, NY: Verso.

Anderson, E. 2004. "The Cosmopolitan Canopy." *The ANNALS of the American Academy of Political and Social Science* 595(1): 14–31.

Angier, Natalie. 2009. "Pigs Prove to be Smart, if not Vain." *New York Times*, November 9. (http://www.nytimes.com/2009/11/10/science/10angier.html).

Anker, Thomas Boysen and Klemens Kappel. 2011. "Ethical Challenges in Commercial Social Marketing." Pp. 284–297 in *The SAGE Handbook of Social Marketing*, edited by Gerard Hastings, Kathryn Angus, and Carol Bryant. London: Sage Publications Ltd.

Arend, P. 2014. "Consumption as Common Sense: Heteronormative Hegemony and White Wedding Desire." *Journal of Consumer Culture*. February 17, 2014. Retrieved July 2, 2015 (http://joc.sagepub.com/cgi/doi/10.1177/1469540514521076).

Arvidsson, A. 2005. "Brands: A Critical Perspective." *Journal of Consumer Culture* 5(2): 235–58.

Ashworth, Laurence, Peter R. Darke, and Mark Schaller. 2005. "No One Wants to Look Cheap: Trade-offs Between Social Disincentives and the Economic and Psychological Incentives to Redeem Coupons." *Journal of Consumer Psychology* 15(4): 295–306.

Aspers, P. and F. Godart. 2013. "Sociology of Fashion: Order and Change." *Annual Review of Sociology* 39(1): 171–92.

Azzarito, Laura and Louis Harrison Jr. 2008. "'White Men Can't Jump': Race, Gender and Natural Athleticism." *International Review for the Sociology of Sport* 43(4): 347–64.

Bain, R. 1937. "Technology and State Government." *American Sociological Review* 2(6): 860–74.

Ball, Stephen J. 2003. *Class Strategies and the Education Market: The Middle-Classes and Social Advantage*. New York: Routledge.

Banet-Weiser, Sarah. 2012a. *Authentic. The Politics of Ambivalence in a Brand Culture*. New York: New York University Press.

Banet-Weiser, Sarah. 2012b. "'Free Self-Esteem Tools?' Brand Culture, Gender, and the Dove Real Beauty Campaign." Pp. 39–56 in *Commodity Activism: Cultural Resistance in Neoliberal Times*, edited by Roopali Mukherjee and Sarah Banet-Weiser. New York: New York University Press.

Bank Muñoz, Carolina. 2008. *Transnational Tortillas: Race, Gender, and Shop-Floor Politics in Mexico and the United States*. Ithaca: Cornell University Press.

Barnard, A. 2011. "'Waving the Banana' at Capitalism: Political Theater and Social Movement Strategy among New York's 'Freegan' Dumpster Divers." *Ethnography* 12(4): 419–44.

Bauman, Zygmunt. 2007. *Consuming Life*. Malden, MA: Polity Press.

Baumann, Shyon. 2008. "The moral underpinnings of beauty: A meaning-based explanation for light and dark complexions in advertising." *Poetics* 36(1): 2–23.

Bautista, Jose. 2015. "Are You Flipping Kidding Me?" *The Players Tribune*, November 9. (http://www.theplayerstribune.com/jose-bautista-bat-flip/).

Beagan, B., G. E. Chapman, A. D'Sylva, and B. R. Bassett. 2008. "'It's Just Easier for Me to Do It': Rationalizing the Family Division of Foodwork." *Sociology* 42(4): 653–71.

Beagan, B., G. Chapman, J. Johnston, D. McPhail, E. Power, and H. Vallian.tos. 2015. *Acquired Tastes: Why Families Eat the Way They Do*. Vancouver, BC: University of British Columbia Press.

Beck, Julie. 2016. "The Decline of the Driver's License," *Atlantic Monthly*. January 22, 2016. (http://www.theatlantic.com/technology/archive/2016/01/the-decline-of-the-drivers-license/425169/).

Belasco, Warren. 2008. *Food*. New York: Berg.

Belk, Russell W. 1988. "Possessions and the Extended Self." *Journal of Consumer Research* 15(2): 139–68.

Benjamin, Walter. 1999. *The Arcades Project*. Trans. H. Eiland and K. McLaughlin. Cambridge, MA: Presidents and Fellows of Harvard College.

Best, Amy. 2006. *Fast Cars, Cool Rides: The Accelerating World of Youth and their Cars*. New York: New York University Press.

Bittman, Mark. 2014. "The True Cost of a Burger." *New York Times*, July 15. (http://www.nytimes.com/2014/07/16/opinion/the-true-cost-of-a-burger.html?hp&action=click&pgtype=Homepage&module=c-column-top-span-region&region=c-column-top-span-region&WT.nav=c-column-top-span-region&_r=2).

Blay, Zeba. 2016. "This Powerful Campaign is Tackling Colorism in Communities Everywhere." *Huffpost Black Voices*, March 9, 2016. (http://www.huffingtonpost.com/entry/this-powerful-campaign-is-tackling-colorism-in-communities-everywhere_us_56e03b2ae4b0860f99d74d05).

Bookman, Sonia. 2013. "Coffee Brands, Class and Culture in a Canadian City." *European Journal of Cultural Studies* 16(4): 405–23.

Bordo, Susan. 2003. *Unbearable Weight: Feminism, Western Culture & the Body*. Berkeley, CA: University of California Press.

Bourdieu, Pierre. 1974. "The School as a Conservative Force: Scholastic and Cultural Inequalities." Pp. 32–46 in *Contemporary Research in the Sociology of Education*, edited by J. Eggleston. London: Methuen.

Bourdieu, Pierre. 1984. Distinction: *A Social Critique of the Judgement of Taste*. Cambridge, MA: Harvard University Press.

Bourdieu, Pierre. 1986. "The Forms of Capital." Pp. 241–258 in *Handbook of Theory and Research for the Sociology of Education*, edited by J. Richardson. New York: Greenwood.

boyd, danah. 2010. "Friendship." Pp. 79–84 in *Hanging Out, Messing Around and Geeking Out*, edited by Ito et al. Cambridge: MIT Press.

boyd, danah. 2014. *It's Complicated: The Social Lives of Networked Teens*. New Haven, CT: Yale University Press.

Breiding, M. J., J. Chen, and M. C. Black. 2014. *Intimate Partner Violence in the United States—2010*. Atlanta, GA: National Center for Injury Prevention and Control, Centers for Disease Control and Prevention.

Brumber, Joan Jacobs. 1997. *The Body Project: An Intimate History of American Girls*. New York: Random House.

Brustein, Joshua. 2014. "We Now Spend More Time Staring at Phones than TVs." *Bloomberg Business*, November 19. (http://www.bloomberg.com/bw/articles/2014-11-19/we-now-spend-more-time-staring-at-phones-than-tvs).

Bryman, Alan. 2007. "Technological Determinism." In *The Blackwell Encyclopedia of Sociology*, edited by George Ritzer. Malden, MA: Blackwell Publishing.

Buckingham, David. 2006. "Is There a Digital Generation?" Pp. 1–18 in *Digital Generations: Children, Young People, and New Media*, edited by David Buckingham and Rebekah Willett. Mahwah, NJ: Lawrence Erlbaum Associates.

Buckingham, David. 2011. *The Material Child: Growing up in Consumer Culture*. Cambridge: Polity Press.

Buijzen, Moniek, and Patti M. Valkenburg. 2003. "The Unintended Effects of Television Advertising: A Parent-Child Survey." *Communication Research* 30, 5: 483–503.

Bureau of Labor Statistics. 2014. "News Release: Union Members—2014." US Department of Labor. January 23, 2015. Retrieved June 13th, 2015. (www.bls.gov/news.release/pdf/union2.pdf).

Buse, Peter, Ken Hirschkop, Scott McCracken, and Bertrant Taithe. 2005. *Benjamin's Arcades: An Unguided Tour*. Manchester: Manchester University Press.

Cahn, Naomi and June Carbone. 2010. *Red Families v. Blue Families: Legal Polarization and the Creation of Culture*. New York: Oxford University Press.

Cairns, Kate and Josée Johnston. 2015. *Food and Femininity*. New York, NY: Bloomsbury.

Campbell, Colin. 1987. *The Romantic Ethic and the Spirit of Modern Consumerism*. Oxford: Basil Blackwell.

Carbone, June and Naomi Cahn. 2014. *Marriage Markets: How Inequality is Remaking the American Family*. New York: Oxford University Press.

Carolan, Mike. 2012. *Sociology of Food and Agriculture*. New York: Routledge.

Caronna, C. 2010. "Project 2: McDonaldization at Towson University." Syllabus published in *TRAILS: Teaching Resources and Innovations Library for Sociology*. Originally published 2002 in *Organizational*, edited by E. Borland. Washington DC: American Sociological Association. (http://trails.asanet.org).

Carr, Deborah. 2007. "Body Work." *Contexts* 6(1): 58.

Carrabine, Eamonn, and Brian Longhurst. 2002. "Consuming the Car": Anticipation, Use and Meaning in Contemporary Youth Culture." *The Sociological Review* 50(2): 181–96.

Carroll, Megan. 2015. "Beyond legal equality for LGBT Families." *Contexts: Understanding People in their Social Worlds* Blog. July 7. Retrieved July 28, 2015 (http://contexts.org/blog/beyond-legal-equality-for-lgbt-families/).

Cashmore, Ellis. 2007. "Cool." In *Blackwell Encyclopedia of Sociology*, edited by George Ritzer. Blackwell Publishing. Blackwell Reference Online. Retrieved March 15, 2015 (http://www.sociologyencyclopedia.com.myaccess.library.utoronto.ca/subscriber/tocnode.html?id=g9781405124331_yr2014_chunk_g97814051243319_ss1–136).

Castellano, Rebecca L. Som. 2015. "Alternative Food Networks and Food Provisioning as a Gendered Act." *Agriculture and Human Values* 32(3): 461–474.

Catalano, Shannan, Erica Smith, Howard Snyder, and Michael Rand. 2009. *Bureau of Justice Statistics Selected Findings: Female Victims of Violence*. US Department of Justice. NCJ 228356.

Catterall, M., P. Maclaran, and L. Stevens. 2005. "Postmodern Paralysis: The Critical Impasse in Feminist Perspectives on Consumers." *Journal of Marketing Management* 21(5–6): 489–504. (http://doi.org/10.1362/0267257054307444).

CCC (Clean Clothing Campaign). 2013. *Breathless for Blue Jeans: Health Hazards in China's Denim Factories*. London: War on Want. (cleanclothes.org).

Chapman, Michelle. 2015. "Quarterly Loss Narrows at Sears." *The New York Times*, February 27. (http://www.nytimes.com/aponline/2015/02/26/business/ap-us-sears-results.html).

Cherlin, Andrew J. 2013. "In the Season of Marriage, a Question. Why Bother?" *New York Times*, April 27. (http://www.nytimes.com/2013/04/28/opinion/sunday/why-do-people-still-bother-to-marry.html?pagewanted=all&_r=0).

Cherlin, Andrew. 2014a. *Labor's Love Lost*. New York: Russell Sage.

Cherlin, Andrew. 2014b. "The Real Reason Richer People Marry." *The New York Times*, December 6. (http://www.nytimes.com/2014/12/07/opinion/sunday/the-real-reason-richer-people-marry.html).

Chertoff, Emily. 2012. "The Racial Divide on . . . Sneakers." *The Atlantic*, August 20. (http://www.theatlantic.com/national/archive/2012/08/the-racial-divide-on-sneakers/261256/).

Chin, Elizabeth J. 1999. "Ethnically Correct Dolls: Toying with the Race Industry." *American Anthropologist* 101(2): 305–321.

Chin, Elizabeth. 2001. *Purchasing Power: Black Kids and American Consumer Culture*. Minneapolis: University of Minnesota Press.

Chriss, James J. 2007. "Networks." In *Blackwell Encyclopedia of Sociology*, edited by George Ritzer. Blackwell Publishing, 2007: Blackwell Reference Online. Retrieved January 29, 2015. (http://www.sociologyencyclopedia.com.myaccess.library.utoronto.ca/subscriber/tocnode.html?id=g9781405124331_chunk_g978140512433120_ss1–14).

Clark-Ibáñez, Marisol. 2004. "Framing the Social World with Photo-Elicitation Interviews." *American Behavioral Scientist* 47(12): 1507–27.

Clay, Andrea. 2012. *The Hip-Hop Generation Fights Back: Youth, Activism, and Post-Civil Rights Politics*. New York: New York University Press.

Cohen, Stanley. 1972. *Folk Devils and Moral Panics: The Creation of the Mods and Rockers*. London: McGibbon and Kee.

Cole, N. L. and K. Brown. 2014. "The Problem with Fair Trade Coffee." *Contexts* 13(1): 50–5.

Cole, Nicki Lisa, and Jenny Chan. 2015. "Despite Claims of Progress, Labor and Environmental Violations Continue to Plague Apple." *Truthout*, February 19, 2015. (http://www.truth-out.org/news/item/29180-despite-claims-of-progress-labor-violations-and-environmental-atrocities-continue-to-plague-apple-s-supply-chain).

Cole, Nicki Lisa and Tara Krishna. 2013. "Apple Exposed: The Untold Story of Globalization." Pp. 331–351 in *Censored 2014: Fearless Speech in Fateful Times*, edited by Mickey Huff and Andy Lee Roth. New York: Seven Stories Press.

Collins, Caitlyn and Michelle Janning. 2014. "The Stuff at Mom's House and the Stuff at Dad's House: The Material Consumption of Divorce for Adolescents." Pp. 163–177 in *Childhood and Consumer Culture*, edited by David Buckingham and Vebjorg Tingstad. New York: Palgrave MacMillan.

Collins, Patricia Hill. 1991. *Black Feminist Thought; Knowledge, Consciousness, and the Politics of Empowerment*. New York, NY: Routledge.

Collins, Patricia Hill. 1998. "It's All in the Family: Intersections of Race, Gender and Nation." *Hypatia* 13(3): 62–82.

Collins, Patricia Hill. 2009. *Another Kind of Public Education: Race, Schools, the Media, and Democratic Possibilities*. Boston: Beacon Press.

Comstock, Sandra Curtis. 2011. "The Making of an American Icon: The Transformation of Blue Jeans during the Great Depression." Pp. 23–50 in *Global Denim*, edited by D. Miller and S. Woodward. New York, NY: Berg.

Cook, Daniel Thomas. 2003. "Spatial Biographies of Children's Consumption: Market Places and Spaces of Childhood in the 1930s and Beyond." *Journal of Consumer Culture* 3(2): 147–69.

Cook, Daniel Thomas. 2010. "Commercial Enculturation: Moving Beyond Consumer Socialization." Pp. 63–79 in *Childhood and Consumer Culture*, edited by David Buckingham and Vebjørg Tingstad. Basingstoke, UK: Palgrave.

Cooley, C. H. 1964 [1902]. *Human Nature and the Social Order*. Schocken, New York.

Coontz, Stephanie. 2005. *Marriage, A History: How Love Conquered Marriage*. New York: Penguin.

Coontz, Stephanie. 2014. "The New Instability," *The New York Times*. July 26, 2014.

Cooper, Britney. 2014. "Iggy Azalea's Post-Racial Mess: America's Oldest Race Tale, Remixed." *Salon*, July 15. (http://www.salon.com/2014/07/15/iggy_azaleas_post_racial_mess_americas_oldest_race_tale_remixed/).

Cotgrove, Stephen, and Andrew Duff. 2009. "Middle-Class Radicalism and Environ-mentalism." Pp. 75–83 in *The Social Movements Reader: Cases and Concepts*, edited by Jeff Goodwin and James M. Jasper. Malden, MA: Blackwell.

Cowan, Brian. 2005. *The Social Life of Coffee: The Emergence of the British Coffeehouse*. New Haven, CT: Yale University Press.

Craig, Lyn, and Janeen Baxter. 2016. "Domestic Outsourcing, Housework Shares, and Subjective Time Pressure: Gender Differences in the Correlates of Hiring Help." *Social Indicators Research* 125(1): 271–88.

Crane, Diana. 1997. "Globalization, Organizational Size, and Innovation in the French Luxury Fashion Industry: Production of Culture Theory Revisited." *Poetics* 24: 393–414.

Crane, Diana. 2000. *Fashion and its Social Agendas*. Chicago: University of Chicago Press.

Crenshaw, Kimberlé W. 1989. "Demarginalizing the Intersection of Race and Sex: A Black Feminist Critique of Antidiscrimination Doctrine, Feminist Theory and Antiracist Politics." University of Chicago Legal Forum, special issue: *Feminism in the Law: Theory, Practice and Criticism* 1989: 139–67.

Crenshaw, Kimberlé. 2015. *Black Girls Matter: Pushed Out, Overpoliced, Underprotected*. New York: African American Policy Forum.

Croghan, Rosaleen, Christine Griffin, Janine Hunter, and Ann Phoenix. 2008. "Young People's Constructions of Self: Notes on the Use and Analysis of the Photo-Elicitation Methods." *International Journal of Social Research Methodology* 11(4): 345–56.

Cross, Gary. 2002. "Toys and the Shaping of Children's Culture in the 20th Century." Pp. 124–150 in *Childhood and Children's Culture*, edited by Flemming Mouritsen and Jens Qvortrup. Campusvej: University Press of Southern Denmark.

Current, Emily, Meritt Elliot, and Hilary Walsh. 2014. *A Denim Story: Inspirations from Boyfriends to Bellbottoms*. New York: Rizzoli.

Curtin, Sally C., Stephanie J. Ventura, and Gladys M. Martinez. 2014. "Recent Declines in Nonmarital Childbearing in the United States." *NCHS Data Brief No. 162*. Hyattsville, MD: National Center for Health Statistics.

D'Antonio, Virginia. 2015. "Vette-ing the American Dream: Nostalgia, Social Capital and Corvette Communities." Presented at the American Sociological Association Meetings, August 2015. Chicago, USA.

Dadush, Uri and Samelse Ali. 2012. "In Search of the Global Middle Class: A New Index." The Carnegie Papers: *International Economics*. Washington, DC: Carnegie Endowment for International Peace.

Das Dasgupta, S. 2009. "Arranged Marriages." Pp. 41–44 in *Encyclopedia of Gender and Society*, edited by J. O'Brien. Thousand Oaks, CA: Sage Publications. (http://doi.org/10.4135/9781412964517).

Davidson, Adam. 2012. "Making it in America." *The Atlantic*, January/February, 2012. (http://m.theatlantic.com/magazine/archive/2012/01/making-it-in-america/308844/).

Daviron, Benoit and Stefano Ponte. 2005. *The Coffee Paradox: Global Markets, Commodity Trade, and the Elusive Promise of Development*. New York: Zed Books.

Deflem, Mathieu. 2007. "Anomie." In *Blackwell Encyclopedia of Sociology*, edited by George Ritzer. Blackwell Publishing, 2007: Blackwell Reference Online. (http://www.sociologyencyclopedia.com.myaccess.library.utoronto.ca/subscriber/tocnode.html?id=g9781405124331_yr2014_chunk_g97814051243317_ss1–54).

DeGusta, Michael. 2011. "The REAL Death of the Music Industry." *Business Insider*, February 18. (http://www.businessinsider.com/these-charts-explain-the-real-death-of-the-music-industry-2011–2).

Department for Business Innovation and Skills. 2014. *Trade Union Membership 2013 Statistical Bulletin*.

DeVault, Marjorie L. 1991. *Feeding the Family: The Social Organization of Caring as Gendered Work*, Chicago and London: University of Chicago Press.

Dodge v. Ford Motor Co., 170 N.W. 668 (Mich. 1919).

Dries, Kate. 2014. "New York Fashion Week: Diversity Talks, but White Faces Walk." *Jezebel*. February 14. Retrieved July 24, 2015 (http://jezebel.com/new-york-fashion-week-diversity-talks-but-white-faces-1522416724).

Duffy, Matt J. 2011. "Smartphones in the Arab Spring." Pp. 53–56 in *IPI Report: Media and Money*, edited by M. Steffens, R. Smith, and A. McCombs. Vienna: International Press Institute.

Duggan, Lisa. 2002. "The New Homonormativity: The Sexual Politics of Neoliberalism." Pp. 175–194 in *Materializing Democracy: Toward a Revitalized Cultural Politics*, edited by R. Castronovo and D. Nelson. Durham, NC: Duke University Press.

Duke, Lisa. 2000. "Black in a Blonde World: Race and Girls' Interpretations of the Feminine Ideal in Teen Magazines." *Journalism and Mass Communication Quarterly* 77(2): 367–92.

Dunham, Lena. 2015. "The Bride in Her Head." *The New Yorker*, July 10. (http://www.newyorker.com/culture/cultural-comment/the-bride-in-her-head).

Durkheim, E. 1964 [1893]. *The Division of Labor in Society*. Trans. G. Simpson. Free Press, New York.

Durkheim, E. 1970 [1897]. *Suicide: A Study in Sociology*. Trans. J. A. Spauldin and G. Simpton. New York, NY: Routledge.

Dworkin, Shari and Faye Linda Wachs. 2009. *Body Panic: Gender, Health, and the Selling of Fitness*. New York: New York University Press.

Dyson, Michael Eric. 2010. *Know What I Mean?: Reflections on Hip-hop*. New York: Basic Books.

Edson, John and Ernest Beck. 2012. *Design Like Apple: Seven Principles for Creating Insanely Great Products, Services, and Experiences*. Hoboken: John Wiley & Sons.

Edwards, Ferne and Dave Mercer. 2012. "Food Waste in Australia: The Freegan Response." *The Sociological Review* 60: 174–91.

Ekpo, Akon. 2014. "Digital Escapes: Escaping Discrimination through Information Technology Use." Conference Paper. AMA Winter Marketing Educators' Conference, at Orlando, FL.

Ellin, Abby. 2014. "Blame the Princess," *New York Times*. November 21, 2014. (http://nyti.ms/1yzYg01).

England, Paula, Michelle Budig, and Nancy Folbre. 2002. "Wages of Virtue: The Relative Pay of Care Work." *Social Problems* 49: 455–73.

Erickson, Bonnie. 1996. "Class, Culture, and Connections." *American Journal of Sociology* 102(1): 217–51.

Fairchild, Caroline. 2014. "Number of Fortune 500 Women CEOs Reaches Historic High." *Fortune*, June 3. (http://fortune.com/2014/06/03/number-of-fortune-500-women-ceos-reaches-historic-high/).

Fairtrade International. 2013. *Monitoring the Scope and Benefits of Fairtrade—Fifth Edition*. (http://onlinelibrary.wiley.com/doi/10.1002/cbdv.200490137/abstract).

Fair Trade USA. 2013. "Fair Trade Certified™ Coffee Imports Hit Record High in 2012." (http://fairtradeusa.org/press-room/press_release/fair-trade-certified-coffee-imports-hit-record-high-2012).

Falasca-Zamponi, Simonetta. 2010. *Waste and Consumption: Capitalism, the Environment, and the Life of Things*. New York: Routledge.

Fantasia, Rick. 1995. "Fast Food in France." *Theory and Society* 24(2): 201–43.

FAO, IFAD and WFP. 2013. *The State of Food Insecurity in the World 2013. The Multiple Dimensions of Food Security*. Rome, FAO. (http://www.fao.org/publications/sofi/2013/en/).

Farrey, Tom. 2008. *Game On: The All-American Race to Make Champions of our Children*. New York: ESPN Books.

Featherstone, Mike. 1987. "Lifestyle and Consumer Culture." *Theory, Culture & Society* 4(1): 55–70.

Featherstone, Mike. 1991. "The Body in Consumer Culture," Pp. 170–196 in *The Body: Social Process and Cultural Theory*, edited by M. Featherstone, M. Hepworth, and B. S. Turner. London: Sage.

Ferguson, Ann Arnett. 2001. *Bad Boys: Public Schools in the Making of Black Masculinity*. University of Michigan Press.

Fincham, Ben. 2006. "Bicycle Messengers and the Road to Freedom." *The Sociological Review* 54: 208–22.

Fingleton, Eamonn. 2013. "Same Car, Different Brand, Hugely Higher Price: Why Pay an Extra $30,000 for Fake Prestige?" Forbes.com (http://www.forbes.com/sites/eamonnfingleton/2013/07/04/same-car-different-brand-hugely-higher-price-why-pay-an-extra-30000-for-fake-prestige/#2706fe0d49ee). Accessed on August 3, 2016.

Finnegan, William. 2014. "Dignity: Fast-Food Workers and a New Form of Labor Activism." *The New Yorker*. September 15, 2014.

Firat, A. F. and Venkatesh, A. 1995. "Liberatory Postmodernism and the Re-Enchantment of Consumption." *Journal of Consumer Research* 22(December): 239–67

Fischer, Claudia. 1992. *America Calling: A Social History of the Telephone to 1940*. Berkeley: University of California Press.

Fitzsimmons, Terrance W., Victor J. Callan, and Neil Paulsen. 2014. "Gender Disparity in the C-suite: Do Male and Female CEOs Differ in How They Reached the Top?" *The Leadership Quarterly* 25(2): 245–66.

Forbes. 2015. "The World's Billionaires," edited by Luisa Kroll and Kerry A. Dolan. March 5. (http://www.forbes.com/billionaires/).

Francis, Andrew M. and Hugo M. Mialon. 2014. "'A Diamond is Forever' and Other Fairy Tales: The Relationship between Wedding Expenses and Marriage Duration." September 15, 2014. *SSRN*. (http://ssrn.com/abstract=2501480 or http://dx.doi.org/10.2139/ssrn.2501480)

Francis, Becky. 2010. "Gender, Toys and Learning." *Oxford Review of Education* 36(3): 325–44.

Frank, Robert. 2011. *The Darwin Economy: Liberty, Competition, and the Common Good*. Princeton, NJ: Princeton University Press.

Frank, Thomas. 1997. *The Conquest of Cool*. Chicago: University of Chicago Press.

Frassanito, Paulo and Benedetta Pettorini. 2008. "Pink and Blue: The Color of Gender." *Child's Nervous System* 24(8): 881–2.

Freedom to Marry. 2015. "History and Timeline of the Freedom to Marry in the United States." June 26, 2015. (http://www.freedomtomarry.org/pages/history-and-timeline-of-marriage).

Freire, Paulo. 2014 [1968]. *Pedagogy of the Oppressed*. New York, NY: Bloomsbury.

Friedman, Hilary Levey. 2013. *Playing to Win: Raising Children in a Competitive Culture*. Berkeley and Los Angeles: University of California Press.

Frisby, Cynthia and Erika Engstrom. 2006. "Always a Bridesmaid, Never a Bride: Portrayals of Women of Color in Bridal Magazines." *Media Report to Women* 34(4): 10–14.

Frosch, Dominick L., Seupattra G. May, Caroline Tietbohl, and José A. Pagan. 2011. "Living in the 'Land of No'? Consumer Perceptions of Healthy Lifestyle Portrayals in Direct-to-Consumer Advertisements of Prescription Drugs." *Social Science & Medicine* 73: 995–1002.

Fulton, L. 2013. "Worker Representation in Europe." *Labour Research Department and ETUI*. (http://www.worker-participation.eu/National-Industrial-Relations).

Gabrielli, V. 2013. "Consumption Practices of Fast Fashion Products: A Consumer-based Approach." *Journal of Fashion Marketing and Management* 17: 206–24. (http://doi.org/10.1108/JFMM-10–2011–0076).

Gaddis, Michael. 2014. "Discrimination in the Credential Society: An Audit Study of Race and College Selectivity in the Labor Market." *Social Forces*. Online first: November 20, 2014.

Galameau, Diane and Thao Sohn. 2013. "Insights on Canadian Society: Long-term Trends in Unionization." *Statistics Canada*.

Gallagher, Dan. 2015. "Apple's iPhone on the Clock." *Wall Street Journal*, March 10. (http://blogs.wsj.com/moneybeat/2015/03/10/apples-iphone-on-the-clock/).

Gardner, Howard and Katie Davis. 2014. *The App Generation*. New Haven, CT: Yale University Press.

Gartman, David. 1994. *Auto Opium: A Social History of American Automobile Design*. New York: Routledge.

Gartman, D. 2004. "Three Ages of the Automobile: The Cultural Logics of the Car." *Theory, Culture & Society* 21: 169–95.

Gates, Gary J. 2015. "Adoption Equality is Not a Sure Thing." *Contexts: Understanding People in their Social Worlds*. (http://contexts.org/blog/adoption-equality-is-not-a-sure-thing/).

Gems, Gerald R. 2012. *The Athletic Crusade: Sport and American Cultural Imperialism*. Lincoln and London: University of Nebraska Press.

Getz, Christy, and Aimee Shreck. 2006. "What Organic and Fair Trade Labels Do Not Tell Us: Towards a Place-Based Understanding of Certification." *International Journal of Consumer Studies* 30(5): 490–501.

Gibbs, Lindsay. 2016. "Then and Now: Cam Newton and the Ongoing Plight of the Black Quarterback." *Think Progress*, February 3. (http://thinkprogress.org/sports/2016/02/03/3745544/cam-newton-marlin-briscoe-black-quarterback/).

Giddens, Anthony. 1991. *Modernity and Self-Identity*. Stanford, CA: Stanford University Press.

Gimlin, Debra. 2007. "What Is 'Body Work'? A Review of the Literature." *Sociology Compass* 1: 353–70.

Goffman, Erving. 1961. *Asylums: Essays on the Social Situation of Mental Patients and Other Inmates*. New York: Anchor Books.

Goffman, Erving. 1963. *Stigma: Notes on the Management of Spoiled Identity*. Simon & Schuster, New York.

Goldstein, Darra. 2006. "Feeding Desire." *Gastronomica* 6(2): iii–iv.

Graham, Ian. 2010. *Automotive Industry: Trends and Reflections*. International Labour Office: Geneva.

Gralnick, Jodi. 2012. "Apples are Growing in American Homes." *CNBC*, March 28. (http://www.cnbc.com/id/46857053).

Granovetter, M. S. 1973. "The Strength of Weak Ties." *American Journal of Sociology* 78(6): 1360–80

Graham, Ian. 2010. *Automotive Industry: Trends and Reflections*. International Labour Office: Geneva.

Green, Nicola. 2007. "Telephone." In *Blackwell Encyclopedia of Sociology*, edited by George Ritzer. Blackwell Publishing, 2007: Blackwell Reference Online. Retrieved February 27, 2015. (http://www.sociologyencyclopedia.com.myaccess.library. utoronto.ca/subscriber/tocnode.html?id=g9781405124331_yr2014_chunk_g978140 512433126_ss1–13).

Greenhouse, Steven. 2014. "Fast-food Workers Intensify Fight for $15 an Hour." *New York Times*, July 27. Retrieved August 25, 2014 (http://www.nytimes.com/2014/ 07/28/business/a-big-union-intensifies-fast-food-wage-fight.html?smid=fb- nytimes&WT.z_sma=BU_FFW_20140729&bicmp=AD&bicmlukp=WT.mc_id &bicmst=1388552400000&bicmet=1420088400000&_r=4&utm_content=buffer dfca5&utm_medium=social&utm_source=facebook.com&utm_campaign=buffer).

Greenhouse, Steven, and Jana Kasperkevic. 2015. "Fight for $15 Swells into Largest Protest by Low-wage Workers in US History." *The Guardian*, April 15, 2015 (http://www.the guardian.com/us-news/2015/apr/15/fight-for-15-minimum-wage-protests-new- york-los-angeles-atlanta-boston).

Grewal, Interpal. 2005. *Transnational America: Feminisms, Diasporas, Neoliberalisms*. Durham, NC: Duke University Press.

Gunn, Simon. 2002. "City of Mirrors: The Arcades Project and Urban History." *Journal of Victorian Culture* 7(2): 263–75.

Guptill, Amy, Denise Copelton and Betsy Lucal. 2013. *Food & Society: Principles and Paradoxes*. Malden, MA: Polity Press.

Haenfler, Ross. 2010. "Hip-hop: 'Doing' Gender and Race in Subculture." *Goths, Gamers, and Grrrls: Deviance and Youth Subcultures*. New York: Oxford University Press.

Haiven, Max. 2013. "Walmart, Financialization, and the Cultural Politics of Securiti- zation." *Cultural Politics* 9(3): 239–62.

Hamilton, B. E., et al. 2015. *National Vital Statistics Reports* Vol. 64, No 12. Hyattsville, MD: National Center for Health Statistics.

Hampton, Keith, Lauren Sessions Goulet, Eun Ja Her, and Lee Rainie. 2009. Social Isolation and New Technology. *Pew Research Center*. November 4. (http://www.pewinternet.org/2009/11/04/social-isolation-and-new-technology/).

Harper, Douglas. 2002. "Talking about Pictures: A Case for Photo Elicitation." *Visual Studies* 17(1): 13–26.

Harris, Elizabeth A. and Tanzina Vega. 2014. "Race in Toyland: A Nonwhite Doll Crosses Over." *New York Times*, July 26. (http://www.nytimes.com/2014/07/27/business/a-disney-doctor-speaks-of-identity-to-little-girls.html?emc=eta1&_r=0).

Hartman, Douglas. 2003. "The Sanctity of Sunday Football: Why Men Love Sports." *Contexts* 2(4): 13–21.

Hartung, Adam. 2016. "Why Cheating in Sports is Prevalent—And We Can't Stop it." *Forbes*, January 23. (http://www.forbes.com/sites/adamhartung/2016/01/23/why-cheating-is-prevalent-and-we-cant-stop-it/2/#3f486d0c2ae5).

Hayes, Dennis and Robin Wynyard (eds). 2002. *The McDonaldization of Higher Education*. Westport, CT, and London: Bergin and Garvey.

Hayward, Keith. 2007. "Arcades." In *Blackwell Encyclopedia of Sociology*, edited by George Ritzer. Blackwell Publishing, 2007: Blackwell Reference Online. Retrieved January 19, 2015. (http://www.sociologyencyclopedia.com.myaccess.library.utoronto.ca/subscriber/tocnode.html?id=g9781405124331_yr2014_chunk_g97814051243317_ss1–62).

Hearn, A. 2008. "'Meat, Mask, Burden': Probing the Contours of the Branded 'Self'." *Journal of Consumer Culture* 8(2): 197–217.

Herring, S. 2008. "Questioning the Generational Divide: Technological Exoticism and Adult Constructions of Online Youth Identity." Pp. 71–92 in *Youth, Identity, and Digital Media*, edited by D. Buckingham. Cambridge, MA: MIT Press.

Herzog, Hal. 2010. *Some We Love, Some We Hate, Some We Eat*. Toronto: Harper Perennial.

Hill, Thomas Edie. 1887. *Hill's Manual of Social and Business Forms: A Guide to Correct Writing*. Chicago: Hill Standard Book Co.

Hines, Alice. 2013. "Meet the New Teen Sneakerheads Flipping Shoes for Cash, Fast." *New York Magazine*, March 4. (http://nymag.com/thecut/2013/03/new-teen-sneakerheads-making-thousands-fast.html).

Hochschild, Arlie. 2003. *The Second Shift*. New York: Penguin.

Hoehner, Christine M., Carolyn E. Barlow, Peg Allen, and Mario Schootman. 2012. "Commuting Distance, Cardiorespiratory Fitness, and Metabolic Risk." *American Journal of Preventive Medicine* 42(6): 571–8.

Holmes, Seth. 2013. *Fresh Fruit, Broken Bodies*. Berkeley and Los Angeles: University of California Press.

Holt, Douglas. 2002. "'Why Do Brands Cause Trouble? A Dialectical Theory of Culture and Branding.'" *Journal of Consumer Research* 29(1): 70–96.

Holtz Kay, Jane. 1997. Asphalt Nation. New York, NY: Crown Publishers Inc.

Hornsby, Anne M. 2007. "Solidarity, Mechanical and Organic." In *Blackwell Encyclopedia of Sociology*, edited by George Ritzer. Blackwell Publishing, 2007: Blackwell Reference Online. Retrieved January 19, 2015. (http://www.sociologyencyclopedia.com.my access.library.utoronto.ca/subscriber/tocnode.html?id=g9781405124331_yr2014_ chunk_g978140512433125_ss1–210).

Horton, Donald. 1957. "The Dialogue of Courtship in Popular Songs." *American Journal of Sociology* 62(6): 569–78.

Houle, Jason and Michael Light. 2014. "The Home Foreclosure Crisis and Rising Suicide Rates, 2005–2010," *American Journal of Public Health* 104(6): 1073–9.

Howard, Vicki. 2003. "A 'Real Man's Ring': Gender and the Invention of Tradition." *Journal of Social History* 36(4): 837–56.

Hui-Tzu, Grace Chou and Nicholas Edge. 2012. "They are Happier and Having Better Lives than I Am": The Impact of Facebook on Perceptions of Others' Lives.'" *Cyberpsychology, Behavior and Social Networking* 15(2012): 117–21.

Human Rights Watch. 2014. "Russia: Sochi Games Highlight Homophobic Violence." February 3. (http://www.hrw.org/news/2014/02/03/russia-sochi-games-highlight-homophobic-violence).

Iber, Jorge, Samuel Regalado, Jose Alamillo, and Arnoldo De Leon. 2011. *Latinos in U.S. Sport: A History of Isolation, Cultural Identity, and Acceptance*. Champaign: Human Kinetics.

IGLHR. 2014. "Rana Plaza: A Look Back, and Forward." *Institute for Global Labour and Human Rights*. April 24. Retrieved July 29, 2015 (http://www.globallabourrights.org/alerts/rana-plaza-bangladesh-anniversary-a-look-back-and-forward).

Ignatiev, Noel. 1995. *How the Irish Became White*. New York: Routledge.

"ILO–IPEC and Chocolate and Cocoa Industry Partnership to Combat Child Labour in West Africa." 2012. *United Nations*. (http://business.un.org/en/documents/10982).

Ingraham, Chrys. 2005. "Introduction: Thinking Straight." Pp. 1–14 in *Thinking Straight: The Power, the Promise, and the Paradox of Heterosexuality*, edited by C. Ingraham. New York: Routledge.

Ingraham, Chrys. 2008. *White Weddings: Romancing Heterosexuality in Popular Culture*. New York: Routledge.

International Cocoa Initiative. 2014. "Cocoa—From Trees to Treats." (http://www.cocoa initiative.org/en/about-us/child-labour-in-cocoa).

Intersex Society of North America. 2008. "How Common is Intersex?" (http://www.isna.org/faq/frequency).

Isley, Natalie. 2016. "Somali Refugees Take to the Ice to Play for Sweden." *Newsweek*, January 5. Retrieved March 28, 2016 (http://www.newsweek.com/somali-refugees-ice-play-sweden-bandy-411246).

Ito, Mizuko, et al. 2010. *Hanging Out, Messing Around, Geeking Out: Living and Learning with New Media*. Cambridge: MIT Press.

Izberk-Bilgin, E. 2012. "Infidel Brands: Unveiling Alternative Meanings of Global Brands at the Nexus of Globalization, Consumer Culture, and Islamism." *Journal of Consumer Research* 39(December): 663–87. (http://doi.org/10.1086/665413).

Jacobson, Ivy. 2015. "Average Wedding Cost Hits National All-Time High." *The Knot 2014 Real Weddings Study.* (https://www.theknot.com/content/average-wedding-cost).

Jaffee, Daniel. 2007. *Brewing Justice: Fair Trade Coffee, Sustainability and Survival.* Berkeley, CA: University of California Press.

Jarosz, Beth and Rachel T. Cortes. 2014. "In U.S., New Data Show Longer, More Sedentary Commutes." *Population Reference Bureau.* (http://www.prb.org/Publications/Articles/2014/us-commuting.aspx).

Jenkins, Henry. 2006. *Convergence Culture: Where Old and New Media Collide.* New York: New York University Press.

Johnston, Holly. 2015. "The State of American Credit Card Debt in 2015." *The Simple Dollar*, June 3. (http://www.thesimpledollar.com/the-state-of-american-credit-card-debt-in-2015/).

Johnston, Josée and Shyon Baumann. 2015 [2010]. *Foodies: Democracy and Distinction in the Gourmet Foodscape* (2nd edition). New York, NY: Routledge.

Johnston, Josée and Judith Taylor. 2008. "Feminist Consumerism and Fat Activists: A Comparative Study of Grassroots Activism and the Dove Real Beauty Campaign." *Signs* 39(3): 941–66.

Johnston, Josée, Michelle Szabo, and Alexandra Rodney. 2011. "Good Food, Good People: Understanding the Cultural Repertoire of Ethical Eating." *Journal of Consumer Culture* 11(3): 293–318.

Johnston, Josée, Shyon Baumann, and Kate Cairns. 2010. "The National and the Cosmopolitan in Cuisine: Constructing America through Gourmet Food Writing." Pp. 161–183 in *The Globalization of Food*, edited by David Inglis and Debra Gimlin. New York: Berg.

Jow, Lauren. 2015. "UCLA's Williams Institute Research Played Role in Historic Same-sex Marriage Decision." *UCLA Newsroom.* (http://newsroom.ucla.edu/stories/ucla-s-williams-institute-research-played-role-in-historic-same-sex-marriage-decision).

Kahne, J., N. Lee, and J. Feezell. 2013. "The Civic and Political Significance of Online Participatory Cultures among Youth Transitioning to Adulthood." *Journal of Information Technology & Politics* 10(1): 1–20.

Kaiser, Amanda. 2009. "Hello Kitty Turns 35 With a Splash," *Women's Wear Daily.* 198(38): 16.

Kang, Jay Caspian. 2016. "The Unbearable Whiteness of Baseball." *The New York Times Magazine*, April 6. (http://www.nytimes.com/2016/04/10/magazine/the-unbearable-whiteness-of-baseball.html).

Kang, Miliann 2010. *The Managed Hand: Race, Gender and the Body in Beauty Service Work.* Berkeley and Los Angeles: University of California Press.

Kantor, Jodi. 2014. "Working Anything But 9 to 5." *New York Times*, August 13. Retrieved August 25, 2014. (http://www.nytimes.com/interactive/2014/08/13/us/starbucks-workers-scheduling-hours.html?_r=0).

Katz, James E. and Mark Aakhus. 2002. *Perpetual Contact: Mobile Communication, Private Talk, Public Performance*. Cambridge: Cambridge University Press.

Kennedy, S. and S. Ruggles. 2014. "Breaking Up Is Hard to Count: The Rise of Divorce in the United States, 1980–2010." *Demography* 51(2): 587–98. (http://doi.org/10.1007/s13524–013–0270–9).

Kennelly, Jacqueline and Paul Watt. 2011. "Sanitizing Public Space in Olympic Host Cities: The Spatial Experiences of Marginalized Youth in 2010 Vancouver and 2012 London." *Sociology* 45(5): 765–81.

Keyser, A. V. 2015. *Sneaker Century: A History of Athletic Shoes*. Minneapolis: Twenty-First Century Books.

Khazan, Olga. 2014. "The Divorce-Proof Marriage." *The Atlantic*, October 14. (http://www.theatlantic.com/health/print/2014/10/the-divorce-proof-marriage/381401/).

Kimport, K. 2012. "Remaking the White Wedding? Same-Sex Wedding Photographs' Challenge to Symbolic Heteronormativity." *Gender & Society* 26(6): 874–99.

Kincheloe, Joe L. 2002. *The Sign of the Burger: McDonald's and the Culture of Power*. Philadelphia: Temple University Press.

Klein, Naomi. 1999. *No Logo*. Toronto: Random House.

Koppman, Sharon. 2014. "Making Art Work: Creative Assessment as Boundary Work." *Poetics* 46: 1–21.

Kunstler, James. 1993. *Geography of Nowhere*. New York: Touchstone.

Kusow, Abdi M. 2007. "Stigma." In *Blackwell Encyclopedia of Sociology*, edited by George Ritzer. Blackwell Publishing, 2007: Blackwell Reference Online. Retrieved May 29, 2015. (http://www.sociologyencyclopedia.com.myaccess.library.utoronto.ca/subscriber/tocnode.html?id=g9781405124331_yr2014_chunk_g978140512433125_ss1–264).

Kwan, S. and M. Trautner. 2009. "Beauty Work: Individual and Institutional Rewards, the Reproduction of Gender, and Questions of Agency." *Sociology Compass* 3(1): 49–71.

Lachance-Grzela, Mylène, and Geneviève Bouchard. 2010. "Why Do Women Do the Lion's Share of Housework? A Decade of Research." *Sex Roles* 63(11–12): 767–80.

LaFrance, Adrienne. 2015. "America's Top Killing Machine." *The Atlantic Monthly*. January 12, 2015. (http://www.theatlantic.com/technology/archive/2015/01/americas-top-killing-machine/384440/). Accessed on August 3, 2016.

Lagi, Marco, Karla Z. Bertrand, and Yaneer Bar-Yam. 2011. "The Food Crises and Political Instability in North Africa and the Middle East." arXiv:1108.2455 [physics.soc-ph] (arxiv.org).

Laird, Gordon. 2009. *The Price of a Bargain: The Quest for Cheap and the Death of Globalization*. Toronto: McClelland & Steward Ltd.

Lancaster, Jen. 2007. *Bright Lights, Big Ass: A Self-Indulgent, Surly Ex-Sorority Girl's Guide to Why it Often Sucks in the City, or Who are these Idiots and Why do They All Live Next Door to Me?* New York: New American Library.

Lane, Jeremy F. 2000. *Bourdieu: A Critical Introduction*. London: Pluto Press.

Lane, Robert. 2000. *The Loss of Happiness in Market Democracies*. New Haven, CT: Yale University Press.

Langer, Beryl. 2002. "Commodified Enchantment: Children and Consumer Capitalism." *Thesis Eleven* 69: 67–81.

Lareau, Annette. 2003. *Unequal Childhoods: Class, Race and Family Life*. Berkeley, CA: University of California Press.

Lawson, Jennifer. 2012. "Sociological Theories of Intimate Partner Violence." *Journal of Human Behavior in the Social Environment* 22: 572–90.

Leach, William R. 1993. *Land of Desire: Merchants, Power, and the Rise of a New American Culture*. New York: Vintage.

Lee, M. 2007. "Fast Fashion." *The Ecologist* (May): 0–22.

Leibovich, Mark. 2012. "Candidates have College, Spicy Chicken and 'Star Trek' in Common." *New York Times*, June 2. (http://www.nytimes.com/2012/06/03/us/politics/intersecting-worlds-of-romney-and-obama.html?pagewanted=all&_r=1).

Leidner, Robin. 1993. *Fast Food, Fast Talk: Service Work and the Routinization of Everyday Life*. Berkeley and Los Angeles: University of California Press.

Lenhart, Amanda. 2012. "Teens, Smartphones and Texting," *Pew Internet and American Life Project*. March 19, 2012. (http://pewinternet.org/Reports/2012/Teens-and-smartphones.aspx).

Leonard, David J. 2015. "Scoreboard: Sports and American Jewish Identities." Pp. 340–52 in *The Routledge Handbook of Contemporary Jewish Cultures*, edited by Lawrence Roth and Nadia Valman. New York: Routledge.

Lepkowska, Dorothy. 2008. "Playing Fair?" *The Guardian*, December 16. (https://www.theguardian.com/education/2008/dec/16/play).

"Let Toys Be Toys." 2015. (http://www.lettoysbetoys.org.uk/).

Lichtenstein, Nelson. 2010. *The Retail Revolution: How Wal-Mart Created a Brave New World of Business*. New York: Picador.

Lieu, Nhi T. 2014. "Fashioning Cosmopolitan Citizenship: Transnational Gazes and the Production of Romance in Asian/American Bridal Photography." *Journal of Asian American Studies* 17(2): 133–60.

Link, B. and J. Phelan. 2001. "Conceptualizing Stigma." *Annual Review of Sociology* 27(3): 363–85.

Lipinski, B., C. Hanson, and J. Lomax. 2013. "Reducing Food Loss and Waste. Creating a Sustainable Food Future." Washington DC. (http://unep.org/wed/docs/WRI-UNEP-Reducing-Food-Loss-and-Waste.pdf).

Lipkin, Elline. 2012. "Something Borrowed, Something Blue: What's an Indie Bride to Do?" Pp. 179–90 in *Fashion Talks: Undressing the Power of Style*, edited by Shira Tarrant and Marjorie Jolles. Albany: State University of New York Press.

Lipsitz, George. 2011. *How Racism Takes Place*. Philadelphia: Temple University Press.

Livingston, Gretchen. 2014. "Less than Half of U.S. Kids Today Live in a 'Traditional' Family." *PEW Research Center*. (http://www.pewresearch.org/fact-tank/2014/12/22/less-than-half-of-u-s-kids-today-live-in-a-traditional-family/).

Livingston, Sonia and Leslie Haddon (eds). 2009. *Kids Online: Opportunities and Risks for Children*. Portland: Policy Press.

Lloyd, Carli. 2016. "Why I'm Fighting for Equal Pay." *New York Times*, April 10. (http://www.nytimes.com/2016/04/11/sports/soccer/carli-lloyd-why-im-fighting-for-equal-pay.html).

Lombardo, Kayla. 2016. "The Debate Over Equal Pay in Tennis, Explained." *Sports Illustrated*. March 25. (http://www.si.com/tennis/equal-pay-raymond-moore-billie-jean-king-venus-williams-novak-djokovic-andy-murray).

Lopes, Paul. 2002. *The Rise of a Jazz Art World*. Cambridge, England: Cambridge University Press.

Lovejoy, Meg. 2001. "Disturbances in the Social Body: Differences in Body Image and Eating Problems among African American and White Women." *Gender & Society* 15: 239–61.

Lowrie, Annie. 2011. "Protesting on an Empty Stomach: How the Egyptian Economy is Fueling Unrest in Egypt" *Slate.com*, January 31. (http://www.slate.com/articles/business/moneybox/2011/01/protesting_on_an_empty_stomach.html).

Lury, Celia. 2004. *Brands: The Logos of the Global Economy*. London, UK: Routledge.

Lustig, Deborah Freedman. 2004. "Baby Pictures: Family, Consumerism and Exchange among Teen Mothers in the USA." *Childhood* 11(2): 175–93.

Madden, Mary, Amanda Lenhart, Maeve Duggan, Sandra Cortesi, and Urs Gasser. 2013. "Teens and Technology 2013." *Pew Internet and American Life Project*. March 13. (http://www.pewinternet.org/2013/03/13/teens-and-technology-2013/).

Manjoo, Farhad. 2015. "Slack, the Office Messaging App that May Finally Sink Email." *New York Times*, March 11. (http://www.nytimes.com/2015/03/12/technology/slack-the-office-messaging-app-that-may-finally-sink-email.html).

Manning, Wendy D., Marshal Neal Fettro, and Esther Lamidi. 2014. "Child Well-Being in Same-Sex Parent Families: Review of Research Prepared for American Sociological Association Amicus Brief." *Population Research and Policy Review* 33: 485–502.

Market Wired. 2014. "BRIDES Reveals Trends of Engaged American Couples with American Wedding Study." *Market Wired*. July 10, 2014. (http://www.marketwired.com/press-release/brides-reveals-trends-of-engaged-american-couples-with-american-wedding-study-1928460.htm).

Marvin, Carolyn. 1988. *When Old Technologies were New: Thinking about Electric Communication in the Late Nineteenth Century*. New York: Oxford University Press.

Masci, David, Elizabeth Sciupac, and Michael Lipka. 2015. "Gay Marriage Around the World." *Pew Research Center.* (http://www.pewforum.org/2015/06/26/gay-marriage-around-the-world-2013/).

Matchar, Emily. 2013. *Homeward Bound: Why Women are Embracing the New Domesticity*, New York: Simon & Schuster.

Matthews, Hugh, Mark Taylor, Barry Percy-Smith, Melanie Limb. 2000. "The Unacceptable Flaneur: The Shopping Mall as a Teenage Hangout." *Childhood* 7(3): 279–94.

Mayer, Gerald. 2004. *Union Membership Trends in the United States.* Washington DC: Congressional Research Service.

Mazzarella, Sharon R. 2007. *20 Questions About Youth and the Media.* New York: Peter Lang.

McAdam, Doug. 1982. *Political Process and the Development of Black Insurgency, 1930–1970.* Chicago: University of Chicago Press.

McAdam, Doug. 2010. *Political Process and the Development of Black Insurgency, 1930–1970.* Chicago: University of Chicago Press.

McCarthy, John D. and Mayer N. Zald. 1977. "Resource Mobilization and Social Movements: A Partial Theory." *American Journal of Sociology* 82(1): 1212–41.

McCarthy, Tom. 2009. *Cars, Consumers, and the Environment.* New Haven, CT: Yale University Press.

McClendon, Alphonso D. 2015. *Fashion and Jazz: Dress, Identity and Subcultural Improvisation.* London: Bloomsbury Academic.

McCracken, G. 1988. *Culture and Consumption: New Approaches to the Symbolic Character of Consumer Goods and Activities.* Indiana University Press: Bloomington.

McPherson, Miller, Lynn Smith-Lovin, and James M. Cook. 2001. "Birds of a Feather: Homophily in Social Networks." *Annual Review of Sociology* 27(1): 415–44.

McPherson, M., L. Smith-Lovin, and M. E. Brashears. 2006. "Social Isolation in America: Changes in Core Discussion Networks over Two Decades." *American Sociological Review* 71(3): 353–75.

McRobbie A. 1997. "Bridging the Gap: Feminism, Fashion and Consumption." *Feminist Review* 55: 73–89.

McWilliams, James. 2012. "A Spy in the Slaughterhouse." *The Atlantic.* June 5, 2012. (http:(http://www.theatlantic.com/national/archive/2012/06/a-spy-in-the-slaughterhouse/258110/). Accessed on June 28, 2014.

Mead, G. H. 1962 [1934]. *Mind, Self, and Society: From the Standpoint of a Social Behaviorist.* Chicago: University of Chicago Press.

Mears, Ashley. 2010. "Size Zero High-End Ethnic: Cultural Production and the Reproduction of Culture in Fashion Modeling." *Poetics* 38(1): 21–46.

Mears, Ashley. 2011. *Pricing Beauty.* Berkeley, CA: University of California Press.

Milkie, Melissa. 1999. "Social Comparisons, Reflected Appraisals, and Mass Media: The Impact of Pervasive Beauty Images on Black and White Girls' Self-Concepts." *Social Psychology Quarterly* 62(2): 190–210.

Millard, Bill. 2014. "Challenging Motorism in New York City." *Contexts* 13: 32–7.

Miller, Daniel. 1995. *Acknowledging Consumption*. London, UK: Routledge.

Miller, Daniel. 2010. *Stuff*. New York: Polity Press.

Miller, Daniel and Sophie Woodward (eds). 2011. *Global Denim*. New York, NY: Berg.

Miller, Daniel and Sophie Woodward. 2012. *Blue Jeans: The Art of the Ordinary*. Berkeley, CA: University of California Press.

Miller, Patrick B. 2015. "The Anatomy of Scientific Racism: Racialist Responses to Black Athletic Achievement." Pp. 70–81 in *Sociological Perspectives on Sport: The Games Outside the Games*, edited by David Karen and Robert E. Washington. New York: Routledge.

Morgan, David H. J. 2007. "Marriage." In *Blackwell Encyclopedia of Sociology*, edited by George Ritzer. Blackwell Publishing, 2007: Blackwell Reference Online. Retrieved February 20, 2015. (http://www.sociologyencyclopedia.com.myaccess.library. utoronto.ca/subscriber/tocnode.html?id=g9781405124331_yr2014_chunk_g978140 512433119_ss1–31).

Muggleton, David. 2007. Subculture. In *Blackwell Encyclopedia of Sociology*. Edited by George Ritzer. Blackwell Reference Online. 15 March 2015.

Muñiz, Albert M. 2010. "Brands and Branding." In *Blackwell Encyclopedia of Sociology*, edited by George Ritzer. Blackwell Publishing, 2010: Blackwell Reference Online. Retrieved June 2, 2015. (http://www.sociologyencyclopedia.com.myaccess.library. utoronto.ca/subscriber/tocnode.html?id=g9781405124331_yr2014_chunk_g978140 51243318_ss1–47).

Muñiz, Albert and Thomas O'Guinn. 2001. "Brand Community." *Journal of Consumer Research* 27(4): 412–32.

Murray, Jeff. B. 2002. "The Politics of Consumption: A Re-inquiry on Thompson and Haytko's (1997) 'Speaking of Fashion.'" *Journal of Consumer Research* 29(3): 427–40. (http://doi.org/10.1086/344424).

Musick, Nathan and Amy Petz. 2015. *Public Spending on Transportation and Water Infrastructure, 1956 to 2014*. Report Released March, 2015. Congressional Budget Office. (www.cbo.gov/publications/49910).

Nack, Jack. 2014. "A Decade in, Dove's 'Real Beauty' Seems to be Aging Well." *Advertising Age* 85(2): 6.

Newman, Jared. 2011. "Six Things You Would Never Guess about Google's Energy Use." *Time Magazine*, September 9. Retrieved May 30, 2014. (http://techland.time.com/ 2011/09/09/6-things-youd-never-guess-about-googles-energy-use/).

Nielsen. 2015. "Hip-Hop Nation: How the Genre is Turning it Up in 2015." *Nielson*, July 28. (http://www.nielsen.com/us/en/insights/news/2015/hip-hop-nation-how-the-genre-is-turning-up-in-2015.html).

Nieuwenhuis, Paul. 2008. "From Banger to Classic—a Model for Sustainable Car Consumption?" *International Journal of Consumer Studies* 32(6): 648–55. Retrieved December 2, 2014. (http://doi.wiley.com/10.1111/j.1470–6431.2008.00721.x).

Nightengale, Bob. 2015. "MLB Showing Gains in Diversity," *USA Today*, April 15, p. C.1.

Norton, Michael and Sorapop Kiatpongsan, Forthcoming. *Perspectives on Psychological Science.* Profiled in the Harvard Business Review Blog. (http://blogs.hbr.org/2014/09/ceos-get-paid-too-much-according-to-pretty-much-everyone-in-the-world/).

Oakes, Steve, and Adrian North. 2013. "Dance to the Music!: How Musical Genres in Advertisements Can Sway Perceptions of Image." *Journal of Advertising Research* 53,4: 411–16.

Oldenburg, Ray. 1989. *The Great Good Place: Cafés, Coffee Shops, Community Centers, Beauty Parlors, General Stores, Bars, Hangouts and How They Get You Through the Day.* New York: Paragon House.

Omi, Michael and Howard Winant. 2014 [1986]. *Racial Formation in the United States.* New York: Routledge.

Oppenheimer, Jerry. 2009. "Toy Monster: The Big, Bad World of Mattel." Hoboken: John Wiley & Sons, Inc.

Organic Consumers Association (OCA). 2014. "Five Reasons to Boycott Starbucks," *Organic Consumers Association Website.* June 3, 2014. Retrieved June 9, 2015. (https://www.organicconsumers.org/essays/five-reasons-boycott-starbucks).

Osborne, Peggy and Michelle B. Kunz. 2011. "Identifying which Retailers Survived the Economic Meltdown." *International Journal of Business, Marketing, and Decision Sciences* 4(1): 18–32.

Otnes, Cele and Elizabeth Pleck. 2003. *Cinderella Dreams: The Allure of the Lavish Wedding.* Berkeley, CA: University of California Press.

"Our Locations." *Wal-Mart Stores, Inc.* Website. (http://corporate.walmart.com/our-story/our-business/locations/).

"Oversight of Public and Private Initiatives to Eliminate the Worst Forms of Child Labor in the Cocoa Sector in Côte d'Ivoire and Ghana." 2011. *Payson Center for International Development and Technology Transfer, Tulane University.* (www.child labor-payson.org/Tulane%20Final%20Report.pdf).

Pachirat, Timothy. 2011. *Every Twelve Seconds: Industrialized Slaughter and the Politics of Sight.* New Haven and London: Yale University Press.

Pager, Devah, Bruce Western, and Bart Bonikowski. 2009. "Discrimination in a Low-Wage Labor Market: A Field Experiment." *American Sociological Review* 74(5): 777–99.

Partnership Africa Canada. 2014. *All that Glitters is Not Gold: Dubai, Congo and the Illicit Trade of Conflict Minerals.* Ottawa, Ontario.

Pascoe, C. J. 2007. *Dude, You're a Fag: Masculinity and Sexuality in High School.* Berkeley: University of California Press.

Patel, Raj. 2009. *The Value of Nothing: How to Reshape Market Society and Redefine Democracy.* New York: Picador.

Patterson, Orlando and Ethan Fosse. 2015. *The Cultural Matrix: Understanding Black Youth*. Cambridge, MA: Harvard University Press.

Patterson, Paul G., Jane Scott, and Mark D. Uncles. 2010. "How the Local Competition Defeated a Global Brand: The Case of Starbucks." *Australasian Marketing Journal* 18(1): 41–7.

Payne, Robert. 2008. "Virtual Panic: Children Online and the Transmission of Harm". Pp. 31–46 in *Moral Panics over Contemporary Children and Youth*, edited by Charles Krinsky. Aldershot: Ashgate.

Petz, Sarah. 2015. "A Tribe Called Red Talks Music, Activism with Fans." Saultstar.com August 25, 2015. (http://www.saultstar.com/2015/08/25/tribe-called-red-talk-music-activism-with-fans).

Pew Research Center. 2010. *The Decline of Marriage and Rise of New Families*. Pew Research Center: Social and Demographic Trends Report. November 18. (www.pewsocialtrends.org/2010/11/18/the-decline-of-marriage-and-rise-of-new-families/).

Pew Research Center. 2015. "Same-Sex Marriage, State by State." June 26. (http://www.pewforum.org/2015/06/26/same-sex-marriage-state-by-state/).

Pieters, Rik. 2013. "Bidirectional Dynamics of Materialism and Loneliness: Not Just a Vicious Cycle." *Journal of Consumer Research* 40(4): 615–31. Retrieved September 8, 2014. (http://www.jstor.org/stable/info/10.1086/671564).

Pilcher, Jeffrey. 2012. *Planet Taco*. New York, NY: Oxford University Press.

Piper Jaffray, 2015. "30th Semi-annual Taking Stock with Teens Survey, Fall 2015." Report released October 15, 2015. (http://www.piperjaffray.com/3col.aspx?id=3631).

Pittman, Cassi. 2012. "Race, Social Context, and Consumption: How Race Structures the Consumption Preferences and Practices of Middle and Working-Class Blacks." Doctoral dissertation, Harvard University.

Podberscek, Anthony L. 2009. "Good to Pet and Eat: The Keeping and Consuming of Dogs and Cats in South Korea." *Journal of Social Issues* 65(3): 615–32.

Polletta, Francesca and James M. Jasper. 2001. "Collective Identity and Social Movements." *Annual Review of Sociology* 27: 283–305.

Portes, A. 1998. "Social Capital: Its Origins and Applications in Modern Sociology." *Annual Review of Sociology* 24(1): 1–24. (http://doi.org/10.1146/annurev.soc.24.1.1).

Powell, Matt. 2014. "Sneakeromics: Who Will Be the Next Nike?" *Forbes*. April 28. (http://www.forbes.com/sites/mattpowell/2014/04/28/sneakernomics-who-will-be-the-next-nike/#791bcb8f4013).

Pugh, Allison. 2009. *Longing and Belonging: Parents, Children and Consumer Culture*. Berkeley: University of California Press.

Putnam R. D. 1993. "The Prosperous Community: Social Capital and Public Life." *The American Prospect* 13: 35–42.

Putnam, Robert. 2000. *Bowling Alone: The Collapse and Revival of American Community*. New York: Simon & Schuster.

Radio + Television Business Report. 2012. "Hip-Hop, Consumers and Retail." *Radio + Television Business Report*, March 22, 2012. (http://rbr.com/hip-hop-consumers-and-retail/).

Rafferty, K. 2011. "Class-based Emotions and the Allure of Fashion Consumption." *Journal of Consumer Culture* 11(2): 239–60. (http://doi.org/10.1177/146954051140 3398).

RealtyTrac. 2010. "Record 2.9 Million U.S. Properties Receive Foreclosure Filings in 2010 Despite 30-Month Low in December." *RealtyTrac.* January 12. Retrieved July 3, 2014. (http://www.realtytrac.com/content/press-releases/record-29-million-us-properties-receive-foreclosure-filings-in-2010-despite-30-month-low-in-december-6309).

Rich, Motoko. 2014. "School Data Finds Pattern of Inequality Along Racial Lines." *New York Times*, March 21, 2014. (http://www.nytimes.com/2014/03/21/us/school-data-finds-pattern-of-inequality-along-racial-lines.html?_r=0).

Ritzer, George. 2002. *McDonaldization: The Reader.* Los Angeles: Sage Publications.

Ritzer, George. 2013. *The McDonaldization of Society: 20th Anniversary Edition.* Los Angeles: Sage Publications.

Ritzer, George and Nathan Jurgenson. 2010. "Production, Consumption, Prosumption: The Nature of Capitalism in the Age of the Digital "Prosumer"." *Journal of Consumer Culture* 10(1): 13–36.

Rivers, Sabrina. 2010. *The Tax-Deductible Wedding: More Wedding and Fun, Less Fret and Debt.* Guildford, Connecticut: GPP Life.

Roberts, David. 2006. "Eat the Press." (http://michaelpollan.com/interviews/eat-the-press/).

Rodriquez, Jason. 2006. "Color-Blind Ideology and the Cultural Appropriation of Hip-Hop." *Journal of Contemporary Ethnography* 35(6): 645–68. Retrieved October 31, 2013. (http://jce.sagepub.com/content/35/6/645.short).

Roloff, Julia and Michael S. Aßländer. 2010. "Corporate Autonomy and Buyer–Supplier Relationships: The Case of Unsafe Mattel Toys." *Journal of Business Ethics* 97(4): 517–34.

Rose, Susan and Arun Dhandayudham. 2013. "Towards an Understanding of Internet-based Problem Shopping Behaviours: The Concept of Online Shopping Addiction and its Proposed Predictors." *Journal of Behavioural Addictions* 3(2): 83–9.

Rose, Tricia. 1994. *Black Noise: Rap Music and Black Culture in Contemporary America.* Hanover, NH: Wesleyan University Press.

Roy, William G. and Timothy J. Dowd. 2010. "What Is Sociological about Music?" *Annual Review of Sociology* 36: 183–203.

Ruetschlin, C. and D. Asante-Muhammad. 2015. *The Retail Race Divide.* Baltimore, MD and New York, NY. (http://action.naacp.org/page/-/economic%20opportunity documents/Retail_Race_Divide_Rename.pdf).

Ruzich, Constance M. 2008. "For the Love of Joe: The Language of Starbucks." *Journal of Popular Culture* 41(3): 428–42

Saguy, Abigail. 2013. *What's Wrong with Fat?* Oxford: Oxford University Press.

Sahlins, Marshall. 1976. *Culture and Practical Reason.* Chicago: University of Chicago Press.

Sandlin, Jennifer A., Jennie Stearns, Julie Garlen Maudlin, and Jake Burdick. 2011. "'Now I Ain't Sayin' She a Gold Digger': Wal-Mart Shoppers, Welfare Queens, and Other Gendered Stereotypes of Poor Women in the Big Curriculum of Consumption." *Cultural Studies—Critical Methodologies* 11(5): 464–82.

"Sanrio: Small Gift, Big Smile." 2014. Sanrio Website. (http://www.sanrio.com/characters-hello-kitty/).

Sassatelli, Roberta. 2008. "Consumer Society." In *Blackwell Encyclopedia of Sociology*, edited by George Ritzer. Blackwell Publishing, 2007: Blackwell Reference Online. Retrieved January 7, 2015. (http://www.sociologyencyclopedia.com.myaccess.library.utoronto.ca/subscriber/tocnode.html?id=g9781405124331_yr2014_chunk_g97814051243319_ss1–209).

Sassatelli, Roberta. 2011. "Indigo Bodies: Fashion, Mirror Work and Sexual Identity in Milan." Pp. 127–44 in *Global Denim*. edited by Danial Miller and Sophie Woodward. New York, NY: Berg.

Sauers, Jenna. 2013. "Fashion Week's Models are Getting Whiter." *Jezebel.com*. Retrieved July 24, 2015. (http://jezebel.com/5985110/new-york-fashion-weeks-models-are-getting-whiter).

Schor, Juliet. 1998. *The Overspent American.* New York: Basic Books.

Schor, Juliet. 1999. "The New Politics of Consumption." *Boston Review* (Summer): 1–8.

Schor, Juliet. 2005a. *Born to Buy: The Commercialized Child and the New Consumer Culture.* New York: Scribner.

Schor, Juliet. 2005b. "Prices and Quantities: Unsustainable Consumption and the Global Economy." *Ecological Economics* 55(3): 309–20.

Schouten, J. W. and J. H. McAlexander. 1995. "Subcultures of Consumption: An Ethnography of the New Bikers." *Journal of Consumer Research* 22(1): 43–61. (http://doi.org/10.1086/209434).

Schrank, David, Bill Eisele, Tim Lomax, and Jim Bak. 2015. *2015 Urban Mobility Scorecard*. Report Released August, 2015. Texas A&M Transportation Institute and INRIX.

Schroeder, Jonathan E. 2013. "Brand Culture." In *Blackwell Encyclopedia of Sociology*, edited by George Ritzer. Blackwell Publishing, 2007: Blackwell Reference Online. Retrieved June 2, 2015. (http://www.sociologyencyclopedia.com.myaccess.library.utoronto.ca/subscriber/tocnode.html?id=g9781405124331_yr2014_chunk_g97814051243318_ss1–45).

Schultz, Howard. 1997. *Pour Your Heart into it: How Starbucks Built a Company One Cup at a Time.* New York: Hyperion.

Scott, Robert E. 2015. "Manufacturing Job Loss: Trade, Not Productivity, is the Culprit." Report Released August 11, 2015. *Economic Policy Institute*. (http://www.epi.org/publication/manufacturing-job-loss-trade-not-productivity-is-the-culprit/).

"Seven Countries Raising the Minimum Wage." 2011. *Financial Edge*. January 21 Retrieved November 29, 2011. (http://www.investopedia.com/financialedge/0111/7-Countries-Raising-The-Minimum-Wage.aspx#axzz1f8DCs6uE).

Shade, Leslie Regan. 2011. "Surveilling the Girl Via the Third and Networked Screen." Pp. 261–275 in *Mediated Girlhoods: New Explorations of Girls' Media Cultures*, edited by Mary Celeste Kearney. New York: Peter Lang.

Sharf, Samantha. 2014. "Mondelez to take Bigger Sip of $81B Global Coffee Industry with DE Master Joint Venture." *Forbes*, May 7. (http://www.forbes.com/sites/samanthasharf/2014/05/07/mondelez-to-take-bigger-sip-of-81b-global-coffee-industry-with-de-master-joint-venture/#37603dac3c14).

Sheller, Mimi, and John Urry. 2000. "The City and the Car." *International Journal of Urban and Regional Research* 24, 4: 737–57.

Shirky, Clay. 2008. *Here Comes Everybody: The Power of Organizing Without Organizations*. New York: Penguin.

Short, John Rennie. 2007. *Liquid City: Megalopolis and the Contemporary Northeast*. Washington DC: RFF Press.

Siddiqi, D. M. 2015. "Starving for Justice: Bangladeshi Garment Workers in a 'Post-Rana Plaza' World." *International Labor and Working-Class History* 87(87): 165–73. (http://doi.org/10.1017/S0147547915000101).

Silberg, Gary, Thomas Mayor, Todd Dubner, Jono Anderson, and Leila Shin. 2015. *The Clockspeed Dilemma*. Report Released November, 2015. KPMG.

Simmel, G. 1957 [1904]. "Fashion". *American Journal of Sociology* 62(6): 541–58.

Simon, Bryan. 2009. *Everything but the Coffee. Learning about America from Starbucks*. Berkeley, CA: University of California Press.

Skeggs, Beverley. 2004. *Class, Culture, Self*. New York: Routledge.

Sklair, Leslie. 2001. *The Transnational Capitalist Class*. Malden, MA: Blackwell.

Slater, D. 1997. *Consumer Culture and Modernity*. Cambridge, UK: Polity.

Sniezek, Tamara. 2005. "Is It Our Day or the Bride's Day? The Division of Wedding Labor and Its Meaning for Couples." *Qualitative Sociology* 28(3): 215–34.

Snow, D. and L. Anderson. 1987. "Identity Work among the Homeless: The Verbal Construction and Avowal of Personal Identities." *American Journal of Sociology* 92(6): 1336–71.

Snyder, Rachel Louise. 2009. *Fugitive Denim*. New York: W.W. Norton and Co.

Social Security Administration. 2015. "Wage Statistics for 2012." October 21. (http://www.ssa.gov/cgi-bin/netcomp.cgi?year=2012).

Sohn, Sang-Hee and Yun-Jung Choi. 2014. "Phases of Shopping Addiction Evidenced by Experiences of Compulsive Buyers." *International Journal of Mental Health and Addiction* 12(3): 243–54.

Soron, Dennis. 2009. "Driven to Drive: Cars and the Problem of 'Compulsory Consumption'." Pp. 181–198 in *Car Troubles: Critical Studies of Automobility and Auto-Mobility*, edited by Jim Conley. Burlington, VT: Ashgate.

Sousanis, John. 2011. "World Vehicle Population Tops 1 Billion Units," *Wards Auto*. August 15, 2011. (http://wardsauto.com/news-analysis/world-vehicle-population-tops-1-billion-units).

Spector, Robert. 2005. *Category Killers: The Retail Revolution and Its Impact on Consumer Culture*. Boston: Harvard Business School Press.

Spigel, Lynn. 2001. *Welcome to the Dreamhouse: Popular Media and Postwar Suburbs*. Duke University Press.

Statistics Canada. 2016. "Fertility: Fewer Children, Older Moms." Government of Canada. (http://www.statcan.gc.ca/pub/11–630-x/11–630-x2014002-eng.htm).

Status of Women Canada. 2015. "Women's Representation and Participation in the Labour Force." Government of Canada. (http://www.swc-cfc.gc.ca/initiatives/wesp-sepf/fs-fi/es-se-eng.html).

Stets, Jan E. and Peter J. Burke. 2003. "A Sociological Approach to Self and Identity." Pp. 128–52 in *Handbook of Self and Identity*, edited by Mark Leary and June Tangney. Guilford Press. (http://wat2146.ucr.edu/papers/02a.pdf).

Stone, G. P. 1981. "Appearance and the Self: A Slightly Revised Version." Pp. 187–202 in *Social Psychology through Symbolic Interaction*, edited by G. P. Stone and H. A. Farberman. New York: John Wiley.

Surowiecki, James. 2015. "The Shake Shack Economy." *New Yorker*, January 26. (http://www.newyorker.com/magazine/2015/01/26/shake-shack-economy).

Sutherland, A. and B. Thompson. 2001. *Kidfluence: Why Kids Today Mean Business*. New York: McGraw Hill.

Sweet, Elizabeth. 2014. "Toys are More Divided by Gender Now than They Were 50 Years Ago." *The Atlantic*, December 9. (www.theatlantic.com/business/archive/2014/12/toys-are-more-divided-by-gender-now-than-they-were-50-years-ago/383556/).

Swift, Art. 2015. "Americans Split on How Often They Upgrade their Smartphones." *Gallup*. (http://www.gallup.com/poll/184043/americans-split-often-upgrade-smartphones.aspx?utm_source=Economy&utm_medium=newsfeed&utm_campaign=tiles).

Sypeck, Mia Foley, James J. Gray, and Anthony H. Ahrens. 2004. "No Longer Just a Pretty Face: Fashion Magazines' Depictions of Ideal Female Beauty from 1959 to 1999." *International Journal of Eating Disorders* 36(3): 342–7.

Tasch, Barbara and Giri Nathan. 2014. "Fast Food Workers Across the World Protest Pay." *Time*, May 15. Retrieved August 25, 2014. (http://time.com/100648/fast-food-protest/).

Taylor, Judy, Josée Johnston, and Krista Whitehead. 2014. "A Corporation in Feminist Clothing? Young Women Discuss the Dove 'Real Beauty' Campaign." *Critical Sociology* 20(10): 1–22.

TEDB (Transportation Energy Data Book). 2015. Edition 34. Released September 30, 2015. (http://cta.ornl.gov/data/index.shtml).

The Sentencing Project. 2014. "Facts about Prisons and People in Prison. The Sentencing Project, January 2014." (http://sentencingproject.org/doc/publications/inc_Facts%20About%20Prisons.pdf).

The Wedding Report. 2014. "Wedding Statistics." (https://www.theweddingreport.com/index.cfm/action/wedding_statistics/view/market/id/00/idtype/s/location/united_states/).

Thomas, William Isaac and Dorothy Swaine Thomas. 1928. *The Child in America: Behavior Problems and Programs*. New York: Knopf.

Thomke, Stefan H. and Barbara Feinberg. 2009. "Design Thinking and Innovation at Apple." *Harvard Business School Case 609–066*. (Revised May 2012).

Thompson, C. J. and D. L. Haytko. 1997. "Speaking of Fashion: Consumers' Uses of Fashion Discourses and the Appropriation of Countervailing Cultural Meanings." *Journal of Consumer Research* 24(1): 15–42.

Thompson, Derek. 2013. "Stop Calling Marriage a Luxury Good." *The Atlantic*, October 30. (http://www.theatlantic.com/business/archive/2013/10/stop-calling-marriage-a-luxury-good/280996/).

Thompson, Derek. 2014. "The Shazam Effect." *The Atlantic*, December 2014. (http://www.theatlantic.com/magazine/archive/2014/12/the-shazam-effect/382237/?single_page=true).

Thompson, Derek and Jordan Weissmann. 2012. "The Cheapest Generation." *The Atlantic*, September, 2012. (http://www.theatlantic.com/magazine/archive/2012/09/the-cheapest-generation/309060/).

Thornton, Sarah. 1996. *Club Cultures: Music, Media and Subcultural Capital*. Middletown, CT: Wesleyan University Press.

Thurlow, C. 2007. "Fabricating Youth: New-media Discourse and the Technologization of Young People. Pp. 212–223 in *Language in the Media: Representations, Identities, Ideologies*, edited by S. Johnston and A. Ensslin. London, UK: Continuum.

Tice, Carol. 2013. "The American Fast Food the World Loves: Top Global Brands." *Forbes*, March 11. (http://www.forbes.com/sites/caroltice/2013/03/11/the-american-fast-food-the-world-loves-top-global-brands/).

Treitler, Vilna Bashi. 2013. *The Ethnic Project: Transforming Racial Fiction into Ethnic Factions*. Stanford: Stanford University Press.

Tuchman, Gaye. 1978. "The Symbolic Annihilation of Women by the Mass Media." Pp. 3–38 in *Hearth and Home: Images of Women in the Mass Media*, edited by G. Tuchman, A. Daniels, and J. Benet. New York: Oxford University Press.

Tukachinsky, R., D. Mastro, and M. Yarchi. 2015. "Documenting Portrayals of Race/Ethnicity on Primetime Television over a 20-Year Span and Their Association with National-Level Racial/Ethnic Attitudes." *Journal of Social Issues* 71(1): 17–38. (http://doi.org/10.1111/josi.12094).

Turkle, Sherry. 2011. *Alone Together. Why We Expect More from Technology and Less From Each Other*. New York: Basic Books.

Tuttle, Brad. 2014. "Why People Care So Much About McDonald's One-Minute Drive-Thru Guarantee." *Time,* August 6. Retrieved August 8, 2014. (http://time.com/money/3086843/mcdonalds-one-minute-drive-thru-guarantee/).

Urry, John. 2004. "The 'System' of Automobility." *Theory, Culture and Society* 21(4/5): 25–39.

US Bureau of Labor Statistics. 2014. *Women in the Labour Force: A Databook*. BLS Reports: Report 1052.

US Department of Labor. 2015. "Latest Annual Data." *Women's Bureau*. (http://www.dol.gov/wb/stats/latest_annual_data.htm).

US Department of Transportation. 2011. "Our Nation's Highways: 2011." Retrieved October 2, 2016. (www.fhwa.dot.gove/policyinformation/pubs/hf/pl11028/).

US Energy Information Administration. 2014. "Oil: Crude and Petroleum Products Explained." Retrieved December 15, 2015. (http://www.eia.gov/Energyexplained/index.cfm?page=oil_use and http://www.eia.gov/Energyexplained/index.cfm?page=gasoline_environment).

Valverde, Mariana. 2006. "A New Entity in the History of Sexuality: The Respectable Same-Sex Couple." *Feminist Studies* 32: 155–62.

Veblen, Thorstein. 1967 [1899]. *The Theory of the Leisure Class*. New York: Penguin Books.

Vidal, Matt. 2013. "Inequality and the Growth of Bad Jobs." *Contexts* 12(4): 70–2.

Virilio, Paul. 2007. *The Original Accident*. Cambridge: Polity.

Volti, Rudi. 2004. *Cars & Culture: The Lifestory of a Technology*. Baltimore: Johns Hopkins Press.

Vryan, Kevin D. 2007. "Identity: Social Psychological Aspects." In *Blackwell Encyclopedia of Sociology*, edited by George Ritzer. Blackwell Publishing, 2007: Blackwell Reference Online. Retrieved May 29, 2015. (http://www.sociologyencyclopedia.com.myaccess.library.utoronto.ca/subscriber/tocnode.html?id=g9781405124331_yr2014_chunk_g978140512433115_ss1–6).

Wade, Lisa. 2013. "From Manly to Sexy: The History of the High Heel." *Huffington Post: Style*, February 4. (http://www.huffingtonpost.com/lisa-wade/high-heel-history_b_2613029.html).

Walker, Esther. 2008. "Top Cat: How 'Hello Kitty' Conquered the World." *The Independent*, May 21. (http://www.independent.co.uk/news/world/asia/top-cat-how-hello-kitty-conquered-the-world-831522.html).

Walmart. 2014. *Walmart 2014 Annual Report*. (http://stock.walmart.com/investors/financial-information/annual-reports-and-proxies/default.aspx).

Walmsley, Roy. 2013. *World Prison Population List*, (10th edition). International Center for Prison Studies. (http://www.prisonstudies.org/sites/default/files/resources/downloads/wppl_10.pdf).

Walsh, Frank. 2015. "Union Membership in Ireland Since 2003." Paper presented at the Statistical and Social Inquiry Society of Ireland, February 19, 2015. (www.ssisi.ie/Walsh_union_membership.pdf).

Walsh, Margaret. 2011. "Gender and Automobility: Selling Cars to American Women after the Second World War." *Journal of Macromarketing* 31(1): 57–72.

Walters, S. D. 2013. "Better Not Put a Ring on It." *Contexts* 12(4): 84.

Wang, Jiayu. 2016. "Multimodal Narratives in SIA's 'Singapore Girl' TV Advertisement—From Branding with Femininity to Branding with Provenance and Authenticity?" *Social Semiotics* 26(2): 208–25.

Ward, Michael R. 2011. "Video Games and Crime." *Contemporary Economic Policy* 29(2): 261–73.

Wasserman, Stanley, John Scott, and Peter J. Carrington. 2005. "Introduction." Pp. 1–17 in *Models and Methods in Social Network Analysis*, edited by Peter J. Carrington, John Scott, and Stanley Wasserman. Cambridge: Cambridge University Press.

Watson, James. 2006. *Golden Arches East*: *McDonald's in East Asia* (2nd edition). Stanford, CA: Stanford University Press.

Weber, Max. 1930. *The Protestant Ethic and the Spirit of Capitalism*. Translated by Talcott Parsons. London: Allen and Unwin Ltd.

Weis, Tony. 2007. *The Global Food Economy: The Battle for the Future of Farming*. New York: Zed Books.

Weissman, Jordan. 2013. "Think Artists Don't Make Anything Off Music Sales? These Graphs Prove You Wrong." *The Atlantic*, February 27. (http://www.theatlantic.com/business/archive/2013/02/think-artists-dont-make-anything-off-music-sales-these-graphs-prove-you-wrong/273571/).

Werback, Adam. 2013. "The American Commuter Spends 38 Hours a Year Stuck in Traffic." *The Atlantic Monthly*. February 6, 2013. (http://www.theatlantic.com/business/archive/2013/02/the-american-commuter-spends-38-hours-a-year-stuck-in-traffic/272905/).

West, C. and D. Zimmerman. 1987. "Doing Gender." *Gender & Society* 1(2): 125–51.

Wexler, Sarah Z. 2010. *Living Large*. New York: St. Martin's Press.

Wiedenhoft, Wendy A. 2007. "Department Store." In *Blackwell Encyclopedia of Sociology*, edited by George Ritzer. Blackwell Publishing, 2007: Blackwell Reference Online. Retrieved January 19, 2015. (http://www.sociologyencyclopedia.com.myaccess.library.utoronto.ca/subscriber/tocnode.html?id=g9781405124331_yr2012_chunk_g978140512433110_ss1–30).

Wilk, Richard. 1997. "A Critique of Desire: Distaste and Dislike in Consumer Behavior." *Consumption Markets and Culture* 1(2): 175–96.

Williams, Alex. 2014. "The Sneaker Comes of Age." *The New York Times*. June 11, 2014. (http://www.nytimes.com/2014/06/12/fashion/the-sneaker-comes-of-age.html?_r=1).

Williams, Amanda L. and Michael J. Merten. 2011. "iFamily: Internet and Social Media Technology in the Family Context." *Family and Consumer Sciences Research Journal* 40(2): 150–70.

Williams, Christine. 2006. *Inside Toyland; Working, Shopping and Social Inequality*. Berkeley, CA: University of California Press.

Williams, Raymond. 1983. *Keywords: A Vocabulary of Culture and Society*. New York: Oxford University Press.

Williams, Stereo. 2015. "Amandla Stengberg Understands Appropriation Better than You." *The Daily Beast*, April 17. (http://www.thedailybeast.com/articles/2015/04/17/amandla-stenberg-understands-appropriation-better-than-you.html).

Williams Institute. 2015. "The Business Impact of Opening Marriage to Same-Sex Couples." *University of California School of Law*. (http://williamsinstitute.law.ucla.edu/interactive-economic-impact/).

Willoughby, Teena, Paul J. C. Adachi, and Marie Good. 2012. "A Longitudinal Study of the Association Between Violent Video Game Play and Aggression Among Adolescents." *Developmental Psychology* 48(4): 1044–57.

Wilson, Bee. 2012. *Consider the Fork: A History of How We Cook and Eat*. New York: Basic Books.

Wilson, Ryan. 2014. "Richard Sherman: 'Thug' is Accepted Way of Calling Someone N-word." *CBS Sports*, January 22. (http://www.cbssports.com/nfl/eye-on-football/24417234).

Winetroub, Andrew H. 2013. "A Diamond Scheme is Forever Lost: The Kimberley Process's Deteriorating Tripartite Structure and its Consequences for the Scheme's Survival." *Indiana Journal of Global Legal Studies* 20(2): 1425–44.

Winson, Tony. 2013. *The Industrial Diet*. New York, NY: New York University Press.

Woloson, Wendy. 2012. "Dollar Stores Have a Rich Nickel-and-Dime History." *Edmonton Journal* (December 26): E.4.

Wong, Phoebe, Margaret Hogg, and Markus Vanharanta. 2012. "Consumption Narratives of Extended Possessions and the Extended Self." *Journal of Marketing Management* 28(July): 936–54. (http://eprints.lancs.ac.uk/53949/).

Workneh, Lilly. 2015. "16-year-old Amandla Stenberg Schools Everyone on Cultural Appropriation in this Powerful Video." *HuffPost*, BlackVoices. April 14, 2015. (http://www.huffingtonpost.com/2015/04/14/amandla-stenberg-cultural_n_7064420.html).

World Economic Forum. 2013. *Connected World: Transforming Travel, Transportation and Supply Chains*. (http://reports.weforum.org/connected-world-2013/).

Wu, Timothy. 2014. "The Problem with Easy Technology." *The New Yorker*, February 21. (http://www.newyorker.com/tech/elements/the-problem-with-easy-technology).

Yano, Christine R. 2013. *Pink Globalization: Hello Kitty's Trek Across the Pacific*. London, UK: Duke University Press.

Young, Alex. 2014. "Killer Mike Gives Emotional Speech in Wake of Ferguson Verdict." *Consequence of Sound*, November 25. (http://consequenceofsound.net/2014/11/killer-mike-gives-emotional-speech-in-wake-of-ferguson-verdict-watch/).

Young, Meredith E., Madison Mizzau, Nga T. Mai, Abby Sirisegaram, and Margo Wilson. 2009. "Food for Thought: What you Eat Depends on your Sex and Eating Companions." *Appetite* 53: 268–71.

Zola, Émile. 1883. *Au Bonheur Des Dames*. London, UK: Penguin Books.

Zukin, Sharon. 2004. *Point of Purchase: How Shopping Changed American Culture.* New York: Routledge.

Zukin, Sharon. 2007. "Shopping." In *Blackwell Encyclopedia of Sociology*, edited by George Ritzer. Blackwell Publishing, 2007: Blackwell Reference Online. Retrieved January 8, 2015. (http://www.sociologyencyclopedia.com.myaccess.library.utoronto. ca/subscriber/tocnode.html?id=g9781405124331_yr2014_chunk_g978140512433 125_ss1–113).

GLOSSARY/INDEX

Page numbers in *italics* refer to figures.